Khrushchev's Cold Summer

Khrushchev's Cold Summer

*Gulag Returnees, Crime, and the
Fate of Reform after Stalin*

MIRIAM DOBSON

Cornell University Press

ITHACA AND LONDON

First published 2009 by Cornell University Press
First printing, Cornell Paperbacks, 2011

Printed in the United States of America

Library of Congress Cataloging-in-Publication Data

Dobson, Miriam.
    Khrushchev's cold summer : Gulag returnees, crime, and the fate of reform after Stalin / Miriam Dobson.
        p. cm.
    Includes bibliographical references and index.
    ISBN 978-0-8014-4757-0 (cloth : alk. paper)
    ISBN 978-0-8014-7748-5 (pbk. : alk. paper)
    1. Soviet Union—Politics and government—1953–1985. 2. Political prisoners—Rehabilitation—Soviet Union—History. 3. Ex-convicts—Soviet Union—History. 4. Crime—Political aspects—Soviet Union—History. 5. Political Culture—Soviet Union—History. 6. Soviet Union—Social conditions—1945–1991. I. Title.
    DK274.D637 2009
    947.085'2—dc22   2008047451

Cornell University Press strives to use environmentally responsible suppliers and materials to the fullest extent possible in the publishing of its books. Such materials include vegetable-based, low-VOC inks and acid-free papers that are recycled, totally chlorine-free, or partly composed of nonwood fibers. For further information, visit our website at www.cornellpress.cornell.edu.

Cloth printing   10 9 8 7 6 5 4 3 2 1
Paperback printing   10 9 8 7 6 5 4 3 2 1

Contents

Acknowledgments

I would first like to thank the funding bodies that enabled me to complete this book. During my first three years at the School of Slavonic and East European Studies (SSEES) in London, the Arts and Humanities Research Board offered generous financial support, and a Scoloudi Research Fellowship from the Institute of Historical Research allowed me a precious "writing-up year." Additional grants from the University of London Central Research Funds, University College London, SSEES, and the Royal Historical Society helped enormously with travel costs. I am grateful to the University of Sheffield for granting me research leave during my second year working here, and to the British Academy for funding a much-needed archive trip during that sabbatical.

Over the nine years that I have been working on this project many people have helped me. Susan Morrissey was an amazing adviser, pushing me to think without forcing me toward any one conclusion. On a personal level, she was extraordinarily supportive, seeming to know instinctively when to be demanding, and when to remind me that there's more to life than Russian history. Others also provided important encouragement along the way. Chris Ward was an inspirational undergraduate teacher, and Geoffrey Hosking has given me great support throughout, always asking probing and insightful questions of my work. Two of the most rigorous readings of my work came from Steve Smith and Stephen Lovell, and as I revised and rewrote my manuscript their detailed and incisive comments proved absolutely invaluable. Many others have discussed my ideas, read drafts, or helped with translations and queries, and I would like to thank all of them, in particular Steve Barnes, Yoram Gorlizki, Maya Haber, Cynthia Hooper, Hubertus Jahn, Polly Jones, Ann Livshchiz, Ben Nathans, Holger Nehring, Kevin McDermott, Rachel Platonov, Susan Reid, Kelly Smith, Claudia Verhoeven, Amir Weiner, and Benjamin Ziemann. In the book's final stages, the input from

Cornell University Press has been outstanding: I am particularly grateful to John Ackerman, Karen Laun, Carolyn Pouncy, and the two anonymous reviewers. Sections of chapter 8 appeared in *Slavic Review* (vol. 64, 3 [Fall 2005]) and are reprinted here with the permission of the American Association for the Advancement of Slavic Studies.

The support I received while conducting research in Russia made this project possible. There are many people in the libraries and archives of Moscow, Vladimir, and Cheliabinsk who helped me. Special thanks go to Leonid Weintraub, Elena Drozdova, and Galina Kuznetsova, who started me on the right path. My biggest debt of gratitude must lie with Denis Klimov and Natasha Kurdenkova for sharing their home and friends with me for almost a year. I am also grateful to Pavel, Masha, Dima, and Nastya for their warm hospitality each time I go back. The late Svetlana Zamiatina was an inspiring friend, and I thank Eduard Kariukhin for introducing us and for his support while I was living in Moscow.

During my post-graduate study, SSEES offered a stimulating environment: staff at the library have always been helpful and the Centre for Russian Studies offered a friendly forum for debate. Fellow doctoral students helped make London a great place to live and study, especially Nick Sturdee, Bettina Weichert, and Maya Haber. Penny Wilson and Kate Wilson were incredible friends and flatmates during these years and helped in many ways. Since I moved to Sheffield four years ago my colleagues have been supportive and interested, offering useful guidance as I began the process of revising my manuscript. My family deserves special thanks for their encouragement, and I particularly appreciate the enthusiasm with which my parents Heather and Mike came to visit me in Russia. Last but not least, all my love goes to Thomas Leng—knowing him makes it harder to go to Russia, but so much more fun to be at home.

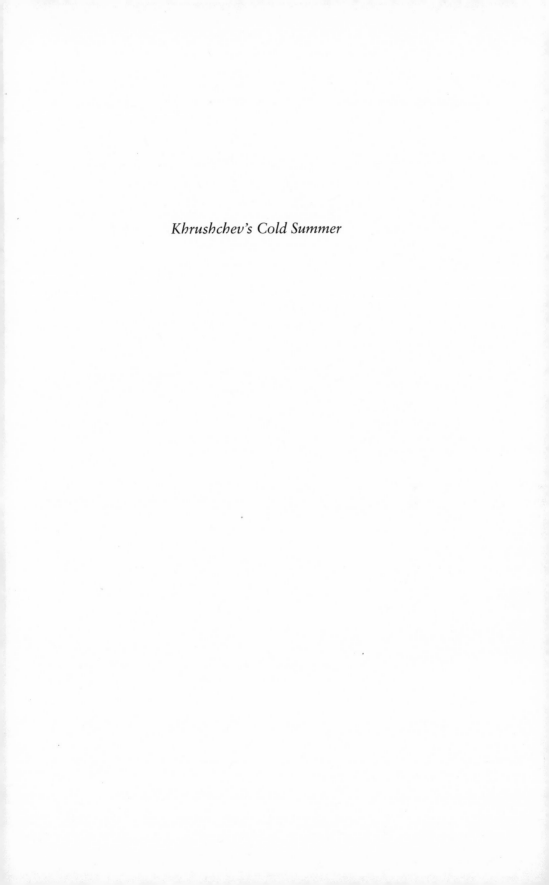

Khrushchev's Cold Summer

Introduction

Cold Summer of '53, a film of the perestroika era, opens in an isolated fishing hamlet. Under the boundless expanse of the northern skies, an unkempt man flirts with a pretty young girl washing the family laundry at the edge of a river.[1] Her mother, a mute, opposes the friendship between the two, at one point throwing a bucket of cold water over them both. Her reasons soon become clear: having served a prison sentence for "treachery" during the Second World War, the man lives in the hamlet as an exile and, although the villagers know him, he remains an outsider to the community.

The first few scenes of *Cold Summer of '53* have an elegiac feel, but the rural calm is soon violently disrupted. Viewed by one critic as the Russian answer to the American western, the film goes on to portray a brutal conflict in which bandits arriving from the outside world rip apart the harmony and security of the tiny rural settlement.[2] In the spirit of a traditional western, the film requires both heroes and villains. The latter come in the form of a group of armed bandits, released from the Gulag by the amnesty of 27 March 1953. Terrorizing the countryside as they make their way back across Russia from the camps, they are organized, violent, and merciless: the villagers are held hostage, the girl narrowly escapes rape but is later killed. The role of hero is taken not, as a Soviet audience might have expected, by a local party official or policeman, but by the shabby exile. Alongside an old comrade, also a former political prisoner, he courageously engages the brigands in a dangerous shoot-out. The risk pays off. The protagonist kills the bandits, and the village is saved. The villagers are forced to recognize that despite his status as exile, the protagonist has rescued them; and yet most

---

[1] *Kholodnoe leto 53*, directed by Aleksandr Proshkin, 1988, USSR.
[2] For comparisons with *The Magnificent Seven* and *The Seven Samurai*, see Anna Lawton, *Kinoglasnost: Soviet Cinema in Our Time* (Cambridge, 1992), 150–151.

I

still remain wary of him. Despite his heroics he is still not fully reintegrated into Soviet society: the last shot of the film sees the hero two years later wandering the streets of the capital carrying his suitcase—alone.

Aleksandr Proshkin's 1988 film told the story of the first wave of Gulag releases following the death of I. V. Stalin on 5 March 1953. Long an outpost for those deemed unfit to remain within the Soviet "family," the Gulag was dramatically downsized between 1953 and 1960. The population of the camps and colonies, which stood at almost 2.5 million on the eve of Stalin's death, would shrink nearly five times over the course of these seven years.[3] In addition to the prisoners in camps and colonies, almost three million people were enduring some form of banishment in 1953, and the majority of these saw their exile status revoked by the beginning of the 1960s.[4] Although the regime tried to protect key cities and major industrial centers by placing restrictions on the movement of some returnees, in practice few points in the Soviet Union remained untouched as millions of Stalin's outcasts began wending their way back from the most remote areas of the country.[5]

How were they regarded by society? Three decades later the filmmaker Proshkin suggested that ordinary people were suspicious of all returnees, regarding political exiles and criminal gangs alike with aversion. The film thus points to important questions: Would those who had been labeled *zeks* (an abbreviation of the Russian word for prisoners) ever lose their alien status in the eyes of the Soviet public? Did Soviet citizens come to distinguish among different categories of returnees? Could returnees hope to create a normal life?

The great exodus of prisoners from the camps marked a significant break with the Stalinist era: although amnesties had been decreed before, there had never been a period in which the size of the Gulag population was reduced so dramatically.[6] A development of such proportion could not pass without

---

[3] In April 1953 the number of prisoners in the MVD's camps and colonies was 2,466,914. The number dipped to 550,882 in 1960. These figures do not include those in prison (who in 1953 constituted an additional 151,247 inmates). See GARF f. 7523, op. 89, d. 4408, l. 82; GARF f. 7523, op. 95, d. 109, l. 27; A. I. Kokurin and N. V. Petrov, eds., *Gulag (Glavnoe upravlenie lagerei), 1918–1960* (Moscow, 2002), 447.

[4] On 1 January 1953, 2,819,776 men and women were serving out some kind of exile. Some were in exile because of the political crimes they or their relatives had allegedly committed, but most had been deported en masse: 2,753,356 were *spetsposelentsy* or "special settlers." The overwhelming majority of the "special settlers" were deported ethnic groups: the most significant categories were Germans (1,224,931), people from the North Caucasus (498,452), and Tartars, Greeks, Bulgarians, Armenians, and others from Crimea (204,698). By 1960 approximately ten thousand "special settlers" remained. It is worth noting that in this book I do not focus on the experiences of the "special settlers" as the complex ethnic issues involved warrant a full-length study in their own right; my focus is primarily on those released from the camps and colonies of the Gulag. The figures given here are taken from V. N. Zemskov, *Spetsposelentsy v SSSR 1930–1960* (Moscow, 2005), 15, 206–212.

[5] The term "Stalin's outcasts" was coined by Golfo Alexolopoulos in her exploration of the petitions written by disenfranchised "former people" in the 1930s. See Golfo Alexopoulos, *Stalin's Outcasts: Aliens, Citizens, and the Soviet State, 1926–1936* (Ithaca, 2003).

[6] The most significant of the Stalin-era amnesties happened in 1945 and released 620,753 prisoners, but this was followed by a steep rise in sentencing and the Gulag population increased

some kind of official explanation. In Proshkin's isolated fishing hamlet newspapers are in short supply and villagers rely on the local policeman to bring news from town, but even here they learn of the event that was splashed across the front pages of *Pravda* in July 1953: Lavrentii Beriia, head of the Ministry of Internal Affairs (MVD), had been arrested. This was the first sign of a shift in what Susan Buck-Morss has called the "political imaginary" (or political landscape), within which stand three "icons": the enemy, the political collective (in this case, Soviet citizenry), and the sovereign agency which wages war in its name (here the party-state).[7] Although Beriia himself was unmasked as an "enemy of the people," Soviet citizens were not asked to root out his accomplices and the press eschewed many of the more violent formulations common in the Stalinist era.[8] This was just the start of a fundamental reevaluation of the status of the enemy which was set to become an important feature of the post-Stalin years.

In 1937 Stalin had argued that the regime's adversaries only became more belligerent and more cunning as the Soviet people advanced toward the light of communism and the figure of the "enemy"—both the foreign foe and the homegrown traitor—became a central tenet of Soviet culture up until 1953.[9] Three years after the dictator died, Nikita Khrushchev openly condemned the term "enemy of the people" (*vrag naroda*), deriding it as a "formula" invented by Stalin. In his famous Secret Speech, delivered at the end of the Twentieth Party Congress, Khrushchev challenged Stalin's dark worldview and mocked Stalin for seeing "enemies," "double-dealers" (*dvurushniki*), and "spies" everywhere.[10] The rabid invective of the Stalinist press now subsided and the rituals of high politics became more moderate, with defeated opponents increasingly condemned for committing "mistakes" and "errors" rather than unmasked as enemies. Khrushchev's vision was based on the belief that in the past the threat of opposition and subversion had been exaggerated and that the Soviet community was far more stable and trustworthy than his predecessor had allowed. If the enemy was a lesser threat than previously imagined, the "sovereign agency" (the party-state) need exert less violence. All this meant that the Gulag—and the practices of surveillance, purging, and imprisonment that had been such a feature of Stalinism—could be reduced.

---

rapidly in the late 1940s. See Golfo Alexopoulos, "Amnesty 1945: The Revolving Door of Stalin's Gulag," *Slavic Review* 64 (2005): 274–306 (279).

[7] Buck-Morss takes the term *politicheskoe voobrazhaemoe* from the work of Valerii Podoroga. See Susan Buck-Morss, *Dreamworld and Catastrophe: The Passing of Mass Utopia in East and West* (Cambridge, 2000), 11–13.

[8] "Nesokrushimoe edinenie partii, pravitel'stva, sovetskogo naroda," *Pravda*, 10 July 1953, 1.

[9] I. V. Stalin, "O nedostatkakh partiinoi raboty i merakh likvidatsii trotskistkikh i inykh dvurushnikov: Doklad na plenume TsK VKP(b) 3 Marta 1937 g.," in *I. V. Stalin: Sochineniia*, ed. Robert H. McNeal (Stanford, 1967), vol. 1, 189–224 (213).

[10] "O kul'te lichnosti i ego posledsvtiiakh: Doklad Pervogo sekretaria TsK KPSS tov. Khrushcheva XX s"ezdu Kommunisticheskoi partii Sovetskogo Soiuza 25 fevralia 1956 goda," *Doklad N. S. Khrushcheva o kul'te lichnosti Stalina na XX s"ezde KPSS: dokumenty* (Moscow, 2002), 51–119 (81).

Khrushchev's Cold Summer explores the massive exodus of prisoners from the Gulag and the reworking of the political imaginary which accompanied it in the first decade after Stalin's death. It also examines popular reactions to such changes. In *Cold Summer of '53,* an elderly captain who acts as har-bormaster is thrown into a state of deep shock by Beriia's arrest and on learn-ing that police officers had been ordered to burn portraits of him passionately denounces their boss as an "enemy of the people." Proshkin's depiction of reactions to de-Stalinization holds at least a grain of truth, and whereas for some people the political and social transformations occurring were liberat-ing (in both literal and figurative senses), for others they represented the start of a painful and disorienting period. The diverse ways in which Soviet men and women—including party members, housewives, workers, children, teen-agers, pensioners, and Gulag survivors themselves—responded to the pro-cess of de-Stalinization is an important theme in this book.

The Legacies of Terror

Proshkin's film was not the only work of the mid- to late 1980s to meditate on the terror and its aftermath.[11] Indeed, as censorship eased under Mikhail Gorbachev's leadership, the atrocities of the Stalin era re-emerged as an im-portant topic in public debate, suggesting that the scars left by the terror years of the 1930s had not healed even fifty years on.[12] This is not perhaps surprising. The experiences of other countries emerging from a period of mass violence and political terror show that recovery is almost always a lengthy and painful process. The task of creating commissions to establish the truth, deciding on the scope and nature of retributive justice, identifying the perpetrators, and designing appropriate rituals to remember the victims can take years, even decades.[13] In Germany the recurring and explosive na-ture of Holocaust commemoration over several decades is a particularly striking example of the difficulty—perhaps impossibility—of "coming to terms" with a genocidal or violent past.[14]

---

[11] For an introduction to the treatment of Stalin's terror in the literature of the perestroika era, see Deming Brown, *The Last Years of Soviet Russian Literature: Prose Fiction 1975–1991* (Cambridge, 1993), 71–78; on filmmakers' treatment of Stalinism, see Lawton, *Kinoglasnost,* 138–166.

[12] Kathleen Smith, *Remembering Stalin's Victims: Popular Memory and the End of the USSR* (Ithaca, 1996); Thomas Sherlock, "Shaping Political Identity through Historical Discourse: The Memory of Soviet Mass Crimes," in *After Mass Crime: Rebuilding States and Communities,* ed. Béatrice Pouligny, Simon Chesterman, and Albrecht Schnabel (Tokyo, 2007), 215–240.

[13] Ruti G. Teitel, *Transitional Justice* (Oxford, 2000); Tina Rosenberg, *The Haunted Land: Facing Europe's Ghosts after Communism* (London, 1995); Martha Minow, *Between Vengeance and Forgiveness: Facing History after Genocide and Mass Violence* (Boston, 1998); Michael Humphrey, *The Politics of Atrocity and Reconciliation: From Terror to Trauma* (London, 2002); David Bloomfield, Teresa Barnes, and Luc Huyse, *Reconciliation after Violent Con-duct: A Handbook* (Stockholm, 2003).

[14] For a useful introduction to the extensive literature on Germany's relationship with its Nazi past, see Robert G. Moeller, "What Has 'Coming to Terms with the Past' Meant in Post-

Stalin's successors saw the re-establishment of the rule of law as the first step to recovery. After Beriia's arrest in 1953 the media enthusiastically embraced the concept of *zakonnost'* (which translates as "legality," or more literally "lawfulness") and condemned arbitrary rule (*proizvol*). New principles developed over the course of the 1950s were meant to ensure that people could be sentenced only when they had broken a law—and not because an official (however powerful) chose to designate them an enemy of the people or a socially harmful element.[15] The Soviet government also began rectifying past errors and, after the amnesty of 1953, a series of commissions were created to review individual cases, leading by 1960 to the rehabilitation of 715,120 victims (many of them no longer alive).[16] Yet once the flaws of Stalinist justice had been acknowledged, however tacitly, difficult questions about blame and culpability emerged, and the party struggled to find answers.

In 1956 Khrushchev told delegates at the Twentieth Party Congress that Stalin himself was responsible for the atrocities, and he repeated such accusations more publicly five years later. Some western observers predicted that formal legislative proceedings against the deceased dictator would follow the first wave of accusations in 1956, but Stalin's successors did not show much appetite for this kind of political ritual, and they certainly balked at the idea of more widespread retributive justice.[17] Khrushchev's son, Sergei, remembers his father telling him in the wake of Beriia's arrest: "You see, the principal accomplices have been punished; some of them have been shot, others are in prison. But millions were caught up in this mincing machine [*miasorubka*]. Millions of victims and millions of executioners—investigators, informants, guards. If we want to start punishing everyone who had a hand in this, as much blood will be shed again. And perhaps even more."[18]

Rather than pursuing the perpetrators, Stalin's successors attempted to build the country's recovery on some kind of recognition of the victims' ordeal, working on the premise (common to many postconflict regimes) that confronting the violence of the past would prevent it from recurring.[19] By

World War II Germany? From History to Memory to the 'History of Memory,'" *Central European History* 35 (2002): 223–256.

[15] With the publication of the "Fundamental Principles of the Criminal Legislation of the USSR" in 1958, the category "enemies of the people" ceased to exist, and courts could no longer sentence offenders as such. The Fundamental Principles also limited the scope of criminal law to acts *specifically* proscribed by law, thus eliminating the doctrine of analogy (embodied in the 1926 Code) whereby a person could be sentenced for committing a "socially dangerous act" not specifically provided for in the code. Harold Berman, *Soviet Criminal Law and Procedure: The RSFSR Codes* (Cambridge, 1966), 26, 47–48.

[16] Between 1954 and 1960, 892,317 counter-revolutionary cases were reconsidered and decisions overturned and amended. Of these 715,120 were granted full rehabilitation. The documentation does not specify how many of these were posthumous rehabilitations. See GARF f. 7523, op. 95, d. 109, l. 11.

[17] On the possibility of legal proceedings against Stalin, see "The New Yalta Conference," *Time*, 8 October 1956, www.time.com/time/magazine/article/0,9171,824407,00.html.

[18] Sergei Khrushchev, *Rozhdenie sverkhderzhavy: Kniga ob ottse* (Moscow, 2000), 89.

[19] On the rationale behind these "Never Again" projects, see chapter 8 of Humphrey, *The*

the early 1960s, the party invited certain purge victims to tell their stories and Khrushchev famously announced: "We can and must explain all and tell the truth to the party and people. . . . This must be done so that nothing similar can ever be repeated."[20] The scope of this truth telling was, however, limited, for the party was interested only in the experiences of a highly select cohort among the millions of Stalin's outcasts. In fact, throughout the first post-Stalin decade the task of defining who had the right to be called a victim proved just as difficult as identifying the perpetrators. Where ordinary criminal justice practices stopped and political terror began was an ongoing source of contestation. Political repressions were only part of Stalin's legacy after all: inside the Gulag, terror victims represented a minority group, with only 22 percent of prisoners serving sentences for "counter-revolutionary" crimes at the time of the dictator's death, meaning almost four out of five Gulag inmates counted as "nonpolitical."[21] Not only did Stalin's successors face the consequences of the regime's political repressions, therefore, they also had to deal with the results of an enormously severe criminal justice system and the bloated prison system it had generated.

The party's repudiation of terror thus raised thorny issues: Who precisely were the victims? Everyone who had endured time in the Gulag, or only former political prisoners? And who was to blame? If crimes were no longer being blamed on the existence of enemies' evil conspiracies and plots, how were they to be explained? The solutions the party leadership offered to these questions were never wholly satisfactory. The problem for Stalin's successors was that they could not reject the past wholesale, for unlike many other countries embarking on the process of transitional justice theirs was not a new regime, but a continuation of the party-state system which had been responsible for the atrocities they now sought to rectify. All attempts to correct past injustices became part of a careful balancing act. Even as the new leaders sought to break with many of the practices developed under Stalin, they were constantly aware that sweeping condemnation of the past might undermine the legitimacy of communist rule.

Politics of Atrocity; and Elizabeth Jelin and Susan G. Kaufman, "Layers of Memories: Twenty Years after in Argentina," in *Genocide, Collective Violence, and Popular Memory: The Politics of Remembrance in the Twentieth Century,* ed. David E. Lorey and William H. Beezley (Wilmington, 2002), 31–52.

[20] Cited in Aleksandr Tvardovskii's preface to "Odin den' Ivana Denisovicha," *Novyi mir* (November 1962): 8.

[21] On 1 January 1953, 21.9% of prisoners in camps and colonies were serving time for counter-revolutionary crimes. See GARF f. R-9414, op. 1, d. 1414, l. 260, and GARF f. R-9414, op. 1, d. 1766, l. 254a, 257–260, both reproduced in A. B. Bezborodov and V. M. Khrustalev, eds., *Istoriia Stalinskogo Gulaga: Konets 1920-kh–pervaia polovina 1950-kh godov,* vol. 4: *Naselenie Gulaga: Chislennost' i usloviia soderzhaniia* (Moscow, 2004), 129–133.

A Revolutionary Agenda

Considering the potential threat the repudiation of terror and the emptying of the Gulag posed to the stability of the regime, it is perhaps surprising that the post-Stalin government embarked on such a path at all. Yet there were pressing reasons to do so. In the 1950s cold war rivalries put pressure on the Soviet system, and, fearful of falling further behind the United States, communist leaders were in a constant battle to drive economic expansion forward.[22] Even before Stalin's death some of his closest advisors, frustrated with existing policies, began developing plans for running the country more effectively.[23] The need to reform the Gulag was a particularly high priority, for it was clear that the country's system of slave labor—far from being a mainstay of the economy—was in fact a huge economic burden. The cost of transporting prisoners and keeping them under armed guard, the harsh climates in which their work was carried out, and the poor physical state of many prisoners made this an expensive enterprise, and one that was far less productive than "free" labor (which after all, did not cost much in the Soviet Union).[24] Moreover, order in the camps was increasingly difficult to maintain with uprisings an increasingly regular feature of Gulag life from the late 1940s onward.[25]

Material or pragmatic considerations were not the only factors, however. Bolshevik ideology was fundamentally based on the notion of progress, and since the late 1940s party theorists had their sights set on the next stage of the revolution: some had suggested that the fourth five-year plan should be seen not only as a chance to recover from the devastation of war but also to begin the transition to communism.[26] In this teleological vision of the world, Stalin's death could be interpreted as a marker of change. Once Khrushchev

[22] Aleksandr Fursenko and Timothy Naftali, *Khrushchev's Cold War: The Inside Story of an American Adversary* (New York, 2006), 23.

[23] In chapter 5 of *Cold Peace,* Yoram Gorlizki and Oleg Khlevniuk suggest that both Beriia and G. M. Malenkov were aware that a policy shakeup was needed in agriculture and the Gulag but were impotent when faced with Stalin's opposition to any significant change. Aleksei Tikhonov has demonstrated that in 1949 and 1951 the MVD was already elaborating plans that would have exiled many offenders to remote areas instead of sending them to the Gulag. See Yoram Gorlizki and Oleg Khlevniuk, *Cold Peace: Stalin and the Soviet Ruling Circle, 1945–1953* (Oxford, 2004); and Aleksei Tikhonov, "The End of the Gulag," in *The Economics of Forced Labor: The Soviet Gulag,* ed. Paul R. Gregory and Valery Lazarev (Stanford, 2003), 67–73.

[24] For example, at the Eniseistroi camp complex in Krasnoiarsk oblast (or region) the cost of producing one thousand bricks was 631 rubles in 1952, while the local regional industry produced the same number at a cost of 210 rubles 49 kopecks. See Galina Mikhailovna Ivanova, *Labor Camp Socialism: The Gulag in the Soviet Totalitarian System* (Armonk, 2000), 118.

[25] On camp disorders in the late Stalin period, see V. A. Kozlov's introduction to the volume on camp rebellions and resistance in V. A. Kozlov, ed., *Istoriia Stalinskogo Gulaga: Konets 1920-kh–pervaia polovina 1950-kh godov,* vol. 6: *Vosstaniia, bunty i zabastovki zakliuchennykh* (Moscow, 2004), 25–100.

[26] Amir Weiner, *Making Sense of War: The Second World War and the Fate of the Bolshevik Revolution* (Princeton, 2001), 33.

emerged as undisputed leader by the late 1950s, a messianic spirit became increasingly strong. This former metal-worker who prided himself on his earthiness was also a dreamer, inspired by the notion that with him at the helm the nation could advance rapidly toward communist paradise.[27]

In seeking to revive revolutionary momentum, Khrushchev paid renewed attention to the task of raising the new Soviet man and woman. He believed the path to the harmonious and productive communist era was through the inculcation of core Soviet values in all citizens, and under his aegis citizens' moral behavior and the concept of *byt* became increasingly important.[28] A deluge of pamphlets and newspaper articles aimed to teach citizens how to behave at work, to conduct their personal lives, to dress, to arrange their living space, and to spend their leisure time. Susan Reid has argued that the party's renewed intervention in "seemingly mundane and intimate matters" was part of a project to form "the fully rounded, socially integrated, and self-disciplined person," linked to the imminent advent of communism. She writes: "Having internalized 'communist morality,' the future citizens of communism would voluntarily regulate themselves, at which point the state could wither away."[29] Although Soviet reality might still be far from this, it was the idyll to which the post-Stalinist leaders strove with renewed determination.

This rediscovered desire to perfect human nature led to the revival of earlier discourses on crime. Employing a metaphor that reflected the industrial spirit of the times, the Bolsheviks had spoken of *perekovka* (reforging) in the 1920s and the early 1930s. Imagining offenders as sick or ailing, criminologists believed that a spell of hard labor could bring them back to full health, or "reforge" them. At first, this did not necessarily involve imprisonment; indeed during the first years of the New Economic Policy (NEP), noncustodial sentences were far more common.[30] Soon, however, doubts as to the wisdom of allowing offenders to remain at loose within Soviet society emerged; and by the early 1930s the Soviet regime encouraged more extensive use of custodial sentences. Confidence in the labor camps' capacity to reform these inmates soon ebbed, however. Increasingly the authorities came

[27] For a fascinating psychological sketch of Khrushchev, see William Taubman, *Khrushchev: The Man and His Era* (London, 2003).

[28] The term *byt* translates as "way of life," often carrying a moralizing overtone about the correct way to behave on a day-to-day basis. In the emerging scholarship on the Khrushchev era *byt* has been recognized as a significant feature of the period. See Victor Buchli, *An Archaeology of Socialism* (Oxford, 1999); Deborah Field, *Private Life and Communist Morality in Khrushchev's Russia* (New York, 2007); Susan Reid, "The Meaning of Home: 'The Only Bit of the World You Can Have to Yourself,'" in *Borders of Socialism: Private Spheres of Soviet Russia*, ed. Lewis H. Siegelbaum (Basingstoke, 2006), 145–170; and Christine Varga-Harris, "Constructing the Soviet Hearth: Home, Citizenship, and Socialism in Russia, 1956–1964," Ph.D. Diss., University of Illinois at Urbana-Champaign, 2005, 132–186.

[29] Susan E. Reid, "Cold War in the Kitchen: Gender and the De-Stalinization of Consumer Taste in the Soviet Union under Khrushchev," *Slavic Review* 61 (2002): 211–252 (216–217).

[30] Peter H. Solomon, *Soviet Criminal Justice under Stalin* (Cambridge, 1996), 52.

to doubt whether offenders could ever really be corrected, worrying that in-herited traits were perhaps too strong, the legacy of their class background too great to shed.[31] By 1936 G. G. Iagoda, then head of the People's Com-missariat for Internal Affairs (NKVD), came to the view that repeat offend-ers were incorrigible and launched a crackdown on recidivist criminals and social marginals.[32] From the mid-1930s onward, the term *perekovka* was dropped and mentions of the Gulag, once extolled as a site of reforging, largely disappeared from the pages of the Soviet press. Inside the camps the story was a little different: in the political education materials produced for use with prisoners, the tropes of correction and redemption were not stamped out. Prisoners were still offered the promise of social reintegration if they could prove themselves worthy.[33] Thus, although the term *perekovka* was largely absent from the mainstream press from the mid-1930s until Stalin's death, the promise to remake, or reforge, wrongdoers had not en-tirely disappeared from Soviet thinking. Reincarnated as *perevospitanie* (re-education), the principle was revived in the 1950s and become a key concept in the Khrushchev era. It seemed to offer useful alternatives to the brutali-ties of the Stalinist system.

Although the new leadership hoped that, once reformed, the Gulag could once more become a site for re-educating offenders, this was not their fa-vored solution to crime and deviant behavior, and in the mid to late 1950s the party returned to ideas of correction *within* society. In keeping with the view that as society progressed, citizens became more politically conscious and socially engaged, the party hoped that the community would help re-ed-ucate offenders. Articles and books informed citizens of their duty not only to pay attention to their own *byt* but also to monitor others' moral trans-gressions. New communal policing measures gave volunteers responsibility for the moral and spiritual re-education of those whose behavior was deemed un-Soviet. Under Khrushchev the party was thus still committed to building a new world and still determined to transform human nature.

Yet this revolutionary project did not necessarily run smoothly. First, Khrushchev's vision contained internal contradictions. In the wake of Stalin's death the party had insisted on the importance of *zakonnost'*, but while com-mitment to the rule of law seems to imply a predictable and stable system of

[31] On the importance of the concept of heredity in discussions of crime during NEP, see Daniel Beer, *Renovating Russia: The Human Sciences and the Fate of Liberal Modernity, 1880–1930* (Ithaca, 2008), 165–204.

[32] Paul M. Hagenloh, "'Socially Harmful Elements' and the Great Terror," in *Stalinism: New Directions*, ed. Sheila Fitzpatrick (London, 2000), 286–308 (286–287). On attitudes toward recidivism, particularly the views of Iagoda and Ezhov, see David Shearer, "Elements Near and Alien: Passportization, Policing, and Identity in the Stalinist State, 1932–1952," *Journal of Modern History* 76 (2004): 835–881 (860).

[33] Amir Weiner, ed., *Landscaping the Human Garden: Twentieth-Century Population Man-agement in a Comparative Framework* (Stanford, 2003), 15–16; Steven Anthony Barnes, "So-viet Society Confined: The Gulag in the Karaganda Region of Kazakhstan, 1930s–1950s," Ph.D. Diss., Stanford University, 2003, 214–220.

government, Khrushchev's own instincts and the implications of the revolutionary ethos he revived favored a society that was constantly evolving and in flux.[34] Second, his campaigns required the participation of enthusiastic and committed volunteers. Ordinary people were told they had a civic duty to assist in the regime's quest to remodel every individual into a citizen of the future. Where once the regime had urged its subjects to participate in the unmasking of enemies, it now mobilized them to assist in the reforging of every erring individual. As this book shows, citizens did not always embrace these new roles in quite the spirit the party-state had hoped.

Popular Opinion under Khrushchev

Embarking on such a radical program, the new leaders were anxious to gauge its success. Their desire to survey popular reactions to the changes being introduced resulted in a wealth of material that survives in the archives: reports on party and workplace meetings, newspaper editors' summaries of letters received, and the letters themselves—including not only letters to the editor but also letters to party leaders, correspondence with party and state institutions, and petitions.

Although disenfranchised, the Gulag population was far from silent. Desperate for release—and upon release for housing, employment, and freedom of movement—*zeks* were required to craft the perfect petition, to effectively explain their life, their errors, and their commitment to the Soviet future. These autobiographies, composed by small-time thieves and victims of political repression alike, have been conserved by the different state and party organizations to which they were addressed. They provide insight into the way the returnees viewed their experience, and how they imagined their tales of exclusion and alienation could be reworked into successful stories of rehabilitation and redemption.

At the other end of the social spectrum stood the seven million party members. The leadership made particular effort to record how this key group reacted to the changing course of Soviet politics. Secretaries at each level reported on their party meetings, particularly when they proved turbulent, and passed the information up the chain to the higher levels of the party hierarchy.

Between these extremes of social experience stood the "ordinary" Soviet citizen, and the authorities were no less interested in charting the mood of this broader public, encouraging citizens to write letters to party leaders and newspapers.[35] At first sight, these unpublished letters preserved in the state

---

[34] As Ruti Teitel writes: "In democracies, our intuition is that the rule of law means adherence to known rules, as opposed to arbitrary governmental action. Yet revolution implies disorder and legal instability" (*Transitional Justice*, 11).

[35] According to Elena Zubkova, newspaper editors increasingly considered the volume of

archives appear to be a "treasure trove" for historians of the Soviet Union who wish to know more of what ordinary men and women thought of the regime under which they lived.[36] Yet such sources are not unproblematic.[37] Even when a bulging file of letters seems to give a rich picture of citizens' views on a topic, it still allows us only to glimpse into the minds of a handful of more than two hundred million Soviet citizens. Citizens who were sufficiently engaged in the country's political life to send a letter about current affairs were not necessarily typical.[38] On occasion, though, the letters' commonalities suggest they are providing us with access to something more than a single author's worldview. In coming to their position, individual authors used the "mental tools" provided by the culture in which they lived.[39] The recurrence of certain ideas and motifs in letters written in far-flung corners of the country suggest the existence of a set of shared beliefs and values that were part of a common oral culture, influenced but not dictated by official media and discourse. The letters can thus tell us something not only about the author but also about the world he or she inhabited.

In using these sources as a means to reflect on popular opinion, a second difficulty presents itself: the question of their candor. Some letter writers did simply speak their mind, but in addressing state functionaries or powerful readers in the party leadership many would formulate their views extremely carefully. Arguing that citizens realized they must learn to play the game, Stephen Kotkin suggests that in the 1930s ordinary people learned the rules of "speaking Bolshevik."[40] This concept has been highly productive in furthering discussion of how surviving texts—letters in particular—can develop our understanding of Soviet mentalities. Yet, as Igal Halfin and Jochen

---

correspondence they received as a matter of prestige. At the Twenty-Second Party Congress, the chairman of the Supreme Court, Aleksandr Gorkin, spoke at length of letter writing, praising citizens who corresponded with the authorities for their political activism. See Elena Zubkova, *Russia after the War: Hopes, Illusions and Disappointments, 1945–1957,* trans. Hugh Ragsdale (Armonk, 1998), 161–162; and "Rech' A. F. Gorkina," *Izvestiia,* 18 October 1961, 3–4.

[36] The term "treasure trove" is taken from Sheila Fitzpatrick, "Supplicants and Citizens: Public Letter-Writing in Soviet Russia in the 1930s," *Slavic Review* 55 (1996): 78–105 (78).

[37] Peter Holquist is particularly critical of approaches that use surveillance materials as a means to explore "what people really thought about the Soviet order." Instead, he argues, the huge information-gathering operation elaborated by the Soviets should be studied primarily for what it can tell us about the state's desire to manage and transform its population. See Peter Holquist, "'Information Is the Alpha and Omega of Our Work': Bolshevik Surveillance in Its Pan-European Context," *Journal of Modern History* 69 (1997): 415–450.

[38] Matthew E. Lenoe suggests that many letter writers came from the higher or aspirational groups within society ("Letter-Writing and the State: Reader Correspondence with Newspapers as a Source for Early Soviet History," *Cahiers du monde russe* 40 [1999]: 139–170).

[39] In his study of sixteenth-century French culture, Lucien Febvre explored the possibility of "unbelief" by asking if individuals had the necessary "mental tools" needed to express an alternative worldview. He argued that if language did not have the right lexical items and syntactical structures, individuals would be unable to form a coherent atheist argument. Stephen Kotkin has used the concept of "mental tools" to think about the beliefs of Soviet citizens in the 1930s. See Lucien Febvre, *The Problem of Unbelief in the Sixteenth Century: The Religion of Rabelais,* trans. Beatrice Gottlieb (Cambridge, 1982), 355; and Stephen Kotkin, *Magnetic Mountain: Stalinism as a Civilization* (Berkeley, 1995).

[40] Kotkin, *Magnetic Mountain,* 198–237.

Hellbeck have argued, if the writing of a text is viewed as a performance or game, it leaves the author's inner mental world unprobed, still hidden from the historian's grasp.[41] The approach taken in this book is a little different and is based on the premise that citizens' ability to speak Bolshevik was rarely perfect, and their performance did not always go without a glitch. Even if we recognize citizens' letters as artifacts purposefully created and intended for a specific audience, they nonetheless offer insight into the author's worldview. First, we get a sense of these letter writers' understanding of the discursive boundaries of the system in which they operated: we have a record of what ordinary people *thought* was an acceptable interpretation or commentary on their lives and on contemporary political events; at the very least we learn what they considered to be successful Bolshevik-speak. Second, we can, with careful attention, get a sense of how their own ideas and beliefs departed from the official script. In seeking to adopt the Bolshevik-speak they found in the newspapers, citizens often went wrong; and these transgressions, permutations, and reworkings of the authoritative text allow us important insight into their worldviews.[42]

However much citizens tried to conform, they did not become identical fonts of party rhetoric. Soviet discourse was far from being stable or monologic in itself, and citizens' diverse attempts to reproduce this Bolshevik-speak in part reflect its fluid, multivocal nature. They also reflect the fact that the Bolshevik vision, thrust onto the Soviet landscape during long years of revolutionary upheaval, had not been taken up uniformly in every corner and milieu of the USSR's vast territory. Existing values and beliefs—religious, political, moral, and sentimental—shaped the way individuals, families, and communities understood the new worldview they encountered. This diversity goes beyond mere acceptance or rejection of Soviet values. Although in the context of the cold war western commentators often searched for signs of "liberated disbelief and active resistance," these are not readily found in the extant texts.[43] The most brazen attacks on party leaders, many anonymous, still remain broadly within the Soviet ethos: the millenarian struggle at the heart of Bolshevik thinking reverberates through many of the surviving texts, however defiant. And even those who thought themselves the most loyal of citizens did not always express themselves in ways that the party leaders would have recognized as correct Bolshevik-speak.

With the party leadership's intervention in the discursive regime in the 1950s—the repudiation of some Stalinist terms, the reintroduction of other,

[41] Igal Halfin and Jochen Hellbeck, "Rethinking the Stalinist Subject: Stephen Kotkin's 'Magnetic Mountain' and the State of Soviet Historical Studies," *Jahrbücher für Geschichte Osteuropas* 44 (1996): 456–463.

[42] For more detailed discussion of letters as a source, see Miriam Dobson, "Letters," in *Reading Primary Sources: The Interpretation of Texts from Nineteenth- and Twentieth-Century History*, ed. Miriam Dobson and Benjamin Ziemann (London: Routledge, 2008), 57–73.

[43] For reflections on the western desire for signs of resistance, see Anna Krylova, "The Tenacious Liberal Subject in Soviet Studies," *Kritika* 1 (2000): 119–146.

half-forgotten concepts—some people felt compelled to defend their own understanding of the Soviet canon. The Gulag releases and the political shifts of the 1950s thus resulted in a complex, sometimes troubled, dialogue about key terms within the Soviet lexicon, and—by extension—about identity, politics, belief, and community in the post-Stalin world.

Three key points of contestation emerge. First, people had to negotiate the party's reappraisal of Stalinist history, and this could have important implications for their own life-stories. For outcasts this rewriting of the past might be a welcome one, for it meant they could try to reinvent themselves, if not as victims then at least as sinners who had atoned for their mistakes. For others this revisionism radically changed the meaning of their lives in less pleasant ways. One MVD worker who was dismissed from his post and expelled from the party, though not arrested, for his role in the *Ezhovshchina*[44] was full of self-pity about this turn of fate: "I don't have my health—I lost it fighting the enemies of my Motherland. I'm going blind, and I'm an invalid of the third category. At the end of the day, there's just nothing for me to live for. Everybody steers clear of me, as if I had the plague."[45] More common perhaps was the experience of men and women who, having suffered during the brutal industrialization of the 1930s or the Second World War, had been encouraged to regard their hardships in terms of service to Stalin; his now ambiguous status inevitably changed the meaning of such sacrifices.

Second, consumers of the Soviet media had to come to grips with the idea that enemies of the people were no longer considered such a deadly threat to Soviet society. In the 1930s the enemy had become a ubiquitous figure: poster art had developed horrifying images of the *vrag;* films told of the cunning and deceit of enemies hidden within the party; show trials of real-life "enemies" were filmed in Moscow and screened across the Soviet Union.[46] As letters of denunciation preserved in the Soviet archives demonstrate, some citizens learnt to participate in the practices of denunciation, employing the vitriolic language deployed in official texts.[47] The "enemy" remained a stalwart in Soviet culture until the 1950s when its validity was suddenly called into question, and for many this reworking of the established political imaginary was unnerving.

Third, vying groups competed over the ascription of honor, with various parties laying claim to the terms *chest'* (honor), *chestnost'* (honesty or in-

---

[44] The term *Ezhovshchina* refers to the purges carried out between 1936 and 1938 when N. I. Ezhov was people's commissar of internal affairs.

[45] GARF f. 7523, op. 107, d. 138, ll. 4–13.

[46] See, for example, Boris Efimov, "Das Faterland," *Izvestiia* (1938), www.soviethistory .org.uk; *Partiinyi bilet,* directed by Ivan Pyr'ev, 1936, USSR; and "Verdict of the Court and Verdict of the People, 1938: The Trial of the Anti-Soviet Right-Trotskyist Bloc," Russian State Film and Photo Archive at Krasnogorsk, www.soviethistory.org.uk.

[47] For letters of denunciation, see Lewis Siegelbaum and Andrei Sokolov, eds., *Stalinism as a Way of Life: A Narrative in Documents* (New Haven, 2004), particularly documents 53 and 81.

tegrity), and the adjective *chestnyi* (which translates as honest, honorable, upstanding, or respectable). From 1953 onward a growing number of letter writers expressed concern that their well-being as *chestnye* citizens was under threat from the unsavory, violent, and subversive subculture that returnees allegedly imported from the camps. In part, this usage of *chestnost'* testifies to the success of the "civilizing mission" the Stalinist state had launched in the wake of collectivization as it attempted to transform the flood of rural newcomers arriving in the cities into the well-behaved, "cultured," new Soviet men and women it desired.[48] Whatever the realities of behavior in the 1950s many people believed they were upstanding, or *chestnye,* citizens deserving of respect and the state's protection. Yet Stalin's outcasts also believed themselves to be worthy members of society: in these years purge victims often claimed their right to have their honor (*chest'*) restored untarnished; and although some *zeks* ascribed to a separate thieves' code of honor, many nonpolitical prisoners were not members of the camps' criminal subculture and desperately hoped they, too, might be recognized as honorable or respectable (*chestnyi*).[49]

Overview

This book explores one of the most important aspects of de-Stalinization—the Gulag releases—from a number of perspectives. De-Stalinization was the result of decisions made by party leaders; and I examine the beliefs and ambitions of those in power, focusing on Khrushchev's political vision, which although full of optimism was riddled with complexities and ambiguities. The reforms Khrushchev and his colleagues introduced had an enormous impact on the lives of ordinary people, and I trace their perceptions of de-Stalinization from 1953 to the early 1960s. Citizens had to respond to both the changing contours of political life and the consequences of the Gulag releases, which some at least came to regard with aversion, fearing that returnees brought with them the culture of an underworld seething with deviance and dissent. I also consider the returnees' experiences of life in the postcamp world.

My book is part of an emerging body of research on the Khrushchev era

---

[48] Vadim Volkov, "The Concept of *Kul'turnost'*: Notes on the Stalinist Civilizing Process," in *Stalinism,* ed. Fitzpatrick, 210–230; David L. Hoffmann, *Stalinist Values: The Cultural Norms of Soviet Modernity, 1917–1941* (Ithaca, 2003); Lynne Attwood and Catriona Kelly, "Programmes for Identity: The 'New Man' and the 'New Woman,'" in *Constructing Russian Culture in the Age of Revolution: 1881–1940,* ed. Catriona Kelly and David Shepherd (Oxford, 1998), 256–290.

[49] The *vory v zakone* (thieves-in-law) formed a fraternity whose rigid observance of a hermetic communal code of behavior led Federico Varese to compare them to the Sicilian Mafia ("The Society of the *Vory-v-Zakone,* 1930s–1950s," *Cahiers du monde russe* 39 [1998]: 515–538).

that uses archival material to explore broad social and cultural changes in the post-Stalin era.[50] This approach departs from earlier scholarship, most of which came from political scientists and literary scholars and depended on published materials.[51] My work questions two basic assumptions of most earlier writing on the period. In the late 1970s Stephen Cohen built on the "conflict model" central to much early Kremlinology in arguing that after Stalin's death Soviet political life coalesced around the "two poles" of reformism and conservatism.[52] I challenge this binary conception. In the fast-changing world of the 1950s few—including political leaders—maintained an unambivalent attitude toward Stalinism, itself a complex and ill-defined entity: people might be enthusiastic about some changes but resentful of others.

My second challenge is to the concept of the "thaw," a term coined by the writer Il'ia Erenburg in 1954 and used as a shorthand for the period in western scholarship ever since.[53] The metaphor defines the period as one of respite and reprieve—not necessarily the experience for all—and implies the existence of a Stalinist "winter." In fact, the nature of the Stalinist past was just one of the issues being debated in the 1950s. Khrushchev himself did not embrace the word *ottepel'* (thaw), even though he believed he was doing something different from his predecessor.[54] Official texts show no appetite for this metaphor taken from nature, with its implication that the seasons might impose their own cyclical patterns onto the Soviet project: in the revolutionary ethos humans transform the natural world, not the other way around. I thus see the period as forward-looking, ambitious, and full of hope on the one hand, but disorienting and potentially unsettling on the other.

Throughout the book I draw on studies that address the procedures and consequences of camp releases. The first monograph devoted to the topic, Nanci Adler's *The Gulag Survivor,* focused on the experience of political prisoners returning from the camps and described the social marginality many of them experienced. Despite its powerful description of the ongoing

[50] A conference organized by Eleonor Gilburd and Denis Kozlov in 2005 brought together much of this recent scholarship. "The Thaw: Soviet Society and Culture during the 1950s and 1960s," University of California, Berkeley, 12–15 May 2005.

[51] On political science approaches, see, for example, George W. Breslauer, *Khrushchev and Brezhnev as Leaders: Building Authority in Soviet Politics* (London, 1982); and Carl A. Linden, *Khrushchev and the Soviet Leadership* (Baltimore, 1966). For literary approaches, see Priscilla Johnson, *Khrushchev and the Arts: The Politics of Soviet Culture, 1962–4* (Cambridge, 1965); Dina Spechler, *Permitted Dissent in the USSR: Novyi Mir and the Soviet Regime* (New York, 1982); and Nancy Condee, "Cultural Codes of the Thaw," in *Nikita Khrushchev,* ed. William Taubman, Sergei Khrushchev, and Abbott Gleason (New Haven, 2000), 160–176.

[52] Stephen F. Cohen, "The Friends and Foes of Change: Reformism and Conservatism in the Soviet Union," in *The Soviet Union since Stalin,* ed. Stephen F. Cohen, Alexander Rabinowitch, and Robert Sharlet (Bloomington, 1980), 11–31 (14). On the "conflict model," see Linden, *Khrushchev and the Soviet Leadership.*

[53] Il'ia Erenburg, *Ottepel': povest'* (Moscow, 1954).

[54] For an extended discussion of the thaw metaphor, see Stephen V. Bittner, *The Many Lives of Khrushchev's Thaw: Experience and Memory in Moscow's Arbat* (Ithaca, 2008), 2–13.

ordeal experienced by many purge victims, Adler's work misses some of the broader social and political tensions created by de-Stalinization and the release of prisoners, the majority of whom were nonpoliticals.[55] In contrast, Marc Elie's doctoral thesis on the Gulag liberations offers a wealth of detail on the release mechanisms; while Amir Weiner describes the problems generated in the Baltic republics, Moldavia, Belarus, and western Ukraine by returning prisoners, many of whom were former nationalist activists.[56] Like Weiner, I see the Gulag releases as an event that affected not only returnees and their families but the whole of society.

This work is divided into three parts, the first of which explores the transitional period 1953–1956. Chapter 1 focuses exclusively on 1953 and suggests that the momentous events of that year—which included Stalin's death, a massive amnesty, and the first campaigns for the restoration of *zakonnost'*—already pointed to many of the difficulties that lay ahead, including problems maintaining law and order and expressions of moral panic from members of the Soviet public. Chapter 2 turns to Stalin's outcasts and uses their petition letters to explore their mindset as the release began. While some letters—particularly ones composed by young men—suggested their authors were alienated by their experiences within the Gulag, those written by purge victims declared their ongoing faith in the communist cause. In 1956, when Khrushchev chose to address to the topic of the terror, he seemed to draw on these self-depictions, using the survival of repressed communists as a sign that the party could survive his bloody revelations. The Secret Speech and its impact are the topic of chapter 3.

Part II examines the impact of the Gulag returns over the course of the 1950s and the government's evolving attitude toward the problem of criminality. Chapter 4 explores the songs, poems, and tattoos that prisoners brought back from the camps and traces the development of a "cult of criminality" among some young people. Faced with a rising crime rate and concerned about Soviet youth, the Soviet government tried various solutions. In the late 1950s, inspired by Khrushchev at his most utopian, it introduced a range of measures for noncustodial sentencing, which were meant to encourage rehabilitation within the community and eradicate the Gulag almost entirely. The development of these new practices and the rhetoric surrounding them are the focus of chapter 5; chapter 6 examines their failure.

Focusing on the final three years of Khrushchev's rule, Part III suggests that although the early 1960s appear to be the high point of de-Stalinization, many important reforms were already being undone. Chapter 7 concentrates on 1961: Stalin was publicly condemned for the first time and purge victims

[55] Nanci Adler, *The Gulag Survivor: Beyond the Soviet System* (New Brunswick, 2002).

[56] Marc Elie, "Les anciens détenus du Goulag: libérations massives, réinsertion et réhabilitation dans l'URSS poststalinienne, 1953–1964," Ph.D. Diss., École des Hautes Études en Sciences Sociales, 2007; Amir Weiner, "The Empires Pay a Visit: Gulag Returnees, East European Rebellions, and Soviet Frontier Politics," *Journal of Modern History* 78 (2006): 333–376.

were exonerated, but at the same time the government introduced policies that encouraged intolerance toward all kinds of small-time offenders and the Gulag began to expand once more. Chapter 8 explores the polemics surrounding the works of two writers (Aleksandr Solzhenitsyn and Iosif Brodskii) and shows that the debate about social boundaries begun in 1953 was still going strong a decade later.

I
RE-IMAGINING THE SOVIET
WORLD AFTER STALIN,
1953–1956

I *1953*

"The Most Painful Year"

> We lost our great friend and father, our beloved and dear Iosif Vissarionovich, and the tears on our face were still not dry, the trepidation in people's hearts over our children's future had not calmed, when the stunning news spread, and the terrible thought pierced people's brains—that enemies of the people are free.
>
> —Anna Karob, letter to V. M. Molotov, 1953

When Stalin died, the most pressing matter for the country's leaders was to lay his body to rest in a meaningful yet orderly manner. It was a daunting task. The new Kremlin bosses drafted every media resource, instructing photographers, writers, and journalists to produce images, poems, and articles for the radio and press. The Hall of Columns where Stalin's body lay in state was transformed into a site for collective displays of grief, reproduced in grainy newspaper images for all those citizens far from Moscow. On the day of Stalin's funeral, Muscovites and visitors to the capital thronged on the streets, forming a vast and overwhelming crowd.[1] Over and over again, the press beseeched the nation to remain unified and called for especial vigilance against the nation's enemies.[2] According to Jeffrey Brooks, "Stalin's final triumph was the enactment of his own funeral." The first few days of March

---

[1] On the day of Stalin's funeral many participants were crushed in the Moscow crowds. In March 1956 Khrushchev would tell the Polish United Workers' Party that 109 people had lost their lives. See Jeffrey Brooks, *Thank You, Comrade Stalin! Soviet Public Culture from Revolution to Cold War* (Princeton, 2000), 234.

[2] On 7 March 1953 *Pravda* carried a front-page headline "The Greatest Unity and Cohesion"; on 8 March "Let Us Unite Tighter Still Around the Communist Party!"; on 11 March "Let The Ranks of the Communist Party Unite Tighter Still!" Also on 11 March the second page bore the headline "Steel Unity," the third "Indestructible Cohesion," and so on.

were Stalin's final show, a finale that drew on "the metaphors of past decades, including the path, family, school, and construction, to bind the nation to him once more."[3]

Citizens grieved in a variety of ways. In addition to the funeral rallies taking place on the streets and in the workplace, many also played out the drama through the act of letter writing, and newspaper editors and Stalin's former colleagues were inundated with letters of condolence.[4] Even as these writers sat alone at home, they presented themselves as participants in a national event. A Leningrad student described how people shared the experience through the radio broadcasts, writing "it was not possible for us all to be there at this hour in Moscow on Red Square, but in thought, with our hearts, we were all there at the Mausoleum."[5] The wireless set directed performances of grief within many homes across the Soviet Union. One housewife described how a group sat together around the radio, sleepless for five days.[6] Another woman wrote to Molotov, saying: "There aren't any words to express my warm feeling towards you! I cried so much listening to your speech on the radio and I cry now writing this letter."[7] Radio broadcasts, on one side, and condolence letters, on the other, constituted a dialogue between leaders and the people and, in the few days of national mourning, became a channel for intense emotion. Many letter writers expressed their own sense of inadequacy, claiming to have no words to convey their grief—yet they too participated in a kind of national graphomania. Referring to the heavy silence that had descended on the country, they nonetheless launched into prolix and often poetic articulations of their woe.

Official and individual formulations achieved remarkable harmony. Model letters published in the press and unpublished letters now preserved in the archives are strikingly similar, in terms of both the emotions expressed and the language used. The media constantly referred to Stalin as the nation's father and depicted children offering flowers to Stalin, and citizens responded with appropriate lamentations of filial loss.[8] One student wrote that she cried more over Stalin's death than when her own father died in 1941.[9] Another young woman told Molotov that she was raised in an orphanage and was personally grateful to Stalin for her upbringing.[10] Other familiar

---

[3] Brooks, *Thank You, Comrade Stalin*, 233–237. For a full account of Stalin's funeral and the mourning ceremonies, see Catherine Merridale, *Night of Stone: Death and Memory in Russia* (London, 2000), 328–336.

[4] In his memoirs, D. T. Shepilov, then editor of *Pravda*, recalled a "flood of telegrams, letters, and articles" from people who wanted to publish testimonials to Stalin. See D. T. Shepilov, "Vospominaniia," *Voprosy istorii* (March 1998): 3–24 (16).

[5] RGASPI f. 82, op. 2, d. 1441, l. 23.

[6] RGASPI f. 82, op. 2, d. 1466, l. 32.

[7] RGASPI f. 82, op. 2, d. 1466, l. 36.

[8] See particularly "Proshchai, Otets!" *Pravda*, 8 March 1953, 4, an article by the author Mikhail Sholokhov which begins "Farewell, father! How suddenly and terribly we have been orphaned!"

[9] RGASPI f. 82, op. 2, d. 1441, l. 24.

[10] RGASPI f. 82, op. 2, d. 1443, ll. 49–50.

tropes of Soviet culture found confident expression in these unpublished letters. A certain Bitiukov wrote that he, along with the whole city of Sverdlovsk, had sworn to build communism in gratitude to Stalin for having brought them to socialism and given them victory over the Germans.[11] Another composed poetry in which he promised "we won't turn from the correct path."[12] The struggle against enemies took a prominent place. While *Pravda* editorials reminded readers how Stalin taught them to be vigilant of their enemies, readers in turn promised to remain strong, to "sharpen their teeth," and to be ever more ferocious with adversaries.[13] Despite their sad tone, the letters suggested that the death of Stalin might serve to reaffirm the shared values of Soviet society.

In the first days after the death, letter writing was used primarily as a means to participate in this collective rite. Eager to preserve the practices of Stalinist culture, many offered their own ideas for rituals and symbols to honor the deceased ruler: Moscow to be renamed after the dead leader; a new military order to be created in his name; every adult citizen to give an oath of loyalty to the motherland.[14] Death, they seemed to claim, should prove no impediment to Stalin's capacity to unify the nation.

For some, of course, Stalin's death promised sought-after change. Andrei Siniavskii described how a friend had called at his apartment, led him away from the neighbors and down to the basement: "I double-locked the door. We stood facing each other, our eyes radiant. We embraced silently."[15] Another memoirist, Janusz Bardach, a Jewish Pole and Gulag survivor, who at the time of Stalin's death was a postgraduate medical student in Moscow, also remembered a closet celebration. With several close friends they gathered in his future wife's apartment and hung drapes to hide their party, which included dancing, drinking, and toasts to a freer future.[16]

Less restrained forms of dissent could be dangerous. The Procuracy archives contain the cases of several men whose lack of caution in the days following Stalin's death cost them dearly. In the Northern Caucasus oblast (region), for example, Iakov Shtyrmer, a twenty-year-old of German origin, attended the mourning session organized by the Chapaev Collective Farm but returned later in the night, tore down the poster of Stalin, and stamped it into the snow.[17] Often incidents happened under the influence of alcohol and not infrequently occurred on trains or at railway stations. On a train traveling between Moscow and Iaroslavl', passengers heard Sergei Drozdov,

[11] RGASPI f. 82, op. 2, d. 1441, l. 108.

[12] RGASPI f. 82, op. 2, d. 1443, l. 62.

[13] "Velichaishaia splochennost' i edinstvo," *Pravda*, 7 March 1953, 1; RGASPI f. 82, op. 2, 1466. l. 23.

[14] RGASPI f. 82, op. 2. d. 1470.

[15] Abram Tertz [Andrei Siniavskii], *Goodnight!* (New York, 1989), 238.

[16] Janusz Bardach and Kathleen Gleason, *Surviving Freedom: After the Gulag* (Berkeley, 2003), 242.

[17] GARF f. 8131, op. 31, d. 38397, ll. 5–8. When using personal records from GARF f. 8131, op. 31, I have changed the names.

a pattern maker from the Academic Institute of the Ministry of Light Industry, say it was a day to be celebrated because there was now one bastard less in the world; the next day he would claim to be too inebriated to remember.[18] On 6 March a rather drunk Nikifor Kurdenkov stood whistling on a station concourse, and when asked by a passerby to show some respect for the occasion, he too began to curse Stalin.[19] In the petition letters they subsequently submitted to the authorities, these men sought to be reclassified as hooligans, not traitors, and they portrayed themselves as hardworking Soviet citizens, temporarily estranged from society and themselves by the dislocating act of travel—and the effects of alcohol. While dissenting attitudes toward Stalin's life and death certainly existed in March 1953, their expression was possible only in the privacy of a locked basement, in the dead of night, or in the surreal world of the drunken train journey.

Initially few letter writers voiced any sort of critical sentiment.[20] Over the coming months, however, such harmony would disappear, and the triumphant trumpeting of national solidarity in March proved premature. As the media clumsily groped for new formulations "after Stalin," citizens were often surprised by the terms and ideas they encountered in the press. Until 1953 the figure of Stalin had functioned as the source of absolute knowledge and truth, a divinity who need obey no rules exterior to him; as one letter writer put it, in complete admiration, "his word was law."[21] With his death, Soviet culture was robbed of what Brooks has called its "prophetic authority."[22] Seeking a new mandate, party leaders did not identify a new figurehead but instead turned to the notion of lawfulness. Rather than relying on Stalin's infallibility, the press now invoked the concept of *sotsialisticheskaia zakonnost'* (socialist legality) to legitimize the new policies it was to introduce.

The term itself was not new but a product of both Lenin and Stalin's rule: although initially Lenin had scorned the law as a weapon used by the old bourgeoisie to exploit the working class, he had come to recognize it as an essential arm of the revolutionary state during the Civil War, adopting the slogan "revolutionary legality" (*revoliutsionnaia zakonnost'*) in 1918;[23] once Stalin had announced the transition to socialism in 1934, the term "socialist legality" coexisted alongside the older "revolutionary legality."[24] The

[18] GARF f. 8131, op. 31, d. 59515, ll. 4–6.
[19] GARF f. 8131, op. 31, d. 68217, ll. 9–12.
[20] There were a handful of exceptions to this. One communist from the city of Gor'kii informed Molotov on 7 March 1953 that the masses expected significant change, hoping for a relaxation of the international situation and improvements in their living standards. He lamented the use of terror within the Soviet system and called for an end to antisemitic policies (RGASPI f. 82, op. 2, d. 1450, l. 103).
[21] RGASPI f. 82, op. 2, d. 1466, l. 75.
[22] Brooks, *Thank You, Comrade Stalin,* 239.
[23] Solomon, *Soviet Criminal Justice,* 18–19.
[24] The journal *Za sotsialisticheskuiu zakonnost'* was published from 1933 to 1935, thereafter becoming simply *Sotsialisticheskaia zakonnost'*.

Bolsheviks' initial reservations about the status of the law did not disappear, however, and the term *zakonnost'* has a checkered history. During the 1930s the Procuracy frequently called for Soviet justice to be administered in accordance with the law and for *zakonnost'* to be fully observed, but such initiatives were submerged by the party's own desire for swift revolutionary justice, and in the siege mentality that accompanied the purges, officials were expected to use their revolutionary instinct to unmask enemies, not to bury their heads in law manuals.[25] And even though N. I. Ezhov, head of the NKVD during the Great Terror, was condemned for his abuse of legality in 1938, this did not mean that the rule of law triumphed afterwards.[26] Indeed, in the 1940s the term *zakonnost'* was used to signify the state's commitment to ensuring all *citizens* acted lawfully rather than its own duty to follow due process: in 1948 a new wave of repression was justified as a sign of refortified *zakonnost'*.[27] In contrast, when the term was taken up once more in 1953, it accompanied the government's admission that certain organs of state power had allowed miscarriages of justice to occur. The word *zakonnost'* peppered newspaper articles, alongside reassurances of the Soviet regime's immense respect for its citizens' rights and its own great "humaneness."

The term *zakonnost'* was mobilized in relation to three of the most significant political events of 1953. The first was the release and acquittal of a group of doctors arrested in January 1953 and charged with poisoning the high-ranking patients they treated at the Kremlin infirmary. In April the newspaper coverage surrounding the repudiation of the notorious "Doctors' Plot" saw a clear admission that legality had not been observed in recent years. Three months later, in July 1953, the term appeared again in the string of accusations laid against the now disgraced Lavrentii Beriia, whose crimes included abusing his position as head of the MVD and violating *sotsialisticheskaia zakonnost'*. The third event—the amnesty decree of 27 March 1953—was chronologically the first, but its impact was significant throughout the year. In a *Pravda* editorial that followed the decree in mid-April, the amnesty and the promises of criminal justice reforms that accompanied it were promoted as a sign that *zakonnost'* was now restored.

Following so close on the heels of Stalin's death, these three events were sensational. They indicated that the new leadership was determined to introduce radical change, particularly in terms of downsizing the Gulag and reforming the criminal justice system. They also suggested the emergence of a new political culture, founded on the law (rather than a single leader's wisdom) and pride in the state's own "humane" treatment of its citizens. This new political rhetoric was not always deployed consistently, however, and throughout 1953 the post-Stalin leadership failed to state explicitly the na-

[25] Chapters 5 and 7 of Solomon, *Soviet Criminal Justice*.
[26] Oleg V. Khlevniuk, *The History of the Gulag: From Collectivization to the Great Terror* (New Haven, 2004), 186–188.
[27] Weiner, *Making Sense of War*, 33.

ture and scope of the changes it was initiating. This left many citizens in a state of anxiety, uncertain of how their own political beliefs fitted with the new formulations found in the Soviet media. Such concerns were redoubled when one of the reforms—the amnesty—led to a wave of crime in the summer of 1953. The popular mood, as recorded in the surveillance materials produced by the Soviet authorities at least, was not simply anxious but at times heated and angry. While some did welcome the restoration of *zakonnost'*, many citizens suggested that the new political course signaled an alarming breakdown in vigilance which placed the Soviet community at risk.

The Doctors' Plot Reversed

On 13 January 1953 *Pravda* announced that enemies had been uncovered at the very core of Soviet power. A group of Kremlin doctors, several of them bearing Jewish-sounding surnames, were accused of murdering Andrei Zhdanov and Aleksandr Shcherbakov, and of hatching further plots against Soviet leaders. The Doctors' Plot, as the conspiracy came to be known, was the culmination of the postwar antisemitic campaigns. Although it did not openly admit to attacking Jews, the late Stalinist press had frequently made allusions to "bourgeois mentality" and "bourgeois nationalism," while showering hostile abuse on those bearing Jewish names. On this occasion *Pravda* had done both, referring in passing to Solomon Mikhoels as the "well-known bourgeois Jewish nationalist," and in a spectacular performance of Stalinist invective, identifying the doctors as every kind of enemy conceivable: "criminals, spies, warmongers, traitors, monsters, loathsome vermin, foul degenerates, contemptible hirelings, a band of beasts in human form, members of a terrorist group, and a gang of doctor-poisoners."[28] The population was urged to be on its guard for similar acts of sabotage. Across the Soviet Union communists and ordinary citizens assembled in local party headquarters and workplaces to read the newspaper communiqué, to collectively voice their outrage toward the unmasked enemies, and to swear their commitment to rooting out further traitors and spies who might be lurking in their midst.[29]

Just under three months later, on Saturday, 4 April 1953, a decree ordered the release and rehabilitation of the accused. On the same day Nikolai Mikhailov, first secretary of the Moscow gorkom (the party's city commit-

---

[28] "Podlye shpiony i ubiitsy pod maskoi professorov-vrachei," *Pravda,* 13 January 1953, 1. Mikhoels, a leader of the Jewish Antifascist Committee and director of the Moscow Jewish Theatre, became one of the most prominent victims of postwar antisemitism when he was assassinated in January 1948.

[29] Mordechai Altshuler, "More about Public Reaction to the Doctors' Plot," *Jews in Eastern Europe* 2 (1996): 22–57. See also Gaël Moullec and Nicolas Werth, eds., *Rapports secrets soviétiques: La société russe dans les documents confidentiels, 1921–1991* (Paris, 1994), 587–591.

tee), sent a special report to Khrushchev on reactions to the reading of the decree in various factories and institutions. In keeping with the etiquette of Soviet reports, Mikhailov first gave examples of the "correct" responses, citing a worker who expressed gratitude that the party always told them the truth, "however bitter that truth might be."[30] Mikhailov was soon obliged, however, to turn his attention to the voices of dissent. After the announcement was read aloud in one factory, workers broke out in noisy protest, posing such questions as "Whom should we believe?" "Why write that they confessed, and then that they didn't?" and "Who's guilty then?" They also shouted "They'll poison again," and "We don't understand anything." The report had to be read aloud three times before the workers would be silenced.[31] By Monday morning, *Pravda* had published a long front-page editorial, providing possible answers to some of the questions workers had posed. The headline "Soviet Socialist Legality Is Inviolable" promoted the concept of *zakonnost'* as the key to understanding the event, although the main thrust of the article in fact highlighted the fragile nature of Soviet legality.[32] The reader discovered how great carelessness and political blindness had allowed MVD deputy M. D. Riumin—a hidden "enemy of the people" and "despicable adventurist"—to abuse his position of authority and to fabricate the case against the doctors. Riumin and his accomplices were accused of inciting "national hostility" and to readers accustomed to reading the Stalinist press, this indicated that the post-Stalinist government was repudiating antisemitism even though this was not spelled out. Foregrounding ideas of Soviet legality, however, the editorial also showed a reluctance to use the media's normally bellicose rhetoric—even with regard to Riumin. Whereas in January the doctors had been branded with every possible term of abuse, Riumin was rarely designated by anything stronger than the relatively mild "despicable adventurist." In place of the hysterical rhetoric of enemies, the term *zakonnost'* was taken up. Those guilty of political blindness were not branded enemies with the same kind of passion the press had shown in January but reprimanded for their failure to safeguard *zakonnost'*. The article had significant implications: first, it suggested that that the government was now committed to ensuring legal due process; second, it implied antisemitism was no longer condoned; and third, it introduced into the Soviet press a new and more restrained approach to correcting error. Although Riumin himself was labeled as a *vrag naroda* (enemy of the people) the press eschewed the more vitriolic formulations so common in Stalinist rhetoric and made no suggestion that further enemies should be unmasked.

How far did the article serve its purpose? Did it successfully calm the rather insubordinate mood described by Mikhailov on 4 April? His subse-

---

[30] RGANI f. 5, op. 30, d. 19, l. 10.
[31] RGANI f. 5, op. 30, d. 19, ll. 14–15.
[32] "Sovetskaia sotsialisticheskaia zakonnost' neprikosnovenna," *Pravda*, 6 April 1953, 1.

quent reports suggest not. He informed the Central Committee (CC) that on 8 and 9 April 1953 *Pravda* had received fifty-two letters, only fourteen of which approved the doctors' release. One reader wrote defiantly: "[Jews] are cowards, liars, and mean-spirited people and no articles in *Pravda* or any other newspaper will make us restore comradely relations with them."[33] In a similar vein, an anonymous letter said: "You think that you can change our views on Jews. No, you can't change them. In our eyes, Jews always were parasites and they always will be."[34]

The *Pravda* editors were not the only recipients of citizens' letters on this matter; so too were party leaders like Molotov (whose personal file contains an extensive collection of such correspondence). Some of his correspondents did greet the doctors' release with alacrity, hoping for an end to legal and judicial malpractice. One anonymous letter arrived from the city of Orel and, after briefly applauding the amnesty decree, the author praised the repudiation of the Doctor's Plot, demanding still greater reform within the MVD. Readily believing in the innocence of the doctors, the author was moved to express his suspicions about the methods used by the MVD more generally.[35] He detailed the kind of corrupt practices that existed, describing an incident that had occurred at a factory in the city of Shchigry in Kursk province in which forty people were interrogated "to find 'spies' among them." This anonymous citizen suggested that the criticisms of the MVD only skimmed the surface of the problem, and that in the regions arbitrary arrest was common. When a similar letter arrived from a certain Popov, who referred to himself as an elderly Russian communist, Molotov's assistants considered it sufficiently important to type their boss a summary. Written in May 1953, Popov's letter stated quite firmly, "Soviet legality has not yet been restored." He even went on to suggest that opponents of Soviet power existed because of the regime's own mistakes: "Where do the enemies within the party and power come from? It is very often as a result of our own bungling." According to Popov, it was easy to recruit enemies from among the Volga Germans, Crimean Tatars, Ingushes, Mingrelians, and Ukrainian and Baltic nationalists because of the mass persecutions they had endured under Stalin.[36] In both letters the regime's much-vaunted restoration of *zakonnost'* was welcome, but only a first step toward the more radical reform they hoped for.

Such appeals for greater reform appear relatively rarely in the extant corpus of letters, however, and the antisemitic sentiment described in Mikhailov's reports also made its way into correspondence addressed to Kremlin leaders. Many of the letters written in the wake of the doctors' re-

---

[33] RGANI f. 5. op. 30, d. 5, l. 10.
[34] RGANI f. 5. op. 30, d. 5, l. 14.
[35] RGASPI f. 82, op. 2. d. 1466, ll. 40–41.
[36] RGASPI f. 82, op. 2. d. 1456, l. 2.

habilitation objected to the implied repudiation of antisemitism. Disturbed by the party's new stance, several letter writers took the opportunity to demand the banishment of Jews. One anonymous letter lamented that Moscow has been flooded with Jews, calling for them to be deported to the "national state of Birobidzhan," where the Jewish Presidium member L. M. Kaganovich could be their leader.[37] A letter from the town of Gor'kii, signed a "group of comrades," argued that nowhere else in the world did Jews have as many "rights" as in the USSR, allowing them to become the wealthiest of all the nationalities, take all the best flats, and seize the best jobs in medicine, trade, theater, music, and so on—"anywhere where physical work is not necessary."[38] Another argued that there had been many Jews among the oppositionists, and that they had given away state secrets, undermining the Soviets' efforts in the war (in which "brave and honest Russian warriors" had lost their lives).[39]

Others drew on more traditional myths about Jews, and one anonymous letter addressed to Molotov is illustrative of the way Soviet language sometimes broke down to reveal violent and unmodified antisemitism.[40] The awkward handwriting and flawed spelling suggest a lack of confidence on paper, yet the author seemed keen to "speak Bolshevik," claiming to write on behalf of "all the workers," and later for "we military workers and peasants." In the opening paragraph, however, he justified his hatred of Jews by dint of a personal anecdote articulated in a language long predating Bolshevik-speak. "I was at the front and I was ill," he explained, "and there was a yid selling vodka. I asked him to sell me some for money, but he said he'd only sell it for my gold watch and rings."[41] The wartime setting suggests that this man's experiences at the front gave such beliefs new meaning, but his formulation also draws on age-old stereotypes of Jews as peddlers, ever greedy for gold. To make his argument even more compelling, the letter writer continued: "And there's still the fact that they bathe their wives in milk and then the milk gets sold in the shops!"[42] Fearing contamination, he projected onto Jewish culture dangerous and secretive rituals and reviled Jews as unhygienic outsiders. In another letter, Anna Karob, a young worker, claimed that Jews love "bloody feasts."[43] Echoing the Beilis case of 1913,[44] when a Jewish worker stood accused of the ritual murder of a child, these letters suggest the

---

[37] Addressing Beriia, Bulganin, and Molotov collectively, the authors of this letter identified themselves as a group of Russian workers (RGASPI f. 82, op. 2, d. 1446, ll. 42–43).

[38] RGASPI f. 82, op. 2, d. 1466, l. 55.

[39] RGASPI f. 82, op. 2., d. 1466, ll. 45–46.

[40] RGASPI f. 82, op. 2., d. 1466, ll. 38–39.

[41] RGASPI f. 82, op. 2, d. 1466, l. 38. The writer uses the offensive Russian word *zhid*, equivalent to the English word "yid."

[42] RGASPI f. 82, op. 2, d. 1466, l. 38.

[43] RGASPI f. 82, op. 2, d. 1449, l. 122.

[44] See Hans Rogger, "The Beilis Case: Antisemitism and Politics in the Reign of Nicholas II," *Slavic Review* 25 (1966): 615–629.

survival of a popular culture that had, in some respects, resisted Soviet re-fashioning.[45]

Letter writers put pen to paper because they feared the party was making a grave mistake in repudiating antisemitism. In fact, some suspected that this "leniency" toward Jews was part of a much wider breakdown in vigilance that would lead to a rise in enemy activity. Anna Karob's visceral anger to-ward Jews was linked to a broader concern that the nation's new leaders were not on their guard. She went on to describe how disorienting young people found the rehabilitation of those condemned only three months previously:

> First of all, I'd like to tell you a little about myself, and then I will ask you to give me an answer. I am a simple worker on the railways and I live in a dormi-tory. Lots of signalmen live here, all young boys and girls coming from differ-ent districts. And I'll tell you honestly, no one reads any newspapers, books, or magazines, though sometimes if there's something alarming on the radio, then you might see the young people gathering round the wireless. And so when it was announced that the doctor-professors were released and that the govern-ment had fully acquitted them of the slander the people had cast on them, no one could get their head round it. Seeing as I read a lot of literature, the girls in our group—twelve of them—came to me for explanations. But I couldn't help them, when I myself had lost my head.[46]

According to Anna, young workers may have appeared impervious to the world of the Soviet media, but they were nonetheless aware of—and dis-turbed by—the changes taking place. Calling 1953 the "most painful year of all we have lived through," she went on to suggest that public confidence, already shaken by Stalin's death, was further destabilized by the specter of enemies at large. She wrote:

> We lost our great friend and father, our beloved and dear Iosif Vissarionovich, and the tears on our face were still not dry, the trepidation in people's hearts over our children's future had not calmed, when the stunning news spread, and the terrible thought pierced people's brains—enemies of the people are free. They once more have the right to commit their dark acts, to wreck mankind's peaceful work, and to receive praise and rewards for their deeds from their American-English bosses.[47]

---

[45] In his examination of the interviews conducted with Soviet refugees by the Harvard Proj-ect, William Korey found that prerevolutionary stereotypes were still entrenched. He suggests that about 10% were ready to voice a violent antisemitism that might, for example, depict Jews as ritual blood drinkers. See William Korey, "Continuities in Popular Perceptions of Jews in the Soviet Union," in *Hostages of Modernization: Studies on Modern Antisemitism 1870–1933/ 39*, ed. Herbert A. Strauss (Berlin: de Gruyter, 1993), vol. 2, 1383–1405.

[46] RGASPI f. 82, op. 2. d. 1449, l. 121.

[47] RGASPI f. 82, op. 2. d. 1449, l. 122.

Experiencing significant distress, Karob attributed her anxiety both to Stalin's death and to the inexplicable exoneration of those who had been so unequivocally cast as enemies. She not only feared the doctors themselves, now able to engage in their dastardly actions once more, but also seemed to suspect that the new reform course indicated a lapse in vigilance.

In some letters, a contrast was established between Stalin, who instinctively knew how to identify an enemy, and his successors, who lacked this insight and were perhaps proving too complacent. One angry letter writer expressed outrage that the new leaders seemed to be questioning Stalin's proficiency in unmasking enemies. He wrote: "It's as if they're saying that when faced with the unmasking of the doctor-wreckers he failed to spot the 'actions of adventurists.' You must understand that this is going too far!"[48] Another letter reminded its intended readers (Beriia, Molotov, and Bulganin) that Gor'kii had warned them that the country was crawling with enemies awaiting their chance to pounce, and that it was important for leaders to be able to "sense" (*chuvstvovat'*) their enemies, even when they hide behind deceptive smiles.[49]

The violent reactions provoked by the doctors' rehabilitation were thus not solely the result of antisemitic traditions but pointed to wider fears about a breakdown in vigilance on the part of the political elite. Significantly, those who *accepted* the doctors' innocence sometimes also sought enemies to blame for the confusing and unsatisfactory situation. Without waiting for the usual prompt from the Soviet press, some launched into their own vitriolic attacks. One anonymous letter affirmed:

We, Soviet citizens of Dnepropetrovsk, like all decent [*chestnye*] people of the Soviet Union and the whole world, heap shame on the former workers of the MGB [Ministry of State Security], raging bourgeois nationalist-antisemites, base betrayers of the multinational Soviet state, bandits and pogrom organizers of the same breed as Petliura, Ezhov, Hitler, who committed cruel violence and torture, in contravention of the laws of the Soviet state, against leading figures in Soviet medicine—the professors Vovsi, Vinogradov, Egorov, Fel'dman, Etinger, B. B. Kogan, M. B. Kogan.[50]

The authors' collective identity seems founded on a combination of Soviet patriotism, local pride, and respectability, but it is strengthened through the act of shaming others and branding enemies. The press treatment of Riumin and his colleagues in the MVD had been restrained, and *Pravda*'s criticisms seem insipid next to the string of abuse offered in this letter. Its writers refused to follow the linguistic shift toward moderation, ignoring the press's

[48] RGASPI f. 82, op. 2, d. 1466, l. 52.
[49] RGASPI f. 82, op. 2, d. 1466, l. 42.
[50] RGANI f. 5, op. 30, d. 5, l. 30.

attempt to find more temperate ways to express criticism. Using all the devices the regime had taught them over the past quarter-century, the letter writers unstintingly piled on layers of abusive terms: ones specific to the case—antisemite pogrom organizers (*pogromshchiki*); more malleable labels such as betrayers, bourgeois nationalists, and bandits; a selection of adjectives to add an extra dash of condemnation—raging, base, cruel—and reference to some of the big names from the Soviet roll call of enemies—Simon Petliura, Nikolai Ezhov, and Adolf Hitler.[51] They constructed compound terms such as "bandits-antisemites-terrorists" (*bandity-antisemity-terroristy*) which, by chaining together insults, became triply virulent.[52] Some Soviet citizens were, it seems, extremely fluent in this language of hate.

Some writers were obedient to the press, calling Riumin merely an "adventurist" (*avantiurist*), but many were more innovative, labeling those who fabricated the cases "foul vermin" (*gnusnaia gadina*) and "sadists from the NKVD" (*sadisty iz NKVD*).[53] Lidiia Timashchuk had been praised in January for unmasking "base spies," but she was now condemned by some as an enemy. A certain S. Grinberg from Moscow labeled Timashchuk a "slanderer and corrupt beast."[54] Chugunov, also from Moscow, wrote to *Pravda*: "That base creature, that certified 'Cheberiachka,' full of Hitlerite ideology, under the guise of a Soviet patriot, committed the most disgusting anti-Soviet acts."[55] In using the word "Cheberiachka," the letter writer referred to Vera Cheberiak, the mother of one of the murdered boy's friends in the Beilis case, found to be the ringleader of a gang of thieves and the mastermind behind the crime.[56] Chugunov used this insulting term, common in Jewish vernacular, to condemn Timashchuk as both an antisemite and a criminal.[57]

The release of the doctors, and the accompanying press materials, thus created a climate of uncertainty: according to one citizen, the "population is buzzing with rumors."[58] Despite the regime's attempt to find a less antagonistic mode of conducting political life, moreover, Soviet readers did not immediately modify their way of viewing the world and the rehabilitation of the Kremlin doctors spurred some citizens to defend a Soviet identity based on pride in their vigilance toward a host of inveterate enemies.

[51] Simon Petliura was the leader of a Ukrainian nationalist movement during the Civil War period and led troops against the Red Army.

[52] In the rhetoric of the Moscow show trials Dermot Fitzsimons identifies compound terms as one of the rhetorical tools used to produce the required mood of excited hatred. See Dermot Fitzsimons, "'Shoot the Mad Dogs!': Appellation and Distortion during the Moscow Show Trials, 1936–8," *Slovo* 13 (2001): 172–187.

[53] RGANI f. 5, op. 30, d. 5, ll. 28–30.

[54] RGANI f. 5, op. 30, d. 5, l. 34.

[55] RGANI f. 5, op. 30, d. 5, l. 8.

[56] Harriet Murav, "The Beilis Ritual Murder Trial and the Culture of Apocalypse," *Cardozo Studies in Law and Literature* 12 (2000): 243–263.

[57] On the term "Cheberiachka," see P. Korolenko, "Ot 'strashnogo' Iudka k 'ne strashnomu' Beilisu: V. G. Korolenko. Noch'iu. Delo Beilisa," *Russkii zhurnal* (March 2001), www.russ.ru/krug/razbor/20010330.html.

[58] RGASPI f. 82, op. 2, d. 1466, l. 47.

An Enemy Unmasked

A second political outrage hit the headlines in July with the arrest of Beriia, one of the most powerful members of the Presidium since Stalin's death as well as minister of internal affairs. In his memoirs, Khrushchev depicts Beriia's ousting as a legitimate move against a nascent dictator.[59] The tussle for political power was perhaps more complex than Khrushchev allowed (and his own motives less blameless), but it certainly seems that by the summer of 1953 relations among the ruling elite were becoming unworkable.[60] On 26 June 1953 Beriia was arrested, and by the end of the year he had been sentenced to death. Beriia did not simply disappear from the public arena: his arrest was announced to the public, and in the press campaign that followed, the concept of socialist legality was used to make sense of this dramatic event.

In *Pravda*'s rendition, Beriia's offenses were many and varied: he had attempted a personal seizure of power; he had tried to promote the MVD over the Soviet government; he had even delayed decisions on rural matters in order to increase social strife in the country. Crucially, he had disobeyed orders to strengthen legality (*zakonnost'*) and had failed to rectify cases of lawlessness and arbitrariness within the ministry. Generous proof was thus presented to demonstrate that Beriia had turned away from communism to become a "bourgeois," a hireling of foreign imperialist powers. These accusations were all made public on the front page of *Pravda* on 10 July 1953.[61]

Beriia was the highest-ranking political figure to be eliminated since the show trials of the 1930s, and the news hit the front pages without any sort of warning or buildup. The tenor of the first article suggests apprehension about introducing this piece of disturbing news. The headline was upbeat— "The indestructible unity of the party, government, and Soviet people"—and roughly the first third of the article was spent reassuring the reader of the great industrial and economic strength of the Soviet Union. This uncertainty also manifested itself in the rather mixed language of the text. To some extent, *Pravda* returned to the hostile and adversarial rhetoric that had been employed under Stalin to condemn enemies, designating Beriia a "bourgeois turncoat," a "traitor," a "renegade," and an "enemy of the people." There was a tentative reference to a "cult of personality" that had been damaging Soviet life.[62] The article did not abandon the new terms of 1953, however, and the more extreme aspects of the Stalinist lexicon *were* avoided. In official rhetoric, for example, neither zoological labels nor metaphors of disease

[59] N. S. Khrushchev, *Khrushchev Remembers*, trans. Strobe Talbott (London, 1971), 321–341.

[60] Taubman, *Khrushchev*, 248–249.

[61] "Nesokrushimoe edinenie partii, pravitel'stva, sovetskogo naroda," *Pravda*, 10 July 1953, 1.

[62] "Kommunisty Moskvy i Moskovskoi oblasti edinodushno odobriaiut postanovlenie plenuma TsK KPSS," *Pravda*, 10 July 1953, 2.

were used to condemn Beriia. Instead the articles repeatedly alluded to the importance of *zakonnost'*, and Beriia's disregard for legality in his work at the MVD. Readers were told that Beriia had opposed the changes of recent months: "Required to fulfill the directives of the Central Committee of the party and the Soviet government on strengthening Soviet legality and eradicating lawlessness and arbitrariness [*bezzakonie i proizvol*], Beriia deliberately hampered the completion of these directives, and in several cases sought to distort them."[63] The lexicon of the socialist legality campaign was now expanded, with the notions of lawlessness and arbitrariness frequently used to condemn Beriia's political style. Thus, on one hand, the public was encouraged to imagine Beriia as an enemy; on the other, readers were told to abhor the arbitrary practices of vilifying adversaries he had encouraged. The ambiguity gave rise to a variety of confused and sometimes passionate reactions.

Beriia's direct victims were among the first to respond. A letter signed by A. E. Nikiforov from the town of Syktyvkar in the Komi ASSR opened with a dramatic self-revelation: "I am not at all Nikiforov and I am no Georgian. I am Nikolai Vasil'evich Kokoev, Ossetian, and for twenty years I have been hiding from the enemy of the people Beriia under the surname Nikiforov."[64] Having fiercely hidden his real identity and endured separation from his family for two decades, he considered the revelations about Beriia sufficient proof of reform to risk confession. Nikiforov/Kokoev was one of the first purge victims to write this sort of plea for rehabilitation, believing that the attack on Beriia and the MVD documented the Soviet leadership's intention to right some of the wrongs of the past. He was not the only purge victim to take such a step, and *Pravda*'s editors reported to the CC that they had several letters, coming in particular from the Caucasus where Beriia worked in the early part of his career.[65]

Most citizens knew of Beriia only from the Soviet media and propaganda, but this did not stop them having strong opinions about him. Between 10 July and 20 August, *Pravda* received three hundred letters from readers about Beriia's arrest. P. Loginov wrote:

> I am seriously ill, I am bedridden, but along with the people, I can still express my indignation over the baseness of the bandit Beriia. As a Soviet person, I have the right to voice my anger and have the right to ask the Supreme Court of the USSR to punish this despicable enemy severely, to punish him in accordance with all the laws of Soviet legality. The bandit Beriia deserves to be hung like a dog.[66]

[63] "Nesokrushimoe edinenie partii, pravitel'stva, sovetskogo naroda," *Pravda*, 10 July 1953, 1.
[64] RGANI f. 5, op. 30, d. 4, l. 133.
[65] RGANI f. 5, op. 30, d. 4.
[66] RGANI f. 5, op. 30, d. 4, l. 140.

Although he gave a nod to the new insistence on Soviet legality, Loginov drew on the rhetoric of the Stalinist press in a manner far more extreme than the *Pravda* editorialists had allowed themselves, labeling Beriia a "bandit," "dog," and "enemy." Z. A. Shomko displayed equal readiness to engage in violent rhetoric against Beriia. Although her letter began conventionally, with images of joyous throngs of Soviet parents unanimously declaring, "We won't allow anyone to destroy our happiness and the happiness of our children," she soon transformed these Soviet parents into a bloodthirsty lynch mob: "I join my voice to the millions of voices of mothers and fathers who say: 'Death to the base enemy of the people Beriia. Death to enemies of humanity! Death!'"[67] More extreme still, M. E. Nud'ko from Kazakhstan claimed Beriia was not a human but a beast (*zver'*) and death too good for him. Like Loginov, who hankered after violent and visible punishment, Nud'ko hoped new public rituals might be elaborated, writing: "He should be put in a cage like a jackal and taken round the cities, the large communist building sites, factories, mines, and collective farms, showing workers his brutal, beastlike [*ozverelyi*] physiognomy."[68] Perhaps remembering the revolutionary celebrations of the late 1920s, when large mannequins representing various enemies were paraded along the streets in cages, Nud'ko now imagined a pageant enlivened by the performance of a living enemy.[69]

Beriia's arrest also offered a possible key to understanding the changes occurring in the country. In the identification of a new enemy, people found a scapegoat for the misfortunes that had befallen them over the past four months. Beriia was imagined as an enemy of great stature who could be made to bear responsibility for all the recent ills, from Stalin's death in March to the release of the Kremlin doctors and the amnesty decree. In a report on workers' reactions to the newspaper readings held in July 1953, Mikhailov listed some of the questions posed: one person asked if Beriia's "sabotage" had caused Stalin's sudden death, while at the Voroshilov Kolkhoz (collective farm) in Moscow oblast another wanted to know if Beriia and his assistants had "shortened the life of Iosif Vissarionovich Stalin."[70] Seemingly reluctant to believe Stalin human and mortal, they preferred to create a more dramatic narrative, in which Beriia starred as the evil plotter, and where death confirmed Stalin's status as hero and martyr.

At such meetings, many also brought up the Doctors' Plot: What role had Beriia played in it? Was it true that the doctors had now escaped abroad? Was the release of the doctors correct, or had perhaps Beriia contrived the release in order to slander colleagues in the MVD?[71] Behind these questions

[67] RGANI f. 5, op. 30, d. 4, l. 140.
[68] RGANI f. 5, op. 30, d. 4, l. 141.
[69] Victoria Bonnell, *Iconography of Power: Soviet Political Posters under Lenin and Stalin*, 2d ed. (Berkeley, 1999), 210.
[70] RGANI f. 5, op. 30, d. 4, ll. 12–13.
[71] RGANI f. 5, op. 30, d. 3, l. 74, and d. 4, l. 12. These questions seem to have appeared in

lay the glimmer of hope that the release of the doctors, the repudiation of antisemitism, and the apparent softening of Stalinist culture were all part of a loathsome plot concocted by Beriia. He was also blamed for the amnesty.[72] One kolkhoz member asked: Was the decree on amnesty linked to Beriia's sabotage?[73] Unwelcome to many citizens, the amnesty could be rebuffed as part and parcel of Beriia's criminal activity. The unmasking of an enemy was a familiar act in Stalinist culture and was interpreted as a signal that recent reforms might be reversed and repudiated.

One colorful rumor wove a complex narrative, offering an inventive explanation for the difficult events of past months. The rumor, attributed to a Moscow party member named Zen'kovich, began with Stalin's death: "At the time of Stalin's illness MVD guards were permanently in the room where he was lying. After I. V. Stalin's death all the guards took an airplane to go on holiday to a resort. During the flight the airplane exploded and all the guards died. This was done on Beriia's instructions to cover up his traces."[74] Zen'kovich went on to claim that Beriia had been the main person responsible for the release of the doctors, and that they had now been rearrested. He finished his tale by claiming that the "amnesty recently decreed was on the whole for Vlasovites, and Beriia wanted to turn them into an army and seize power."[75] Zen'kovich was not alone in his suspicions. One anonymous letter writer noted the sudden nature of Stalin's death and asked if he had died at the hands of "scum of the earth" (*izvergi roda chelovecheskogo*). If this was the case, he urged: "Don't have mercy on them, hand them over to us, the people, and we will tear them to pieces!"[76] Official reports lamented the rapid proliferation of "absurd" rumors.[77]

The letters vilifying Beriia and the rumors blaming him for Stalin's death and the March amnesty suggest the inventiveness of Soviet popular culture. Although their language sometimes drew on the rabid lexicon developed by the Stalinist press, letter writers and rumormongers were original in the way they responded to new developments, seeking to impose their own readings on the events described in the press. By the summer of 1953 it was not only

---

all forums, from the Moscow gorkom and obkom meetings to workers' conversations. A letter to *Pravda* from B. G. Bulatov, a Muscovite, posed similar questions. See RGANI f. 5, op. 30, d. 4, l. 138.

[72] RGANI f. 5, op. 30, d. 4, l. 24.

[73] RGANI f. 5, op. 30, d. 4, l. 13.

[74] RGANI f. 5, op. 30, d. 4, l. 25.

[75] The term "Vlasovites" referred to Soviet soldiers who fought on the German side during the Second World War. Many were prisoners of war who preferred to enlist rather than endure the terrible conditions of German captivity, while others deserted from the Red Army, responding to an appeal made by General Andrei Vlasov. Vlasov, himself captured by the Germans, promised Russian workers and peasants a better life; and his leaflets, dropped behind the Soviet lines near Smolensk in January 1943, inspired several thousand to come in search of him and his "liberation army." See Geoffrey Hosking, *A History of the Soviet Union 1917–1991*, 3d ed. (London, 1992), 289–291.

[76] RGASPI f. 82, op. 2, d. 1466, l. 23.

[77] RGANI f. 5, op. 30, d. 4, l. 20.

that official explanations were unclear or incomplete (although the official descriptions of Beriia's wrongdoing surely raised more questions than they answered) but also that the first post-Stalin reform—the amnesty—had produced unwelcome social change. As the next section shows, the amnesty (and the surrounding press coverage) would produce even more heated responses from the Soviet public than the doctors' release or Beriia's arrest.

Mass Exodus from the Gulag

Decreed on 27 March 1953 by the Supreme Soviet and announced on *Pravda*'s front page the following day, the amnesty had far-reaching impact over the course of 1953.[78] Prisoners who had displayed a conscientious attitude toward work and whose crimes did not represent a "significant danger for the state" were to be amnestied. The first clause released those with sentences under five years, while later ones included pregnant women, mothers with children under ten, children under eighteen, men over fifty-five, women over fifty, those convicted for certain offenses at work or during military service, and those sentenced by laws now under review. The decree also halved sentences of over five years (although some of the gravest offenses, including most counter-revolutionary crimes, were excluded from this clause).[79] The published decree also recognized the need to reconsider the length of sentences given for domestic crimes and work-related offenses, indicating that criminal justice reform was planned.

The Soviet authorities tried to persuade the public that the amnesty was an appropriate decision. Readers were told that this mass release of prisoners was possible as a result of the "consolidation" of the Soviet state and society (*uprochenie obshchestvennogo i gosudarstvennogo stroia*), the improved welfare and raised cultural levels of the population, the growth in citizens' political awareness, and the public's honorable attitude toward its public duty. Soviet society, it suggested, was sufficiently robust to cope with the return. Writing in *Pravda* three weeks after the decree, Minister of Justice K. P. Gorshenin asked readers to interpret the amnesty in the light of "socialist legality" and lauded the decision to allow prisoners to return to their homes and work as evidence of socialist humaneness (*sotsialisticheskaia gumannost'*).[80] In addition to the theme of legality, the editorial also revived the concept of correction. According to Gorshenin, the amnesty decree was evidence that Soviet laws helped those who committed errors "to correct themselves" (*ispravit'sia*) and then return to the "path of honest labor." Gor-

[78] "Ukaz Prezidiuma Verkhovnogo Soveta SSSR ob amnistii," *Pravda*, 28 March 1953, 1.

[79] Marc Elie estimates that the number of "political" prisoners released by the amnesty of 1953 was between thirty thousand and seventy-eight thousand. For detail of the clauses under which they were released, see Elie, "Les anciens détenus du Goulag," 33–34.

[80] "Sotsialisticheskaia zakonnost' na strazhe interesov naroda," *Pravda*, 17 April 1953, 2.

shenin's comments thus revived the notion of redemption, once seen as the main function of the Gulag but long absent from the press. From Gorshenin's article it was not clear, however, if those who benefited from the amnesty had been reformed *entirely* during their stint within the Gulag, or if the process was still ongoing (and the returnees thus only halfway to becoming decent Soviet citizens).[81] This ambiguity regarding the status of the returnees was to become one of the contested features of the Gulag releases, although it would have been apparent to only the most careful of readers in the spring of 1953. Indeed, the general message from the Soviet leadership was that the enormous size of the Gulag was unnecessary and that Soviet society could afford to welcome home a significant portion of its inmates.

Initially some citizens responded enthusiastically, sending letters of goodwill to the Supreme Soviet. Some of these had very personal reasons: they or their relatives could hope for imminent release. One fourth-grade girl from Irkutsk oblast wrote to the chairman of the Supreme Soviet's Presidium: "Dear Grandpa [*dedushka*] Kliment Efremovich Voroshilov. With all my heart I thank you for the amnesty decree. My father was temporarily isolated and was in prison. Now he will be a Soviet citizen again and will return home to our Soviet family."[82] Others were quick to assure their illustrious readers that they personally had never been in trouble, but that they nonetheless appreciated the generosity of the decree. Determined to read it as evidence of the superiority of the Soviet system, some gleefully imagined how unnerved the USSR's enemies would be by the decree's humaneness.[83]

Such confidence was far from universal, however. According to reports on the popular mood composed for the party's CC immediately following the publication of the decree, not all citizens were entirely convinced that the return could happen as seamlessly as Gorshenin had promised. A summary of reactions in Ukraine written on 1 April recorded certain anxieties. Several people apparently voiced concern that the decree would release minors from the colonies who would engage in hooliganism and theft. So widespread in the postwar years, it seems the problem of *bezprizornost'* (homeless children) still weighed heavily on the public's mind. Other citizens suggested that certain prisoners needed an intermediary stage on their return from the periphery, one proposing that prisoners complete a probationary period on remote building sites, before they be allowed to reintegrate fully into Soviet society.[84]

These initial worries would only grow over the coming months. Despite

[81] According to Gorshenin, the amnesty had been applied to prisoners who had shown, through their "conscientious attitude to work," that they could return to a decent working life and "*become* healthy members of society" (my italics).

[82] GARF f. 7523, op. 58, d. 130, l. 6. In this *delo*, ll. 1–30 contain similar letters from relatives of prisoners whom they now hoped would be released and from prisoners themselves. See also GARF f. 7523, op. 85, d. 235, ll. 8–12.

[83] GARF f. 7523, op. 85, d. 235, l. 7.

[84] RGANI f. 5, op. 30, d. 36, ll. 9–13.

the regime's public confidence in the spring of 1953, the amnesty caused significant disturbance. In the first weeks following the decree several serious incidents including drunkenness, violent rioting, stabbings, killings, and rapes occurred on trains carrying released prisoners home from the camps.[85] In one particularly gruesome case in mid-April, fifteen amnestied prisoners entered a carriage reserved for female travelers and raped almost all of the forty women present. All but one of the attackers managed to escape. In several similar cases over the spring and early summer of 1953 the police proved incapable of controlling the returning prisoners. In one incident described in a secret report to the party's CC, a train transporting 1,139 prisoners released from camps in Sakhalin became the site of fights, thefts, and rapes. When it arrived at In station in the Far East, chaos reigned and the local police were overwhelmed. A man wearing a woman's (stolen) coat was arrested, and an enraged crowd of two to three hundred set on the policemen, trying to push the officers onto the tracks. The policemen tried to leave the station, but the throngs of ex-prisoners pursued them, armed with knives, pikes, and stones.[86]

Even once the prisoners finished their long train journeys, they continued to present difficulties for the authorities. In the second and third quarters of the year the number of crimes registered showed increases of up to two-thirds in comparison with the same period in 1952: muggings had increased by 66.4 percent; murders by 30.7 percent; rapes by 27.5 percent; theft of personal property by 63.4 percent; and hooliganism by 19.3 percent.[87] Beneficiaries of the amnesty were certainly blamed for this sudden crime wave: in Leningrad, a full 41 percent of those arrested between April and September 1953 were people released by the March amnesty; in Penza oblast, 45 percent of those convicted for theft and 40 percent of those sentenced for murder had come almost directly from the Gulag.[88] In many cases, the criminal actions were the result of sheer desperation, and the government itself recognized the failure of local authorities to find jobs and homes for the returning prisoners.[89] Particularly alarming for the authorities (and citizens), though, were signs of an organized criminal fraternity alongside the incidents

[85] RGANI f. 5, op. 21, d. 556, ll. 25–36, reproduced in Moullec and Werth, eds., *Rapports secrets soviétiques,* 409–411.

[86] RGANI f. 5, op. 21, d. 556, ll. 84–88, reproduced in Moullec and Werth, eds., *Rapports secrets soviétiques,* 415–416.

[87] GARF f. 8131, op. 32, d. 2386, l. 28.

[88] GARF f. 8131, op. 32, d. 2386, l. 31.

[89] In late May 1953 the Council of Ministers recognized that the reintegration of amnestied prisoners had been poorly managed and issued a resolution on "the elimination of inadequacies in the resettlement of citizens freed by the amnesty." V. P. Pronin, reporting on the Council of Ministers' work regarding the resettlement of returnees in July, acknowledged that the crisis was ongoing, and that 16% of arrivals had still not found work. According to official statistics, in Iaroslavl' oblast, for example, there were 2,272 amnestied prisoners without work; in Molotov oblast 2,243; and in Kirov oblast 3,420. Real unemployment could easily have been higher. RGANI f. 5, op. 30, d. 36, ll. 35–37.

of petty theft and muggings. By the end of the year official reports described several cases of "criminal-recidivists organizing criminal gangs." Not only were they responsible for armed robberies and violent stabbings, but they appeared capable of outwitting the law. In one case a group of eight "bandits," all amnestied over the preceding months, disrupted the court hearing of a criminal ringleader, attempted to murder key witnesses, and even managed to "spring" one of their gang members from a prison convoy.[90]

There were, then, some grounds for citizens' anxieties in 1953. Many people had no direct experience of this crime wave, but rumors of unchecked violence committed by Gulag returnees converged with anxieties regarding the new political course Stalin's successors had chosen, creating a sense of panic among at least some sectors of Soviet society. On 19 June 1953 I. Kiriushkin, head of the Correspondence Section at *Pravda,* reported to Khrushchev on the letters received from the newspaper's readers. "I bring to your attention," he wrote, "the collection of letters received by the editors of *Pravda.* Recent letters report a significant increase in petty crime, and in the number of burglaries and murders committed in many towns and regions. . . . Some authors link these excesses with the amnesty and the release of individuals who don't wish to work but return to the path of crime." As was the custom, Kiriushkin included examples from this body of correspondence. Key themes were established: the unprecedented scale of this phenomenon; the audacity of the criminals who dared to act in the broad light of day; the failure of the police to respond adequately. Letter writers did not see the issue of crime in isolation but presented it as part of a grave crisis. One Leningrader wrote that the climate of fear engendered by the releases "assists the 'work' of the bandits and creates favorable conditions for the enemies of the Soviet Union who use—for their own ends—individuals released from the corrective labor camps." A citizen from the city of Molotov also saw serious political implications, fearing that the rise in crime testified to the state's failure to protect its citizens from enemy action. Lamenting the impunity with which the murderers carried out their "terrorist acts," he wrote: "I don't want to believe that revolutionary legislation is incapable of stopping these social enemies from damaging society, harming the people, and injuring the builders of communism."[91]

Some citizens not only articulated concerns about increased danger on the city streets but also resisted and even derided official calls to view the amnesty as an act of humaneness and legality. Citizens tended to demand a more hostile attitude toward those who violated the social order, expressing fears that the city was becoming a site of criminal and deviant behavior. They contested any implication that returning prisoners had been successfully cor-

---

[90] GARF f. 8131, op. 32, d. 2386, ll. 32–33.

[91] RGANI f. 5, op. 21, d. 539, ll. 108–128, reproduced in Moullec and Werth, eds., *Rapports secrets soviétiques,* 50–52.

rected during their time within the prison complex. Although some letter writers spoke of hooligans, it was more common for the criminals to be branded "bandits."[92] One anonymous letter addressed to Molotov manifested a highly aggressive opposition to the amnesty and labeled the returnees bandits, claiming that "night and day, the returnees, these jailbird-bandits [*vernuvshiesia tiuremshchiki-bandity*] kill and slaughter peaceable citizens, carry out armed break-ins at warehouses, and murder guards and policemen."[93] Antonova, a Moscow tram conductor, employed similar terms, claiming that "such disgraceful horrors happen in Moscow, without even speaking about the Moscow suburbs, where the bandits reign [*tsarstvo banditov*], especially with their lairs in Nikitovka and Obiralovka, stations on the Gor'kii railway line."[94] Whereas the "hooligan"—a figure much feared by the middle classes in early twentieth-century Russia—emerged from deprived slum areas and was a product of the city itself, the "bandit" of 1953 was imagined as man in transit who established his own danger zones around the railway lines and stations.[95] The *bandity* were thus imagined as marauding outsiders preying on urban society but not a part of it.[96]

Antonova's letter continued its attack on "bandits": "Indeed, this dirty water, these Russian 'gangsters' [*gangstery*] are without conscience [*sovest'*] or honor [*chest'*]. We conquered Germany when it was armed to the teeth, can it really be that our state is without the strength to conquer these parasites [*darmoedy*]?"[97] By invoking Germany, she categorically branded the criminals enemies and by labeling them "dirty water" and "parasites," she warned of their contagious nature. The term "gangster" was more unusual. A more recent borrowing than either "bandit" or "hooligan," the word "gangster" was still regarded as a foreign word and indicated her desire to brand the returnees as outsiders, even though the blight was all too familiarly "Russian."[98] Antonova was grappling to find an effective rhetoric with

---

[92] For an example of a letter that spoke of hooligans, see RGASPI f. 82, op. 2, d. 1466, l. 72.

[93] RGASPI f. 82, op. 2, d. 1466, l.71.

[94] RGASPI f. 82, op. 2, d. 1440, l. 78.

[95] On hooligans in the rapidly expanding cities of early twentieth-century Russia, see Joan Neuberger, *Hooliganism: Crime, Culture, and Power in St. Petersburg, 1900–1914* (Berkeley, 1993), 216–278.

[96] The figure of the bandit—*razboinik* or *bandit* in Russian—had a colourful history. According to Jeffrey Brooks' work on popular literature of the late imperial period, the *razboinik* appealed to readers' sympathy because he mocked authority. At this point, the term "bandit" had already been borrowed into the Russian language and featured in Vladimir Dal''s dictionary of 1882 but does not seem common in popular fiction. By the 1930s, however, it had become a core term in the aggressive newspeak of the Stalinist press and was used frequently in the angry letters citizens wrote in 1953 (rather than the term *razboinik*). The foreign origin of the word *bandit* perhaps gave it the power to estrange Gulag returnees more forcibly. See Jeffrey Brooks, *When Russia Learned to Read: Literacy and Popular Literature, 1861–1917* (Princeton, 1985), 166–213. For dictionary definitions, Vladimir Dal', *Tolkovyi slovar' zhivogo velikorusskogo iazyka* (St. Petersburg and Moscow, 1882); D. N. Ushakov, *Tolkovyi slovar' russkogo iazyka* (Moscow, 1935).

[97] RGASPI f. 82, op. 2, d. 1440, l. 78.

[98] According to N. M. Shanskii's *Etymological Dictionary of the Russian Language*, this bor-

which to repel the contingent of ex-convicts as a phenomenon completely alien to the respectable realm of Soviet society. Exposed to Stalinist newspeak for the last quarter of a century, Antonova and the other letter writers manipulated established invective in creative and innovative ways to condemn and vilify the unwanted returnees.

While *Pravda* editorials claimed that those released from the camps had shown a conscientious attitude toward work during their time in the Gulag, readers were more suspicious. Challenging the claims made in the press, one correspondent from Kazan' asked: "Why didn't Stalin—who so valued the people's labor—do this? In the month or so since Comrade Stalin's death, have the criminals really become 'conscious' [*soznatel'nye*] citizens?"[99] The revived notions of "correction" and "humaneness" were also contested. One letter writer wrote that "these 'corrected' [*ispravshiesia*] down-and-outs use their knives to strengthen the forces of darkness in the country"; placed in quotation marks, the term *ispravshiesia* was clearly a source of derision.[100] Another argued that offenders had "animal instincts" and could never be corrected; he proposed putting them to work in mines, dropping them food only when their daily quotas had been met.[101] A third bitterly recounted how the local police force had responded to his complaints simply by reminding him of the importance of re-educating criminals. Sick of the theft and violence he claimed was all around him, the letter writer suggested popular beliefs were slightly different from the official line: "But us, we believe that only the grave can correct thieves and recidivists."[102] The tram conductor Antonova used the same proverb and derided the term *gumannichat'* (to be humane)—a pejorative derivative of *gumannost'*—writing: "There's been too much humaneness shown toward these weeds [*Dovol'no gumannichat' s etim sorniakom*]." Gorshenin's talk of "correction" had clearly failed to convince these citizens that former prisoners deserved the chance to rejoin the Soviet family, and his praise for the regime's "humaneness" in decreeing the amnesty was rejected by those who wished to believe returnees were nothing more than a pack of animals.

Antonova ended her letter with some suggestions for how the authorities should deal with criminals. She wrote: "We ask you to decree a law which says that a thief who is caught, will have five fingers cut off from his left hand. They should be branded, so that people will know that these are thieves and can beware of them. Merciless and severe measures should be taken."[103]

---

rowing came from the United States in the twentieth century. He notes that it appeared for the first time in the *Dictionary of Foreign Words* (*Slovar' inostrannykh slov*) in 1942. N. M. Shanskii, *Etimologicheskii slovar' russkogo iazyka* (Moscow, 1963).

[99] RGASPI f. 82, op. 2, d. 1466, l. 58.

[100] RGASPI f. 82, op. 2, d. 1466, l. 71.

[101] GARF f. 7523, op. 85, d. 235, ll. 13–14.

[102] RGANI f. 5, op. 21, d. 539, ll. 108–128, reproduced in Moullec and Werth, eds., *Rapports secrets soviétiques*, p. 52.

[103] RGASPI f. 82, op. 2, d. 1440, l. 78.

Antonova's urges were perhaps not unique: another letter said that there was frequent talk in Moscow of an ancient Finnish law that allowed for the finger, or even the hand, of a hardened thief to be chopped off.[104] In prerevolutionary Russia physical mutilation had been one method used to permanently brand criminals as outsiders, and it apparently still appealed to some citizens in the 1950s.[105] As with some of the antisemitic responses to the doctors' release, certain aspects of traditional culture resurface here, although a letter writer such as Antonova did not identify them as archaic or prerevolutionary herself, having incorporated them into a set of beliefs she considered loyally Soviet.

Although aware of the new course being taken in the press in 1953, letter writers did not immediately agree that this kind of tolerance toward those once branded outsiders was an important facet of the new Soviet man. One worker from a car factory in Kalinin wrote: "I'm not sure, but it's perfectly possible that our government was counting on the strength of the Soviet collective, and on the gratitude of this riff-raff for what they've been given. But for the working man, it certainly doesn't make things easier that there are these swinish gangs of bandits who commit hooligan acts and refuse to contribute to our enormous work."[106] He understood the government's intentions in issuing the decree but scorned them. He was not alone. Using terminology drawn from Stalinist rhetoric, occasionally peppered with traditional notions and proverbs, many letter writers continued to view those who had committed errors as irredeemable enemies and insisted that it was the state's duty to protect Soviet citizens from these dangerous hordes. These sentiments may not have been universal, but certain commonalities among the letters suggest shared ideas about crime and punishment existed among at least some sectors of the Soviet population. And in putting pen to paper, some individuals were ready to defend these beliefs as being more truly Soviet than the ones currently promoted by the state.

Crisis Management: The Press Promises Punishment

By the beginning of July 1953 the party leadership acknowledged that there was a problem of sorts. At the CC plenum called in early July 1953 to condemn Beriia the first secretary of the Leningrad obkom (the regional party committee), V. M. Andrianov, said:

---

[104] RGANI f. 5, op. 21, d. 539, ll. 108–128, reproduced in Moullec and Werth, eds., *Rapports secrets soviétiques,* 51.

[105] Abby M. Shrader, "Branding the Exile as 'Other': Corporal Punishment and the Construction of Boundaries in Mid-Nineteenth Century Russia," in *Russian Modernity: Politics, Knowledge, Practices,* ed. David L. Hoffmann and Yanni Kotsonis (Basingstoke, U.K., 2000), 19–40 (21–22).

[106] GARF f. 7523, op. 85, d. 235, l. 13.

On the subject of the amnesty, I think that provocateurs within the Ministry of Internal Affairs left their dirty mark. Out-and-out cutthroats were let out, and the police had failed to make even the most basic of preparations. As soon as these people appeared in the city, the knives were out. A very alarming situation developed among the people. Without a doubt, the letters sent in to local authorities and to the government and the Central Committee were justified.[107]

Andrianov's claims are supported by the many internal memoranda describing violent incidents occurring across the Soviet Union in the first half of 1953. Other members of the CC, however, recognized that some of the public's reactions might have been driven by fear and rumor as much as by direct experience of crime. Although Voroshilov also criticized the way Beriia had implemented the amnesty, he suggested that popular anxieties had little basis in reality, stating: "There is much talk, and many letters—both signed and unsigned—have been written about the murders, rapes, and so on which are supposedly the result of the amnesty. When you make inquiries with the various officials responsible for the regions from where these alarming accounts have come, however, it appears that in reality nothing of the sort has occurred."[108] In the unsettled climate of 1953 it was possible for the amnestied prisoner to become a sort of folk-devil even in places where significant criminal incidents had not occurred. Although the Soviet leadership appreciated the need to find new ways of dealing with the "crime problem"—and would devote significant energies to this task in coming years—it also recognized the pressing need to quell public anxieties.

The press was at least part of the solution, and the topic of crime began to appear in Soviet newspapers over the summer of 1953. On Thursday, 18 June, the back page of *Pravda* contained the serial rubric "From the Courtroom" and under the simple headline, "Thief-Recidivist," the reader learned how the criminal Kotov was tried for pickpocketing and sent down for six years—his sixth sentence.[109] One week later, *Pravda* reported that the leader of a gang of armed thieves working in the Moscow suburbs had been sentenced to twenty-five years.[110] Local newspapers took the cue, and there was a dramatic rise in the number of "From the Courtroom" (*Iz zala suda*) articles over the coming months.[111] *Leningradskaia pravda* published three "From the Courtroom" articles in late June, and a further five by the end of the year.[112] *Moskovskaia pravda* had not contained a single crime report be-

[107] RGANI f. 2, op. 1, d. 42, l. 4.

[108] RGANI f. 2, op. 1, d. 42, l. 12.

[109] "Vor-retsidivist," *Pravda*, 18 June 1953, 4.

[110] "Khuligany-grabiteli," *Pravda*, 24 June 1953, 4.

[111] This section is based on a close study of *Pravda, Leningradskaia pravda, Moskovskaia pravda*, and *Prizyv* (the local newspaper for Vladimir oblast) over the course of 1953 and 1954.

[112] The first three were "Vory nakazany," *Leningradskaia pravda*, 23 June 1953, 4; "Grabiteli," *Leningradskaia pravda*, 25 June 1953, 4; and "Prestupniki nakazany," *Leningradskaia pravda*, 28 June 1953, 4.

tween March and August, but six appeared in the final four months of 1953. Not only did these reports acknowledge that serious crimes had been committed, they also promised the reader that the offenders received their due punishment. The last line normally assured the reader that the guilty party had been sentenced, often to a stretch of twenty or twenty-five years.

The rubric "From the Courtroom" was not in itself a new invention: it had been common in the prerevolutionary boulevard press and continued intermittently in Stalinist newspapers.[113] Crime reporting before June 1953 was sporadic, however, and the crimes described posed little real threat to citizens' personal safety.[114] The column was now radically reworked, with accounts of fights, stabbings, and thefts on the city streets. Mirroring the hostile language found in citizens' letters—many of which dated from the spring and early summer—these articles employed the term *bandit* and the headline "Bandit Punished" was repeated many times in the final months of 1953, even in cases where the offense was theft rather than banditry.[115] Several of the articles identified the criminals as amnestied prisoners, and even where the amnesty was not directly mentioned, references to the culprits' "return" in the spring of 1953 marked them as outsiders.[116] In these texts, the criminals worked in bands, preying on the city, but were not a part of it. A *Moskovskaia pravda* article from December 1953, for example, recounted how four criminals met on the platform of the Moscow-Kursk-Donbass rail depot one autumn morning, drank heavily, and then set off for Moscow, with the intention of committing a robbery at Kursk station. Once in Moscow, however, they decided to "travel" (*puteshestvovat'*) around Moscow on the tram—and robbed the conductor.[117]

Tracing the offenders' deviance back to childhood, some journalists implicitly suggested that they were born criminals, incapable of change. No excuses were offered, no extenuating family circumstances put forward to explain their actions. In contrast to the promises of greater humanity and legality made in the press in the spring, these biographies seem to reject the possibility that a criminal might be reformed or "corrected." With apparent delight, the articles gloated over the number of years a criminal had spent

[113] Louise McReynolds, *The News under Russia's Old Regime: The Development of a Mass-Circulation Press* (Princeton, 1991).

[114] In February 1953, for example, an article entitled "Criminal Gang" referred to a racket stealing and selling watches, but the watches were pilfered from a factory, not snatched from passersby; a second article reported on the theft of a fire engine. See "Shaika prestupnikov," *Moskovskaia pravda*, 7 February 1953, 4; and "Plody beskontrol'nosti i rotozeistva," *Moskovskaia pravda*, 12 February 1953, 4.

[115] "Bandit nakazan," *Leningradskaia pravda*, 27 September 1953, 4; "Grabiteli poimany," *Leningradskaia pravda*, 4 December 1953, 4.

[116] "Bandity nakazany," *Leningradskaia pravda*, 23 June 1953, 4; "Shaika vorov-retsidivistov," *Pravda*, 4 December 1953, 4; "Grabiteli," *Leningradskaia pravda*, 27 December 1953, 4; "Bandit nakazan," *Leningradskaia pravda*, 27 September 1953, 4; "Grabiteli poimany," *Leningradskaia pravda*, 4 December 1953, 4.

[117] "Bandity nakazany," *Moskovskaia pravda*, 2 December 1953, 4.

within the camp system as if this offered indisputable proof that he could never escape the criminal life. The articles even seemed to deride the idea that a criminal might return as part of the amnesty and become a valued member of society. One article explained that although the "amnesty offered Vinogradov the chance to start a new life—to become an honorable worker," he was uninterested in returning to a respectable way of life: "'Work? No way!' Vinogradov told his mother, when he arrived in Leningrad last summer."[118] By showing Vinogradov's scorn for the idea of a "new life" and redemption through labor, the article seemed to undermine the official reading of the amnesty. One report even hinted at the contagious nature of the returnees. A report in *Moskovskaia pravda* began: "Despite his youth, N. Vozdvizhenskii has already had a conviction and been in prison. In the spring of this year he was in a hospital for infectious diseases. At the end of May he left the hospital without permission, however, failing to complete the time for cure or to undergo the necessary quarantine. That same day he and three unknown accomplices robbed citizen M."[119] Despite having served his prison sentence, Vozdvizhenskii was not a healthy returnee allowed to return to society but remained a dangerous source of infection.

Throughout 1953 and 1954 these crime reports used a combination of rhetorical strategies to cast criminals as outsiders, as marauders who pillaged and ravaged Soviet society. This was, of course, a rather different reading of the amnesty from the one that had been presented on the front pages of *Pravda* in the spring of 1953. In these back-page reports, the returnees had not "corrected themselves" during their time in the Gulag and were not reformed individuals ready to return to an honest working life, as promised. Here Soviet citizens are cultured, honest people, as the newspapers had claimed when announcing the amnesty decree, but they are also victims. Instead of being able to absorb the return of Gulag veterans, they find themselves at their mercy: stabbed, robbed, abused, they are clearly unable to revel in the "humaneness" of Soviet criminal justice.

By the end of the year several of the country's leading political figures felt that the newspaper-reading public needed even greater reassurance. The call for a sacrificial lamb (or two) came in January 1954 from a commission that had been set up five months earlier to reform criminal justice.[120] Voroshilov, Gorshenin, S. N. Kruglov (Beriia's successor as minister of internal affairs), R. A. Rudenko (general procurator) and A. A. Volin (chairman of the USSR Supreme Court)—the high-profile members of the commission—wrote to the Presidium, arguing that many of the murders committed in the autumn of 1953 were the work of Gulag returnees, often motivated by desires for revenge against those who had previously testified against them or as a warn-

---

[118] "Bandit nakazan," *Leningradskaia pravda*, 27 September 1953, 4.
[119] "Bandity nakazany," *Moskovskaia pravda*, 18 November 1953, 4.
[120] GARF f. 7523, op. 85, d. 33, ll. 1–5.

ing to others. Public anxieties were obviously a key consideration: "More and more frequently people express dissatisfaction with the way murderers are punished more lightly than those who commit theft or other crimes."[121] Instead of simply arguing for a new piece of legislation reintroducing the death penalty (abolished in 1947), the commission suggested using the press to inform the public that even now the murderers *could* be sentenced to death.[122] Their proposal took a rather imaginative approach to the law.

A 1950 act permitting the death penalty in cases of counter-revolutionary crime provided a possible loophole.[123] Members of the commission suggested that if, in the course of his criminal activities, a man had killed a policeman or slandered Soviet power his crime could be classified under article 58, allowing the judge to award the death sentence. Two cases were chosen. The first concerned two previous offenders, I. A. Mitin and A. D. Samarin, leaders of a notorious gang that had carried out twenty armed raids on savings banks and shops in the Moscow region.[124] During their holdups, they had attacked both staff and customers, and in one case Mitin had shot a policeman. The court chose to classify this as the assassination of a state representative (*predstavitel' vlasti*), and as such an act of high treason.[125] In the second case, the culprit was E. G. Verakso, a member of an armed gang responsible for many thefts, burglaries, violent assaults, and killings. Allegedly, he had also made anti-Soviet comments among friends and acquaintances. It was this "slander" (not the violence or killings) that would allow the courts to convict him under article 58 and sentence him.[126] The commission drafted a newspaper article titled "The Soviet Court Severely Punished Murderers and Thieves." In it, the reader would not learn of the legal contortions necessary to sentence these men to death but simply hear the grisly stories of their violent crimes and the state's ruthless justice.[127]

In the end, such legal intricacies were unnecessary: on 30 April 1954 the death penalty was extended to intentional homicide committed under aggravating circumstances.[128] In the back-page crime reports of 1953 offenders had been given prison sentences of up to twenty-five years, but after April 1954 several accounts finish with the execution of the offender. In one such article, the reader learned how N. M. Zinov'ev, who had already served sentences for theft, banditry, and jailbreak, visited the All-Union Agricultural

---

[121] GARF f. 7523, op. 85, d. 33, ll. 6–12 (l. 6).

[122] GARF f. 7523, op. 85, d. 33, l. 7.

[123] The Presidium of the USSR Supreme Soviet had abolished the death penalty for all crimes on 26 May 1947, but on 12 January 1950 it was restored, though only for traitors, spies, subversives, and saboteurs. See Berman, *Soviet Criminal Law*, 44.

[124] For more detail of Mitin's gang and its criminal activities between 1950 and 1953, see Jeffrey Burds, "Bor'ba s banditizmom v SSSR v 1944–1953 gg.," *Sotsial'naia istoriia. Ezhegodnik 2000* (Moscow, 2000), 169–190 (178–179).

[125] GARF f. 7523, op. 85, d. 250, ll. 16–35.

[126] GARF f. 7523, op. 85, d. 250, ll. 36–43.

[127] GARF f. 7523, op. 85, d. 250, l. 15.

[128] Berman, *Soviet Criminal Law*, 46.

Exhibition where he entered into a dispute with another visitor, a postgraduate student, whom he later stabbed in the chest at the tram stop. He was to be shot.[129] So too was another previous offender who had returned home in 1953 and by May of that year attempted to rape a girl, slashed her face, and then smothered her to death.[130] There were several similar pieces.[131]

This did not signal a full-scale reversal of the changes introduced in 1953. The promises of criminal justice reform made in the weeks following Stalin's death were far from forgotten.[132] The rather panicked way that the commission cast around to invent a "murderer sentenced to death" headline is, however, revealing. It clearly shows that leading government figures were aware of popular anxieties following the amnesty and were keen to find ways to assuage them, especially as they could not immediately solve the root cause. Their legislative creativity—and their readiness to sacrifice Verakso and Mitin—also reveals the rather fragile nature of the regime's much-vaunted commitment to the concept of *zakonnost'*.

The young railway worker Anna Karob considered the year an incredibly "painful" one, and she does not seem to have been alone. The paper trail left by the regime's surveillance apparatus tells a story of disorientation and distress, with many apparently troubled by the revised status of Jews and Gulag returnees.[133] Warning against a perceived breakdown in vigilance, some letter writers believed Stalin's successors were failing in the nation's battle against hidden enemies. Although the language they used to articulate these anxieties was not homogenous, with vocabulary and syntactic forms taken from both prerevolutionary and Stalinist lexicons, these citizens believed they were defending essential Soviet values. In their understanding of "Sovietness," the fashionable terms of 1953—"legality," "humaneness," and "correction"—were sometimes an unwelcome intrusion.

Of course, 1953 was not painful for all: over half of the Gulag population was released and several miscarriages of justice—including the Doctors' Plot—were reversed. Yet for Stalin's successors, the first year of experimen-

---

[129] "Ubiitsa prigovoren k rasstrelu," *Moskovskaia pravda,* 21 November 1954, 4.

[130] "Ubiitsa prigovoren k rasstrelu," *Moskovskaia pravda,* 19 June 1954, 4.

[131] See "Vyrodok," *Leningradskaia pravda,* 11 June 1954, 4; "Ubiitsa prigovoren k rasstrelu," *Leningradskaia pravda,* 12 November 1954, 4; "Ubiitsy," *Prizyv,* 17 October 1954, 4.

[132] On 10 January 1955 an edict on the small-scale theft of state or social property instructed judges to give far lighter sentences for a first offense (correctional tasks for six months to one year or deprivation of freedom for three months). A second similar offense would be punished with deprivation of freedom for one to two years. Such sentences compare with the 1947 law in which the minimum penalty for stealing state or social property was seven years' deprivation of freedom. On 20 December 1956 petty hooliganism was made punishable by detention for three to fifteen days, whereas previously the minimum penalty had been for a year (Berman, *Soviet Criminal Law,* 46–47).

[133] On the public's reactions to the first reforms, see also Polly Jones, "From Stalinism to Post-Stalinism: De-Mythologising Stalin, 1953–6," in *Redefining Stalinism,* ed. Harold Shukman (London, 2003), 127–148 (128).

tation already revealed many of the difficulties the reform process would face over the coming years. First, the amnesty raised many practical issues, not least of which was the question of how Gulag returnees could be successfully reintegrated into Soviet society. Second, the contested nature of reactions to key news stories suggested many citizens had deep-rooted and complex ideas of what it meant to be Soviet, and their responses showed that government attempts to reconceptualize social relations and rework political rhetoric would not be accepted unthinkingly. Third, the government's attempt to deal with the emerging crisis in the final months of 1953 and early 1954 demonstrated how difficult the party leadership would find it to adhere to its own principles (like the inviolability of *zakonnost'*) and claims (such as the Gulag's capacity to correct its inmates). The events of 1953 demonstrated that the course of political reform would be far from smooth; and yet it was one that the political leadership would continue to navigate—however uneasily —for several years to come.

2 Prisoners and the Art of Petitioning, 1953–1956

And I recalled my whole life
And my life recalled everything
In that year when from the depth of the seas and the canals
My friends suddenly began returning

—Ol'ga Berggol'ts, "That Year" (1955), *Novyi mir*, August 1956

In March 1956, in the wake of Nikita Khrushchev's Secret Speech, the poet Anna Akhmatova said: "Now those who were arrested will return, and two Russias will look each other in the eye: the one that sent people to the camps and the one that was sent away."[1] This image of two nations "eyeball to eyeball" has been used frequently in western literature to evoke the difficulties Soviet society faced when huge armies of prisoners exited the camps.[2] Although evocative, Akhmatova's suggestion in the spring of 1956 that this uneasy encounter (or series of encounters) still lay ahead was misleading, for they had been taking place for almost three years before the Twentieth Party Congress.[3] The period between Stalin's death and the Secret Speech already saw the dramatic downsizing of the Gulag and the return of large numbers of prisoners.[4]

---

[1] L. K. Chukovskaia, *Zapiski ob Anne Akhmatovoi*, vol. 2, 1952–62 (Paris, 1980), 137.

[2] See, for example, Stephen F. Cohen, "The Stalin Question since Stalin," in *An End to Silence: Uncensored Opinion in the Soviet Union*, ed. Stephen F. Cohen (New York, 1982), 22–50 (27); Adler, *The Gulag Survivor*, 1; and Zubkova, *Russia after the War*, 167.

[3] On 7 March 1955 an entry in the diary of the children's author Kornei Chukovskii described an uncomfortable encounter between a returnee, S. D. Dreiden, and the man who had falsely denounced him, N. G. Dembo, editor of the Leningrad section of the publication *Iskusstvo*. At a Moscow theater, Dembo approached Dreiden and tried to congratulate him on his return, but Dreiden chose to walk straight past him, without turning his head. See Kornei Chukovskii, *Dnevnik, 1930–1969* (Moscow, 1994), 222.

[4] For other accounts of the releases occurring in the years 1953–1955, see Adler, *The Gulag Survivor*, 77–108; and Marc Elie, "Les anciens détenus du Goulag," 62–81.

The amnesty decree of 27 March 1953 began the release of large numbers of prisoners almost immediately after Stalin's death, but the process did not end there. A further 1,300,000 prisoners returned from the Gulag in the years 1954–1955.[5] By 1 January 1956 the population of the camps and colonies had fallen to 781,630, compared to 2,246,914 on 1 April 1953. In the three-year period *prior* to the Twentieth Party Congress, then, the Gulag population had been reduced by almost two-thirds.[6]

These releases were the result of various measures. On 24 April 1954 one Supreme Soviet edict offered release (or the reduction of sentence) to those who had committed offenses as juveniles, while another decreed on 14 July 1954 re-established the practice of parole for prisoners who could prove a conscientious attitude toward their work.[7] The following year the Supreme Soviet granted early release to the sick, the elderly, and mothers with young children.[8] Perhaps more surprisingly, 1955 also saw an amnesty awarded to almost sixty thousand Soviet citizens sentenced for collaborating with occupiers during the Second World War.[9] In addition to these one-off edicts, a system of "work days" was reintroduced, allowing prisoners who overfulfilled the daily norms to reduce their sentence.[10] Existing practices were also expanded. As under Stalin, the Supreme Soviet had the power to grant personal amnesties, and this avenue was pursued by a growing number of petitioners. The section dedicated to processing such petitions dealt with an increasing number of letters each month, with its workload almost doubling between March and December 1953.[11]

Some prisoners started to see their convictions overturned. The process of rehabilitating political prisoners began rather predictably with the release of those closely related to leading political figures—such as Viacheslav Molotov's wife in May 1953—but it soon took on more significant dimensions.[12] The tide turned with the dismantling of the Special Board (*osoboe sove-*

[5] According to one internal memo, 629,143 people were released in 1954; in 1955, a further 671,734 (see GARF f. 7523, op. 89, d. 4408, l. 85). It is important to remember that new prisoners still entered the Gulag: 421,995 in 1954 and 432,670 in 1955 (GARF f. 9414, op. 1, d. 1398, ll. 14–22, reproduced in Kokurin and Petrov, eds., *Gulag*, 435–441).

[6] GARF f. 7523, op. 89, d. 4408, l. 82.

[7] Peter H. Solomon, Jr., *Soviet Criminologists and Criminal Policy: Specialists in Policy-Making* (Basingstoke, U.K., 1978), 42–45.

[8] For a list of the six decrees, see Kokurin and Petrov, eds., *Gulag*, 885.

[9] For interesting commentary on the reasoning behind this 1955 edict (in particular the international dimension), see V. P. Naumov, "Sud'ba voennoplennykh i deportirovannykh grazhdan SSSR. Materialy Komissii po reabilitatsii zhertv politicheskikh repressii," *Novaia i noveishaia istoriia* (March–April 1996): 91–112 (107–110).

[10] GARF f. 7523, op. 89, d. 4403, l. 2. On the gradual reintroduction of work days in the early 1950s and its standardization in 1954, see Elie, "Les anciens détenus du Goulag," 55–61; and Solomon, *Soviet Criminologists*, 42.

[11] GARF f. 7523, op. 69, d. 174, l. 9. See also GARF f. 7523, op. 69, d. 176.

[12] In May 1953 Polina Zhemchuzhina was released and fully rehabilitated, along with seven relatives or acquaintances caught up in her case. See APRF f. 3, op. 32, d. 17, ll. 131–134, reproduced in A. Artizov, Iu. Sigachev, I. Shevchuk, and B. Khlopov, eds., *Reabilitatsiia: Kak eto bylo. Dokumenty prezidiuma TsK KPSS i drugie materialy, mart 1953–fevral' 1956*, vol. 1 (Moscow, 2000), 41–43.

shchanie), an extralegal body attached to the MVD and responsible for so many of the false convictions of the Stalin era. On 1 September 1953, a decree not only announced the board's abolition but also made provision for the review of cases: the Procuracy was given responsibility for assessing the petitions sent in by prisoners and former prisoners whose sentences had been awarded by the Special Board (and other extralegal bodies run by the security organs, such as the NKVD troikas which had played such a significant role in the *Ezhovshchina*).[13]

A more ambitious venture was launched in the spring of 1954. In February Kruglov (minister of internal affairs), Rudenko (general procurator), and Gorshenin (minister of justice) recommended the establishment of a series of commissions that would re-examine the cases of those still serving time in camps, colonies, or exile for counter-revolutionary crimes, if sentenced by the military courts, boards and tribunals, or by the boards and troikas of the security organs.[14] Within three months, the proposed commissions were introduced across the Soviet Union, overseen by a central body headed by Rudenko himself.[15] As a result of the commissions' work, 42,796 prisoners had been released by the beginning of 1956.[16] (It is worth noting, however, that not all of these were yet granted full rehabilitation, as in many cases the commissions chose to reduce sentences or apply the 1953 amnesty rather than fully overturn the conviction.)

Prisoners were thus being released from the camps, not only in large numbers but also from a wide range of categories, including those sentenced for both political and nonpolitical crimes, and through different processes— some by amnesty, Supreme Soviet edict, or through personal pardon; others as a result of the commissions' work. Figures from one particular camp, Kargopol'lag, give some sense of release patterns: of those freed from the camp in 1955, 28 percent were released as a result of one of the Supreme Soviet decrees, 8.5 percent had their case reviewed, and 5.1 percent were pardoned, while 58 percent were released simply because their sentence was at an end—

---

[13] During the Civil War and again during collectivization the secret police had operated tribunals for the purposes of handing down sentences (often death sentences) to political enemies. Although their activities had been curtailed in the mid-1930s, three-person boards composed of the local first party secretary, procurator, and NKVD chief became one of the main agents of the terror. In 1937, 87% of all criminal sentences were made by these troikas. On the troikas, see J. Arch Getty and Oleg V. Naumov, *The Road to Terror: Stalin and the Self-Destruction of the Bolsheviks, 1932–1939* (New Haven, 1999), 113, 469–470. For the document, see APRF f. 3, op. 58, d. 11, ll. 60–61, reproduced in Artizov et al., eds., *Reabilitatsiia: Kak eto bylo*, vol. 1, 70.

[14] GARF f. 9401, op. 2, d. 450, ll. 30–65 (l. 30).

[15] RGANI f. 3, op. 10, d. 79, l. 2; ll. 12–14, reproduced in Artizov et al., eds., *Reabilitatsiia: Kak eto bylo*, vol. 1, 116–117.

[16] GARF f. 9401, op. 2, d 500, l.319. *The Gulag Survivor* contains a short analysis of the commissions' work in different provinces. Adler shows there was great variation among regions: in Chita 37% of convictions re-examined were upheld, whereas in Astrakhan province almost 50% of convictions were upheld by the commissions, and as many as 75% in Stalingrad (*The Gulag Survivor*, 95–97).

though the Gulag official who authored the internal memo containing these figures noted that this category was so large because it included those whose sentences were reduced by being able to count "work days."

There was thus no single legislative mechanism that brought about this massive exodus from the camps, no one state organ with responsibility for the downsizing of the Gulag that was taking place. And yet, although no single act marked the dawn of this era, officials working in any branch of the judiciary, police, or prison system must have been aware that radical change was taking place. Prisoners who were suddenly granted release, and their relatives to whom they returned, must also have sensed that something unprecedented was under way. In 1953 the press had made some attempt to explain the changes, particularly with the assertion that "socialist legality" was now being restored, but for prisoners and their relatives back home these clues to understanding the new era remained confusing and oblique. Like the letters examined in chapter 1, the petitions of those once cast out of Soviet society point to the difficulty ordinary people encountered in the ambiguous climate following Stalin's death.

Crafting a Life Story

The vagaries of this system of release had one very significant result: the primacy of the petition remained. As there was no one surefire way to guarantee release or rehabilitation, many prisoners, ex-prisoners, and their relatives were still obliged to write letter upon letter, explaining their case and desperately seeking to win the interest of bureaucrats in one of the many offices that could potentially offer salvation. The reforms and changes introduced gave new hope to Stalin's outcasts and led to a new frenzy of letter writing.

In February 1954 Anna Akhmatova wrote to Voroshilov begging him to save her only son (L. N. Gumilev) who was in a camp in Omsk and now an invalid.[17] In the same month, the daughter of the Moscow show-trial victim A. I. Rykov appealed directly to Khrushchev asking to be released from exile and given work teaching (for which she was trained).[18] It was not only prominent figures who wrote letters, though, and a great number of prisoners and their families dispatched letters to any state or party organization they thought might offer help. Internal memoranda suggest that senior officials were alarmed by the sheer quantity of petition material their offices now received. At the Supreme Soviet, members of the team responsible for processing pardon petitions felt overstretched by the cascade of letters they received each month, repeatedly appealing to their superiors for extra assis-

[17] GARF f. 7523, op. 85, d. 251, l. 16, reproduced in Artizov et al., eds., *Reabilitatsiia: Kak eto bylo,* vol. 1, 91–92.

[18] APRF f. 3, op. 24, d. 439, ll. 86–87, reproduced in Artizov et al., eds., *Reabilitatsiia: Kak eto bylo,* vol. 1, 90–91.

tance over the course of 1954–1955.[19] In March 1955 D. E. Salin, director of the "special cases" section at the Procuracy, wrote a memo in which he explained that although they had re-examined 13,084 counter-revolutionary cases over the last seven months, their task was only just beginning: 30,000 petitions awaited response.[20]

The necessity of petitions did not stop with release, or even rehabilitation. To re-establish any kind of normal existence, the returnee often had to ask for help with employment, pensions, housing, or even the return of belongings confiscated at the time of arrest.[21] Despite the extra work it required, the authorities seemed intent on preserving this personalized aspect of the Soviet system, perhaps reflecting their still tentative attitude toward the repeal of Stalin's terror. In January 1955 P. G. Moskatov, chairman of the Personal Pensions Commission at the Council of Ministers, wrote to the CC suggesting that the pensions awarded to those rehabilitated and their dependents be raised. Although the principle of a general raise was approved, Moskatov's proposal to introduce some kind of standardized system was refused. In his response, the Presidium member M. A. Suslov insisted that each case should be considered on its own merits, with careful attention paid to the particular circumstances of the individual in question.[22] This meant that the fate of each returnee was highly dependent on the individual official who received and processed his or her appeal. (This was exactly what Moskatov had been trying—unsuccessfully—to avoid because, as he explained in a subsequent letter to Khrushchev, some regions were hostile toward rehabilitated persons—particularly Leningrad, where F. R. Kozlov, first party secretary for the oblast, refused to deal with their pension claims.)[23]

Petitions were thus to remain an integral part of the return to Soviet life. A lot rested on the writer's ability to produce an effective autobiographical account, and it must have been a daunting task for many. Though the ability to craft a compelling life story was an essential skill for all Soviet citizens, it was particularly important for those who had ever been banished from society. Returnees must narrate their personal story in a way that would per-

[19] See GARF f. 7523, op. 69, in particular d. 174, ll. 4–9.

[20] APRF f. 3, op. 24, d. 440, ll. 73–82, reproduced in Artizov et al., eds., *Reabilitatsiia: Kak eto bylo*, vol. 1,, 196–203.

[21] For an interesting analysis of petitions for housing, including the letters written by recently rehabilitated citizens, see Christine Varga-Harris, "Forging Citizenship on the Home Front: Revising the Socialist Contract and Constructing Soviet Identity during the Thaw," in *The Dilemmas of De-Stalinization: Negotiating Cultural And Social Change in the Khrushchev Era*, ed. Polly Jones (London, 2006), 101–116.

[22] RGANI f. 5, op. 30, d. 94, ll. 1, 13–14.

[23] Moskatov told Khrushchev that a rehabilitated communist named Podgorskii, the first secretary of a raikom (a neighborhood or district party committee) in Leningrad oblast before his arrest in 1950, had written to him claiming that Kozlov would not issue pensions to the rehabilitated and their families because he had taken an active part in the drawing up of lists of victims during the Leningrad Affair. When Moskatov tried to intervene, Kozlov told him outright that the Leningrad obkom was not going to deal with the issue of rehabilitated persons' pensions (RGANI f. 5, op. 30, d. 94, ll. 1, 13–16).

suade officials that they were fit to be considered Soviet citizens once more and their existing status as outcasts was erroneous.

In embarking on any kind of autobiographical project, the writer is never fully alone but draws on patterns and models suggested by the culture in which he or she lives. Even though authors write about the unique circumstances of their life, they have access to what the psychologist Jerome Bruner has called a "stock of canonical life narratives" or "tool kit," which they use to shape these experiences into a coherent tale.[24] For those who come under the scrutiny of the law, this tool kit provides an important aide for situating the crime or incident within the overarching frame of a whole life in a way that that the authorities might find acceptable.[25]

Soviet culture certainly provided some guidance for making sense of criminal acts. In the communist imagination the prison camp was a site for social and psychological transformation and, at least at first, had been a source of pride for the Soviet state. In the early 1930s the press had been full of tales of social aliens dispatched to hard labor within the camp system, given intensive re-education, and thereby "reforged" as decent citizens.[26] *Journey to Life* (Putevka v zhizn'), a 1931 film based on the writings of the renowned pedagogue Anton Makarenko, told the story of a group of violent street kids who were taken to a remote commune, taught a profession, and transformed into happy and honorable young workers.[27] On the subject of reforging the most famous text was the collection *Belomor,* written by a number of leading authors including Maksim Gor'kii, which contained the bold claim that "as the result of twenty months of work, the country has a few thousand skilled builders who have gone through a hard but formative experience and have been cured of the creeping infection of petty bourgeois society."[28] The

[24] Jerome Bruner, "Life as Narrative," *Social Research* 54 (1987): 11–32. See also Paul John Eakin, *How Our Lives Become Stories: Making Selves* (Ithaca, 1999).

[25] In her study of sixteenth-century pardon appeals, Natalie Zemon Davis shows how important a culture's existing canon might be for a petitioner hoping to explain his or her criminal actions. Of all the petitions studied, Zemon Davis finds the least convincing to be those written by women convicted of brawling with other women. She suggests that the reason for the "flatness" of their accounts was the absence of stories about women fighting amongst themselves in the storytelling, biblical, and folktale traditions in which they were raised. Because they lacked "guidance," the female petitioners struggled to craft accounts of their actions when found guilty of violence against other women. See Natalie Zemon Davis, *Fiction in the Archives: Pardon Tales and Their Tellers in Sixteenth-Century France* (Stanford, 1987), particularly 101–102.

[26] Katerina Clark, *The Soviet Novel: History as Ritual,* 3d ed. (Bloomington, 2000), 118–119. Accounts of reclaiming criminals were common in the Soviet press. For instance, in 1935 *Izvestiia* proudly recounted the good work of Matvei Pogrebinskii, director of a NKVD labor commune, who devoted his life to converting criminals into loyal members of the Soviet community (A. Zorich, "Serdtse chekista," *Izvestiia,* 4 October 1935, 4). For discussion of this article, see Sheila Fitzpatrick, *Everyday Stalinism: Ordinary Life in Extraordinary Times. Soviet Russia in the 1930s* (New York, 1999), 78.

[27] *Putevka v zhizn',* directed by Nikolai Ekk, 1931, USSR.

[28] Marksim Gor'kii, L. Auerbach, and S. G. Firin, eds., *Belomor: An Account of the Construction of the New Canal between the White Sea and the Baltic Sea,* trans. Amabel Williams-

volume included the stories of several of these reformed offenders, including, for example, the tale of Abram Rothenburg, raised in prerevolutionary
Tbilisi: his father gambled, the family went hungry, and the boy took to stealing; once expelled from school, he spent most of his time hanging out at the
bazaar, where he learnt more tricks of the trade; by the age of fourteen he
was already involved in fraud, and well advanced on the "thorny path."
Only when he found himself, aged almost forty, the target of educational initiatives at the White Sea Canal (Belomor) labor camp was he transformed;
once inside a Soviet labor camp, he was finally convinced of the errors of his
early life, began to work enthusiastically on the project, and was awarded
the Order of the Red Banner of Labor. Whether in print or celluloid, these
stories offered some guidance in writing autobiography and showed how
even the most hardened thief or murderer could make his way from darkness to light.

Yet these "tools" were not unproblematic for the prisoner hoping to craft
the perfect petition in the period 1953–1956. The Belomor model certainly
did not offer a useful template for those wrongly convicted of political
crimes; repressed party members would be unlikely to present themselves as
sinners who had seen the light as a result of their time in the camps. But the
model was also problematic for other categories of prisoner. The characters
of *Belomor* could attribute their errors and sins to ignorance and the nefarious influence of prerevolutionary culture, like Rothenburg who was ne-
glected by his father and corrupted by the bad influences of the capitalist
marketplace; but what of men and women born under Soviet power? How
could they explain their transgressions? How could those raised and educated during the Soviet era explain their digression from the correct path?[29]

Petition writing had never conformed to a one-size-fits-all model and
Golfo Alexopoulos's study of appeals shows the diversity of writing strategies employed even in the 1920s and 1930s.[30] Yet by the 1950s the episte-
mological challenges facing the petitioning prisoner were greater still. First,
the ongoing existence of crime in Soviet society was a phenomenon that
politicians and petitioners alike struggled to explain. Second, the decision to
release, and in some cases rehabilitate, large groups of the prison population

---

Ellis (London, 1935), 338. For an interesting study of this work, see Greg Carleton, "Genre in
Socialist Realism," *Slavic Review* 53 (1994): 992–1009.

[29] Aminda Smith's recent dissertation on Chinese attempts to "re-educate" beggars, prostitutes, vagrants, pickpockets, and petty thieves (identified as members of the "parasitic population") after the 1949 revolution offers interesting parallels, both in terms of the Chinese and
Soviet regimes' initial pride in their allegedly successful conversion stories and their subsequent
difficulty when crime and deviancy failed to disappear in the new, postrevolutionary society
("Reeducating the People: The Chinese Communist and the 'Thought Reform' of Beggars,
Prostitutes, and other 'Parasites,'" Ph.D. Diss., Princeton University, 2006).

[30] Golfo Alexopoulos writes: "narrative patterns in the appeals of the disenfranchised
demonstrate that despite an implicit imperative to speak the language of power, the disenfranchised produced effective narratives with considerable stylistic diversity" (*Stalin's Outcasts,*
100).

clearly suggested an important change of direction. The creation of the commissions seemed to imply that some *zek*s should never have been in the Gulag at all, but the state provided little guidance as to how such developments should be understood. For those who benefited from the amnesty matters were still less clear. In the spring of 1953 Gorshenin's comments in *Pravda* suggested that returnees were not dangerous, but he had offered little hard assurance about the success of "correction" practices inside the Gulag. The Belomor model was now perhaps outdated, but new models for prisoners' life stories were as yet lacking.

The letters prisoners and former prisoners wrote in the years 1953–1956 suggest how difficult their authors found it to explain their experiences in a way they believed would suit their all-powerful readers, especially when given such limited guidance from the press. The enormous body of correspondence dispatched to government and party offices on a daily basis communicated to the authorities the returnees' potential to ask challenging and disturbing questions. Some prisoners tried to shape their stories according to the Belomor model, but others broke with this now outmoded pattern: a number of young men explicitly challenged the concept of the Gulag as a site of personal salvation, others began to look for other models, creatively elaborating on scattered hints in the Soviet press or even the illicit foreign media. A significant number of political prisoners, particularly the older generation, looked to other traditions within Soviet culture, in particular to early radical fiction. Thus, while the official media went rather silent on the meaning of the prisoner releases in 1954 and 1955, petitioners were busy interpreting the Gulag and its place in the Soviet past and present.

The Belomor Model

Some prisoners were prepared to admit that they had indeed sinned before the Gulag brought enlightenment. The petition of Il'ia Simonov, a young man from a peasant family convicted in 1953, offers an example of the classic conversion model.[31] While serving as an army recruit, Simonov went on a drinking binge one evening and ignored instructions from a senior officer to return to barracks, taking refuge in the house of a collective farmer; when found hiding in the oven, he was promptly arrested. In his narration of the events of this fateful night, Simonov twice asserted that he was unaware that he was committing a crime: neither when he went AWOL, nor when he started drinking, did he realize he was doing anything wrong. Now, however, he realized his mistake: "I made a very, very grave error. And that's why I am making every effort to atone [*iskupit'*] for my guilt. During my time in the I.T.L. [corrective labor camp], I haven't been given any penalties. By

31 GARF f. 7863, op. 22, d. 2325.

working honestly and being disciplined, I just want to atone for my guilt in the eyes of the people, the party, and our Soviet government. Having been in the I.T.L. for more than two years, I have deeply and fully recognized my guilt."[32] Simonov thus narrated his life as a journey from darkness to light: crimes were committed out of ignorance, but the Gulag brought self-awareness and recognition of guilt. He argued that he was ready for release because he had already been through the transformative experience of the camps. In June 1955 the Supreme Soviet decided to pardon him.[33]

A second petitioner was even more explicit in presenting the Gulag as a life-changing experience. In the immediate postwar period, a teenager named Iurii Kuznetsov was employed at a railway station in Sakhalin where he lived with three other young, unmarried men. Struggling to get by on their meager salaries, they were often forced to borrow from friends and acquaintances to tide them over between pay packets, which then disappeared on debt repayments. Kuznetsov's descent into crime began one night with the theft of some herring. Later, aided and abetted by a roommate, he stole ten children's baths, ten basins, one box of apples, and two boxes of canned foods. In his petition, Kuznetsov expressed horror at his past actions, explaining them as the misdeeds of a young man "lacking life experience" and "fallen under the influence of depraved comrades." Although only twenty-five when he wrote the petition, Kuznetsov distanced himself from this younger, erroneous self: "being young and not having any firm and independent opinions on life, I was like a barbarian [*varvar*] mocking life."[34] As fitting, it was his experience of the camps that had allowed him to be transformed: "In the camps I realized my mistakes and understood everything." Accepting the narrative structure found in the Belomor conversion tales, Kuznetsov rejected every aspect of his former self, totally admitting his error, the distasteful nature of his past, and the importance of the Gulag experience in making this transition. His plea for pardon was also successful, and in February 1954 the Supreme Soviet approved his release.[35]

Yet although many prisoners understood that recognizing their guilt and promising atonement through labor were important elements of a good petition, relatively few wrote a full conversion story of the kind found in the petitions of Simonov and Kuznetsov.[36] Not all were willing to present their

---

[32] GARF f. 7863, op. 22, d. 2325, l 5.

[33] GARF f. 7863, op. 22, d. 2325, l. 11.

[34] GARF f. 7863, op. 20, d. 1274, l. 7.

[35] GARF f. 7863, op. 20, d. 1274, l. 14.

[36] For example, Viktor Perfilov, another twenty-four-year-old in trouble for drunken misdemeanors, wrote: "During my sentence, I have recognized [*osoznal*] this as my first mistake in the eyes of society and atoned for my guilt through an honest and conscientious attitude toward life and through work for the good of the Motherland." Nikolai Danilov, sentenced for theft of grain, recognised his guilt, and blamed his youth: "Considering . . . my youth—I was born in 1928—and the fact that I fully recognize my guilt, and the real punishment I've already endured, and that this is a one-time event which will never be repeated . . . I beg you not to refuse me a *personal amnesty*." In neither case, however, did the petitioner offer the kind of full con-

past in entirely negative terms, as the case of Gerasim Rumiantsev demon-strates. Convicted in 1948 for appropriating money from the state farm where he worked, Rumiantsev wrote a petition letter in October 1953 in which he assured his readers that he was working hard and studying dili-gently inside the Gulag.[37] Although he presented himself as a model Gulag inmate, he did not go further with the Belomor model; and in writing about his past life, Rumiantsev clearly felt there was still much of which he could be proud. In fact, Rumiantsev presented his former self as a true Soviet worker:

> All of my conscious life I have done socially useful labor. I finished only four classes at school, and because my parents were old, I had to begin my working life very young.
>
> From 1939 to 1946 I served in the Soviet army without a break. I was a par-ticipant in the battles of the Great Patriotic War and fought for the freedom and independence of our motherland from the German fascists and Japanese impe-rialists. I was rewarded with a medal.[38]

Instead of rejecting his first thirty years as part of a dark, criminal pre-exis-tence, he believed that his achievements made him a deserving Soviet sub-ject. This left Rumiantsev with the rather tricky task of explaining how such a good Soviet citizen came to commit a criminal act. His story continued: "In the hard years of rationing I was materially provided for very badly and had a seventy-year-old father and a daughter to care for." Then a new para-graph began: "I admitted my guilt toward my motherland at every stage of the investigation."[39] The narrative contains an important ellipsis, or to bor-row a term from Natalie Zemon Davis's study of sixteenth-century petitions, a "wound."[40] Rumiantsev hinted that during the years of rural famine, he was forced by sheer deprivation to steal, yet while he acknowledged his guilt, he did not attempt to recount the theft within his autobiographical petition. Rumiantsev had no interpretative tools at his disposal with which to make sense of this act. The narrative line thus skips from the description of his hardship to the sentencing, making the reader insert the criminal act. Despite the frailties of his petition, Rumiantsev was pardoned and released in May 1954.[41]

---

version tale provided by Kuznetsov. See GARF f. 7863, op. 22, d. 2034, l. 1; and GARF f. 7863, op. 21, d. 2126, l. 14.

[37] GARF f. 7863, op. 21, d. 6031, l. 3.

[38] GARF f. 7863, op. 21, d. 6031, l. 2.

[39] GARF f. 7863, op. 21, d. 6031, l. 2.

[40] Natalie Zemon Davis describes the men and women pleading for the king's pardon as "people with a corpse to explain." Unpicking their texts, she finds that their narrative accounts often have "wounds" in them, by which she means "open cuts or gaps in the argument" (*Fiction in the Archives*, 47).

[41] GARF f. 7863, op. 21, d. 6031, l. 23.

This kind of narrative ellipsis or wound was not uncommon, and it could take various forms. In petitioners' autobiographies the consumption of large quantities of vodka often marks the transition from good citizen to prisoner, with drunkenness obliterating both memory of the crime and the possibility of narration. Like Rumiantsev, Mikhail Tumanov, arrested for making anti-Soviet comments in March 1953, was proud of his wartime record: in 1941 he had been taken prisoner but managed to hide from the occupiers for four months and then rejoined the Soviet army, fighting at the front until the end of the war, despite three injuries. His petition described his family's loyalty to the Soviet regime and told how they had chased off the *isplaktatory* (a garbled version of the Russian word for "exploiters") during collectiviza-tion. How then, could he explain the fact that on 6 March 1953 he was heard slandering and cursing the recently deceased Stalin? Tumanov claimed igno-rance and incredulity. His account was thus very simple: he got on a train at Kozel'sk, already drunk, and went straight to sleep on a bench, despite ha-rassment from the conductor. When he tried to get off the train at the next station, the police were already waiting for him. With little memory of the night in question he made no attempt to explain his actions. Is it really pos-sible, he mused, that he could have said all these things? The reader is led to question the veracity of the story, and there is even a gentle hint that he might have been falsely denounced, perhaps by an overzealous conductor. Tu-manov only raised this question, however, and shied away from setting up an alternative version of the night. The incident remains a black hole, an in-explicable rupture, in what he believed was otherwise an exemplary life story.[42]

Aleksandr Gorbunov was also arrested in 1953 for slandering Stalin and was sentenced to eight years.[43] His petition began: "I, Aleksandr Vasil'evich Gorbunov, was born in 1909. I come from a worker family. I was born in the town of L'gov in Kursk oblast. In 1929 I was called up to the Soviet army where I honestly [*chestno*] served two years. On leaving the army I worked at the sugar factory in the city of L'gov."[44] During the war years Gorbunov served in the army again, and although he was left an invalid he nonetheless managed to provide for his family. Having asserted his credentials as a de-cent Soviet citizen, his petition moved on to narrate the day of the alleged crime:

> On 2 April 1953 I was at the market selling meat. After work I went into the pub [*pivnaia*] where I drank vodka. Various people were sitting around and we got talking about [G. M.] Malenkov and about his achievements and aptitude as head of the Soviet government. Along with everyone else, I drank a large mea-

[42] GARF f. 8131, op. 31, d. 59688, ll. 9–10.
[43] GARF f. 8131, op. 31, d. 43260.
[44] GARF f. 8131, op. 31, d. 43260, l. 12.

sure of vodka in honor of our government and Malenkov. For a period of time after this I don't remember anything, as I was obviously very drunk. I don't really remember how, but I woke up on 3 April at the L'gov police station and was called in to see the investigator.[45]

Again there is an ellipsis in the narrative: from a happy scene where citizens toast their leaders, the reader is taken straight to the moment of arrest and police investigation. The narrator failed to explain the transition, twice repeating "I can't remember." Gorbunov's requests for release were twice rejected by the Supreme Soviet in 1955.[46]

Petitioners were thus in a quandary. On one hand, they knew the camps should be seen as a site of correction and redemption. On the other, they wanted to present themselves as deserving, loyal Soviet people, not as dark degenerates whose prearrest lives were futile and unwholesome. They were reluctant to erase or downplay what they saw as their contribution to Soviet society, which often included labor in Soviet industry and military service. Unable to explain how they as men raised during the Soviet era could have committed a crime, they recoiled from the task of exegesis, leaving a blank, or wound, in their narrative.

This reticence was not universal, however. The case of Nikolai Korolev suggests that some prisoners came to resent the canonical narratives offered by the Belomor model. In a letter written to the editors of *Izvestiia* in March 1954, Korolev told his readers that as a young man he had served in the army, participated in the Komsomol, and gone through "all the stages of upbringing [*vospitanie*] as any person coming out of a Soviet school." He admitted, however, that as a nineteen-year-old he had committed a "deed that subsequently became a crime," though he did not elaborate further on the nature of this misdemeanor which he ascribed to "wild fantasy, quixotry [*donkikhotstvo*], and the desire to stand out." More radically, Korolev rejected the notion that the Gulag was a possible site for atonement, condemning the terrible, violent state of the camps. In a passionate exposé of life in the Gulag he wrote:

Having made me out to be an anti-Soviet person, they sent me to the faraway camps of Dal'stroi. They decided to educate [*vospityvat'*] me in a "corrective-labor camp." And do you know what this is? These are places where they raise criminals, where they make criminals out of people who aren't already, where they brutally kill those who don't want to become one. The "corrective-labor camps" are nests that fill our country with new cadres, specialists in murdering, thieving, and swindling, not people. It is impossible to be a human being here, and if someone does manage to hold out and to retain a human spirit [*che-*

[45] GARF f. 8131, op. 31, d. 43260, l. 12.
[46] GARF f. 8131, op. 31, d. 43260, ll. 22–26.

lovecheskii oblik], then they will have very bitter feelings towards the Soviet government and party.[47]

Korolev was highly distressed by the murder of his friend Ivan Pichugov, a crime which he believed exposed the Belomor concept to be a sham. As a sinner bent on self-improvement, Pichugov had exemplified the Belomor prisoner: working as a lathe operator, he always overfulfilled the daily norms; despite having received little formal education, he studied hard and hoped to enter the physical-mathematics institute on release; he loved Belinskii. His elderly mother, to whom Pichugov wrote regularly, "was happy that her son was 'correcting himself.'" Upset by his friend's death, Korolev condemned the authorities for allowing the camps to destroy the one person who was actually trying to follow the impossible path set by the Belomor model.

The boldness of Korolev's letter perhaps echoed the assertive moods that flourished as insurrections and strikes swept through several camps in 1953–1954.[48] Certainly Korolev was not alone in daring to say that far from *curing* them, the Gulag had been a site of further corruption and contamination. One young man used this claim in a petition he addressed to Khrushchev. Boris Nesterov already had several years' experience of the Gulag when he found himself in court charged with theft in 1954; and on receiving another lengthy sentence, he could not contain a great vent of angry spleen, which the authorities deemed "anti-Soviet" and which resulted in yet another conviction. Explaining the outburst in his petition Nesterov blamed his actions on the time he had spent in the camps as a youth: "I was sentenced several times for theft. From the children's colony, I ended up in the adult camp, that's to say with the fascists. That's where I learnt the words I used in court. From the age of fourteen I have been in prison, with only a nine-month break [*sic*] between 10 May 1953 and 9 December 1953."[49] Rather than putting him on the straight path in life, time in the camps had corrupted him further and led him deeper into crime.

While Nesterov and Korolev argued that the kind of educational measures promised by the Belomor model were entirely absent in the camps, other young Gulag veterans audaciously suggested that the upbringing they had received as children *within* society had also been less than perfect. Far from

[47] APRF f. 3, op. 58, d. 169, ll. 106–113, reproduced in Artizov et al., eds., *Reabilitatsiia: Kak eto bylo*, vol. 1, 105–109.

[48] Steven A. Barnes, "In a Manner Befitting Soviet Citizens": An Uprising in the Post-Stalin Gulag," *Slavic Review* 64 (2005): 823–850; Marta Craveri, "Krizis Gulaga: Kengirskoe vosstanie 1954 goda v dokumentakh MVD," *Cahiers du monde russe* 36 (1995): 319–344; Andrea Graziosi, "The Great Strikes of 1953 in Soviet Labor Camps in the Accounts of Their Participants: A Review," *Cahiers du monde russe et soviétique* 33 (1992): 419–445. For primary material on the disorders, see V. A. Kozlov, ed., *Istoriia Stalinskogo Gulaga: Konets 1920-kh–pervaia polovina 1950-kh godov*, vol. 6: *Vosstaniia, bunty i zabastovki zakliuchennykh* (Moscow, 2004), 317–648.

[49] GARF f. 8131, op. 31, d. 50509, l. 28.

enjoying the happy childhood promised by Stalin, they had in fact been deprived of proper care and attention. Although less explicitly critical of the regime, this approach nonetheless raised deeply troubling questions for the authorities.

Viktor Telegin, born in 1929 in Moscow province, believed that the neglect he had experienced as a child was to blame for his failure to conform in later life. He was sentenced to ten years' imprisonment in February 1953 for the theft of an overcoat, two pairs of gloves, and a cheese; and although his subsequent petition claimed that he had been experiencing extreme financial hardship while waiting for his first wage packet after demobilization, he too chose to focus on his childhood experiences. His petition recounted how his two brothers had been killed at the front, his father hung himself in 1941, and his mother, unable to cope with the losses and the experience of evacuation to Alma-Ata, died in a psychiatric hospital. Rather than focusing on the emotional distress these events must surely have caused him, he preferred to talk of them in terms of the "upbringing" they had denied him. "I ask the Presidium of the USSR Supreme Soviet to consider my request for mercy," he wrote, "and to take into consideration the circumstances laid out here and my heavy and unhappy childhood. At an early age I was deprived of my parents and my elder brothers, and I grew up among strangers and didn't receive an appropriate upbringing, experiencing all possible deprivations, both material and moral."[50] The immediate hardships that led him to steal in 1953 were rapidly glossed over, for Telegin seemed to believe that only an inadequate upbringing could explain why he was so morally weak as to succumb to the lure of crime, whatever the circumstances. In both destroying his immediate family—and implicitly, preventing the Soviet system from providing adequate in loco parentis guardianship—the war had kept him from obtaining a "Soviet" education. Telegin's sentence was halved by the amnesty decree of 1953; he was then pardoned and released in April 1955.[51]

When he was released by the amnesty in the spring of 1953, Aleksei Smirnov had served several sentences for a range of crimes, included theft of personal property. By the autumn, he was under arrest again. Drunk at Manzovka station in the Far East, he had attempted to steal a wallet, threatened the victim with a knife, resisted arrest, and then cursed Soviet power. Back within the penitentiary system, Smirnov wrote a petition letter containing a long and detailed account of his life: "I was born in Leningrad where I lived with my mother and father until the war in 1940 [*sic*] with the German occupiers. Then I was evacuated to Cheliabinsk in the Urals. I was left without the supervision of family or friends who could have put me on the true path in life, so that I could have lived and through work been useful to the fa-

[50] GARF f. 7863, op. 22. d. 2564, l. 2.
[51] GARF f. 7863, op. 22. d. 2564, l. 8.

therland."[52] In keeping with the regime's own rhetoric, he recognized that there was a "true path in life" and regretted that fate—in the form of the German offensive—had diverted him from it. Embarking on a life of theft in early adolescence as a result of the lack of "supervision" he had experienced, he had become an outsider to society. After his last release from the camps as part of the 1953 amnesty, he sought work in the mines of the Far East but was refused registration. He wrote in his petition: "With sadness in my soul, I was once more forced to roam the different provinces of the Soviet Union like a Gypsy, until I received another prison sentence for something or other."[53] Instead of heading toward the bright future promised by Soviet culture, Smirnov endured a nomadic existence with no clear direction and blamed the authorities for his fate. His case was supported by the review commissions created in May 1954, and several high-ranking legal officials became involved in the case, including Rudenko himself, who argued that as Smirnov was semiliterate and "politically underdeveloped," a ten-year term was too "harsh."[54] Despite objections from Rudenko's deputy, N. I. Khokhlov, who believed Smirnov's "personality" (by which he made it clear he meant the fact that he was an unemployed transient) justified the courts' severity, Smirnov saw his sentence halved.[55]

The stories Smirnov, Nesterov, and Telegin presented in their petitions reveal the scars of war: the Soviet system had not been able to provide adequate provision for all its children, pushing many into a life of hardship and marginality from which they still had not escaped a decade later.[56] Their petitions posed unsettling questions: How far were the new leaders prepared to go in their criticism of the Stalinist system? Might even those who *had* committed an offense in fact still be victims in some way? In the discussion of legal cases that went on behind closed doors, some high-ranking figures (like Rudenko) were sympathetic toward the petitioners' claims that poor upbringing and limited education had led them into crime, but others continued to see them as disagreeable outcasts. The petitions of this cohort of young men who had come of age in the camps thus raised very difficult questions about the extent and scope of de-Stalinization.

In Search of New Narrative Forms

The petitioners thus far molded their life stories on the Belomor model: some attempted to write tales of personal redemption but found it difficult to pro-

---

[52] GARF f. 8131, op. 31, d. 43332, l. 27.
[53] GARF f. 8131, op. 31, d. 43332, l. 28.
[54] GARF f. 8131, op. 31, d. 43332, ll. 15–16.
[55] GARF f. 8131, op. 31, d. 43332, ll. 21, 33.
[56] Margaret K. Stolee, "Homeless Children in the USSR, 1917–1957," *Soviet Studies* 11 (1988): 64–83.

duce a coherent text, leaving gaps and breaks in their accounts; others challenged the idea of the Gulag as a site of salvation or claimed they had been forced into a marginal existence as a result of the regime's own failings. Belomor was proving a rather problematic "tool kit." Petitioners began to cast around for new tools with which to make sense of their lives as outcasts.

A few looked outside the Soviet world for interpretative frameworks. Voice of America, a radio station created by the U.S. government with the goal of destroying communism from within, offered some daring citizens access to alternative sources of knowledge.[57] Vladimir Surin, sentenced in 1949 for theft, aged sixteen, and then released by amnesty, was reconvicted in 1955 for writing anti-Soviet leaflets and listening to Voice of America. When he crafted his petition, he disputed his sentence on the grounds that it was expensive and the money could be better spent helping the "people." He claimed his incarceration was costing the state 640 rubles a day, or 14,600 rubles a month, figures that he had perhaps gleaned from listening to foreign broadcasts.[58] The procuracy officials who rejected the plea in 1957 were certainly unconvinced by such arguments.[59]

More petitioners, though, looked to their own media for possible solutions. One aging mother hoped that the revoking of the Doctors' Plot might mean that her daughter, arrested in connection with the Jewish Antifascist Committee, would be declared innocent. In a petition written to Voroshilov in February 1955 P. M. Teumin explained: "Considering that the investigation of my daughter's case took place at a time when accusations against the doctors and other public figures (like Mikhoels) were being fabricated, and that when she was arrested enemies of the people like Abakumov and others—later unmasked—were in charge of the MGB [Ministry of State Security, later amalgamated into the MVD] and the Investigation Department, I ask you to reconsider the case." She went on to remind Voroshilov that if her daughter had signed a confession, it was obtained by "methods forbidden by Soviet laws." "Confined to bed," she continued, "I think about my daughter night and day, wondering where she is and what has happened to her."[60] In November 1955 her daughter was rehabilitated posthumously: in 1952 E. I. Teumin had been given the death sentence.[61]

For others the key event of 1953 was not the release of the Kremlin doctors but the arrest of Beriia. In April 1954 A. A. Kalmykova began her petition to Anastas Mikoian with a reminder that reports on the radio and in the press in July 1953 had revealed senior figures within the MGB and the MVD

[57] Gene Sosin, *Sparks of Liberty: An Insider's Memoir of Radio Liberty* (University Park, 1999), 2.

[58] GARF f. 8131, op. 31, d. 67339, l. 13.

[59] GARF f. 8131, op. 31, d. 67339, ll. 17–18.

[60] GARF f. 7523, op. 107, d. 123, ll. 39–41.

[61] RGANI f. 3, op. 8, d. 316, ll. 118–123, reproduced in Artizov et al., eds., *Reabilitatsiia: Kak eto bylo*, vol. 1, 265–267 (see also 459).

had long been using criminal methods. She then continued: "There is no doubt—and I say this with great certainty—that one of the victims of the vile provocation and the slanderous actions of Beriia and his accomplices was my husband Betal Kalmykov and indisputably, in connection with this, I was also a victim of the arbitrariness and lawlessness created by Beriia."[62] The media's treatment of Beriia's arrest had given direct victims, at least, "approved" terms with which to make sense of their ordeal. By accusing Beriia of arbitrariness and lawlessness, *Pravda* enabled Kalmykova to explain why she and her husband had been repressed.[63] Due to her close ties to those in power, Kalmykova could hold Beriia directly responsible for the injustices committed. In 1938 Kalmykova's husband had held the prestigious position of party obkom secretary in the Kabardin Autonomous Republic and the family had very close connections to the Ordzhonikidze family—Sergo Ordzhonikidze's wife took responsibility for the Kalmykov children after the arrest of their parents. In the narrative constructed in Kalmykova's petition, Beriia's personal hatred for Sergo Ordzhonikidze led to their arrest.[64]

The wife of the former first secretary of the Komsomol, Aleksandr Kosarev, likewise wrote a version of her husband's arrest in which Beriia played the leading role. She explained that Beriia took offense at a critical toast Kosarev had made in front of guests. Beriia had contrived Kosarev's downfall, she argued, within four months of succeeding Ezhov, even carrying out the arrest in person.[65]

Not only direct victims of Beriia's violence tried to use the terminology presented—but not fully explained—in the press. In February 1955 a certain N. E. Korviakov began his petition to Voroshilov in terms that were remarkably similar to Kalmykova's opening line. He too used the terms "arbitrariness" and "lawlessness" furnished by *Pravda* in its attack against Beriia: "I will tell you something about my 'case.' This tale, in my opinion, should show you the arbitrariness, lawlessness, and the bureaucratism that exists in our system, and especially in the judicial-procuracy sector."[66] As he was not a figure of such prominence as either Kalmykova or Kosareva, Korviakov had to show greater ingenuity in the writing of his petition.[67] A lawyer and journalist before the war, he had been arrested in 1944 for allegedly taking goods from the Moscow Benefit Fund for War Invalids and

[62] RGANI f. 5, op. 30, d. 78, l. 66.

[63] "Nesokrushimoe edinenie partii, pravitel'stva, sovetskogo naroda," *Pravda*, 10 July 1953, 1.

[64] RGANI f. 5, op. 30, d. 78, ll. 66–69.

[65] APRF f. 3, op. 24, d. 439, ll. 31–32, reproduced in Artizov et al., eds., *Reabilitatsiia: Kak eto bylo,* vol. 1, 79–80. Aleksandr Kosarev was rehabilitated posthumously in August 1954.

[66] GARF f. 7523, op. 107, d. 186, l. 4.

[67] The fact that Kalmykova's petition was treated by the Central Committee and preserved in the archives at RGANI, while Korviakov's petition was reviewed within the regular mechanisms of the Supreme Soviet and preserved in the more extensive archives at GARF is symbolic of the difference in their status.

selling them on the black market; now released but not rehabilitated, he could not find work. In his letter he claimed that the case was the result of forgeries created by the investigators. In his case, Beriia personally played no role, so although he tried to model his letter on the press articles attacking Beriia, Korviakov was obliged to incorporate a larger cast of villains. "I didn't doubt for a minute," he wrote, "that I was not dealing with Soviet judges but with the objective or subjective accomplices of enemies of the people. I, a patriot raised during Soviet power (I am now forty-four), realized that to label an innocent Soviet citizen and invalid from the Second World War as a counter-revolutionary and enemy of the people could only be the work of (actual) enemies of the people and their accomplices."[68] In making these accusations, Korviakov seemed to realize he was on shaky ground, and his idiosyncratic term for the judges—"objective or subjective accomplices of enemies of the people"—points to some uncertainty: Did he have the right to point the finger at a whole group of people? Was it legitimate to identify enemies of the people? Was this in the spirit of the times? In the second half of the letter he went on to accuse Chairman of the USSR Supreme Court Volin of malpractice, claiming that Volin had been charged with reviewing Korviakov's case but was too scared to rehabilitate him.

As a war veteran and a man proud to have been raised during the Soviet era, Korviakov believed himself to be an upstanding Soviet citizen. He interpreted the press campaigns of 1953 as an invitation to right the wrongs of the past and to point the finger at "enemies" within the MVD or judiciary. In blaming Soviet judges and Volin personally, Korviakov went much further than the prescription of the socialist legality campaign had allowed. Korviakov seemed to imagine a world where Soviet people were locked in mortal combat with their enemies, and he sought a reversal of fates: the victims were to be rehabilitated and welcomed home, and their accusers arrested, sentenced, and cast out.

Ivan Cherkasov, arrested in 1943 during what he modishly called the *Berievshchina,* was also looking for some kind of settling of scores. In May 1955 Cherkasov composed a letter to the man he held responsible for his arrest, an engineer named Shteinman, whom he believed denounced him after taking credit for his scientific discoveries. As he did not know Shteinman's address, Cherkasov was "obliged" (to use his word) to send his letter via the Chief Military Procuracy, and Cherkasov clearly hoped for intervention in the case. He wrote that he "naively" hoped that after Beriia's arrest, "what was left" of Shteinman's conscience would drive him to confess his own crimes to the appropriate authorities.[69] He went on to ask Shteinman to assist in his application for rehabilitation and release from exile, begging him to correct past injustices. Directed to the authorities, it was more of a threat

[68] GARF f. 7523, op. 107, d. 186, l. 4.
[69] RGANI f. 5, op. 30, d. 232, l. 71.

than a plea for help: "If my letter falls into the hands of someone tough, strong-willed, influential, and completely dedicated to the party, then you will be forced to confess and you will be required to tell the truth about how you hunted down party members."[70] This letter was thus a rather transparent device through which Cherkasov requested not only his own rehabilitation but also retribution. He suggested that Shteinman might like to present himself to the Procuracy and the Party Control Commission and to recount who employed him as a provocateur. In the final paragraph he expressed his hope that Shteinman would experience all the "unhappiness" that he had inflicted on Cherkasov.

For those who had themselves once worked within the MVD, the question of retribution was even more complex. Writing to Voroshilov in November 1953, M. I. Belkin explained that his 1951 conviction as a Jewish "bourgeois nationalist" had recently been overturned, and both he and his wife had been legally rehabilitated. Despite this apparent vindication, however, he had not been allowed to return to his work at the MVD. Indeed, new attempts had been made to discredit him. He explained: "The thing is that among the MVD staff there are still people—like Akimov, Samarin, Nabalov, Grishaev, Golub', Degtiarev, Nekrasov, Matavkin, Bad'in and the procurator Novikov—who have been allowed to remain in their posts and not brought to justice, even though they are responsible for the criminal methods used in my case during a nineteen-month period, and indeed in many other cases. These people fully understand that my full rehabilitation will at the same time mean they are deeply compromised."[71]

Another petitioner who proudly identified himself as a former "Chekist" was still more embittered against his erstwhile colleagues. In June 1954 A. A. Grib wrote his twenty-first petition, this time addressed to the CC. Having spent six and a half years in prison and camps, he had been rehabilitated in 1954, but like Belkin prevented from returning to his work, in his case in espionage. He wrote: "I am now pure in your eyes, in the eyes of the party, my relatives and friends. But Serov, Kruglov, and their men [*cheliad'*] cannot forgive me for criticizing their shameful work; even now they are weaving a web of lies and slander around me and the other Chekists with whom I used to work."[72] He believed their intrigues were preventing him from rejoining the party, receiving confiscated awards, and returning to the high-status work to which he had devoted twenty-two years of his life. In his letters Grib mentioned the names of many people whom he considered responsible for the injustice and violence he and other prisoners experienced, including such prominent figures as Kruglov and I. A. Serov, chairman of the KGB (Committee of State Security). Grib argued that Presidium members had become the puppets of enemies hidden within the apparatus of the MVD

---

[70] RGANI f. 5, op. 30, d. 232, l. 74.
[71] GARF f. 7523, op. 58, d. 141, l. 85.
[72] GARF f. 7523, op. 58, d. 141, l. 145.

and asked, in despair: "What more can I do to convince you that there are enemies in your very midst?"[73] Those who continued to discredit him were not simply in error, but vile foes of Soviet power whom he labeled "bastards" (*merzavtsy*), provocateurs, double-dealers, and "super-Hitlerites."

Beriia's arrest and execution had provoked a round of purging among the higher echelons of the MVD, but its scope had been relatively limited.[74] In the years 1954–1955 it was unclear—perhaps even to the leaders themselves—how far the party was going to take the process of identifying, judging, and sentencing those responsible for the many miscarriages of justice now being revealed. While former members of the party elite such as Kalmykova and Kosareva could blame Beriia alone, others like Cherkasov, Korviakov, Belkin, and Grib began to identify a wider cast of people whom they believed bore responsibility for their suffering. Their letters listed the names of leading governmental figures and investigators whom they considered part of Beriia's band, including Volin, Serov, and Kruglov. Once the rehabilitation of process had begun, the implicit admission that errors had occurred in the past raised the question of who was to blame for these mistakes. Drawing on the combative rhetoric that Stalinist culture had created, petitioners often identified their accusers as enemies who must be crushed. Their demands for full-scale retributive justice surely made disconcerting reading matter not only for government and party officials across the country (some of whom had built their own careers on dubious practices) but also for the political leaders who profoundly feared the new round of purging which identifying those responsible for past injustices would inevitably bring.

Resurrected Heroes

As they attempted to make sense of their experiences of punishment and exile, a certain group of petitioners chose to look not to the contemporary media but instead to older traditions within Soviet culture. Some purge victims, in particular the 1937 generation, presented their life stories in a style reminiscent of early radical fiction and their approach to the horrors of Stalinism began to suggest new, perhaps more fruitful ways to make sense of the country's bloody past.

Nikolai Kochin typed a fourteen-page petition to Voroshilov in September 1954.[75] The main focus of the text was the interrogation and the confession forced out of him; he continued to feel deep anger that the inves-

---

[73] GARF f. 7523, op. 58, d. 141, l. 150.

[74] In his memoirs Pavel Sudoplatov, one of the most significant figures in the Soviet intelligence network until his arrest in August 1953, remembers Rudenko telling him he was one of fifty of Beriia's "conspirators" who had been arrested. See Pavel Sudoplatov, with Anatoli Sudoplatov, Jerrold L. and Leona P. Schecter, *Special Tasks: The Memoirs of an Unwanted Witness—A Soviet Spymaster* (London, 1994), 384.

[75] TsADKM f. 85, op. 1, d. 491, ll. 16–29.

tigation had turned his biography "into one black blot [*chernoe piatno*]."[76] Through the act of petitioning, he hoped to take back the authorial rights over his own life. Although he was angered at the mistreatment he received at the hands of his interrogators, Kochin showed no desire for retribution; nor, however, did he rely on the rhetorical props offered by the media. Instead, he wrote about his life as the story of a true revolutionary.

His petition began by asserting his revolutionary credentials under the subheading "A Little Bit about Myself." Born in 1902, he was the son of a peasant family from Gor'kii oblast. He embarked on Soviet work at the age of nineteen as a member of the village poor committees and later fought against kulaks, counter-revolutionaries, saboteurs, and speculators in the village. As the model personification of a Bolshevik revolutionary, he was upwardly mobile, receiving an education at the pedagogical institute that allowed him to return to the provinces as a teacher in 1924. His life provided material for various novels and tales, and in the 1930s he became an author and member of the Writers' Union. In this most exemplary of Soviet narratives, his transformation reached its zenith in 1939 when he was awarded a state prize for literature, joined the party, and was elected a deputy of the Gor'kii oblast soviet. As he chose to present it, Kochin's story reflects socialist realist narrative, for his tale is that of a young man successfully coming to consciousness. It was not a life without mistakes: "I have never claimed to be someone who never makes mistakes or has no doubts and hesitations. I didn't become [*sformirovat'sia*] a Marxist-Leninist straight off. I didn't immediately overcome the many vestiges of the past within me [*ne srazu preodolel v sebe mnogie perezhitki*]. But I was never for a moment a counter-revolutionary."[77] With a certain pride, Kochin narrated his early life as a process of inner transformation, the act of *becoming* a revolutionary, yet any erring committed by Kochin was well within the bounds allowed even to a Soviet hero.[78]

The influences on Kochin's autobiography came from the Soviet canon, but perhaps particularly from the literary traditions of his youth. In her study of the Soviet novel, Katerina Clark examines the qualities given to the early socialist realist hero, suggesting that he shared similarities with figures from various genres of old Russian written tradition, including hagiography and sections of the chronicles that recount the secular virtues of princes.[79] If me-

---

[76] TsADKM f. 85, op. 1, d. 491, l. 22.

[77] TsADKM f. 85, op. 1, d. 491, l. 27.

[78] The Soviet belief system did not require its subjects to have been perfect from birth but allowed for some error in the process of self-fashioning. Catriona Kelly suggests that "the actual moment of being broken and remade, and the sense of humility and gratitude to the higher authority it inspired, held as much importance as adherence to political orthodoxy in itself." See Catriona Kelly, "'Thank You for the Wonderful Book': Soviet Child Readers and the Management of Children's Reading, 1950–75," *Kritika* 6 (2005): 717–753 (753).

[79] Clark, *The Soviet Novel*, 47. She suggests, for example, that these qualities are found in Pavel, the hero of Gor'kii's *Mother*.

dieval princes had a strong sense of honor, duty, valor, and service, so too did early Bolshevik heroes—and so indeed did many purge victims like Kochin. In their petitions they emerge as highly honorable revolutionaries, tied to the party by strong kinship or family bonds, and ready martyrs to the Bolshevik cause.

In claiming their rights to rehabilitation, many petitioners presented themselves or their relatives as heroes for whom honor was everything. In October 1954 N. Z. Pertsovskii wrote to Voroshilov with a request for the rehabilitation of his late father, who was arrested in 1938. In his petition he made no demands for any sort of material recompense but expressed concern only for his father's honor, writing, "my conscience cannot be clear while my father's honor is still stained by these serious accusations."[80] Despite the brevity of his letter, the issue of honor recurred twice more.[81] Employing similar language, I. V. Kirenko applied for both her own rehabilitation and the rehabilitation of her late husband, who had been a senior engineer within the military, writing: "I consider that it is my duty to cleanse the honor of my husband, even posthumously, as I know how much he valued his stainless [*nezapiatannaia*] honor."[82] The privations she experienced obliged Kirenko to plead for practical aid in the process of finding work and registration, but for her dead husband the issue at stake was only his honor (*chest'*).

Many found it agonizing to think they had acted against the dictates of communist honor. Kochin repeatedly stressed his remorse for the false testimonials he signed under duress, for he believed that nothing could "excuse a communist signing false documents, not even torture."[83] Although ordinary mortals might succumb to physical torment, a communist belonged to a higher order and should have absolute fortitude. Those who *did* refuse to sign false confessions used it as further proof of their heroism. S. Filipovich, a doctor who had once worked for Voroshilov, sent him an intimate letter in April 1953, reminding him that they had worked together between 1924 and 1938: "In the fifteen long and heavy years since then, I have always remembered you saying that anyone who tells you an untruth, whatever it might be, loses your trust forever. Now I can repeat to you, that I only ever told you the truth." Later in the letter, he wrote: "The desire always to be truthful in your eyes gave me strength in 1938 to resist the 'refined' methods investigators used to force me into giving false testimonial against myself."[84] His formulations suggested the existence of an honor code among Old Bolsheviks, where commitment to "truth" was unbreakable. Although it would

[80] GARF f. 7523, op. 107, d. 123, l. 20.
[81] GARF f. 7523, op. 107, d. 123, l. 20. Pertsovskii was rehabilitated in October 1955 (l. 22).
[82] GARF f. 7523, op. 107, d. 123, l. 83.
[83] TsADKM f. 85, op. 1, d. 491, l. 19.
[84] GARF f. 7523, op. 107, d. 123, l. 1.

seem that Voroshilov had offered no practical assistance against his arrest, Filipovich's petition insisted on the existence of kinship bonds linking Bolsheviks and sustaining them in their most extreme suffering. In January 1955 the Military College of the USSR Supreme Court rehabilitated him and ordered his release.[85]

This kind of kinship bond was another of the symbolic patterns surrounding the revolutionary hero in early radical fiction.[86] Just as the revolutionary hero belonged to a radical "family," the letters of repressed communists often fiercely asserted their membership in a closed community. Sometimes their entitlement came through blood ties. Kirenko, for example, wrote that she was descended from a family of teachers and that between 1898 and 1911 their apartment had served as a safe house for political exiles on the run and as a store for illegal propaganda, including the underground Bolshevik newspaper *Iskra*.[87] The wife of a communist repressed in 1937, Antonina Veiner, informed Voroshilov that her husband's mother was a Bolshevik, and that her father was a Baku railway worker and party member from 1905.[88] In both letters, genealogy was used to strengthen revolutionary credentials. In other cases, the journey toward revolution forged these tight bonds. Barkhonov, a senior figure within the military management in 1938, was supported in the petitioning process by General Khrulev, who wrote: "I know Barkhonov from childhood, when we used to go together to the local *zemstvo* school and my brother and I used to stay over at his home. I knew him later when he worked with my father at the Putilov works."[89] A childhood friendship initiated in the local school for poor children, flourished in adulthood at the Putilov factory—a key site for the forging of the revolutionary spirit before 1917.

The revolutionary hero of early Bolshevik fiction led an ascetic life of extraordinary dedication and self-deprivation, and this ideal also shaped purge victims' petitions. Clark writes that while the hero in mature socialist realism was "a *bogatyr* figure," "a dynamic figure, a veritable *perpetuum mobile*" and a "vessel of inexhaustible revolutionary energy," his precursor in prerevolutionary radical hagiography had been "the typical martyr prince."[90] Although Soviet prisoners were far from inactive for much of their incarceration, and the years, even decades, of forced labor could have offered plenty of material for strenuous and dynamic scenes, many petitioners preferred to present themselves as "martyr princes." They wrote highly abridged versions of their sentences, often nothing more loquacious than "I honestly served seventeen years in the camps" or "I spent ten years working

[85] GARF f. 7523, op. 107, d. 123, l. 3.
[86] Clark, *The Soviet Novel*, 49.
[87] GARF f. 7523, op. 107, d. 123, l. 84.
[88] GARF f. 7523, op. 107, d. 123, ll. 9–11.
[89] GARF f. 7523, op. 107, d. 123, l. 13.
[90] Clark, *The Soviet Novel*, 72–73.

honestly in prison."[91] Instead it was the experience of incarceration and torture that enhanced their life stories as saintly revolutionary heroes. In the late tsarist era, prison was an inevitable chapter in the autobiography of a committed radical, and paradoxically, the solitary cell still remained a key site for the symbolic formation of a true revolutionary identity.[92] Many of these petitioners focused their narratives on the harrowing experiences of Lefortovo and Butyrka, for it was in the torture chambers where their right to be called a communist was doubted and disputed, that their faith was most sorely tested. In their narratives, survival required mental and spiritual strength rather than physical might. Kochin, for instance, described all that he had lost—a decade of his life, his health, reputation, citizenship, family, friends, and work—but then assured the reader: "But not for a moment did I lose faith in the cause of communism, which I have served all my life. I didn't lose confidence that justice would triumph, and being in prison didn't turn me against Soviet power even for a moment. I didn't become bitter, for I found inside myself the strength and integrity of conviction that makes one recognize the inexorable motion of history and its unavoidable costs."[93] He wrote that even prison failed to rock his faith in the party, and in the darkest of circumstances he was aided in his battle against internal demons by his belief in the Marxist-Leninism creed. If anything, his time banished to the wilderness made him a stronger Bolshevik.[94]

In radical Bolshevik fiction, the hero should ideally be ready to make the supreme sacrifice of his life. If he died, the event was commonly followed by a secularized version of the Christian death-and-transfiguration pattern, with the hero's "resurrection" symbolized, for example, by a comrade-in-arms taking up his banner.[95] Still in exile in April 1955, one former political prisoner wrote home describing how a friend had recently been released from the camps: "It is the greatest happiness to witness the miracle of a person resurrected from death. . . . Butsenko carried his cross for eighteen years. He came to his Golgotha and was crucified, but he was not killed. Now his cross has been removed and he has been brought back to life."[96] Some petition writers likewise interpreted their arrest as a symbolic death, their return as rebirth. Barkhonov, released early for good work, wrote: "I was born on earth a second time, everything is new for me, even buses."[97] For others, however, "rebirth" would be possible only when their honor was restored.

---

[91] GARF f. 7523, op. 107, d. 123, l. 14; TsADKM f. 85, op. 1, d. 491, l. 28.

[92] Susan Morrissey, *Heralds of Revolution: Russian Students and the Mythologies of Radicalism* (New York, 1998), 34.

[93] TsADKM f. 85, op. 1, d. 491, l. 28.

[94] By the end of 1956 his petitions had paid off and Kochin was fully rehabilitated (TsADKM f. 85, op. 1, d. 492, ll. 16–17).

[95] Clark, *The Soviet Novel*, 49.

[96] RGASPI f. 560, op. 1, d. 17, ll. 32–34.

[97] GARF f. 7523, op. 107, d. 123, l. 14. Barkhonov was rehabilitated in June 1955 (l. 19).

After eight years in prison and six in exile, Aleksandr Langovyi returned to Moscow, but only rehabilitation could offer him resurrection. He explained: "For sixteen years I was disgraced [*oplevannyi*—literally, spat upon] and every further month of bureaucratic red tape lies on my soul like a stone, especially as I still hope to be born again as a human being [*vozrodit'sia chelovekom*]."[98]

Allowed home, some returnees clamored for the restoration of their honor and their party cards. In writing their petitions, they were interested not only in what they hoped the party might do for them but also in what they might offer the party. Langovyi wrote: "I am fifty-nine years old, I have aged considerably, but I am mentally hale and hearty [*dushevno bodr*], and in those years that are left to me I would like to work with all my strength for the cause to which I have devoted all my life."[99] These former "enemies" hoped to serve the revolution once more.

In the mid-1950s Elena Stasova, Lenin's former colleague and an Old Bolshevik aged over eighty years, received many letters from repressed communists seeking help with their appeals. Curiously, she was also petitioning on her own behalf: in 1948 she had received a severe reprimand for a lecture in which she apparently praised Bukharin, and she now hoped that either Khrushchev or Malenkov might help wipe her record clean.[100] Despite her own difficulties and her age, she became a source of support for many old party members, some of whom had worked with her in the early years of the revolution.[101] In this less formal forum, the returnees were sometimes more explicit about the difficulties they encountered in daily life, but they were just as passionate in their loyalty to the revolution.

E. M. Rikhter, a former Bolshevik, had been in correspondence with Stasova since 1944, and it was to Stasova that he articulated both his frustrations and aspirations on return from the camps.[102] Released from the camps in 1954, he was rehabilitated the following year. He lived in a tiny room of six square meters in Novgorod and was disappointed that staff at the gorkom and obkom failed to treat him with sufficient respect: "I try not to lose heart and to be patient, but a bitter taste remains: I expected that after eighteen years of undeserved suffering, I would have a right to a minimum of sensitivity and not to repeated questioning and interrogations, which painfully touch unhealed wounds."[103] After almost a decade of cor-

---

[98] GARF f. 7523, op. 107, d. 123, l. 33.

[99] GARF f. 7523, op. 107, d. 123, l. 34.

[100] RGASPI f. 356, op. 2, d. 37, ll. 1–3 (both dated September 1953).

[101] Stasova maintained a correspondence with some of these former colleagues throughout their imprisonment and, when they reported ill health, she sometimes tried to use her renown to persuade camp authorities to find less arduous work for them. After their release, she occasionally sent money. See particularly the case of Mariia Shaver (RGASPI f. 356, op. 2, d. 25).

[102] Rikhter asked Stasova to support his demand to be allowed to go and fight in the Second World War. She refused, arguing that she did not know him sufficiently well to grant such a request. Their correspondence continued, however, and appears to have become more intimate.

[103] RGASPI f. 356, op. 2, d. 34, ll. 11–12.

respondence with Stasova, he did not hesitate to share the tribulations he faced and his annoyance with the hostile attitudes occasionally shown by local authorities. Yet none of this led him to question the party—quite the opposite. Patiently battling against these further injustices was also part and parcel of the extraordinary test of faith he had endured for so long. Throughout 1955 he admitted to thinking about only one thing: "I have been patient and will continue to be patient, but I will never stop striving for the main aim of my whole life: returning to the party."[104] Elsewhere he talked of the importance of returning to the "family of the party" (*v rody partii*). His battle to clear his name could thus not be satisfied by legal rehabilitation alone. Until the party admitted him, the torment would continue, and he claimed: "Compared to Vorkuta, I feel much better here, but it is painful that I, a new person, am still cut off from social life."[105] Although he wanted to believe that he had been reborn, he felt he remained an outcast until the party recognized him fully.[106]

Sofiia Shpits, Stasova's former colleague, became another of her regular correspondents in 1954.[107] A German communist, Shpits had arrived in Moscow in 1934 and worked with Stasova until a false denunciation in 1937 led to her being exiled to Kazakhstan for five years. Rehabilitated as early as 1953, she now asked for Stasova's help in navigating the red tape that prevented her from drawing a personal pension. From her letters, it seems that Shpits's life was governed by daily privations and ill health, on one hand, and by an overwhelming faith in the party, on the other. She wrote: "Sixteen years have passed. From a young woman and passionate revolutionary I have been transformed into an old woman whose health is shattered. Every month, every day, it becomes harder to go to work. I don't have any relatives or anyone close to help me." And yet there was still hope: "My rehabilitation is a bright ray of sunlight in front of the sunset. It is a victory for truth. I am a sick person, and there is already little left to live for."[108]

In the epistolary exchange that followed, the hope of reinstatement into the party became increasingly important to Shpits. As the pension she was eventually granted was insufficient to allow her to stop working, life continued to be onerous, but in the autumn of 1955 she excitedly announced to Stasova that she had written to the CC: "I want to tell you that I can't stand by on the sidelines any more. I must be in the party once more and again

[104] RGASPI f. 356, op. 2, d. 34, l. 17.

[105] RGASPI f. 356, op. 2, d. 34, l. 35.

[106] In December 1956, Rikhter received 2,000 rubles in compensation, though he was dismissive of this, saying he received "compensation for that which it is impossible to compensate." In the summer of 1957 he found work—possibly with Stasova's intervention—at an editorial staff in Moscow and, with the housing issue eventually solved, Rikhter and his wife could return to the capital. After this, the correspondence between Stasova and Rikhter dropped off.

[107] The correspondence began when Shpits asked Stasova for information concerning their work in the 1930s, which the authorities required to assess her pension.

[108] RGASPI f. 356, op. 2, d. 41, l. 1.

bear the distinguished title of member of the Communist Party."[109] Worried that Stasova might question her delay in addressing the party, Shpits explained in detail the emotional distress she had experienced over the last few months, especially as rehabilitation had brought on a nervous breakdown, the result of years of extreme stress. First, she interpreted her ordeal as an assault on her honor, which she imagined "amputated" almost as if it was a part of her physical being: "I don't know, Elena Dmitr'evna, if you will understand that kind of state? It was a terrible reaction. My misfortunes had dragged on for nineteen years. It wasn't just that no one had any sympathy or pity for me and no one needed me—it was the misfortune of a clean, honest revolutionary-communist, who had been shamed, whose honor had been cut off [*chest' otrezali*]." Second, she promoted herself as a ready martyr for the cause, a believer whose faith knew no bounds: "Whom could I show that I was clean, without guilt, and that I was ready at any moment to give up my life for the cause of communism, revolution, the working class, the fatherland, for everything that is dear to us? But I had no one to tell, no one would believe me." Third, she adopted a quasi-religious language, replete with burning souls, death throes, and salvation: "For nineteen years my soul has burnt. Then, when salvation came, the organism didn't hold out, and I found myself in hospital. The spiritual agonies have passed [*dushevnaia agoniia otoshla*], and now I want to live and with all my strength to catch up with everything that I lost, with all my soul and burning love to deserve the title of member of the party, our dear [*rodnoi*] party." Like other petitioners, Shpits presented her story of exile and rehabilitation as one of death and rebirth, in which full rebirth could only happen with the party's reacceptance. Finally, she cast Stasova as her confessor. "Elena Dmitr'evna!" she wrote, "Please forgive me for writing so much, and forcing you to read what is in my soul."[110] For Shpits the vocabulary of religious belief best described the total nature of her devotion, and she desperately desired the party to take the time to re-examine the inner recesses of her being and to reverse the moral judgment made almost two decades earlier.[111]

In her letter, Shpits voluntarily replicated the rituals that gripped the party in the 1920s and 1930s. She urged Stasova to collaborate in what Igal Halfin has labeled the "communist hermeneutics of the soul," by which he means "the complex ritual of words and deeds that permitted the party to determine who was worthy to belong to the brotherhood of the elect."[112] Shpits was not alone in wanting such rituals renewed, this time leading not to ex-

[109] RGASPI f. 356, op. 2, d. 41, l. 6.

[110] RGASPI f. 356, op. 2, d. 41, l. 7.

[111] Shpits's return to the party was made additionally difficult by the fact she was a member of the German Communist Party. She was told that the only way to be reinstated was to make the journey to Germany, but she was too ill to embark on this and well into the mid-1960s was still writing petitions asking for party rehabilitation.

[112] Igal Halfin, *Terror in My Soul: Communist Autobiographies on Trial* (Cambridge, Mass., 2003), 7. See also Michel Foucault, "About the Beginning of the Hermeneutics of the Self: Two Lectures at Dartmouth," *Political Theory* 21 (1993): 198–227.

pulsion but to reinclusion in the brotherhood. The sister of Ia. B. Gamarnik, first secretary of Belorussia until 1937, wrote to Khrushchev in 1954 asking the party to re-examine not just her case but her whole being: "I understand that anything written by me cannot serve as evidence, but I know that you are able to verify my whole life [*proverka vsei moei zhizni*], and it is this that I'm begging you to do."[113] Rather than fearing retrials and renewed interrogation, several petitioners implored the authorities to recall them and to read their souls in—to borrow Kochin's terms—the "light of truth" (*v svete pravdy*).[114]

The significant aspect of these petitions is that not only did the authors want the reader to grant requests for housing, jobs, rehabilitation, or renewed party membership, but they also wanted the revised narrative of their lives to be accepted by the party, replacing the false biographies written for them by interrogators in the prison cells. By eschewing the desire for revenge or recrimination, they presented themselves as the most noble and self-sacrificing of communists who, despite suffering inordinately for the party, retained a fervent and steadfast faith. In looking back to the early days of the revolution, however unintentionally, they found a heritage that predated Stalinism. Moreover, this pre-Stalinist literary tradition enabled them to present a self that was honorable and heroic, yet did not require the authorities to hunt down the guilty or identify a new enemy.

In the years 1953 to 1955 the Soviet leadership introduced a wide range of reforms that allowed a significant contingent of *zeks* to leave the camps and make their way home. A combination of amnesty decrees, pardons, early release for good work, and the re-examination of cases ensured that prisoners from all categories were part of these returning masses. Even as some of the problems seemingly associated with the return, such as rising criminality and escalating public anxiety, became apparent, the government did not retreat. In January 1956 the Presidium created new commissions to re-examine the cases of those serving time for political or work-related crimes, with officials now instructed to visit the camps in person and make decisions on the spot.[115] As a result of the commissions' work, a further 100,139 prisoners were released by October 1956, approximately half of them politicals.[116] The following year another amnesty was passed, this time in honor of the fortieth anniversary of the October revolution, resulting in the release of almost 200,000 more prisoners by the end of 1958.[117]

---

[113] RGANI f. 5, op. 47, d. 89, ll. 32–33, reproduced in Artizov et al., eds., *Reabilitatsiia: Kak eto bylo*, vol. 1, 182–183.

[114] TsADKM f. 85, op. 1, d. 491, ll. 16.

[115] RGANI f. 3, op. 10, d. 218, ll. 17–18, reproduced in Artizov et al., eds., *Reabilitatsiia: Kak eto bylo*, vol. 1, 308.

[116] APRF f. 3, op, 57, d. 110, ll. 99–100, reproduced in Artizov et al., eds., *Reabilitatsiia: Kak eto bylo. Fevral' 1956– nachalo 80– kh godov*, vol. 2 (Moscow, 2003), 193–194.

[117] A report sent by the MVD to the CC in December 1958 stated that 196,713 prisoners had been released by the 1957 amnesty (GARF f. 9401, op. 2, d. 500, l. 316).

Despite its evident commitment to downsizing the Gulag, the government made little attempt to state its purpose openly. Although 1953 saw the press make some tentative moves toward explaining the changes occurring, with announcements about Beriia's arrest and the abuse of power at the MVD, in 1954 and 1955 the party was almost entirely silent on the subject. Large numbers of prisoners returned, some even had their cases revoked, but the Soviet leadership failed to provide interpretative tools with which citizens could make sense of these changes.

Prisoners, ex-prisoners, and their relatives were not allowed, however, to remain silent. In these years the petition was a staple element of the release process. Many texts communicated to the authorities the alienating nature of the Gulag experience. In trying to explain how they had ever come to be cast out from Soviet society, some petitioners started to raise thorny issues. If they were innocent, was someone to blame for their ordeal? Should the people responsible be held to account for the miscarriages of justice they had perpetrated? And even if the petitioner had indeed committed an offense, what had led him into crime? Had the regime failed to provide adequate care for its young people? The problem of how to explain the ongoing existence of crime within socialist society was one that would plague the authorities throughout the Khrushchev era.

Yet with regard to political terror at least, a few petitions started to offer some solutions. With their tales of heroic martyrdom the petitions of purge victims pointed to the final service this older generation could do for the party. Instead of blaming the party, many victims of the *Ezhovshchina* presented themselves as endlessly devoted to the cause, noble warriors whose only desire was to be allowed to rejoin the faithful. In early 1956, when he began to proffer explanations for a process of reform begun almost three years earlier, Khrushchev would draw on these stories of heroic self-sacrifice.

3 Heroes, Enemies, and the Secret Speech

> When she got home from the party activists' meeting, Algaya
> didn't know what to do with herself. She drank some vodka, then
> some valerian drops, then more vodka. She lay down, jumped up,
> ran around the room thinking, but she couldn't understand how
> it could all have happened. After such words had been spoken, it
> was impossible to carry on living the same old way—or perhaps
> at all. Khrushchev had said it; Mikoyan had supported him; Molo-
> tov, Malenkov, Voroshilov and Kaganovich had kept silent. . . .
> What had happened to them? Had they gone insane? Had they
> turned out to be traitors?
>
> —Vladimir Voinovich, *Monumental Propaganda*, 2002

Looking back on his political career, Khrushchev suggested that one of the
driving forces behind his most notorious speech, delivered on 25 February
1956 at the close of the Twentieth Party Congress, was the fate of Stalin's
victims. In his account of the February days, he describes how, during a re-
cess between sessions, he had desperately sought to convince his colleagues
in the Presidium of the need to talk openly about the purges and the fate of
Stalin's victims. In his memoirs he quoted his speech verbatim: "'We now
know that the people who suffered during the repressions were innocent. We
have indisputable proof that, far from being enemies of the people, they were
honest men and women, devoted to the party, devoted to the revolution, devoted to the Leninist cause and to the building of socialism and communism
in the Soviet Union. We can't keep people in exile or in the camps any longer.
We must figure out how to bring them back.'"[1]

[1] Khrushchev, *Nikita Remembers*, 378.

Some aspects of this account have now been challenged, in particular the timing: the archival records show the Presidium agreed to the Secret Speech before the congress had even started.[2] Somewhat selective and self-aggrandizing, Khrushchev's memoirs give an idealized account of his actions, charting a journey of discovery in which Stalin's crimes gradually came to light, his own mounting horror, and the great importance he placed on releasing and rehabilitating his victims. He thus explained how Beriia's arrest had led to further investigations into the Ministry of Internal Affairs and wrote of his personal shock on discovering that M. S. Kedrov, a hero of the Civil War, had been executed as an enemy of the people and of his mounting desire to find out more about the arrests.

Many have questioned the true extent of Khrushchev's knowledge, suggesting that he knew much more about the terror than he later admitted, but it is certainly true that over the course of 1953–1955, the dismantling of the Special Board allowed Khrushchev and his colleagues to discover greater detail about the arrest and execution of former heroes such as Kedrov.[3] They also received, read, and processed petitions from those who had survived. As early as June 1953, for example, Molotov forwarded to Khrushchev a petition from I. M. Gronskii, erstwhile editor of *Izvestiia,* suggesting that the letter warranted the attention of the Central Committee. Khrushchev in turn passed it on to P. N. Pospelov (CC secretary) who recommended that Gronskii be legally rehabilitated, given employment at the Gor'kii Institute of World Literature, and considered for reinstatement into the party.[4] Gronskii's letter was typical of other petitions of repressed communists. He told Molotov (and thus Khrushchev and Pospelov): "Imprisonment did not break me either physically or morally. I came out of the camps a convinced communist just as I was before, just as you knew me. I came out entirely healthy and fit for work. Solid, revolutionary, party tempering [*solidnaia, revoliutsionnaia, partiinaia zakalka*] gave me the strength to endure and overcome the ordeal." He insisted that to be bitter or to "take offense," would be a sniveling, bourgeois, philistine reaction.[5]

It is impossible to know how many of these letters Khrushchev personally

---

[2] Using archival documents to show that other members of the Presidium had approved the Secret Speech on 13 February 1956, Iurii Aksiutin dispels the myth that the other leaders had not agreed to the speech right up to the last minute. Aksiutin writes: "there was no personal improvisation by Khrushchev, and no secret decisions [*keleinosti ne bylo*]. Khrushchev followed the norms of collective decision making." See Iu. V. Aksiutin, "Novoe o XX s″ezde KPSS," *Otechestvennaia istoriia* (March–April 1998): 108–123 (110). For a detailed narrative of the Presidium discussions and the drafting of the speech, see Taubman, *Khrushchev,* 270–300.

[3] On the extent of Khrushchev's knowledge regarding Stalin's terror, see, for example, V. P. Naumov, "N. S. Khrushchev i reabilitatsiia zhertv massovykh politicheskikh repressii," *Voprosy istorii* (April 1997): 19–36.

[4] RGANI f. 5, op. 30, d. 36, ll. 45–56. According to a petition written by Gronskii's friend in the summer of 1954, he was legally rehabilitated and readmitted to the party but still living in poverty. He was yet to be granted living space. GARF f. 7523, op. 58, d. 142, l. 79.

[5] RGANI f. 5, op. 30, d. 36, l. 48.

read, but there can be little doubt that from 1953 on the cases of leading party members, and their petitions, were handled at the highest levels. Having read the petitions of both the living and the dead, Khrushchev used the Secret Speech to present an image of the victims that was in keeping with their own self-portrayal as honest, courageous, and devoted communists. Khrushchev drew on the testimony of several victims of Stalinist terror, including A. V. Snegov, who had recently returned from the camps, and several leading party figures such as R. I. Eikhe, Ia. E. Rudzutak, M. S. Kedrov, P. P. Postyshev, S. V. Kosior, V. Ia. Chubar', and A. V. Kosarev, who all perished as "enemies of the people." With remarkable symmetry to the petitions written in the 1950s, Khrushchev depicted these victims as the true heirs of the revolution. The motifs of truth, honor, and belief prevailed. Khrushchev quoted from Eikhe's letter to Stalin: "If I were guilty of even a hundredth of the crimes they're pinning on me, I wouldn't dare to address this dying letter to you, but I haven't committed a single one of the crimes I am charged with, and there has never been a shadow of baseness on my soul. I have never in my life told you even a half-word of untruth, and now, with both feet in the grave, I am also not lying to you."[6] Referring to himself as a faithful son of the party, Kedrov wrote: "To die in a Soviet prison labeled a despicable traitor of his country—what can be more terrible for an honorable person? . . . I firmly believe that truth and justice will triumph. I believe, I believe."[7] Struggling against the "enemy" label forced on him, Kedrov reaffirmed his undying faith in the Bolshevik creed. Using the victims' own words, Khrushchev suggested that those long vilified as "enemies of the people" must now be regarded as honorable revolutionaries.

The Secret Speech can be understood as an attempt by Khrushchev to resolve some of the uncertainties generated by the political changes occurring since Stalin's death. Although it did not clarify the status of all Gulag returnees—for the Secret Speech was concerned solely with political prisoners—the party leadership was at last offering some kind of explanation for the reforms of 1953–1955. The key term of 1953, "socialist legality," was not abandoned, though Khrushchev now spoke more often of "revolutionary legality," and the speech fleshed out its meaning more fully than the oblique newspaper references of three years earlier. Suggesting the arbitrary application of the label "enemy of the people" had led to gross miscarriages of justice, particularly in the key years 1936–1938, Khrushchev spoke of an "unprecedented violation of revolutionary legality." Legality, or rather its violation, was now more clearly associated with the *Ezhovshchina*, and with the destruction of noble men and women who had been the true sons and daughters of the revolution. In his attempt to find a salutary narrative, Khrushchev drew on the stories of purge victims, once erroneously and unlaw-

---

[6] "O kul'te lichnosti i ego posledstviiakh," 75.
[7] Ibid., 102.

fully branded as enemies, now reinstated as honorable revolutionaries and symbols of party truth.

Khrushchev's speech was neither included in the official records of the Twentieth Party Congress nor mentioned in the Soviet media (at least initially), but it was far from secret. Following instructions from the CC, sections of it were read out, or summarized, at party and Komsomol meetings across the Soviet Union in the spring of 1956: from the rank-and-file members at workplace party meetings to the elite assembled as delegates at the gorkom and obkom level, communists at every step on the party hierarchy were privy to the text.[8]

Recognizing their new status, some rehabilitated communists felt that local party meetings held to discuss the Secret Speech were an ideal opportunity to speak of their experiences. In Kalinin oblast, for example, the chief engineer of the Kalinin artificial leather complex summarized the key points in his biography: "I have been a communist since 1928. I am from a worker family, educated by the Komsomol, and I was made out to be an enemy of the people, a spy, and a saboteur. . . . I am happy that I kept a profound belief in the party. When it was possible, I applied to the Central Committee with this faith intact." In keeping with the language of victims' petitions and of the Secret Speech, he presented himself as a martyr whose faith in the party had sustained him through all the trials and tribulations thrown at him.[9] At the party meeting held at the Communist Avant-Garde factory in Vladimir oblast, another victim of the *Ezhovshchina*, B. S. Shukhman, also presented his life story, describing how in 1937 he had been working as deputy director of the factory when the raikom secretary personally stripped him of his party ticket and called him "first a wrecker and then an enemy of the people." As a result, he was arrested and imprisoned. Shukhman's attitude toward this suffering was also impeccable: "Our duty," he said, "is to lead a decisive battle to overcome any remnants of the cult of personality, to rally around the Leninist CC even more tightly, and to mobilize all our energy and skill to fulfill the decisions of the historic Twentieth Party Congress."[10] Even though he incorporated his experiences of Stalinist terror into a highly conformist response to the speech—invoking a collective battle against the cult, increased party unity, the fulfillment of obligations—local officials were clearly worried that he had spoken at all. The party secretary at Sobinskii raikom included it in his report to superiors at oblast headquarters under the heading "critical remarks."

This chapter begins by using reports and transcripts from the meetings

---

[8] According to Iurii Aksiutin, over seven million members of the Communist Party of the Soviet Union and eighteen million members of the Komsomol were informed of the main content of the speech. See Iurii Aksiutin, "Popular Responses to Khrushchev," in *Nikita Khrushchev*, ed. Taubman, Khrushchev, and Gleason, 177–208 (182–183).

[9] RGANI f. 5, op. 32, d. 45, ll. 37–38.

[10] GAVO, f. p-830, op. 3 d. 213, l. 47.

held in the wake of the Secret Speech to explore communists' attitudes toward the new narrative of the terror presented. Was the caution of the Sobinskii raikom typical, or were returning party members given a warmer welcome elsewhere? The focus here is on responses to the vindication of former "enemies"—the issues that Khrushchev as memoirist would later consider so central to the whole venture. It was not, however, the only aspect of the Secret Speech that was discussed and disputed in the spring of 1956. The second half of this chapter explores other issues raised by the speech, in particular Khrushchev's attack on the *concept* of the "enemy of the people." The Secret Speech not only suggested that Stalin had attacked and destroyed innocent victims, but that the warlike mentality nurtured under him, on which the purges drew, was in itself wrong. The collective hunt for enemies—so long the central aspect of Soviet culture—was being called off, and this shift sparked debate outside the party as well as within.

Although the party reports and unpublished letters that survive in the archives allow only partial insight into reactions to the speech, they at least give a sense of the information that was flowing into the party's central headquarters about the party and public mood in the aftermath of the Twentieth Party Congress. It was not necessarily a cheering picture. The body of correspondence shows a diverse set of responses, but it certainly seems to suggest that Khrushchev's keynote speech failed to bring any firm resolution to the doubts and uncertainties that had first begun to surface in 1953.

From Victims to Heroes?: Responses at Two Moscow Meetings

When eleven hundred party members in Moscow's Sverdlov raion (neighborhood or district) met on 14 March 1956, the first party secretary spoke for one hour and twenty minutes. In that time, although he covered a range of issues including housing, industrial growth, building plans, and the need to establish more reading rooms in the district, he did not mention the Secret Speech. When the meeting was opened to questions from the floor, however, the implications of the speech dominated discussion. One person asked if this promised return to Leninism would mean that the extravagant salaries paid to bosses under Stalin would now be reduced; a second queried whether Stalin's portrait would be removed from workplaces; and a third demanded to know what members of the CC had been doing while Stalin was alive, and what had happened to their revolutionary "intransigence" (*neprimirimost'*). Another even rebuked the first secretary of the raion: "Comrade Riabkin, you still haven't given us your assessment of Stalin!"[11]

There was, however, only a single mention of the victims themselves. One of those attending commented: "The fact that in 1937–1938 lots of com-

[11] TsAODM f. 82, op. 34, d. 12, l. 33.

munists and honest Leninists were arrested, convicted, and destroyed was already known to the whole party in 1939. This was said at the Eighteenth Party Congress. We already discussed it then. Why do we need to talk about this again?"[12] Seeing little reason to reopen old wounds, he showed no appetite for transforming purge victims into new heroes. It was a heated meeting, with some apparently welcoming the changes that the speech might bring—such as more equal pay—while others simply wanted information and clarification. Yet, in all this passionate discussion the victims were mentioned only once—and that was a plea to stop any further discussion of their fate.

From the transcripts of another party meeting taking place at the same time in Moscow, a different picture emerges. In contrast to the party *aktiv* (activists) in Sverdlov raion, members of the capital's literary elite awarded the returnees significant attention when they met at a combined meeting for writers at the *Sovetskii pisatel'* publishing house, the board of the Writers' Union, and members of the Writers' Foundation (*Litfond SSSR*). One of those attending the meeting was a certain comrade Bliakhin, who spoke at length about the fate of purge victims and warned against premature self-congratulation. He claimed it was too early to speak of Bolshevik legality and justice being restored, and voiced strong criticism of the slow pace of reform:

> The simple fact that of the tens of thousands of innocent people repressed only seven to eight thousand have as yet been rehabilitated shows that overcoming the consequences of the cult of personality is creaking along [*pod skripom*], slowed down by the resistance of the government bodies assigned this task. Comrade Khrushchev's speech about the paltry number of people rehabilitated and restored their rights was very distressing for the delegates. Involuntarily everyone had the same thought: how many decades will those who have been expunged from life have to languish [*tomitsia*] and suffer, if these cases will be considered only at a rate of two to three thousand a year?[13]

The slow pace of rehabilitation concerned others present at the writers' meeting. A certain Rudnyi criticized the speech made by A. A. Surkov, first secretary of the Writers' Union of the USSR, which he considered too conservative, particularly with regard to the status of surviving victims. While Surkov had, according to Rudnyi, spoken correctly of the need to rehabilitate various people and works, he had chosen to talk primarily about authors who had died during the purges. Rudnyi considered this important, but insisted on the need to rehabilitate the living as well.[14]

---

[12] TsAODM f. 82, op. 34, d. 12, l. 34.
[13] TsAODM f. 8132, op. 1, d. 6, l. 10.
[14] TsAODM f. 8132, op. 1, d. 6, l. 64.

The fact that many of those present knew of people who had been purged and were already aware of their return could not help but influence discussion. They drew on personal experience or on the tales of friends who had survived prison and the camps to talk about the importance of overcoming the cult of personality. Demanding greater dynamism from his colleagues, Rudnyi, for example, referred to the critic Charnyi, who had been repressed and recently rehabilitated: "He needs moral support. But when I, as the deputy secretary of our party organization, talked with Comrade Kedrina at *Literaturnaia gazeta* and asked her to ring him and commission an article, she passed me on to someone else, saying it needed approval." He went on to ask: "Why haven't Subbotskii, Isbakhu, Brovman, and others who have also been rehabilitated and readmitted to the party had articles commissioned?"[15] The hall erupted in applause. Direct references to the ordeals of fellow writers, apparently known personally to many, drew emotional responses from the audience.

Delegates at the meeting were not, it seems, afraid to voice criticism of those who were hampering the return and reintegration of purge victims, but the mood was not only one of dissatisfaction. Although Bliakhin had been downcast, others followed Khrushchev's example and found the seeds of the party's spiritual revival in the stories of returning purge victims. When a party member named Voitinskaia spoke of their many colleagues, including one present, who were still unable to find work because previous convictions or doubts over their political reliability, she presented them as heroic figures. She described how one acquaintance who had spent eighteen years in camps was asked by the CC what had given her the strength to survive, to which she replied "the party."[16] Voitinskaia not only demanded recognition of purge victims' right to fair treatment but also presented the returnee as a true believer in the party cause. At the same meeting, Comrade Ermashov concluded that the party had proved that Leninism was "stronger than Stalinism" (which brought applause), and that the Secret Speech had "saved the party."[17] For him, purge victims such as Postyshev, who bravely stood up to Stalin, were heroes. Their resurrection imbued the party with fresh glory, for *their* courage was the *party*'s courage. Here at least, party members welcomed these returning heroes, cast them as the party's saviors, and suggested that, far from being damaging, a rewriting of party history was fortifying.

The atmosphere at the Writers' Union thus seems quite different from that of the Sverdlov raion party meeting, where there were no references to the purge victims, except for a single comment disputing the need to discuss them at all. Perhaps the difference can be attributed to the greater likelihood that members of the cultural intelligentsia would have close contact with those

[15] TsAODM f. 8132, op. 1, d. 6, l. 65.
[16] TsAODM f. 8132, op. 1, d. 6, l. 77.
[17] TsAODM f. 8132, op. 1, d. 6, l. 70.

returning for the camps. The diaries of the children's author Kornei Chukovskii certainly suggest that in the years 1954–1955 the writers' community had already welcomed back many old friends who had survived long
sentences, and this might explain the alacrity with which those present at the
Writers' Union meeting pounced on elements of the Secret Speech that referred to the victims' rehabilitation.[18]

In fact, although rank and file party members in Sverdlov raion had shown
little interest in knowing more about the terror and its victims, this was not
true for the whole party. Indeed, the writers, though particularly outspoken,
were not alone in their desire to uncover the truth about the party past and
to heroize returnees. Nor were they alone in their readiness to criticize the
way the rehabilitation process was being handled. The records of meetings
at the gorkom and obkom level show that the Moscow writers were not radical dissenters but rather party members who articulated ideas and view-
points current among the higher ranks of the organization, where experience
of the purges—direct or secondhand—was more likely.

The Party's Search for Truth and Purity

At the gorkom and obkom level the party also gathered activists together to
hear the main content of the speech. Attendance at such meetings could reach
almost a thousand.[19] The proceedings were led by the first secretary, with
other party officials, kolkhoz chairmen, and deputies on the local soviets
playing a key role. The activists were there by invitation: these were committed, devoted communists, and their contributions and questions differed
markedly in tenor and content from those made by rank-and-file members
at some meetings at the raion level.

As with the writers, some who attended these meetings had known people directly affected by the purges, and they welcomed the opportunity to in-
quire about their fate and to garner information about events in their own
locality during the Great Terror.[20] Members frequently called for further information about the events detailed in the Secret Speech, wanting to know—
among other things—which of the CC members shot had now been found
innocent, which military leaders sentenced in 1937–1938 were now reha-

---

[18] For example, on 5 January 1954 Chukovskii learnt that B. I. Zbarskii, one of Lenin's em-
balmers, and his wife had been released from the camps, and on 29 January he visited the family. In November of the same year he met up with Katia Boronina, another children's writer,
who had recently returned from exile (Chukovskii, *Dnevnik*, 207–208, 216–217).

[19] In Stalingrad, for example, the obkom called a meeting on 12 March 1956 attended by
962 people (RGASPI f. 556, op. 1, d. 1031). For more on the Stalingrad party structures, see
Philip D. Stewart, *Political Power in the Soviet Union: A Study of Decision-Making in Stalingrad* (Indianapolis, 1968).

[20] RGASPI f. 556, op. 1, d. 304, l. 142; RGASPI f. 556, op. 1, d. 638, l. 93.

bilitated, how many had died as a result of the Leningrad Affair, and whether any Leningrad party leaders repressed in 1937 were still alive.[21]

From one region to another there was great variation in the nature of discussions taking place at party meetings, often reflecting the stance taken by the local leadership. Some first secretaries clearly discouraged party members from discussing the terror and the fate of its victims. This was certainly the case at the meeting of party activists in the Leningrad obkom. In the time allocated for questions and discussion, one party member challenged the fact that Kozlov, first secretary of the Leningrad obkom, had mentioned only those rehabilitated posthumously, asking if there were any more, particularly among the living. Kozlov answered: "I know of only two . . . , Comrade Utkin, a former party worker, and Comrade Pikin, who used to work for the Komsomol and is now studying at the Higher Party School. Comrade Utkin is a pensioner. In my opinion, no other comrades who are still alive have been rehabilitated. I certainly haven't met them."[22] Considering the number of returnees, the answer is clearly disingenuous; indeed Kozlov had already been criticized for his reluctance to meet and assist those rehabilitated, in particular his refusal to consider their pension claims.

The extent and mood of debate depended to a degree on the lead given by the party secretary chairing the session. The first secretary invariably opened the meeting with his or her own evaluation of the Twentieth Party Congress. Some local leaders were conservative, repeating almost word for word sections of Khrushchev's speech and restricting free discussion. In Moscow, for example, the gorkom meeting suppressed discussion; and its chair, a candidate member of the Presidium, E. A. Furtseva, stuck close to Khrushchev's text.[23] In Irkutsk and Vladimir, both lead speaker and delegates reproduced Khrushchev's words faithfully, and the subsequent debate was limited as a result.[24] At the meeting of the Gor'kii obkom, the opening speaker focused on the financial tasks posed by the Twentieth Party Congress and paid scant attention to the cult of personality, so most delegates followed suit, with the exception of an editor who dared to raise the issue.[25] At these more restrained meetings, party members often expressed satisfaction that *zakonnost'* had been restored, but it remained an abstract concept, with few signs of appetite for more detailed exploration of its meaning in relation to

[21] RGASPI f. 556, op. 1, d. 304, l. 142.

[22] RGASPI f. 556, op. 1, d. 601, l. 133.

[23] RGASPI f. 556, op. 1, d. 705. The meeting made little mention of the Secret Speech, and the floor was not opened to delegates. Their views could be expressed only in written notes handed to the speaker. Furtseva referred to these in her summing-up and gave answers to selected questions, but she claimed that many of the questions had a personal character and were not worth the attention of the whole party *aktiv*.

[24] Irkutsk gorkom (RGASPI f. 556, op. 1, d. 304); Vladimir obkom (RGASPI f. 556, op. 1, d. 197).

[25] RGASPI f. 556, op. 1, d. 243 (especially ll. 91–93).

the purges.[26] Elsewhere, however, some party secretaries wrote their own "speeches." The transcripts of obkom and gorkom meetings in Rostov and Magadan, alongside reports from other regions, provide insight into how narratives of party history were now being rewritten in some localities.

On 10 March 1956 N. V. Kiselev, obkom secretary, opened proceedings in Rostov. Like Khrushchev and first secretaries everywhere, he described the torture inflicted on show-trial victims and others in Moscow, but Kiselev was quick to remind his audience that atrocities occurred in their city too. Having decided to go beyond mere regurgitation of Khrushchev's narrative, he had commissioned his own research into local archives. In a five-month period in 1937, he informed the party faithful, no less than 1,006 communists had been excluded from the Rostov party and arrested on the grounds of fabricated confessions. By February 1938 a further 1,178 had joined them, and many were shot. Presumably on the basis of contact with purge survivors or possibly their petitions, he continued: "Those who stayed alive recount the terrible torture that went on in Rostov prisons. Here there were the same horrors of which the Old Bolshevik Kedrov wrote about from within Lefortovo prison, where the enemy Beriia was handling his case. Here we had cretinous hangmen [*kretiny-palachi*] of the same ilk as Rodos, about whom Khrushchev talked in his speech."[27] Where Khrushchev quoted from the interrogation transcripts of Postyshev, Rudzutak, Eikhe, and other leading party figures, Kiselev used the words of a Rostov communist, I. T. Efimenko, party member since 1920 and formerly a plenipotentiary of the Ministry of Supplies for Rostov oblast. From inside a Rostov prison Efimenko had written: "Comrade Stalin, I am obliged to turn to you for a second time in search of the truth, for Rostov investigators are afraid to look truth in the face and [instead] fabricate rotting, cowardly cases."[28] Like Eikhe, whose letter to Stalin was cited in the Secret Speech, Efimenko also invoked "truth," and through Efimenko's own words, Kiselev allowed the former prisoner to embody integrity in a disintegrating world.

The decision to write his own narrative of local party history when other colleagues—in Moscow, Leningrad, Irkutsk, Gor'kii, and Vladimir—used Khrushchev's words, suggests Kiselev's profound support for the Secret Speech. Rejecting the safe option, he committed himself to radically new versions of the party past and promoted a former enemy as hero. In their oblast, seven hundred people had already been rehabilitated, many posthumously, and yet this was only a small part of the caseload facing the KGB and the Procuracy, he said. Kiselev interpreted the Secret Speech as an invitation for party organizations to rethink and reformulate their own experiences.

Three days later many of the Rostov party activists met again, this time at

---

[26] Gor'kii obkom (RGASPI f. 556, op. 1. d. 243, l. 41); Moscow obkom (RGASPI f. 556, op. 1, d. 691, l. 52).

[27] RGASPI f. 556, op. 1, d. 875, ll. 86–87.

[28] RGASPI f. 556, op. 1, d. 875, l. 88.

the gorkom meeting.[29] The opening speech, made by gorkom secretary Comrade Lobanov, also drew on research from the local archives. Briefly detailing the lives of a number of the Rostov party's victims, he promoted the city's own heroes. He commemorated A. A. Semiakin, party member since 1917, A. I. Larichev, party member since 1911, V. S. Viktorov, party member since 1917, and A. A. Konovko, party member since 1918 and former chairman of the Rostov soviet.[30] With the mood of the meeting set by Lobanov and Kiselev before him, others present at the meeting discussed the fate of former colleagues. One delegate spoke of Ivan Chentsov. A party member from as early as 1904, Chentsov had been sentenced to seven years in 1906 for owning a printing press and had "served his sentence, as a Bolshevik ought, asking no one for pardon. He had never been a part of any opposition and had always behaved as a revolutionary." The speaker listed other purge victims, adding the date they joined the party for each one, and it was invariably prior to 1917.[31] Party members chose to depict purge victims as almost exclusively Old Bolsheviks, unswerving in their commitment to the party, unquestioning in their faith.[32]

Not content with praising Chentsov, however, the same delegate went on to demand retribution against those who had participated in the terror. "Now they are rehabilitated," he said of the purge victims. "But they were considered enemies of the people. Why have I raised this question? I raised this question because there were lackeys who in fact had no party qualities. If these members of the party slandered people, then it is necessary for our party organizations at town and oblast level to take retribution against them for those who died in vain." His suggestion was popular, receiving applause and shouts of "hear, hear." Someone called out, "And were you arrested too?" Responding by telling his own story, the speaker recounted how they had tried to stitch him up with Chentsov and to prove that he too was an "enemy of the people." He drew the conclusion that the party organization should investigate thoroughly, and that "maybe there will be more than one swine to find."[33] Thus for a second time he called for measures to be taken against those who had labeled others "enemies." The implications of this are highly significant. At meetings where the leading officials chose to engage in a rewriting of party history, calls for retribution began to surface. Khru-

[29] At the gorkom meeting, one delegate mentioned that many of them had already heard Kiselev speak at length about Rostov's victims (RGASPI f. 556, op. 1, d. 881, l. 53).

[30] RGASPI f. 556, op. 1, d. 881, l. 32.

[31] RGASPI f. 556, op. 1, d. 881, l. 53.

[32] Revisionist research on the purges has suggested that Old Bolsheviks were not singled out during the purges but were victimized primarily as a result of their job or status. This pattern is not reflected in the portrayal of terror victims found here, perhaps because speakers felt the suffering of Old Bolsheviks provided the most powerful stories. See J. Arch Getty and William Chase, "Patterns of Repression among the Soviet Elite: A Biographical Approach," in *Stalinist Terror: New Perspectives,* ed. J. Arch Getty and Roberta T. Manning (Cambridge, 1993), 225–246 (243).

[33] RGASPI f. 556, op. 1, d. 881, l. 54.

shchev had made no reference to finding the guilty, but to some party members this was a crucial step toward restoring the party to health.

These transcripts suggest not only the speech's potential to revitalize the party but also its inherent danger. At both meetings, the audience appears to have been stirred by the first secretaries' rewriting of local party history. Yet one activist audaciously suggested that alongside rehabilitation of the innocent, the party should find those responsible for these miscarriages of justice and punish them. Although such comments were relatively rare, this delegate was not alone.

As in Rostov, the meeting held by the Magadan obkom to discuss the Secret Speech became heated. Here the address given by the first secretary was in itself cautious, reproducing sections from the Secret Speech rather formulaically, but senior figures soon took the discussion in unexpected directions.[34] A certain Comrade Potnov gave a very long speech in which he welcomed Khrushchev's text, not least because it reasserted the importance of re-educating those serving time in the prison camps, and he attacked the current situation within the Gulag. He openly criticized those raion party secretaries who helped local bosses avoid using convict labor from the camps, meaning that many prisoners were deprived of the opportunity to "redeem" themselves through work. More controversially still, he suggested that some camp workers continued to commit acts of "arbitrariness and lawlessness."[35] This senior figure in the camp administration used the Secret Speech as an opportunity to tackle local problems head on, and he did not hesitate to point the finger at those he thought were responsible. Perhaps inspired by his lead, the secretary of Pen'kin raion, who was the next to take the floor, also offered his own interpretation of the Secret Speech. Comrade Markov detailed the purges in Magadan and hinted at the need for reprisals. He described how 70 percent of the Dal'stoi party had been arrested in 1937–1938; how the head of Dal'stroi, Pavlov, had personally ordered the shooting of every third prisoner in the mines without any sort of investigation or trial; and how those guilty of terrible crimes—for example, those responsible for the Kirov murder—were treated like heroes. "We are submitting to the oblast party committee," he concluded, "a proposal for the creation of a commission to review the cases of all communists shot on the territory of Magadan oblast. We don't doubt that many will be rehabilitated posthumously and request that their families also be rehabilitated and that those guilty of massacring communists and honorable Soviet people in Kolyma be held responsible. These are our conclusions from Comrade Khrushchev's speech on the cult of personality."[36] Although Markov's wording was cautious, his demands—like those made in Rostov—pointed to a desire

[34] RGASPI f. 556, op. 1, d. 638, ll. 1–39.
[35] RGASPI f. 556, op. 1, d. 638, l. 52.
[36] RGASPI f. 556, op. 1, d. 638, ll. 66–68.

for some kind of settling of scores. In the question time that followed the speeches, another delegate asked what measures would be taken against those who participated in mass terror.[37] Markov appears to have found support for an initiative that not only sought the truth about the past but would also bring those responsible for the crimes to justice.

In the spring of 1956 communists were expected to express their support for the restoration of legality and the end to arbitrary rule, and at some obkom and gorkom meetings this was done without straying too far from the canonical text that Khrushchev had issued. Some party members took a more imaginative approach to the script, responding to it with attempts to seek out the truth about the party's past, particularly at a local level.[38] This could be seen as part of the party's revival, a flourishing of local initiative in contrast to the centralizing, homogenizing forces of Stalinism. Yet this insistence on uncovering the "truth" about the past was often accompanied by calls for more dramatic change, in particular to find those responsible for the atrocities committed under Stalin. They wanted to see not only the victims rehabilitated but also their executioners punished.

Purging and Truth

One man wrote to Khrushchev, repeatedly thanking him for telling the "truth": "On behalf of many citizens, I thank you for openly telling the people the whole truth about Stalin. This is your big service, and everyone will remember it. The fact that you have said this truth will guarantee that everything bad will be thrown out—and only the good will remain."[39] For this letter writer, re-establishing truth also meant ejecting or excising the bad from the party.

Paradoxically, renunciation of the terror brought a revival of purge rhetoric. Writing about the purges of the 1930s, Igal Halfin argues that, "messianic truth, according to party doctrine, spoke in a single voice. Since there was only one path to the light, and only one platform indicating that course, it followed that . . . disputants had somehow to be 'in opposition' to what subsequently became proletarian 'truth.'"[40] When party members embraced the Secret Speech as the restoration of truth, some imagined that the Twentieth Party Congress marked a return to the correct path, a victory of

[37] RGASPI f. 556, op. 1, d. 638, l. 90.

[38] A lecturer in Marxism-Leninism spoke at the Stalingrad obkom meeting of the need to bring the social sciences "back to life," a process she associated with the revival of local history. She lamented that there was still no collection of memoirs by Stalingrad's Old Bolsheviks, compared to the many tomes devoted to Moscow and Leningrad heroes (RGASPI f. 556, op. 1, d. 1031, ll. 70–72).

[39] RGANI f. 5, op. 30, d. 140, ll. 185–186.

[40] Igal Halfin, "The Demonization of the Opposition: Stalinist Memory and the 'Communist Archive' at Leningrad Communist University," *Kritika* 2 (2001): 45–80 (48).

light over darkness. In some people's eyes, reestablishing the party's integrity and purity after the degeneration of the Stalin years required a return to "cleansing."

At some meetings, communists began to wonder if there would now be a new purge (*chistka*).[41] Indeed, some apparently imagined not a small-scale search for those who committed the worst atrocities under Stalin but a broader attack on those who had stood in the way of "truth." At the Gor'kii Institute of World Literature, a speech made by a certain Comrade Bialik caused substantial concern at the highest levels of party organization. Asserting that the party apparatus included a layer of people whose careers were built on the purges, Bialik said that many responsible for the deaths of thousands of innocent people were still in power. Moreover, he remarked, they were now charged with fulfilling the tasks of the Twentieth Party Congress. As the party had not organized a purge for over twenty years, he suggested one should be implemented. Bialik did not envisage token retribution against a handful of individuals but far more sweeping changes within the party ranks. The renunciation of terror alone could not purify the party; it needed to be cleansed through renewing the practices of questioning, investigating, and expelling. Apparently his comments were acceptable to members of the audience, as party authorities noted their failure to condemn Bialik: two others made "demagogic comments" and no one spoke out against him until the final summing up led by the chief editor of *Kommunist,* which was greeted with hisses and boos.[42]

The concepts of cleanliness and purity were so essential to the Bolshevik faith that even in the moment of repudiating the grotesque forms they took during the Great Terror, some party members could not do without them. Even though the quest for party purity had once led to the terror, the very phenomenon now being repudiated, some party members continued to think of their organization's recovery in these same terms.

The ambiguous implications of this resurfacing rhetoric of hygiene and purity were never fully explored, even within party circles. Bialik, for one, was silenced. It was a reading of the Secret Speech that on one level supported Khrushchev's initiative but also departed from it. Khrushchev imagined a restoration of truth and the party's return to health, but in his canonical text this was to be achieved without needing to "excise" the rotten and unhealthy. In fact, the numbers actually ousted from the party for their role in the terror were incredibly low. Only a small number of communists seem to have been expelled from the party for unlawful behavior.[43] In the years between

---

[41] RGANI f. 5, op. 32, d. 45, l. 62.

[42] RGANI f. 5, op. 32, d. 45, ll. 2–3.

[43] In the records from Vladimir obkom, I found only one case of a party member expelled for his role in the purges. Avraam Fishman, who joined the party in 1939 at the age of thirty, was expelled from it in April 1957. In 1937–1939 he had worked for the MVD in Poltava oblast and had taken an "active role in the fabrication of cases," using "physical" methods to extract

the Twentieth and Twenty-Second Party Congresses, the Party Control Commission expelled only 347 members for "violating legality."[44] Many of these were high-ranking figures at the MVD, including Kruglov (its chief from 1953 to 1956), demonstrating the party's reluctance to probe deeper into issues of personal accountability when they could lay the blame on a handful of men easily written off as Beriia's associates.[45]

By the end of the year, members of the Presidium began to openly question the wisdom of "uncovering the truth." At a meeting between representatives of the Writers' Union and party leaders on 10 December 1956, Pospelov criticized the chief editor of *Novyi mir*, Konstantin Simonov, the poet Ol'ga Berggol'ts, and other leading authors for their insistence on writing "only the truth" (*tol'ko pravda*). Pospelov reminded them that there was no such thing as abstract truth, just as there was no such thing as abstract democracy.[46] Heralded by writers—and some party members—as the cornerstone of revived party integrity, "truth" came to be considered a potentially dangerous heresy.

The Enemy At Large: Broader Social Responses

As already suggested, the term the "Secret Speech" is a misnomer. The contents of Khrushchev's midnight address were made known to all party members, and there is little to suggest they kept such astonishing events to themselves. A student project conducted in the 1990s seems to indicate that at least two-thirds of Muscovites remember hearing about the Secret Speech in 1956.[47] At the time, one letter writer told Molotov that even though the speech had not been made public yet, everyone knew its content.[48] Another complained that despite Khrushchev's instructions to limit dissemination of

---

false confessions. The primary organization at the Meat Industry Trust in Vladimir voted to issue a serious warning on his party record, but the obkom decided expulsion was more appropriate (GAVO f. p-830, op. 3, d. 269, l. 278).

[44] See RGANI f. 6, op. 6, d. 1165, l. 40, reproduced in A. Artizov, Iu. Sigachev, I. Shevchuk, and B. Khlopov, eds., *Reabilitatsiia: Kak eto bylo*, vol. 2, 365.

[45] Ironically, S. N. Kruglov took over from Beriia at the MVD and oversaw many of the releases of the years 1953–1956. He was expelled from the party in January 1960 for his role in the repressions of the Stalin era. See Artizov et al., eds., *Reabilitatsiia: Kak eto bylo*, vol. 2, 860.

[46] Iu. V. Aksiutin and A. V. Pyzhikov, *Poststalinskoe obshchestvo: Problema liderstva i transformatsiia vlasti* (Moscow, 1999), 137–138.

[47] Aksiutin cites a survey conducted between 1994 and 1997 by students in the History Faculty of the Moscow Pedagogical University. The survey asked 568 people who were alive in 1956 about their reactions to the speech: 163 said they had approved, 185 had disapproved, and 220 said they knew nothing at the time of Stalin's demotion *or* were uncertain how to react to it—although the two might not be the same, they are banded together in the results of the survey. Although it is difficult to know how accurately people would remember their reactions forty years on, the figures would suggest that a majority knew of the speech, and that positive and negative reactions were fairly evenly represented. Aksiutin, "Novoe o XX s"ezde KPSS," 120.

[48] RGASPI f. 82, op. 2, d, 1458, l. 2.

the speech to party circles, it had been read to nonparty members and even to schoolchildren.[49] Two schoolgirls informed Molotov that after Khrushchev's speech was read in the city's factories, children heard about it from adult conversation, and the "cult of personality" became a "subject of discussion at home and at school."[50]

Previously I suggested that Stalin's funeral was the final masterpiece in the Stalinist performance, a media event that created a sense of public solidarity and shared suffering across the Soviet Union. With Khrushchev's Secret Speech falling less than two weeks before the third anniversary of the funeral, some letter writers remembered this event. For several of Molotov's correspondents, memories of Stalin's funeral came to symbolize the demise of a certain way of life. One letter writer seemed almost nostalgic for the sense of belonging the leader's death had brought: "Although three years have already passed since the death of I. V. Stalin, your graveside speech still rings in my ears. You read your speech with such pain in your heart . . . on the loudspeakers we could hear how your voice shook. . . . We all cried listening to you . . . we cried because our love for Stalin was boundless." Three years earlier letter writers had expressed their grief in grandiose rhetoric, some elaborating formulaic poems, but here the author repeatedly let her sentences trail off, as if failing to find conclusive meaning. She continued: "And now they say—or rather they don't say, and I have to rely on rumors, for I am not a party member, and here in the city of Barnaul Khrushchev's letter was read only to party members—that Stalin was little short of an enemy of the people, and they're taking down his portraits, burning literature, and so on."[51] Again she voiced doubt—was it just in Barnaul that the people were denied access to the speech? And was it right that Stalin should be rejected as a quasi "enemy of the people"?

Such responses suggest that the Secret Speech only exacerbated the anxieties of 1953. The desire to learn more of the victims' fate articulated by some writers and party members at the higher levels of the organization was not necessarily shared by rank-and-file communists, or by nonparty citizens. As had happened at the Sverdlov raion meeting in Moscow, some questioned the need to revisit the terror. One war veteran reminded Molotov that at the close of 1938 he and Stalin had already told the party that "enemies had wormed their way into the organs of the MVD and slaughtered party cadres," and he claimed that this earlier discussion was sufficient.[52] In a similar vein, an anonymous collective farmer called the terror a "completed stage" (*proidennyi etap*), needing no further examination.[53] He told Molotov that by mentioning these things, "we won't bring back those people who

[49] RGASPI f. 82, op. 2, d. 1467, l.18.
[50] RGASPI f. 82, op. 2, d. 1461, l. 87.
[51] RGASPI f. 82, op. 2, d. 1466, l. 131.
[52] RGASPI f. 82, op. 2. 1467, l. 29.
[53] RGASPI f. 82, op. 2, d. 1446, l. 160.

at the present moment aren't among the living"—an odd reference which, by obscuring the finality of death, apparently refused to recognize the victims as human beings who lived once and died once.

If not the terror and its victims, what other issues were at stake? The Barnaul letter points to some of the most important ones: clarification of Stalin's new status, concerns for the symbols and rituals established under Stalin, and anxiety regarding "enemies of the people."

It is worth returning for a moment to the text of the speech itself. In addition to the revelations about the purges, Khrushchev's text also had important implications for some of the fundamentals of the Soviet belief system. Khrushchev ridiculed the idea that Stalin was "superhuman" (*sverkhchelovek*): while official propaganda had long proclaimed Stalin a hero of the Bolshevik underground, Khrushchev now questioned his revolutionary credentials; and although Stalin had been worshipped as the nation's savior during the Second World War, Khrushchev now suggested that he had been a rather flawed military leader, responsible for the catastrophic setbacks of 1941. Stalin was not only found to be an unsuitable hero, however; the existence of living idols per se was said to be harmful and contrary to Lenin's teaching. Khrushchev reminded his audience that Lenin had counted modesty as one of the most important attributes of a Bolshevik and had criticized the practice of idolizing living people. Khrushchev condemned the fact that many cities, factories, farms, and cultural institutions were named after party figures still alive and well. Although he prescribed caution, he hinted that renaming should be undertaken. His speech can thus be read as a tentative attack on one of the central aspects of Soviet culture in which heroes were promoted and revered.

In addition to the demotion of heroes, Khrushchev also queried the practice of labeling and casting out "enemies." He told his audience that it was Stalin who introduced the concept of "enemies of the people." "When engaged in any sort of polemic, this term immediately freed him from any need to provide proof of the person's ideological error," he said.[54] Later in the speech he referred to the term "enemy of the people" as a "formula" that allowed all sorts of abuses. Deriding Stalin for seeing "enemies," "double-dealers," and "spies" everywhere, Khrushchev undermined key terms in the established lexicon, and in his own attacks on Stalin he circumvented the rabid rhetoric used in the press until 1953. Accusing Stalin of "arbitrary rule" and "lawlessness" and of committing abuses or distortions of "revolutionary" or "socialist legality," Khrushchev promoted the language developed in the press three years earlier. In the place of hostile invective, he deliberately avoided labeling Stalin an "enemy." Khrushchev instead identified both positive sides (Stalin "played a positive role" in the ideological battles of 1928–1929) and negative characteristics (his rudeness and despotism). By depict-

[54] "O kul'te lichnosti i ego posledstviiakh," 58.

ing a human being who was neither all good nor all bad, it seemed that the era of absolute evil versus heroic good was over.

When he talked of Beriia, admittedly, Khrushchev used more venomous terms: "In the organization of several dirty and shameful affairs, the out-and-out enemy of our party, the agent of foreign spies Beriia, who had wormed his way into Stalin's confidence, played a major role."[55] Although he wanted to break with the poisonous invective of Stalinist culture, Khrushchev showed how important the enemy remained in the Soviet political imagination. Even the initiator of the new rhetoric, it seems, found it hard to abandon Stalinist concepts.

Despite the inconsistencies, the general argument behind Khrushchev's rewriting of history was that the enemy camp had been far less dangerous than Stalin had claimed so famously in 1937. Rather than seeing the Trotskyists as a mounting threat the further they progressed along the revolutionary path, Khrushchev believed that the party's opposition was almost defeated by the mid-1930s. It was totally unthinkable, he claimed, that 70 percent of those elected to the CC in 1934 were enemies. Based on this reading of party politics in the 1930s, Khrushchev argued that the party had long been moving away from the era of conflict (*bor'ba*); and as a result, he said, the party should be oriented toward not the extermination of deviants but the goal of correction. Khrushchev reintroduced the idea that people might err but not immediately be cast out as "enemies." Urging a return to the practices of the Leninist era, he reminded his audience that the early years of the revolution witnessed many occasions when people who had vacillated and erred from the party line were given the chance to return to the party path (*put' partiinosti*). He cited the example of Lenin's forgiving approach to Lev Kamenev and Grigorii Zinov'ev after the revolution. Khrushchev's portrayal of Lenin was complex, though, for he also admitted that enemies had existed in the early stages of the revolution, and Lenin had shown no mercy toward exploiters from the old regime. The following thesis emerged: in the early years of the revolution there *were* enemies, but Lenin still strove to "correct," not "destroy," wherever possible; under Stalin, though the actual threat declined, fear of the enemy escalated, and with it came the most extreme "terroristic" measures. In recognition of the relatively small threat the "enemy" represented, the order of the day was now correction, not punishment.

Responding to this dramatic revision of the Soviet political imaginary, many citizens struggled to understand how they were supposed to think about Stalin and to treat the symbols and rituals that embodied their reverent relationship to him. One of the most important issues was the body itself, which lay in the Red Square Mausoleum next to Lenin, whose remains had by now become a kind of "holy relic."[56] After such condemnation of

[55] Ibid., 99.

[56] Visits to the Mausoleum had become an enduring ritual in Soviet culture by this time. See Nina Tumarkin, *Lenin Lives! The Lenin Cult in Soviet Russia* (Cambridge, Mass., 1983), 173.

Stalin, the proximity of his body to the saintly Lenin was problematic. Although Khrushchev had made no mention of Stalin's body in the Secret Speech, many were desperate for an answer. At almost every lower level party meeting, the list of questions posed by the audience included the fate of the deceased leader's remains.[57] As news leaked after the party meetings elsewhere, gossip in one shop queue held that Stalin was soon going to be removed.[58] By August 1956 a CC report stated that "many communists and nonparty workers have made speeches or written letters to the CC with proposals for the removal of Stalin's body from the Mausoleum on Red Square."[59]

For both supporters and opponents of de-Stalinization, the body was rich in meaning. In a passionate defense of Stalin, one Stalingrader wrote to Molotov informing him that the people still loved Stalin. Pinning his hopes on Stalin's right-hand man, he entreated Molotov to intervene: "It's clear now that Khrushchev's band is getting ready to liquidate Stalin's body. Speak with Mao Zedong, and ask him whether, if this should happen, he would take the body to his country on a temporary basis."[60] For Ivanov, a poorly educated, middle-aged man working as a night watchman on a building site in Stavropol', the body signified something quite different. In an emotional letter addressed to Voroshilov, Ivanov called Stalin a "grasping beast" who stole from the people and asked why he had not been wiped from history yet. He demanded that the leaders dispose of the body because it stank.[61] In Orthodox theology saints' bodies do not decompose, and for Ivanov the alleged smell of putrefaction betrayed Stalin as a false icon.[62] The handwriting and spelling of their letters suggest that both men were uncertain scribes, yet both risked committing themselves to paper because they believed the location of the body was significant—whether as symbol of rotting leadership or as an icon of great Soviet power.

Although its most powerful embodiment lay in the Mausoleum, Stalin's iconography was reproduced in public places, offices, and homes across the country. As with his body, many were anxious to know what to do with his portraits. A frequent question raised at local party meetings was, "What should we do with his portraits?" or, translated more literally, "How should

---

[57] At the Suzdal raion meeting in Vladimir oblast, for example, one delegate asked how the question of the Mausoleum was to be resolved, while another party member wished to know what was going on at the Mausoleum and whether Stalin was still lying next to Lenin (GAVO f. p-830, op. 3, d. 212, ll. 65–66. See also GAVO f. p-830, op. 3, d. 212, ll. 109–110, 170).

[58] RGANI f. 5, op. 32, d. 46, l. 177.

[59] APRF f. 3, op. 57, d. 110, ll. 75–80, reproduced in Artizov et al., eds., *Reabilitatsiia: Kak eto bylo*, vol. 2, 173–176.

[60] RGASPI f. 82, op. 2, d. 1467, l. 3. There was precedent for this: during the Second World War Lenin's body had been transported to Siberia and away from the front. See Merridale, *Night of Stone*, 194.

[61] GARF f. 8131, op. 31, d. 82269, l. 42.

[62] On the Bolsheviks' attempts in 1919 to prove that saints' bodies did rot like any normal corpse, see Merridale, *Night of Stone*, 161.

we be with portraits of Stalin?" (*Kak byt's portretami Stalina?*).[63] One party member asked what action should be taken with the portraits of Stalin hanging in the red corners.[64] Children told Molotov that in the neighboring school, the pupils were taking pictures off the walls and ripping them up, and no one was punishing them. "Did this mean it was right?" they asked.[65] Students wondered whether Stalin's portrait would be carried during the 1 May celebrations.[66] One subscriber to *Bolshevik* told the editors that many local party officials were taking down portraits of Stalin, and this "upsets the people" (*vozmushchaet narod*). She described in detail the confusion that reigned at a local factory:

> Yesterday workers from Workshop 34 came to the bursar and cursed him for taking down the portraits of Stalin, calling him an overzealous fool. In my opinion they were right.
>
> Twice a member of the factory party bureau came running up to one of the department managers in the factory's administration and asked why he hadn't taken down the portrait of Iosif Vissarionovich Stalin in his office. The manager said that he wouldn't allow anyone to touch the portrait.[67]

She also described the tremendous fear experienced by the manager's wife on learning that her husband was acting against orders. Despite his wife's warnings that he might be arrested as a "cult of personality" (*sic*), the manager was resolute that the portrait remained where it was, though he then fell ill with stress.

Whereas in some workplaces Stalin's loyal supporters resisted instructions from local party cells to take down portraits, in others people leaped to destroy them. According to the reports of raion officials, some party members became so impassioned during the reading of materials from the Secret Speech that they immediately began ripping portraits off the wall. Such incidents were not rare. In the small town of Gus'-Khrustal'nyi alone, for instance, two incidents were reported to superiors in the oblast capital Vladimir: in the Red Labor workshop, one worker took a poster of Stalin and burned it in the stove, while at the Lenin Club, "hooligans" defaced a statue of the dead leader.[68] At the Volzhskii raion meeting in Saratov oblast, a man tried to remove Stalin's picture from the foyer of the gorkom library where the meeting was being held.[69]

---

[63] GAVO f. p-830, op. 3, d. 212, ll. 50–51, 65–66, 109–110, 126, 170; TsAODM f. 82, op. 34, d. 12, l. 33.

[64] GAVO f. p-830, op. 3, d. 212, l. 75.

[65] RGASPI f. 82, op. 2, d. 1461, l. 87.

[66] RGANI f. 5, op. 30, d. 179, l. 27. For the author of this report from the Komsomol to the CC, one of the worrying features was that students seemingly preferred to discuss issues among themselves rather than turn to party or Komsomol organizations for clarification.

[67] RGASPI f. 599, op. 1, d. 82, l. 117.

[68] GAVO f. p-830, op. 3, d. 213, l. 7.

[69] RGANI f. 5, op. 32, d. 45, l. 60.

It is apparent from their reports that party leaders were deeply concerned by the spontaneous desecration of portraits and statues, acts perhaps worryingly reminiscent of the anarchic destruction of imperial monuments and symbols following the 1917 revolution.[70] Katherine Verdery has suggested that tearing down statues "not only removes that specific body from the landscape as if to excise it from history, but also proves that because it can be torn down, no god protects it."[71] Some officials perhaps feared this was the case, anxious that iconoclastic acts presented a lack of respect for the authority of the party. Mikhail Yampolsky, however, offers a rather different insight into such acts: "Attacks on monuments, characteristic for certain stages of change in Russia, cannot, in my opinion, be described in terms of pure iconoclasm. Rather, they express the deep dependence of the masses on the monument they are attacking."[72] With valiant efforts to save monuments alongside attempts to desecrate them, the reactions of 1956 illustrate the great importance attached to such symbols. Moreover, they suggest citizens experienced difficulty in viewing Stalin as a composite being who had both positive qualities and flaws. In Stalinist public culture there had been no place for such ambiguity, and now many citizens continued to see Stalin as either a true hero maligned by his enemies or the über-enemy gloriously unmasked.

Rejecting his portrayal as a man who both committed errors and achieved great feats, some put pen to paper to demand that he either be reinstated as the personification of "good" or be conclusively unmasked as the icon of "evil." One of Molotov's anonymous correspondents, taking on the role of amateur sociologist, classified different kinds of responses to the speech, one of which he attributed condescendingly to collective farmers and petty philistines (*melkie obyvateli*) and summarized in the following way: "Stalin is an enemy of the people and an accomplice to Beriia: we must throw his body out of the Mausoleum."[73] Letters show, though, that the opposite reaction was also possible. Believing that the Secret Speech required them to label Stalin an enemy, some rebelled. One exclaimed, "We are sure that Stalin wasn't an enemy of the people!" Another wrote, "We don't believe that our Stalin was an enemy of the people!"[74] One letter writer suggested that the "masses" were deeply confused and that people frequently asked whether Stalin should be considered an enemy of the people and a traitor.[75] Certainly there were many who, desperate to understand the essence of the matter cor-

[70] In 1917 and 1918 portraits of the monarchy were burned on huge bonfires as part of the destructive force of revolution. See Christel Lane, *The Rites of Rulers: Ritual in Industrial Society—The Soviet Case* (Cambridge, 1981), 200; and Richard Stites, *Revolutionary Dreams: Utopian Vision and Experimental Life in the Russian Revolution* (New York, 1989), 64–72.

[71] Katherine Verdery, *The Political Lives of Dead Bodies: Reburial and Postsocialist Change* (New York, 1999), 5.

[72] Mikhail Yampolsky, "In the Shadow of Monuments: Notes on Iconoclasm and Time," trans. John Kachur, in *Soviet Hieroglyphics: Visual Culture in Late Twentieth Century Russia*, ed. Nancy Condee (Bloomington, 1995), 93–112 (105).

[73] RGASPI f. 82, op. 2, d. 1467, l. 43.

[74] RGASPI f. 82, op. 2, d. 1466, ll. 106, 119.

[75] RGASPI f. 82, op. 2, d. 1461, l. 48.

rectly, called for clarification. One letter from a Komsomol member briefly listed five questions he needed answering, the first of which was simply: "Was Stalin ever an enemy of the people?"[76]

The concept of the "enemy of the people" did not simply disappear from people's vocabulary. In fact, the new party leader was soon labeled one himself. For those who opposed the Secret Speech, the concept offered a convincing explanation for unwanted change. One letter from Moscow, whose anonymous authors identified themselves as workers and war veterans, began "Down with Khrushchev!" It accused Khrushchev of "pouring dirt" on Stalin, called him a cunning beast (*ukhidnaia tvar'*), and hoped the world would come crashing down on his "bald head." The authors threatened to follow the Georgian example (hinting that public protests like the one that had occurred in Tbilisi were possible elsewhere) and demanded a public decree to say that Stalin was *not* an enemy of the people and that his body would not be touched.[77] The Stalingrader who had proposed Mao as guardian of Stalin's body also adroitly adopted the rhetoric of enemies to attack Khrushchev. Referring to Khrushchev's speech as an "unbridled and exaggerated campaign of slander against the great Stalin which only enemies of socialism want," he praised Stalin at length and concluded that "only a cretin, an ignoramus, or a malicious enemy would deny [his greatness]."[78] Both letters expressed concern about Stalin's body, both contested the labeling of Stalin as "enemy," and both hinted that Khrushchev himself might be the true villain.

Others did not go so far but were still concerned that his leadership left the country at the mercy of its enemies. In November 1956 Vasilii Taran wrote to Molotov that Khrushchev and his cronies were aiding "reactionaries and enemies." Referring to events in Georgia, Poznań, and Hungary, Taran claimed that "day after day, these smart operators play into the hands of our enemies—both at home and abroad."[79] Once, he implied, the knowing gaze of Stalin had protected the USSR from enemy attacks, but without him as sentry—particularly after his "second death" of February 1956—the country was perilously at risk. Another vehement opponent of the Secret Speech dismissed Khrushchev's assertion that Stalin had conducted the war just by looking at the globe, saying that "even without a globe, he knew every

[76] RGASPI f. 82, op. 2, d. 1464, l. 13.

[77] RGASPI f. 82, op. 2, d. 1466, ll. 114–115. In Tbilisi and other Georgian cities, crowds insisted on commemorating Stalin's death as they had done in previous years, and four days of demonstrations were quelled only by the arrival of Soviet troops, mass arrests, and bloodshed. See Vladimir A. Kozlov, *Mass Uprisings in the USSR: Protest and Rebellion in the Post-Stalin Years*, trans. Elaine McClarnand MacKinnon (Armonk, 2002), 112–129.

[78] RGASPI f. 82, op. 2, d. 1467, l. 1.

[79] RGASPI f. 82, op. 2, d. 1461, l. 47. In the Polish city of Poznań workers protested against Soviet domination in June; and in Hungary protest against the country's Stalinist leader, Mátyás Rákosi, was particularly strong, with street demonstrations, strikes, and rallies lasting until November, when they were bloodily suppressed by Soviet forces.

village and remembered every little hamlet," while Khrushchev would get lost "even with a map."[80] In this man's mind Stalin was an all-seeing, all-knowing figure whose careful watch had saved the nation in the Second World War; in contrast, Khrushchev's sanguinity put them all at risk of enemy attack.

Many citizens, then, were bewildered by the speech. It could not easily be fitted into the interpretive framework developed by Stalinism, for it did not allow them to easily distinguish the good from the bad, the hero from the enemy, and indeed discouraged them from trying to do so. Even for those who welcomed criticism of Stalin, it was a difficult text to negotiate. Demands for further explanation and clarification were common. An article was published in *Pravda* at the end of March, but it contained no mention of the purges or of Stalin's wartime failures, and the Soviet public was left to make its own interpretation of most of the speech.[81] This "silence" provoked protest from some within Soviet society. One man wrote to Molotov: "I am begging you to speak out in the newspapers and to explain to the people how they should regard Stalin, and whether their appreciation of him can continue, or if it is necessary to evaluate him differently now."[82] Another letter writer believed that the absence of public commentary reflected the speech's dubious political worth, arguing in a letter to Molotov:

> The fact that this letter wasn't read out on the radio and in the newspapers like the other materials from the Twentieth Party Congress shows that the person who wrote the letter wasn't certain himself that it would be approved, and it shows the criminality and the slander of the letter. At the congress you weren't afraid to read it in front of the foreign guests, but in front of the people you are afraid to read it at the top of your voice. You whisper like cowards in the corners of party and Komsomol meetings.[83]

Hostile to the Secret Speech, the writer's anger was redoubled by his feeling that he, as a nonparty man, was excluded from discussions and debates surrounding it. Indeed, some party members realized that the silence surrounding the speech had only served to heighten the crisis. After giving a series of open lectures in Leningrad on the meaning of the Secret Speech, the renowned historian A. M. Pankratova also informed the CC of the need to produce more explanatory material. Attracting over six thousand listeners and with the auditorium bursting on each occasion, her lectures clearly re-

---

[80] RGASPI f. 82. op. 2, d. 1466, l. 114.

[81] On 28 March 1956 pages 2 and 3 of *Pravda* featured a long piece under the headline "Why Is the Cult of Personality Alien to the Spirit of Marxism-Leninism?" On 2 July 1956 the topic was blazoned across the front cover of *Pravda,* but this reading of the Secret Speech was even more conservative.

[82] RGASPI f. 82, op. 2, d, 1445, l. 104.

[83] RGASPI f. 82, op. 2, d. 1467, l. 22.

sponded to a need within Leningrad society. Reporting on the opinions she encountered at her lectures, she summarized the questions raised in the eight hundred written notes submitted by those attending and warned that one *Pravda* article was far from sufficient.[84]

Many who entered into dialogue with the state hoped that their letters might themselves serve as the basis for a public debate. Seeking to spark a reaction in the press, a lawyer and party member from Minsk ordered the editors of *Kommunist* to publish his letter. He believed that the failure to talk openly about the cult detracted from any attempts at reform.[85] Another letter writer, this one wholly opposed to the spirit of the Secret Speech, suggested his letter be published alongside Khrushchev's text and the public be given the chance to vote for their favorite.[86] Just as many were uncertain how the authorities wanted them to respond to the Secret Speech, many also believed that their leaders were unaware of the mood of the people. They urged their readers to listen to their opinions. Convinced that his own views were widespread, one opponent of de-Stalinization suggested that leaders should find out the true opinion of rank-and-file members of the party on the subject of the cult of personality.[87] Another regretted that they did not have an "institute of public opinion" like they did in America.[88]

The aims of the Secret Speech were enormous. Khrushchev not only initiated a huge and, for some, devastating attack on Stalin's reputation but also sought to transform the political imaginary. Building on the initiatives of 1953, Khrushchev adopted the idea of "legality" (rather than a single leader's infallibility) as the regime's guiding principle. Renouncing the notion of the "enemy of the people" he suggested a less belligerent vision of the world was possible. In doing so, however, he robbed citizens of a heuristic device that had been used to make sense of the nation's confusing and turbulent political life for over two decades. This ideological shift—presented in a document of ambiguous, semiofficial status and accompanied by little explanatory material—left Soviet people hopelessly adrift. The calls for clarification had been heard, but the answer did not prove satisfactory for many members of Soviet society.

The attacks on Stalin in the Secret Speech caused confusion. For many citizens "heroes" and "enemies" were central components of the political language they had learnt over preceding decades and Khrushchev's wholesale rejection of the enemy concept wrong-footed them. The rhetoric of the Stal-

[84] RGANI f. 5, op. 32, d. 46, ll. 212–217.
[85] RGASPI f. 599, op. 1, d. 101, l. 67. On Pankratova's complex life, see Reginald E. Zelnik, *Perils of Pankratova: Some Stories from the Annals of Soviet Historiography,* Donald W. Treadgold Studies on Russia, East Europe, and Central Asia (Seattle, 2005), 59.
[86] RGASPI f. 82, op. 2, d. 1466, l. 106.
[87] RGASPI f. 82, op. 2, d. 1467, l. 19.
[88] RGASPI f. 82, op. 2, d. 1467, l. 25.

inist era with its repertoire of hostile invective did not immediately disappear from the texts composed by Soviet citizens as they entered into dialogue with their political leaders. As in 1953 some citizens proved imaginative and skillful in using this repertoire, with a handful even ready to turn it against Khrushchev himself.

Even among those who welcomed change, the speech was problematic and inconclusive. For those who embraced the search for the truth about the party's past and supported the rehabilitation of former "enemies," the speech had a significant omission: it left unresolved the fate of those responsible for the miscarriages of justice committed under Stalin. From the higher ranks of the party and some members of the cultural and academic intelligentsia came calls for the guilty to be called to account. The leadership's attempts to avoid a process of retributive justice did not satisfy all, and the association between "truth" and purging—a staple in party thinking for so long—was particularly dangerous.[89] Khrushchev had tried to craft an answer to the questions articulated in the years 1953–1956, but his interpretation of party history and his attempt to reshape the beliefs underpinning Soviet culture were not entirely successful, proving complex and alienating for many party and nonparty citizens alike.

Faced with a heterogenous array of interpretations, the party had to decide how to deal with these responses to the Secret Speech. Party officials struggled to find the correct terminology to describe the unexpected interpretations of the speech they faced. Aware that it was no longer appropriate to simply label anyone who disagreed with the party position an "enemy," and uncertain now where the boundaries of permissible debate lay, officials spoke of antisocial moods, anti-Soviet statements, slander, demagoguery, and hostile comments.[90] The party did continue to define some beliefs as unacceptable, and in some cases it expelled members who proved unwilling to accept the new line, but on the whole there was a reluctance to arrest and convict people for espousing erroneous views in the Secret Speech year.[91] De-

---

[89] In an excellent study of responses to Vladimir Dudintsev's *Not by Bread Alone*, Denis Kozlov also finds that there are certain continuities with Stalin-era rhetoric, in particular the use of metaphors of social hygiene to attack adversaries ("Naming the Social Evil: The Readers of *Novyi mir* and Vladimir Dudinstev's *Not by Bread Alone*, 1956–59 and beyond," in *Dilemmas of De-Stalinization*, ed. Jones, 80–98).

[90] Polly Jones, "From the Secret Speech to the Burial of Stalin: Real and Ideal Responses to De-Stalinization," in *Dilemmas of De-Stalinization*, ed. Jones, 41–63 (46).

[91] In Vladimir oblast, for example, at least two members were expelled for defending Stalin's reputation and criticizing Khrushchev. G. M. Vozhankov, born 1911, said in late March 1956 that "in the speech, they groundlessly blacken the reputation of Stalin and belittle [*umaliat'*] his achievements," adding that he didn't believe that Stalin had made mistakes, and that it was all an attempt on Khrushchev's part to win himself political capital. He was excluded in April 1956. A collective farmer, A. P. Pronin, born in 1904, said at a kolkhoz party meeting that the line taken against Stalin was incorrect. Despite several warnings, he continued to express such views and was expelled in September 1956. See GAVO f. p-830, op. 3, d. 148, l. 276; f. p-830, op. 3, d. 269, l. 59. In a more notorious case from the Academy of Science Thermo-Technical Laboratory, three young academics and a technician were removed from the party ranks for

spite the widespread articulation of unorthodox views in the wake of the Secret Speech, few people were sentenced for their political beliefs: in 1956 only 558 people were sentenced under article 58, far fewer than in preceding, or indeed following, years.[92]

For a short period following the unrest in Poland and the Hungarian uprising, party leaders were to interpret unorthodox views with greater suspicion. By the end of 1956, and in the light of the protests in Budapest, the CC was clearly unsettled by the reports on party and popular mood it received. These anxieties are reflected in a CC document circulated to all party organizations on 19 December 1956 which warned of an increase in "enemy activity." The letter suggested not only the leaders' readiness to speak of enemy elements in moments of crisis but also their entrenched suspicion of former prisoners (including political ones). The letter primarily blamed the social unrest on the Hungarian uprising and foreign influences such as Voice of America, the BBC, and Radio Free Europe, but it also pointed the finger at returnees from the camps:

> Party organizations do not always take into consideration the fact that a significant number of people have recently returned from places of imprisonment, either as a result of amnesty or rehabilitation, or because their sentence was over. Most are now carrying out productive work, are actively engaged in social and political life, and conscientiously fulfill their civic duties. There are also those among the returnees, however, who have taken a spiteful stance toward Soviet power, especially among the former Trotskyists, right opportunists, and bourgeois nationalists. They form groups around anti-Soviet elements and politically unstable people, trying to renew their hostile anti-Soviet activity. Party organizations should increase their educational work among those who have been amnestied and rehabilitated.

Although it seems likely that concerns about former prisoners were particularly related to the nationalist insurgents returning from the Gulag to Ukraine, this sudden volte-face in the treatment of political prisoners suggested an ominous retraction of the promises made in the Secret Speech.[93] Reservations concerning the political reliability of former prisoners continued to be expressed in early 1957, with the Party Control Commission advising regional committees to check the credentials of repressed communists carefully before allowing them to rejoin the party.[94] The numbers of former

their attacks on the limited nature of Soviet democracy. See RGANI f. 3, op. 14, d. 13, l. 20, ll. 76–79, reproduced in Artizov et al., eds., *Reabilitatsiia: Kak eto bylo,* vol. 2, 63–65.

[92] GARF f. 7523, op. 95, d. 4, l.58.

[93] Marc Elie notes that early drafts of the letter primarily targeted students and intellectuals and that the reference to returning political prisoners was an addition suggested by the first secretary of the Ukrainian party. See Elie, "Les anciens détenus du Goulag," 164.

[94] RGANI f. 6, op. 6, d. 1076, ll. 11–18, 20–22, 29–35, 39, reproduced in Artizov et al., eds., *Reabilitatsiia: Kak eto bylo,* vol. 2, 252–268.

political prisoners regaining their party card increased in 1957, however, and there was no permanent repeal of the principles laid out in the Secret Speech.[95]

The course of reform was far from consistent, but the CC letter of December 1956 proved to be a panicked response from a government that felt itself besieged: it did not mark a permanent change in political direction. Despite the worries and equivocations of 1956, the party leadership would revisit the subject of the country's bloody history in 1961. In his second major foray into historical interpretation at the Twenty-Second Party Congress, Khrushchev was to promise the restoration of "truth," again proclaim the re-establishment of Soviet legality, and speak in even more glowing terms of the heroism displayed by Stalin's victims. Nevertheless, 1956 left difficult questions unanswered: Did the crimes of the Stalin era need to be reinvestigated and culprits punished? Should enemies be identified? Could one, indeed, still talk of enemies? Moreover, other problems that had been ignored in 1956 continued to fester: What kind of status should be given to other Gulag returnees? What should be done with ex-*zeks* who could not so easily lay claim to being the party's martyred heroes? Did de-Stalinization entail a complete repudiation of the Gulag?

With a dramatic flourish, Khrushchev's speeches in October 1961 would try to resolve these issues in one stroke. The political vision he championed at the Twenty-Second Party Congress is examined in Part III. The solutions he proposed in 1961 were heavily influenced by events in the intervening years, in particular by the difficulties the government encountered in dealing with crime, recidivism, and the reintegration of prison returnees more broadly. These difficulties are the focus of Part II.

---

[95] Miriam Dobson, "POWs and Purge Victims: Attitudes towards Party Rehabilitation, 1956–7," *Slavonic and East European Review* 86 (2008): 328–345.

II
STALIN'S OUTCASTS
RETURN

Moral Panic and the Cult of Criminality

4 Returnees, Crime, and the Gulag Subculture

> I have never conducted anti-Soviet agitation or even thought about it. . . . Personally, I would classify my words as drunken shouts. I acted like this to prove myself a "hero." . . . I myself don't know where this attitude toward life comes from. Maybe it's from the camps where I served my sentence. There were anti-Soviet conversations there, and we listened to Voice of America. In the camp I learned not to give a damn about anyone else and to always blame somebody else for any problems.
>
> —Viktor Martyrshin, court statement, February 1958[1]

In the first five years after Stalin's death, approximately four million prisoners were released from the corrective-labor camps and colonies.[2] Even though new persons were sentenced in these years, the Gulag's release rate significantly exceeded its intake, and the population of the camps and colonies continued to shrink dramatically. By 1960 it was a fifth of its size on the eve of Stalin's death.[3]

---

[1] In February 1958 twenty-six-year-old Viktor Martyshin was sentenced to six years for anti-Soviet agitation: on three different occasions in 1957 Martyshin was heard talking about the imminence of war and his intention to "hang" and "slaughter" (*rezat'*) communists and to throw bombs at them. Martyshin had already spent two years inside the camps, and he blamed his misdemeanors on the Gulag experience (GARF f. 8131, op. 31, d. 88282, l. 45).

[2] A statistical report sent from the MVD to the Central Committee in December 1958 suggested that between the beginning of 1953 and September 1958, 4,118,414 prisoners were released from the corrective-labor camps and colonies. These releases were the result of Supreme Soviet decrees and the work of the commissions described earlier, as well as prisoners simply finishing their sentences (GARF f. 9401, op. 2, d. 500, ll. 316–320).

[3] GARF f. 7523, op. 95, d. 109, l. 27.

For the prisoners released from the camps, the return to civilian life did not always prove as easy as they might have hoped. The authorities continued to place limitations on the movement of many former prisoners. Although prisoners who were rehabilitated were given a "clean" passport, and those released under amnesty were allowed to settle where they wished (at least in theory), others were more restricted. Many prisoners were released because their sentence had been reduced (rather than overturned), and among this cohort those sentenced for an "especially dangerous crime" were subject to passport restrictions which prevented them from living in certain strategic areas such as capital cities, industrial centers, border zones, and ports. Marc Elie estimates that in the mid-1950s about half of returnees experienced these passport restrictions, which stopped them from living in many parts of the Soviet Union and often prevented them reuniting with their family.[4]

In practice, former prisoners from all categories—not only those with passport restrictions—encountered difficulties, particularly in terms of housing and jobs. In 1953 the authorities struggled to organize employment and accommodation for more than a million prisoners released by the amnesty.[5] With releases continuing throughout the 1950s, the problem did not disappear. In April 1956 an MVD report to the party's CC admitted that they had received many letters from former prisoners who had been unable to find work or housing and had encountered hostility from the local authorities. Some bosses explained they did not wish to "dirty" (*zasoriat'*) their workplace.[6] In December 1958 instructions from the Council of Ministers declared that released prisoners must be given work in their profession within two weeks of arriving home, but a subsequent investigation suggested that this ruling was not enforced universally. While in some areas ex-*zeks* found work and residency very quickly, the authorities in other places were so lax in their treatment of returnees that they did not even know how many released prisoners had arrived back.[7]

In 1956 one senior official at the Supreme Soviet, I. Babukhin, spoke of the "moral stigma" (*moral'noe piatno*) that former prisoners carried for many years after release. In a report condemning the vulnerable status of camp returnees, he provided several examples, including the case of N. I. Zinchenko, released from the camps in 1953, who had worked conscientiously in Kiev for three years until one day his right to residency in the city was revoked and he was sacked from his job. Babukhin lamented the fact that restrictions on movement meant that families were still separated, citing the example of Z. A. Zinov'eva, a middle-aged and sickly woman who

---

[4] Elie, "Les anciens détenus du Goulag," 250.

[5] See GARF f. 7523, op. 85, d. 41; and RGANI f. 5, op. 30, d. 36, ll. 35–37.

[6] GARF f. 9401, op. 2, d. 479, ll. 388–399, reproduced in Kokurin and Petrov, eds., *Gulag*, 164–181 (171).

[7] GARF f. 7523, op. 32, d. 6706, ll. 1–30.

was forced to work as a live-in domestic even though she had a daughter with a flat in Moscow. Teachers, engineers, and other specialists, he said, were obliged to take low-paid, unskilled work.[8] High-ranking government figures were thus aware of the problems generated by the passport regime, but although they discussed reform repeatedly, the restrictions remained in place throughout the decade.[9] Official attitudes toward returnees thus continued to be characterized by ambivalence: although all former prisoners were expected to become law-abiding, hard-working citizens, many of them were under constraints that made this almost impossible.

Even for those rehabilitated, the process of reintegration could be difficult. In December 1956 N. G. Alekseev, a party member since 1918, now rehabilitated, wrote to the CC secretary, A. B. Aristov, to complain about the treatment he was receiving from the CC staff.[10] Despite his frequent phone calls and visits, officials had made little effort to find him appropriate work, treating him as a nuisance to be fobbed off. This quest for employment—or as Alekseev termed it, his "road to Calvary"—had already lasted a year. Readmitted to the party, he still had only one room with two beds and no bedding or curtains. Not enough for a "cultured person," he complained.

For others, the experience of return could prove even more traumatic. One man amnestied in 1955 later wrote a petition laying out the difficulties returnees faced and his own unbearable circumstances: after release he had gone to live with his sister in Ioshkar-Ola, but despite all his applications he had failed to gain employment, and after getting drunk one day and arguing with her, his sister threw him out; he was then without a job or home and often went hungry. He wrote to the KGB asking to be given work or else be sent back to the camps. When no response was forthcoming, he composed anti-Soviet leaflets and pinned them directly on to the wall of the local MVD building—the act of a man totally bereft of hope. While Rudenko, who considered the case as part of the Procuracy's regular sampling of cases, believed the man should be released, Serov, chairman of the KGB, said that his alleged motives could not be used as justification for his actions and, indeed, that if he was without work it was his own fault.[11]

Many returnees were forced into a nomadic existence, some because of passport restrictions, others because enterprises and factories refused to hire former convicts. Traveling from city to city across the Soviet Union by train, they became part of a transient underclass, often clashing with the law once

---

[8] GARF f. 7523, op. 89, d. 4408, ll. 138–144.

[9] Elie, "Les anciens détenus du Goulag," 239–250.

[10] GARF f. 5, op. 30, d. 192, ll. 5–10. When he investigated the case, the head of the Personal Pensions Commission found that Alekseev was now receiving 1,200 rubles a month and had received compensation amounting to 11,900 rubles. Moskatov also suggested that Alekseev was without work because he refused the positions offered him (GARF f. 5, op. 30, d. 192, l. 11).

[11] GARF f. 8131, op. 31, d. 71418.

again. The experiences of a certain Vasilii Barsukov are illustrative.[12] Released from the camps in October 1958, Barsukov had tried to return to his wife and children in Moscow, but when denied registration he had taken to the road (*poekhal brodiazhnichat'*). He traveled to Iaroslavl', Kaluga, and then Tula in search of work, but without success. At Tula, he decided to head for the city of Kozel'sk. Unable to find anywhere to stay, he decided to sleep rough at the station. After spending the evening in the buffet, he was drunk and angry. According to one witness, Barsukov began shouting about the nation's leaders, saying that Khrushchev and Furtseva gadded about together, gorging themselves (*raz"ezhaiut i piruiut*), whereas he had been separated from his wife. Incensed that he was homeless and far from his partner, he railed against the authorities that denied him a family home, saying that he hated Soviet laws and wanted to hang communists. He soon found himself back inside the camps.

This chapter explores in detail more cases of men whose post-Gulag experience once more brought them into conflict with the law. Of the millions who came back from the camps, many no doubt *did* return home and find work, but stories of successful reintegration leave little trace in the archives. It was the tales of the rebellious or the tragic that were recorded, primarily because they were of interest—and a source of anxiety—for the authorities. The government's suspicion of former prisoners (reflected in their ambivalent policies) was ultimately a self-fulfilling prophecy. Many ex-*zeks* continued to feel marginalized and persecuted, and a significant number found themselves on the wrong side of the law once more.

Previous offenders were often blamed for the rising levels of recorded crime that became a feature of the 1950s. Although the numbers of registered crimes dipped slightly as the impact of the 1953 amnesty eased, the problem did not disappear. Far from it. If in 1953 a total of 552,281 crimes had been registered, by 1956 this figure had reached 717,582, and by 1957 it was 745,812. The number of cases of banditry recorded did not reach the 1953 levels again, but other violent crimes were certainly on the rise: in 1953, 8,394 murders were registered; in 1956, 9,670; and in 1957, 12,230.[13] N. P. Dudorov, minister of internal affairs from 1956 to 1960, reported that in 1958 in the country as a whole, recidivists committed 27 percent of crimes overall, and 30 percent of crimes committed on the railways (a further sign that ex-*zeks* were more likely than other citizens to lead a peripatetic existence on the margins of Soviet society).[14] For some time Dudorov had also

---

[12] GARF f. 8131, op. 31, d. 88119.

[13] GARF f. 9401, op. 2, d. 497, l. 347.

[14] GARF f. 9401, op. 2, d. 505, l. 178. Reports from the provinces also frequently identified recidivism as a major factor contributing to high levels of offending. For example, a 1956 report from Molotov oblast acknowledged that the authorities often failed to find employment for those returning from the Gulag and suggested that this might in part explain the fact that 23% of crimes committed the previous year had been done by people with previous convictions (GARF f. 8131, op. 32, d. 4593, l. 62).

been harboring suspicions that Gulag returnees were casting a deleterious influence on young people and claimed that "former convicts and people without permanent living place or work . . . do not just commit crimes themselves but entice unstable citizens, most commonly young people, into criminal activities."[15]

Exploring the nature of the Gulag return as it is refracted through the paperwork generated by the law-enforcement agencies—the Ministry of Internal Affairs, the Procuracy, and the Supreme Soviet—this chapter argues that those charged with maintaining order in the Soviet Union came to view the massive exodus of prisoners from the camps as a major problem. The danger apparently lay not only in the thefts, rapes, or murders that some former convicts committed on return from the camps but also in the ideas and beliefs imported back from the camps and the impact of these on young people.

The Gulag Subculture

For one category of crimes the level of recidivism was substantially higher than others: counter-revolutionary crimes. Of those sentenced under article 58 in 1957, 39 percent already had previous sentences, substantially more than for crime generally. This was not the result of a rounding up of those already identified as politically unreliable (as happened with the rearrests of purge victims in 1948).[16] In 1957–1958 former *political* prisoners accounted for only 11 percent of the total sentenced under this notorious article. In fact, 28 percent of those now convicted under article 58 had previously served time for *non*political crimes.[17] This means that almost one in three of those now accused of anti-Soviet activity was a person who had already spent time within the Gulag but had not previously been convicted of a *political* crime. Although this phenomenon was in part caused by the authorities' mistrust of former prisoners, it also reflected the alienating nature of the Gulag experience. Far from converting its inmates into ideal citizens as the Belomor model had promised, it had transformed at least some prisoners into angry critics of the regime. In the 1950s this subversive subculture was imported back into Soviet society in at least four ways: tattoos, leaflets (*listovki*), verbal outbursts, and song.

The criminal tattoo, which had originated in tsarist prisons and camps, flourished during the Soviet era.[18] For those who knew how to decode their

---

[15] GARF f. 9401, op. 2, d. 479, l. 334.

[16] On the 1948 rearrests, see Ivanova, *Labor Camp Socialism*, 56.

[17] Elena Papovian, "Primenenie stat'i 58–10 UK RSFSR v 1957–1958 gg.: po materialam Verkhovnogo suda SSSR i Prokuratury SSSR v GARF," in *Korni travy: Sbornik statei molodykh istorikov*, ed. L. S. Eremina and E. B. Zhemkova (Moscow, 1996), 73–87 (85).

[18] Abby M. Schrader, "Branding the Other/Tattooing the Self: Bodily Inscription among

Fig. 1. "The extra rations of a convict-hero of socialist labour." *Russian Criminal Tattoo Encyclopaedia*, vol. 2. Danzig Baldaev. Published by FUEL © 2006.

meanings tattoos often contained a wealth of information about the bearer's identity and status: sexual preference, marital status, the number of prison convictions served, and membership in a thieving fraternity.[19] Others were more overtly political. Due to its prominence in the propaganda campaigns of the early Stalinist period, the Belomor project was a favored subject, and references to its horrors were etched on the bodies of returnees. For example, in 1956 firemen pulled an unconscious man with a head wound out of the Fontanka River in Leningrad and found his body bore a tattoo with the initials BBK (standing for the Belomor-Baltic Canal) and the title "The extra rations of a convict-hero of socialist labor," below which were symbols of the prisoners' subjugation. The tattoo contained Soviet imagery (the hammer and sickle and carnations—the flower of the revolution) but these were juxtaposed with symbols of oppression such as barbed wire and shackles (Figure 1).[20]

Five years later an elderly man was found frozen to death on the bank of Vvedenskii Canal near Vitebsk station in Leningrad and the students at the Military Medical Academy who carried out the autopsy would have discovered a depiction of Belomor's brutalities on his left shoulder. Under the heading "Dig deeper, throw further, farting steam, 1931–33," the depiction of the skeletons at work not only condemned the use of slave labor on the canal but also displayed a dark (and vulgar) humor alien to official culture (Figure 2).[21]

What the young students at the Military Medical Academy made of the tattooed bodies brought in for examination goes unrecorded. Perhaps for

---

Convicts in Russia and the Soviet Union," in *Written on the Body: The Tattoo in European and American History*, ed. Jane Caplan (London, 2000), 174–192.

[19] Nancy Condee, "Body Graphics: Tattooing the Fall of Communism," in *Consuming Russia: Popular Culture, Sex, and Society since Gorbachev*, ed. Adele Marie Baker (Durham, 1999), 339–361; Alexei Plutser-Sarno, "All Power to the Godfathers!" in *Russian Criminal Tattoo Encyclopaedia* (London, 2006), vol. 2, 32–59.

[20] "The extra rations of a convict-hero of socialist labour," *Russian Criminal Tattoo*, vol. 2, 158.

[21] "Dig deeper, throw further, farting steam, 1931–1933," *Russian Criminal Tattoo*, vol. 2, 159. The artist whose drawings make up this fascinating collection, Danzig Baldaev, born in 1925, was sent to an orphanage when his parents were arrested as "enemies of the people." In 1948 he was ordered by the NKVD to work as a warden in a Leningrad prison where he started drawing the tattoos of criminals.

Fig. 2. "Dig deeper, throw further, farting steam, 1931–1933." *Russian Criminal Tattoo Encyclopaedia*, vol. 2. Danzig Baldaev. Published by FUEL © 2006.

some this kind of glimpse into the Gulag underworld was shocking. Such sights occurred in public places too, at the municipal baths for example, or even at the railway station, as the case of Konstantin Ponamarev demonstrates.[22] Ponamarev was a former prisoner whose body carried indelible markers of the many sentences he had served for acts of theft and hooliganism. Released by the 1953 amnesty, he worked as a laborer mixing concrete in Moscow for a few weeks until arrested under article 58.[23] Ponamarev's offense was to get drunk at the station buffet at Moscow's Kiev station and then, angered by the absence of hot food for sale, to slander the country's leaders (particularly Beriia, who had just been arrested) and rip open his shirt to display tattoos of Lenin and Stalin. His choice of chest tattoo was not unusual among prisoners, and some commentators have argued that it reflected the belief that no firing squad would ever shoot at a portrait of the leaders.[24] The way Ponamarev exhibited his chest at Kiev station suggests his choice of tattoo had another dimension, however; as he exposed his torso he allegedly shouted, "I wear these [bastards] on my chest," a declaration that seems to imply his sense of ownership over these icons of Soviet power, as well as his loathing of them.[25] Ponamarev's pride in his Gulag branding and his desire to exhibit the tattoos in public give some indication as to why the Gulag return was potentially so explosive.

Other prisoners spread the message through other media. Ivan Lopatkin came back from the camps armed with a set of subversive texts he wished to share with the world. First sentenced in 1952 for theft, but released early, Lopatkin was sentenced a second time in 1956 for forging documents and during this stint became acquainted with another prisoner, Mikhail Zverev, who gave him a set of fifty anti-Soviet leaflets, all signed "The Underground Russian Committee." Zverev, a twenty-seven-year-old fellow inmate, took responsibility for writing the leaflets, saying that he was the sole member of the committee, although this confession did not exempt Lopatkin, for even

[22] *Russian Criminal Tattoo Encyclopaedia* (London, 2003), vol. 1, 125.
[23] GARF f. 8131, op. 31, d. 43168.
[24] Anne Applebaum, "Introduction," in *Russian Criminal Tattoo*, vol. 2, 16–25.
[25] The official record does not give Ponamarev's exact curse, but instead refers to "unprintable words." GARF f. 8131, op. 31, d. 43168, ll. 7–10.

on his way back from the camps he had begun distributing them. After drinking at Cheliabinsk station with another recently released prisoner, he passed on a number of leaflets to his new acquaintance with instructions to give them out to participants at the international youth festival being held in Moscow.[26] Betrayed by his drinking partner, Lopatkin was arrested a few hours later and subsequently given a five-year sentence. While the exact role played by Lopatkin in the composition of the leaflets was not entirely resolved during the investigation, the texts offer useful insight into the kind of subversive thinking that was possible within the camps. One of the leaflets read as follows:

> Workers and collective farmers, students!
> Fight against the existing system!
> Down with the government!
> Demand an amnesty for prisoners suffering in our jails!

Another read:

> Down with deceit, down with the government of Bulganin, Khrushchev, and Voroshilov!
> Long live Malenkov, Molotov!
> Warm greetings [*goriachii privet*] to all peoples fighting against their government.

A third one said:

> Soldiers and students!
> Speak out against Bulganin and Khrushchev's policies as there is no truth in them!
> Fight for the shining future [*borotes' za svetloe budushchee*]!
> Long live Malenkov![27]

Although the form of the *listovki* shows the author's desire to register some kind of opposition to the political status quo, he was also strangely conformist. Some features suggest the author was highly dependent on the political language deployed by the very system he attacked: for example, he exhorted his audience to fight for a "shining future," and extended a "goriachii privet" to other exploited people. And although he repeatedly condemned the deceit of the Soviet leaders, in particular Khrushchev and

---

[26] For more on the festival, see Kristin Roth-Ey, "'Loose Girls' on the Loose? Sex, Propaganda, and the 1957 Youth Festival," in *Women in the Khrushchev Era*, ed. Melanie Ilič, Susan E. Reid, and Lynne Attwood (Basingstoke, U.K., 2004), 75–95.

[27] GARF f. 8131, op. 31, d. 81879, ll. 7–8.

Bulganin, he praised Molotov and Malen'kov: bound within the regime's political vision, he simply inverted official values, championing Molotov and Malen'kov because they had been officially denigrated. Thus, the Soviet system, which constantly sought to project a single, coherent, political line in fact provided the potential for subversion in the form of the values, people, and places it rejected.

Even prisoners who left the camps with no plans to spread political messages sometimes found that the perspective on the world they had acquired in the camps ran them into trouble, especially when drunk or provoked. The authorities were particularly concerned about the verbal attacks some returnees launched against the Soviet system.[28] As with Lopatkin's *listovki*, verbal tirades against Soviet power often adopted official language and beliefs but inverted them. In September 1953 Viktor Zhukov, a twenty-four-year-old recently released from the Gulag, was drinking beer with a new acquaintance at a station buffet in Kuibyshev oblast when he became rowdy, attracting the attention of the police. After the police hauled him into their office to check his documents, Zhukov spat in the face of one officer, kicked another, and shouted: "Down with Soviet power!" and "Long live capitalism!"[29] With its ubiquitous slogans, the language of revolution had created the template for Zhukov's protest; the Gulag—itself the mirror of the Soviet world—had, it seems, taught him to reverse the official values.

As they rejected Soviet power, some former prisoners broke all taboos and brashly announced themselves to be fascists.[30] In this postwar period, however, a new archenemy had emerged, and it was capitalist America that more often became a rallying symbol for former *zek*s. The case of Boris Nesterov, a young man in his early twenties with several years' Gulag experience under his belt, illustrates the violent pro-American and procapitalist sentiment sometimes found among former prisoners. Back in court in May 1954 on a further count of theft, Nesterov began cursing Soviet leaders, shouting that he had been sentenced unlawfully. According to a witness, he went on to claim that Truman would come to free him and slaughter everyone and, finally, that the "Trumanites will come and they'll hang everyone" in the Soviet government.[31] In February 1957, when V. G. Marutenkov, a former

---

[28] In 1956–1957, 57% of convictions for anti-Soviet agitation and propaganda related to oral comments, and only 13% to the writing of *listovki*. See GARF f. 8131, op, 32, d. 5080, ll. 17–18, reproduced in V. A. Kozlov, "Kramola: Inakomyslie v SSSR pri Khrushcheve i Brezhneve, 1953–1982," *Otechestvennaia istoriia* (July–August 2003): 93–111 (100).

[29] GARF f. 8131, op. 31, d. 60332, ll. 5–8. Zhukov was from a peasant family near Omsk, and had been sentenced for various nonpolitical crimes, including theft and attempted escape from the Gulag. Back in the Gulag in 1954, he became an active participant in a camp uprising.

[30] In May 1957, only five days after his release from prison, Aleksandr Kuterev was on the Vorkuta–Moscow train when he broke a window and allegedly started shouting: "Citizens, don't believe the communists—they are deceiving the people!" and "I hate Soviet power, I am a fascist" (GARF f. 8131, op. 31, d. 81639, l. 1).

[31] GARF f. 8131, op. 31, d. 50509, ll. 22–25.

prisoner currently without a permanent job or living place, was arrested at Kazan' station, he shouted at the police: "Soon Truman and Adenauer will come, and they'll hang you all."[32] In December of the same year, the police detained a twenty-year-old electrician with two previous convictions, V. V. Kariakin, who began to shout that when "Grandpa Truman" (*dedushka Trumen*) came, he would hang all communists.[33] On his way home from the camps in March 1958, A. A. Panfilov told other passengers that it would be good if Eisenhower started the war as soon as possible because in the camps prisoners were dying of hunger, and he suggested that instead of dogs they should put Khrushchev himself in the sputnik.[34] The names Truman and Eisenhower resonated in the cosmogony of the *zek* as mythical figures, avenging angels who would come to save Soviet unfortunates. This championing of American presidents was almost exclusively the preserve of the prisoner and ex-prisoner, with over 85 percent of cases in which U.S. leaders were mentioned committed by people who already had experience of the Gulag.[35]

The parallels between the cases are striking. When goaded, these ex-*zeks* rallied behind the same idols—America and capitalism—though they often knew little about either. One returning prisoner told fellow travelers that in the camps he had met American workers who were mining uranium, and that he had learned that all Americans lived very well—"better than any Soviet manager": "Each one has his own car, suits, and nice hats. They work for ten days, and then they're able to get drunk [*pianstvovat'*] for half a year, whereas here people work really hard but all the same have nothing." This returnee dreamed of cars and nice clothing as signs of the wealth and status denied him, and as he drank vodka on his triumphant journey home, he imagined the United States as a haven where there would be tolerance for a way of life frowned on by respectable Soviet society.[36] Actual knowledge

---

[32] GARF f. 8131, op. 31, d. 81375, summarized in V. A. Kozlov and S. V. Mironenko, eds., *58-10: Nadzornye proizvodsvta prokuratury SSSR po delam ob antisovetskoi agitatsii i propagandy, mart 1953–1991* (Moscow, 1999), 328.

[33] GARF f. 8131, op. 31, d. 80953, summarized in Kozlov and Mironenko, eds., *58-10*, 486.

[34] GARF f. 8131, op. 31, d. 84255, summarized in Kozlov and Mironenko, eds., *58-10*, 459.

[35] Kozlov and Mironenko, eds., *58-10* catalogues cases that were verified by the Procuracy, with information about 4,855 people convicted of sedition (*kramol'niki*). The authors calculate this to be about 60% of the total number sentenced between 1953 and 1991. Thirty-one of the cases summarized in this collection mention Truman, and of these twenty-five were committed either by prisoners or by people with previous convictions. Similarly, fifty-one of the sixty-one cases that mention Eisenhower were committed by *zeks* or ex-*zeks*. This suggests that the notion of an American president coming to save Russia and taking revenge on the communists was far more popular among those with experience of the Gulag than with ordinary Soviet citizens, even those who might speak "seditiously." V. A. Kozlov also suggests that this championing of Truman was most common among prisoners who imagined him as some kind of liberator (*Mass Uprisings*, 154).

[36] GARF f. 8131, op. 31, d. 43334, ll. 11–13.

about America was not necessary, or perhaps even desirable, for ex-*zeks* could project onto America all their fantasies; indeed, its appeal lay in the fact that it could stand as the polar opposite of everything they hated about the Soviet Union. In Stalinist culture change had been conceivable only through a violent showdown between opposing forces; these ex-*zeks* chose to embrace the "pole" that had been officially rejected and demonized. As Stalinist ideology had divided the world into a set of pairs—communism versus capitalism, the Soviet Union versus the west, respectability versus unculturedness, sobriety versus drunkenness, light versus darkness—it provided, in the form of the rejected values, ready-made formulas for dissent. In 1957 another man in his twenties who had been in and out of prison since adolescence, knifed an overly officious librarian and then allegedly shouted at the police "soon the black forces will come out [*skoro vyidut chernye sily*] and then we will slaughter all the chekists." If the Soviet battle was for the light of the shining future, this young Gulag survivor willfully embraced the darkness.[37]

It has sometimes been argued that the Stalinist system destroyed the potential for "unbelief." In this regard, Jochen Hellbeck's work has stimulated important discussion, in particular his suggestion that the Soviet citizens lacked "an outside frame of reference," meaning that they could only articulate dissent by using the regime's own doctrines. Hellbeck argues that although the state might be condemned for failing to deliver on its promises, the ideology on which the regime was founded could not be challenged because there were no alternatives on offer.[38] Certainly in the postwar period, though, some citizens did have broader horizons: many ordinary army recruits had seen western Europe; by the Khrushchev era, officially sanctioned cultural contacts had increased and foreign stations such as Radio Liberty and Voice of America sent seditious programs across Soviet airwaves. Yet the cases studied here suggest it was not only from outside the Soviet Union that these alternative beliefs could originate. The Gulag—the Soviet regime's own creation—had produced its own subculture with a unique set of ideas and beliefs. Official Soviet culture certainly shaped thinking even among its most embittered prisoners; but in enacting their inversion of official paradigms *zeks* also produced something new. Although this subculture embraced the negative pole established by official binary models, once adopted, prisoners fleshed it out in original ways.

It is particularly in the music and verse produced within the Gulag that the complexity of its subculture reveals itself, for song and poetry were an important medium in which prisoners expressed their alienation from Soviet society. Songs about prisons had long existed within Russian folklore, often

[37] GARF f. 8131, op. 31, d. 84187, l. 13.
[38] Jochen Hellbeck, "Fashioning the Stalinist Soul: The Diary of Stepan Podlubnyi, 1931–9," in *Stalinism*, ed. Fitzpatrick, 77–116 (105).

expressing moral approval or sympathy for the convict, and these musical traditions (as with tattoos) survived and evolved post-1917.[39] Some songs told of isolation, loneliness, and lost love, many invoking the theme of *nevolia*, or lack of freedom. Others were barbed with hatred, lamenting the prisoner's misfortunes and railing against the tyranny of the courts and police. One Soviet-era song went: "They finished me, the bastards, they finished me / They destroyed my youth / My golden hair turned white / And I am on the edge of ruin."[40] Many of these tropes originated in the songs of the prerevolutionary era, but new elements also appeared in the Gulag canon. One popular song that began "Behind the Kremlin Walls Sit the *Narkomy*" reminded listeners that Soviet achievements such as industrialization, road building, and the construction of the Belomor Canal were all the work of prisoners.[41] The song thus accepted the idea that Soviet achievements in canal digging and construction were inherently valuable, but it also made the subversive claim that society's outcasts—the *zeks*—were the real heroes. Camp song culture was thus a dynamic form that, though it preserved many traditional features, was also shaped and influenced by its subversive relationship with official Soviet culture.

Songs that overtly criticized the Soviet regime most concerned the authorities and sometimes landed ex-prisoners in serious trouble. A collection of verses discovered on one returning prisoner show how the traditional themes of loneliness and isolation could be combined with more daring contemporary commentary. On 11 June 1957 twenty-one-year-old Aleksei Babaikov was released early from a three-year sentence, but just two days later, before he had even finished his journey, he was re-arrested. When Babaikov was found to be traveling without a ticket, he was taken to the police post at the station of Kishmurin, where he drunkenly smashed up a seat, spilt ink over the paperwork, ripped a policeman's shirt, and shouted obscene comments about the party leaders. He was also found to be carrying an album of verse, including "The Kremlin," "The Nineteenth Party Congress," "The Criminal World," and "Kengir."[42] "The Kremlin" condemned the false and mercenary nature of those in power and lamented the suffering of ordinary, innocent people, especially the young "swallowed up" by the prisons. "The Nineteenth Party Congress" imagined Lenin awakening in the Mausoleum

---

[39] Stefano Gardzonio, "Tiuremnaia lirika i shanson. Neskol'ko zamechaniia k teme," *Toronto Slavic Quarterly* 14 (2005), www.utoronto.ca/tsq/14/garzonio14.shtml; Aleksandr Glotov and Natal'ia Guliaigrodskaia, "Russkaia fol'klornaia tiuremnaia pesnia i pesni Iuza Aleshkovskogo," *Studia Metodologica* 12 (2003): 74–81 (74–75); Gerald Stanton Smith, *Songs to Seven Strings: Russian Guitar Poetry and Soviet 'Mass Song'* (Bloomington, 1984), 71–87.

[40] Mihajlo Mihajlov, *Moscow Summer* (London, 1966), 80.

[41] Mikhail Dzhekobson and Lidiia Dzhekobson, *Pesennyi fol'klor GULAGa kak istoricheskii istochnik (1940–1991)* (Moscow, 2001), 93.

[42] Some witness statements said that Babaikov had been reading the verses aloud on the train, though he denied this, claiming the album had been given to him by another prisoner on his last day in the camps and that he was unaware of its content. Eventually his defense was accepted, and he was released again in 1960 (GARF f. 8131, op. 31, d. 88449).

and, with biting sarcasm, encouraged him to look around and see people's torments, particularly prisoners'.[43] "The Criminal World" offered the fullest account of Gulag conditions, describing how prisoners lived off little more than water and slept in the snow and how the half-dead were left to rot in damp solitary confinement cells. It detailed the many different ways that prisoners might self-harm—including chopping off their own feet and hands—in order to win temporary reprieve in the prison hospital. "Kengir," subtitled "Colonel Kuznetsov," provided a detailed version of the uprising that had occurred in 1954.[44] The first stanzas described the brutal regime imposed by the "chekists" and the prisoners' mounting rage, which flared when they heard the cries of women being abused in the neighboring complex. "Kengir" went on to describe how six thousand prisoners took part in an armed protest, putting up barricades, organizing a headquarters and system of guards, and forging weapons. After forty days and nights, the prisoners' limited arsenal was spent, but, the song promised, although their struggle was defeated its spirit survived. For those who died in the uprising, revenge must be taken: "Although the enemy is strong, the masses are breaking their fetters," the song warned. At the end of eighteen stanzas in which myths of the prisoners' courage, integrity, and independence were applauded, the author of the verse identified an enemy by adopting a Marxist metaphor, though—crucially—he had flipped its meaning to make the Soviet state enemy, not defender, of the masses.

Over the long years of Stalin's rule, a unique camp culture had thus been created. Although not detached from official categories, the subculture was in itself new—and, in the authorities' eyes—highly seditious. Immersion in this subculture continued to set its inmates apart after their release, even when the individual prisoner did not conceive of his own thinking or actions as politically dangerous. In the 1950s the nation saw not only a rise in violent crime but also a spate of incidents involving former *zeks* that the state chose to label as "political." Long sentences had apparently equipped these convicts with unique "mental tools" that made their reintegration back into Soviet society remarkably difficult. Their experience of alienation led at least some prisoners to embrace alternative beliefs and to rebelliously champion their fellow outcasts as constituting a worthy community deserving of respect, not contempt. Songs and poems were cultural artifacts of this other world, easy to remember, easy to pass on.

The massive release of prisoners in the 1950s made the containment of this subculture increasingly difficult. Iulii Daniel, one of two writers put on trial in 1966 for publishing work abroad, wrote a short story set in the late 1950s in which he said: "It was a time when songs from the camps were becoming

---

[43] For a full copy of this poem and commentary on its origins, see Dzhekobson and Dzhekobson, *Pesennyi fol'klor GULAGa*, 112–116.

[44] For a full account of the uprising, see Barnes, "In a Manner Befitting Soviet Citizens."

popular. They were gradually seeping through from Siberia and the Far North, and you kept hearing snatches of them in refreshment rooms at railway junctions. It sounded as if the amnesty decree were being sung through clenched teeth. They wound their way round the suburbs like the vanguard of an advancing army. Suburban trains pounded out their rhythm. At last they marched into town on the backs of the 'rehabilitated' offenders. There they were picked up by the intelligentsia."[45] When the Yugoslav academic Mihajlo Mihajlov visited Moscow State University in 1964, he remembered the popularity of such songs in student dormitories, while the poet Evgenii Evtushenko criticized this phenomenon with his barbed verse "The 'intelligentsia' are singing *blatnye pesni* [criminal songs]," in which he lamented the fact that doctors, actors, and writers were all crooning about the death of the criminals' moll Murka, rather than taking up revolutionary songs.[46]

This penetration of the intellectual world, however, was not the only concern for the Soviet authorities in the 1950s. The popularity of Gulag culture among much broader sections of Soviet youth, particularly those who had dropped out of the system—those who had escaped what Anne Gorsuch calls the "civilizing eye of the school, youth club, or workplace"—was an equally worrying trend.[47]

The Cult of Criminality

The "problem" of Soviet youth is a well-known feature of Khrushchev's Russia.[48] Contemporary commentators and historians alike have paid attention to the growth of social phenomena such as the *stiliagi*—fashion-conscious youth who rejected Soviet styles, adopting and reworking American trends— and the rise of hooliganism.[49] Two pupils at one of Saratov's elite schools later recalled how criminality had a certain cachet even among their milieu. In an oral history interview conducted in 2003, Aleksandr Trubnikov remembered the influence of the *dvor* (courtyard) where children spent much of their free time and admitted that by the time he was eight in 1958 he had tried drinking and smoking hash. He recollected: "Well, our courtyard was not all that far from what was considered the center of Saratov's criminal

[45] Yuly Daniel [Nikolai Arzhak], "Atonement," *This Is Moscow Speaking* (London, 1968), 77–78.

[46] Mihajlov, *Moscow Summer*, 76–84; Evgenii Evtushenko, "Intelligentsia poet blatnye pesni," cited in Smith, *Songs to Seven Strings*, 81–82.

[47] Anne E. Gorsuch, *Youth in Revolutionary Russia: Enthusiasts, Bohemians, Delinquents* (Bloomington, 2000), 165.

[48] For discussion of the "youth problem," see chapter 1 in Kristin Roth-Ey, "Mass Media and the Remaking of Soviet Culture, 1950s–1960s," Ph.D. Diss., Princeton University, 2003.

[49] Mark Edele, "Strange Young Men in Stalin's Moscow: The Birth and the Life of Stiliagi, 1945–53," *Jahrbücher für Geschichte Osteuropas* 50 (2002): 37–61; Juliane Fürst, "The Arrival of Spring? Changes and Continuities in Soviet Youth Culture and Policy between Stalin and Khrushchev," in *Dilemmas of De-Stalinization*, ed. Jones, 135–153.

world, Glebuchev Ravine. And all sorts of people lived there, not exactly the dregs of society, but . . . Therefore, the influence came from there. I can't say what it was like in other parts of the city, but I rubbed shoulders with those who came from there, almost all of whom ended up in jail."[50] As part of the same project, Aleksandr Konstantinov also spoke of the existence of criminal gangs, commenting: "your prestige at school—in the restroom where the pupils smoked—was dependent on who your 'protectors' were. I was protected since the 'king' of the riverbank neighborhood nicknamed the 'Italian' lived in our building and was friendly to me. This gang world was a fact of life for us boys."[51] Konstantinov spoke of the "deep criminalization" of their schools.

The Soviet youth movement, the Komsomol, was alarmed that the criminal milieu had a certain allure for young people. In 1956, for example, Komsomol leaders in Rostov oblast reported to the organization's Central Committee that youth crime was escalating: in 1953 teenagers had committed 39 criminal acts, rising to 123 in 1954 and to 191 in 1955. To illustrate the situation, the report described how schoolchildren and young workers had formed a gang in the city of Azov: they adopted nicknames like John Silver and Billy Bones; made membership cards embossed with a skull and crossbones; and announced that their ethos was "not to study, not to work, to travel, and to live the good life." Incredibly, these seemingly childish exploits led to murder when two members of the gang were killed during a dispute over guns. In the city of Rostov teenagers had also formed a gang and taken over the cellar of a house, where they played cards and learnt thieves' jargon and tricks. To pay debts accrued while gambling, the members also committed criminal acts.[52] The problem was not unique to Rostov: in 1958, for example, 47 percent of crimes committed in the Soviet Union were by people under the age of twenty-five.[53]

Other societies faced similar problems in the wake of the Second World War.[54] In western Europe, too, "youth" emerged as a problematic category as never before and foreign influences were regularly blamed for the perceived corruption of the postwar generation.[55] Richard Hoggart's famous

---

[50] Donald J. Raleigh, trans. and ed., *Russia's Sputnik Generation: Soviet Baby Boomers Talk about Their Lives* (Bloomington, 2006), 224–225.

[51] Ibid., 32.

[52] RGASPI f. M-1, op. 32, d. 813, ll. 8–18.

[53] GARF f. 9401, op. 2, d. 505, l. 179.

[54] On the immediate postwar problem in Germany, see Alan Kramer, "'Law-Abiding Germans'?: Social Disintegration, Crime, and the Reimposition of Order in Post-War Western Germany, 1945–9," in *The German Underworld: Deviants and Outcasts in German History*, ed. Richard J. Evans (London, 1988), 238–262.

[55] Several commentators are keen to note that youth misbehavior was not in itself new: it was the level of social panic that was exceptional. See John Clarke, Stuart Hall, Tony Jefferson, and Brian Roberts, "Subcultures, Cultures, and Class," in *Resistance through Rituals: Youth Subcultures in Post-War Britain*, ed. Stuart Hall and Tony Jefferson (London, 1993), 9–74; Geoffrey Pearson, *Hooligan: A History of Respectable Fears* (Basingstoke, U.K., 1983).

study of postwar life in Britain was typical in its scorn for the American mass culture that seemed to have swept away Britain's working-class traditions, and many commentators blamed this "Americanization" for the allegedly galloping crime rate in the United Kingdom.[56] In both East and West Germany in the immediate postwar period, American culture, especially the popular westerns, was held responsible for adolescent misbehavior. According to one recent study, in West Germany, however, there was a conceptual shift in the mid-1950s, where some limited youth rebellion became a permissible stage in an individual's life cycle, and involvement in hooligan acts or rioting came to be seen as part and parcel of becoming adult.[57]

The Soviet authorities, in contrast, were never ready to agree that hooliganism was a rite of passage. The authorities were convinced that this younger generation—which, after all, had never known the debilitating effects of capitalism—should be brimming with altruism and more committed than ever to the communist project and continued to blame the influence of the bourgeois west. Increasingly, though, they admitted that nefarious influences might also come from the east, and the criminal returnee began to be portrayed as a potentially sinister figure. By 1960 this menacing character was portrayed in literature, namely in G. A. Medynskii's children's novel, *Chest'* (Honor).[58] Clearly influenced by the work of the Soviet pedagogue Anton Makarenko, Medynskii recounted one adolescent's descent into crime and his subsequent rehabilitation within a youth colony.[59] In the novel a Gulag returnee, the twenty-six-year-old Vit'ka Buzunov, is highly instrumental in the hero's fall from grace, always pushing the group of teenagers living on his block toward more serious crimes. Buzunov, nicknamed the Rat, is an entirely objectionable character: having spent time in prison he was freed by the amnesty and returned to his old home even though he was denied a *propisk* (residence permit) and continued to make a living off petty crime.

Medynskii created the figure of Buzunov at the end of the 1950s, but anxieties about the detrimental nature of the Gulag return on young people had been voiced from the outset. As early as December 1953 the Procuracy had identified this problem: "A large number of especially dangerous crimes are committed by people released from imprisonment by the amnesty. They draw unstable elements, especially young people, to their criminal activity."[60] Such anxieties resurface throughout the decade. In March 1956 the

---

[56] Richard Hoggart, *The Uses of Literacy* (Harmondsworth, U.K., 1958). On the perceived association between increased crime and Americanization, see Pearson, *Hooligan*, 16–20.

[57] Uta G. Poiger, "A New, 'Western' Hero? Reconstructing Masculinity in the 1950s," in *The Miracle Years: A Cultural History of West Germany, 1949–1968*, ed. Hanna Schissler (Princeton, 2001), 412–427.

[58] G. A. Medynskii, *Chest'* (Moscow, 1960).

[59] A. S. Makarenko, *The Road to Life: An Epic of Education (Putevka v zhizn': Pedagogicheskaia poema)*, trans. Ivy and Tatiana Litvinov (Moscow, 1951); Kari Murto, *Towards the Well Functioning Community: The Development of Anton Makarenko and Maxwell Jones' Communities* (Jyväskylä, Finland, 1991).

[60] GARF f. 8131, op. 32, d. 2386, l. 23.

procurator of Molotov oblast compiled a report on the state of criminality in the area. Identifying young workers as a problem group, he blamed the factory administrations for failing to organize proper educational activities and for allowing the influence of criminal recidivists to penetrate the workplace and living quarters. "In many young workers' hostels there are no newspapers, no games table, no political or cultural activities, and the young are not involved in the work of the club or in the amateur cultural or sporting groups. As a result, a certain portion of working youth is won over by ideas and beliefs that are alien to us, falling under the influence of criminal elements." He gave several examples: a young worker at the Uritskii mine was persuaded by Nagaev, who had recently been released from the camps, to take part in robbing a shop, from which they took 50,000 rubles. Another young worker fell under the sway of the thief-recidivist Aref'eva and participated in a major robbery.[61] V. Bulochnikov, the procurator in Cheliabinsk oblast, reported that in 1959 crime in the city had risen steeply compared to the previous year, in particular the category of "especially dangerous crimes." Of these, 42 percent were committed by people previously convicted—a percentage noticeably higher than the national average. "The danger of the recidivist," opined Bulochnikov, "lies in the fact that he creates criminal gangs, which draw in people without previous convictions, particularly young people." In Magnitogorsk, for example he said, the recidivist A. Gavrilov had formed a group to carry out muggings, with at least one teenaged member, while elsewhere in the province the thief-recidivist V. N. Ivanov organized a gang of nine members, of whom five were minors.[62]

The perceived danger of the recidivist criminal lay not only in his talent for recruiting young people to take part in actual criminal acts. His influence could be much more insidious. There was a growing anxiety that young people had begun to emulate the criminal's bravado, to adopt his insubordinate style, and to rebel against the behavioral norms nurtured by Soviet schools and by the Komsomol. In a collective letter to the leadership, inhabitants of Cheliabinsk wrote: "The worst of it is that these rotten criminals affect the health of Soviet society, especially Soviet youth, which includes young people ready to imitate these criminals and even to join their ranks. In certain circles, criminal tendencies are even becoming fashionable. Thieving jargon [*blatnoi zhargon*] and even tone of voice [*blatnoi ton*] have become trendy."[63] Other letters also testify to public concerns regarding criminal influence. According to Ann Livschiz's work on Soviet childhood, Komsomol leaders and law-enforcement officials not infrequently blamed young people's moral failings on adult criminals, principally those now returning from the camps.[64] A cult of criminal behavior was emerging, they feared. One

---

[61] GARF f. 8131, op. 32, d. 4593, l. 57.
[62] GU OGAChO f. 288, op. 24, d. 108, l. 12.
[63] GU OGAChO f. 288, op. 21, d. 93, l. 13.
[64] Ann Livschiz, "De-Stalinizing Soviet Childhood: The Quest for Moral Rebirth," in *Dilemmas of De-Stalinization*, ed. Jones, 117–134 (121).

leading Komsomol figure stated in 1954: "We have a lot of hooliganism on the streets and in school and for some kids, [criminals] look like heroes, which is one of the main difficulties."[65]

Songs and poems from the Gulag's criminal subculture proved particularly attractive to young people who wanted to break away from the confines of official Soviet culture and to prove their credentials as rebels. Iurii Gretskii, a nineteen-year-old from the city of Nizhnii Tagil, left school at an early age and worked as a metal worker in one of the city's factories until he was sacked for absenteeism. A week later, he tried to run away from home but was arrested at Sverdlovsk station for carrying handwritten copies of two songs. The first, "Cranes," was a version of "Behind the Kremlin Walls Sit the *Narkomy*" described above; the second, "My father Was Lenin," was considered even more seditious. It began irreverently:

My father was Lenin, and my mother was Nadezhda Krupskaia
My grandfather was Mikhail Kalinin
We all lived happily in Moscow on Red Square
But I was born the one thief in the family.

The stanza that caused most offense read:

Down with the raikom and the sovraikom[66]
And down with Soviet power
Our youthful strength will take care of the CC
And we will take the Bolsheviks in an iron vice and crush them

In the final verses of the poem, anger gave way to a longing for a different, freer world, and the prisoner was imagined as a trapped bird:

Only the centuries-old cedars will cry for us
The Siberian taiga will sing us a song
And those who cannot bear correction
Right, left, and you're shot

Abroad, where there is no Stalin
There is another law
I would fly there on a steel bird
But migration over the border is forbidden.[67]

---

[65] RGASPI f. M-1, op. 5, d. 556, l. 27, cited in Livschiz, "De-Stalinizing Soviet Childhood," 119.

[66] The term "raikom" refers to the district (raion) committee of the CPSU, but within the party structures there was no such thing as a "sovraikom." This suggests that the authors of the song were not fluent with party terminology (or deliberately chose not to use it correctly).

[67] GARF f. 8131, op. 31, d. 81439, 18.

Although Gretskii tried to claim that a stranger he met on the train taught him the songs, the investigation identified the source as a fellow worker at the factory, Aleksandr Pokachev, who, though only twenty, had already spent three years in the camps, where he learned the songs. On 13 February 1957, while out walking in a deserted area on the edge of the city, Gretskii, Pokachev, and another friend had sung songs that the court would later identify as "hooligan." Pokachev had apparently decided to "show off" (*pokhvastat'sia*) by showing that he also knew "forbidden songs," and Gretskii, suitably impressed, asked his friend for copies. The court's harsh treatment of the two young men reflected common fears that the "criminal world" had penetrated the ranks of Soviet youth and that certain groups of young people were falling prey to this rival ethos.[68]

Gretskii may have been lying when he said that he had learned the songs from a stranger on a train, but this kind of encounter at stations or on the railways was not impossible. From the age of eight to eighteen, Nina Fateeva was raised in a children's home, but when she started work in 1955 in one of the mines in Shakhtii, she went to live with her sister. Sacked from her job the following year, she set off for Baku (where an aunt lived) and was discovered traveling without a ticket. She was thrown off the train in the town of Mineral'nye Vody, where she began to hang out with some rather shady characters. First she got to know N. A. Krysin, with whom she drank vodka and went begging. A few days later, in the station garden, the couple met twenty-eight-year-old Boris Mukhorin, who was there with his wife and child. Freed from the camps in August 1957 after a four-year stretch for theft, Mukhorin had been traveling from city to city in search of work. Witnesses claimed that while sitting in the station garden reading the newspaper, he criticized an article on vagrancy in the United States, arguing that they had even more tramps in the USSR. Mukhorin himself denied this part of the case but admitted that he had recited a poem he had learnt in the camps, a version of "The Nineteenth Party Congress."[69] At their request, he had also written out a copy for Fateeva and Krysin. Fateeva was sentenced to five years, Mukhorin to seven. In the many petitions that followed, Mukhorin was incredulous that he, an uneducated man, could be convicted as a political prisoner and voiced indignation that he had been sent back to the Gulag because of an "infection" (*zaraza*) that he had caught the first time around.[70]

The cases of Gretskii and Fateeva are both tragic. They were in the later stages of adolescence but had not yet carved out a niche for themselves in the Soviet world, having neither a steady job nor a stable, independent home

---

[68] GARF f. 8131, op. 31, d. 81439. Both Gretskii and Pokachev were sentenced to eighteen months' imprisonment by Sverdlov oblast court, though the following year the Supreme Court overturned the conviction, setting the two youths free.

[69] GARF f. 8131, op. 31, d. 84974, ll. 17–20.

[70] GARF f. 8131, op. 31, d. 84974, l. 39.

life. They clearly found the subversive texts learnt from camp returnees appealing. Songs and poems they would have learned at school intoned praise for a way of life from which they probably felt alienated, whereas the texts that they now so enthusiastically copied articulated seductive rebellion. In his memoirs Gennadii Molchanov, who would himself later spend many years in prison camps, remembers growing up in a provincial town in the early 1960s. Keen smokers and cursers even in the early grades at school, he and his friends embraced anything frowned on by their teachers. When older brothers or friends returned from prison, they brought with them songs that were seized on by youngsters desperate for ways to articulate their frustrations.[71]

For such limited rebellion, Gretskii and Fateeva found themselves in prison, their unsettled existence within Soviet society interrupted, simply because they had been impressed by songs they heard from Gulag veterans. Yet the story of Mukhorin, the source of these songs in Fateeva's case, is no less sad. After his sentence he had returned home but was unable to find work, forced into a nomadic life, and, after some vodka in a station garden, recited verses which he had learned in the camps. He claimed to have been contaminated by his first stint in the camps, imbued with a set of ideas that he neither wanted nor fully understood.

KGB Clampdown

The heavy sentence handed out to Mukhorin for teaching two youths songs from the camps was not atypical. Increasing numbers of men who had previously served time for nonpolitical crimes now found themselves accused of anti-Soviet activity. Such was the case with Nikolai Zolotarev, a man in his mid-forties who had been in and out of the camps from the age of twenty-three. In December 1957 he was released early by amnesty and began to make his way home on the Arkhangel'sk–Onega train. With five other prisoners on the train, he decided to drink in the restaurant car to celebrate his release. At the station of Isakagorka, his fellow travelers reminded him that he needed to go to his own carriage to ensure that he was in the right part of the train when it was uncoupled. Having taken his suitcase and tickets from the others in the group, he made his way to his seat but discovered en route that the chocolates he had bought for his family were missing from his luggage. Realizing the other prisoners must have eaten them, Zolotarev was outraged but continued to his reserved place. The lights in the carriage were broken and in the dark, upset and a little drunk, Zolotarev struggled to find his papers. When the conductor demanded to see his ticket, Zolotarev began

[71] Gennadii Molchanov, "Lagernyi kanon: popytka opredeleniia zhanra," *Volia: zhurnal uznikov totalitarnykh sistem*, no. 2–3 (1994): 381–388.

to curse. This led a fellow passenger to start quizzing him about his journey. On learning that he was coming from the camps, the stranger said: "The party and the government try to correct you, but it seems you don't want to be corrected!" At this, Zolotarev exploded, spewing out foul language [*mat*], and stormed back off to the train's buffet car.[72]

At least that was how Zolotarev chose to remember the evening in his subsequent petitions. The official story was slightly different and included Zolotarev slandering the party's leaders, praising life in America, and condemning conditions in the USSR, as well as drunken swearing.[73] Zolotarev claimed this was all a fabrication crafted by the local KGB. "I can't understand why the KGB fabricated this article against me and turned me into a state or political criminal," he said.[74] He had certainly been drunk and disorderly—crime enough at his age, he admitted—but he had not made the political statements with which he was charged. According to Zolotarev, he had been framed because of his previous convictions. In summing up the case, he claimed, the procurator had said: "Citizen judges, this man has been convicted so many times and hasn't been corrected. I ask you to give him the most severe sentence possible." In his case, it was ten years.

Zolotarev, convicted of a political offense for the first time in 1958, believed that he had been framed, unfairly classified as a counter-revolutionary because of his past record as a repeat offender. Certainly, there was a rise in the number of people sentenced for political crimes in 1957–1958, perhaps reflecting the government's renewed determination to identify and punish certain "anti-Soviet" elements.[75] Elena Papovian attributes the rise in convictions under article 58 to the CC letter of 19 December 1956, but she suggests that there was a subtle difference between the message given by the party leaders and the practices of the justice system. According to Papovian, the CC letter primarily targeted the cultural intelligentsia and students, whereas subsequent circulars from the Procuracy were aimed at anti-Soviet agitation in oral form and gave examples of the kind of anti-Soviet, pro-American statements that were particularly common among ex-*zeks*. Panovian refers to the low "cultural level" among investigators, arguing: "The policies of the reforming wing of the party leadership, aiming to apply punitive measures to the guilty and to explain their motives, met with incomprehension in the localities."[76] She argues that the people convicted during the campaign of 1957–1958 were not members of a liberally minded intelligentsia but in fact little educated and "uncultured." Almost 30 percent had already spent time in the Gulag for nonpolitical crimes. These were not the

[72] GARF f. 8131, op. 31, d. 84656, ll. 5–7.
[73] GARF f. 8131, op. 31, d. 84656, ll. 23–24.
[74] GARF f. 8131, op. 31, d. 84656, l. 5.
[75] In 1956, 558 people were sentenced for counter-revolutionary crimes; 2,244 were sentenced in 1957; and 1,668 in 1958 (GARF f. 7523, op. 95, d. 4, l.58).
[76] Elena Papovian, "Primenenie stat'i 58–10," 76.

thoughtful intellectuals that historians of Soviet dissidence have tended to seek, but men like Zolotarev who existed precariously on the margins of society.

In these years the KGB was increasingly likely to classify skirmishes and clashes with the police as counter-revolutionary acts rather than hooliganism. An internal report produced by the Supreme Court in early 1958 stated that "in considering cases where individuals, often in a drunken state, make cynical comments regarding government and public figures, there is a growing tendency to classify them not as incidents of malicious hooliganism [*zlostnyi khuliganizm*] but instead as acts of anti-Soviet agitation."[77] For camp returnees who now found themselves classified not as hooligans but for the first time as political criminals, this shift was an unwelcome one.

Other former prisoners, rearrested and sentenced under article 58 like Zolatarev, argued that they had been the victim of a setup simply because they were former criminals. Valentin Seriakhin, from a poor peasant family in Kursk oblast, had left school early to fight in the war; after twelve years of military service he returned to his collective farm but in March 1957 was sentenced for setting fire to a neighbor's hut (a conviction later overturned). Released at the end of 1957, he was rearrested just months later following a drunken evening when he slandered party leaders.[78] In a subsequent petition, Seriakhin complained about the difficulties he had experienced following his release from prison, speaking of the "economic blockade" that the local authorities had erected to prevent him from making an honest living in his home village. His accusations against the local police went further still: "The *brigadmilitsiia* scurry about like some kind of mythical vision. Handcuffs, straitjackets, unprintable obscenities, curses—all this reminds me of some kind of super-Gestapo."[79] This second conviction, he claimed, was a fabrication invented by the Kursk KGB.

Fedor Molokoedov also blamed the local police authorities for his arrest. Having spent twenty-seven years in prison for a range of crimes including hooliganism and banditry, Molokoedov headed for Mineral'nye Vody upon release. This was perhaps a bad choice of destination. Many prisoners released from the camps headed for spa towns such as Mineral'nye Vody, attracted by the more temperate climates of the south, and local officials were

[77] GARF f. 9474, op. 16s, d. 648, l. 9, cited at length in Elena Papovian and Aleksandr Papovian, "Uchastie Verkhovnogo suda SSR v vyrabotke repressivnoi politiki, 1957–1958 gg.," in *Korni travy*, ed. Eremina and Zhemkova, 54–72.

[78] One evening in March 1958 Seriakhin joined a gathering of local women and young girls in the home of one of the collective farmers. Arriving very drunk, he then argued with one of the women who had been a witness in the earlier arson case, criticized the party's agricultural policies, and called the government a gang of criminals. His case got worse when the police searched his home. In addition to some *listovki* in German, which a kolkhoz shepherd had found and apparently asked Seriakhin to store (but which no one could read), they also discovered a letter that he had written to the United Nations in which he recounted the injustice of his first sentence (GARF f. 8131, op. 31, d. 84944).

[79] GARF f. 8131, op. 31, d. 84944, l. 55.

particularly alarmed about the large presence of recidivists.[80] In a crime hot spot like Mineral'nye Vody, local officials were anxious to find ways to rid the area of undesirables, or at least this was how it seemed to Molokoedov. In 1958 he was arrested for anti-Soviet agitation, accused of insulting the country's leaders and saying he would like to kill Khrushchev and all the members of the CC.[81] In his petition Molokoedov claimed that he had long known the key witness, a man named Orlov, to be a police informant and argued that had he been harboring any anti-Soviet feelings, he would hardly have expressed them in his presence. The courts had chosen to use a false witness statement, he said, simply because he was a "former criminal" (*byvshii ugolovnik*). Molokoedov believed he was a marked man whom the local authorities would persecute by any means possible.[82] And in 1959 Rudenko's right-hand man, A. Mishutin, seemed to accept such assertions.[83] In a written objection against the sentence, the deputy to the general procurator of the USSR wrote: "As is clear from the petition, the court incorrectly interpreted the fact that he had spent twenty-seven years in prison, considering it to be an aggravating factor," instead of the extenuating one he believed it should be.[84] Mishutin thus backed Molokoedov, suggesting that the court took such a hard line primarily because he was already known to be a former criminal.

Back inside the Gulag, Zolotarev, Molokoedov, Seriakhin, and Mukhorin all realized that their postcamp existence had gone bitterly wrong. Mukhorin blamed the prison world itself, which—far from transforming him into an ideal citizen who would be welcomed back into the Soviet family—had saddled him with dangerously seditious ideas. In different ways, Zolotarev, Seriakhin, and Molokoedov all blamed the KGB and the court system, believing that as ex-*zek*s they had faced impossible discrimination. In seeking to understand the sharp rise in article 58 convictions in 1957–1958, these two explanations are perhaps not incompatible. First, some Gulag returnees did come home with beliefs and values that were at odds with official Soviet culture. Forced to live in highly precarious conditions, ex-*zek*s sometimes lost their cool, allowing the subversive views learned in the camps to break out. Second, the local police force, seeking to enforce law and order in their fiefdom, tended to treat those coming back from the camps with deep dis-

---

[80] In August 1960 the head of the Stravropol' Soviet wrote to the Presidium of the Supreme Soviet requesting that certain towns in his oblast—Kislovodsk, Essentuki, Piatigorsk, Mineral'nye Vody, Zheleznovodsk, and Pregornyi raion—be designated "special passport regime" status once more. In these towns there were 5,409 people with previous convictions, and over half of all crimes were committed by people with previous convictions—a figure substantially higher than the national average (GARF f. 8131, op. 32, d. 6413, l. 170).

[81] GARF f. 8131, op. 31, d. 46981, l. 21.

[82] GARF f. 8131, op. 31, d. 46981, ll. 41–43.

[83] Vladimir Kozlov suggests that by 1959 there was some redressing of cases ("Kramola").

[84] GARF f. 8131, op. 31, d. 46981, ll. 31–32.

trust. The enthusiasm with which some young people embraced the Gulag subculture—coupled with concerns about youth offending—only heightened such suspicions. The application of article 58 provided a loophole that allowed local courts to dispatch unwanted figures for long stretches, but it did not prove a wholly satisfactory solution. Chapters 5 and 6 explore how the government sought more enduring solutions to the ongoing problem of criminal behavior.

5 *The Redemptive Mission*

We believe that no such thing exists as a person who cannot be corrected.

—N. S. Khrushchev, May 1959

Fedor Medvedev included the following passage in an anonymous pamphlet he produced in honor of the Twenty-First Party Congress in 1959:

In our country, the following flourish: hooliganism, banditry, theft, and terribly bad manners. All this is the fruit the "wise" gardener Khrushchev [*mudryi sadovnik Khrushchev*] has been cultivating. For three and half decades there was none of this, because the country was in the hands of Leninist leaders. When Khrushchev talks of building communism, he's pulling the wool over people's eyes, and only the dim-witted can believe in his utopian fantasies [*utopicheskie bredni*]. The Soviet people know that we shouldn't even be thinking about constructing real communism when there is such disorder [*bezobrazie*] going on in our country.[1]

The decision to produce and disseminate anti-Soviet pamphlets was relatively rare, and Medvedev's own story was certainly unusual: he had been convicted twice (in 1934 and 1945) but despite this checkered past had joined the party and secured a management position at the Saratov hydroelectric power station in the 1950s. The metaphors Medvedev chose to use in his pamphlet are revealing.

Medvedev saw society as a garden, its leader as the cultivator. This im-

[1] GARF f. 8131, op. 31, d. 86890, l. 31.

agery had long been employed by the Soviet regime itself. In 1936, for example, *Pravda* proudly commended Stalin's role in the wives' volunteer (*obshchestvennitsa*) movement by speaking of his commitment to nurturing his subjects: "Ploughed up by the revolution, the soil of our land again and again bears new and remarkable fruit. The Soviet land has become a vast and magnificent garden where the talents of the people blossom and the great Bolshevist gardener nurses them as though they were his favorite tree."[2] A poem, also published in *Pravda* in the 1930s, began: "Wise master, Marxist gardener! Thou art tending the vine of communism."[3]

Such metaphors are reminiscent of Zygmunt Bauman's definition of modernity as the emergence of a "gardening state."[4] Influenced by Bauman, recent work on the Stalinist era emphasizes the state's use of education, culture, and science to nurture and shape the minds and bodies of its citizens.[5] Stalinist gardening techniques included not only nurturing but also the destruction of anything that might damage the health of the nursery. Arguing that the postwar period saw growing anxiety regarding the purity of the Soviet population, Amir Weiner has shown how the Stalinist state became ever more committed to the task of uprooting and excising human "weeds" in its final years.[6] Ripped out by their roots, the "weeds" would be either destroyed or transplanted elsewhere. The results of this excisionary practice are well-known: violence, purging, and the expansion of the Gulag.

Khrushchev's attempts to reduce the Soviet state's use of violence did not, apparently, please all. The pamphleteer Medvedev considered Khrushchev a lazy horticulturist: less ready to engage in the practices of excision, he had allegedly let his plot become overgrown and disordered. For this ill-fated pamphleteer, it was contradictory that while promising the imminence of the perfect society, Khrushchev was allowing such problems to thrive in his own backyard.

Yet the authorities were highly concerned about the apparent rise in criminal behavior, and its possible impact on young people, and Medvedev was quite wrong to think that Stalin's successors were not acting on this problem. Throughout the 1950s the Soviet leadership discussed, drafted, and tested different measures that they hoped would solve the problem of crime. Party and law-enforcement officials held no illusions about the effect of the

[2] "A remarkable conference," *Pravda*, 10 May 1936, reproduced in Rudolph Schlesinger, ed., *Changing Attitudes in Soviet Russia: The Family in the USSR* (London, 1949), 235–238.

[3] "To the *Vozhd'*, to Comrade Stalin," *Pravda*, 29 November 1932, cited in Robert C. Tucker, "The Rise of Stalin's Personality Cult," *American Historical Review* 84 (1979): 347–366 (365).

[4] Bauman writes: "The gardening posture divides vegetation into 'cultured plants' to be taken care of, and weeds to be exterminated." See Zygmunt Bauman, *Modernity and the Holocaust* (Cambridge, 1989), 18.

[5] See Hoffmann, *Stalinist Values*, 7. Juliane Fürst has suggested ways in which Bauman's work could be useful in understanding Soviet youth during the Khrushchev period. See Fürst, "The Arrival of Spring?"

[6] Weiner, *Making Sense of War*, 34–35.

Gulag, and Khrushchev seemed to conclude that instead of being cured by a stint within the camp system, offenders were further damaged. As a result, one of the main characteristics of the new initiatives was the increased role of the Soviet public, or *obshchestvennost'*. If the community could be effectively mobilized, the leaders hoped, the task of re-educating wrongdoers could happen within society, and the Gulag could be reduced further still. In itself, the mobilization of volunteers was not new to Soviet society, but whereas in the 1930s voluntary work had largely been the domain of the elite (or at least elite wives), the post-Stalin era saw the party encourage far more extensive community involvement.[7] The alleged imminence of the communist era—and the "withering away" of the state which Marxist theory prophesied—made public participation in the running of the country ever more pressing.[8] Contrary to Medvedev's line of argument, then, the party leadership maintained that building communism was possible primarily because new approaches *were* being taken toward crime.

As with the concept of *obshchestvennost'*, many of the community initiatives introduced were not in themselves new. Brigades of volunteers (*druzhiny*) patrolling the city streets—which were to become a key feature of the law-and-order campaigns of the 1950s—had precedents dating from before Soviet power: in 1905 and 1917 revolutionary attachments were created to maintain law and order; in 1928 the practice was revived in the form of the *osodmil* (societies for assisting the police), renamed *brigadmil* (police-assistance brigades) in 1932.[9] Similarly, comrade courts, another important element in Khrushchev's reform of Soviet justice, had a long heritage: they were a feature of factory life by 1919, and although they fell into abeyance in the wake of the Great Terror, they were revived in 1951 as a means for dealing with small infractions of labor discipline.[10] Khrushchev had already shown his enthusiasm for involving citizens in administering justice: in 1948 he introduced into Ukraine (where he was party leader) measures granting collective-farm assemblies the right to exile members identified as "parasites."[11] What *was* new about the community initiatives introduced in the

---

[7] Under Stalin, the term *obshchestvennost'* tended to refer to the activities of party and Soviet officials or their relatives. The *obshchestvennitsa* was a public-spirited woman or female activist who was invariably married to a manager, engineer, or member of the armed forces. It was almost inevitable that these female volunteers came from society's elite, as only women from more comfortable families could afford to labor without pay. The activities encouraged in the 1950s were to be in *addition* to work, however, and as George Breslauer has noted, by the late 1950s the word *obshchestvennost'* "referred to a stratum of mobilizers drawn from all groups in society." See Mary Buckley, "The Untold Story of *Obshchestvennitsa* in the 1930s," *Europe-Asia Studies* 48 (1996): 569–586; and George W. Breslauer, "Khrushchev Reconsidered," in *The Soviet Union since Stalin*, ed. Cohen, Rabinowitch, and Sharlet, 50–70 (57).

[8] Theodore H. Friedgut, *Political Participation in the USSR* (Princeton, 1979), 236.

[9] Oleg Kharkhordin, *The Collective and the Individual in Russia: A Study of Practices* (Berkeley, 1999), 285.

[10] Ibid., 284.

[11] Taubman, *Khrushchev*, 206–207.

1950s was the enlarged scope of their activities, the extensive coverage they were given in the media, and the great hope the political leaders placed on them as one of the essential elements for building communism.

This chapter follows the changing representation of the criminal in official sources and the development of policy toward criminality between Stalin's death in 1953 and Khrushchev's key intervention in 1959. At the end of the 1950s a truly radical mood seemed to prevail: the Gulag was scorned, and the healing powers of Soviet society exalted. In this chapter I hope to recapture this brief moment of optimism in Soviet criminal justice policy, when alternatives to Stalinist repression were embraced not as a retreat from revolution but as the correct way to reach the promised communist paradise.

The Turn to *Byt*

In December 1956 a campaign targeting petty hooliganism introduced the widespread use of short prison sentences (normally a matter of days) for minor offenses such as swearing, disrespect to other citizens, drunkenness, and rowdiness. Although the punishments were relatively light, this measure was significant because it turned conduct that had previously been tolerated by the authorities into "deviant" behavior.[12] The roots of the campaign against petty hooliganism can be traced back to 1954 and the growing importance attached to *byt* in the mid-1950s.

On 17 August 1954 the front page of *Leningradskaia pravda* led with the headline "Toward Soviet Man's Healthy *Byt*" (*Za zdorovyi byt sovetskogo cheloveka*).[13] Although the article opened with a positive picture of the "cultured" way most Soviet citizens lived, it soon went on to lament the vestiges of the capitalist past that still lingered within Soviet society. Claiming it was imperative to fight against all that impeded the Soviet man's "cultured" leisure time, the article identified drunkenness as a social ill that must be eradicated without delay. In the same year, the publication of a series of new pamphlets and books reflected the current importance of *byt*. The *Yearbook of Soviet Publications* included the category of *byt* for the first time in 1954, with fourteen new titles in that year and a steady increase recorded over the decade.[14] The new publications included titles like *Communist Morality and Byt, Toward a Healthy Byt*, and *The Culture of Correct Behavior among Soviet Young People*, with many texts devoted to the dangers of alcoholism.[15]

[12] Brian LaPierre, "Making Hooliganism on a Mass Scale: The Campaign against Petty Hooliganism in the Soviet Union, 1956–1964," *Cahiers du monde russe* 47 (2006): 349–376.

[13] "Za zdorovyi byt sovetskogo cheloveka," *Leningradskaia pravda*, 17 August 1954, 1.

[14] Catriona Kelly, *Refining Russia: Advice Literature, Polite Culture, and Gender from Catherine to Yeltsin* (Oxford, 2001), appendix 5.

[15] *Ezhegodnik knig SSSR 1954: II-polugodie* (Moscow, 1955), 256; *Ezhegodnik knig SSSR 1955: II-polugodie* (Moscow, 1956), 294.

This new emphasis on *byt* was reflected in an important shift in crime reporting. In 1953 "From the courtroom" reports had consistently portrayed the criminal standing trial as a bandit, inveterate criminal, and veteran of the Gulag. In every respect this "bandit" stood outside of Soviet society. Although such depictions did not immediately disappear in 1954, new sorts of offenders began to populate crime reports.[16] Increasingly they depicted ordinary citizens taking to a life of crime. Rather than strangers from an alien world, transgressors might be members of the Soviet community who had been allowed to lapse into an unhealthy and un-Soviet way of life. Instead of simply lamenting the rise in crime as in 1953, newspapers claimed citizens could play a positive, instructive role in preventing the emergence of these new deviants.

In August 1954 an article headlined "In Drunken Intoxication" opened by telling readers that, "young joiner V. Eroshin was often seen drunk. He didn't spend his free time with his family, but with his drinking companions."[17] With neighbors cast as witnesses to his debauched ways, Eroshin was identified as a member of the Soviet community, not an outsider. The reader was given to understand that Eroshin's problems began with apparently minor misdemeanors which then escalated dramatically. While drunk one summer evening, he insulted a girl on the street, and when one of her young companions tried to reason with him, Eroshin stabbed him. In a second article entitled "Hooligan," an eighteen-year-old from Leningrad was sentenced for attacking a young girl who had rejected his amorous advances at the youth-club dance.[18] Again the roots of the problem lay with the protagonist's daily conduct. Preferring "hooligan" behavior to hard work or study, Gennadii Fedorov drank, insulted passersby on the street, and organized wild parties (*deboshi*) at home at night. The reader was to infer that it was only one short step from minor hooligan acts to violent assault. Neither Eroshin nor Fedorov were presented as members of a prison subculture, yet their dissolute lifestyle led them to commit heinous crimes. Replacing the marauding bandit of 1953, the press now targeted the "hooligan" who was a product of an urban habitat. The publication of such articles seemed to remind citizens of the importance of *byt*. Drinking, swearing, and rowdy behavior, readers were implicitly warned, must be strongly discouraged, for they were the first warning signs that an individual was on the path to full-blown criminal acts.

[16] One example is "Bandit nakazan," *Leningradskaia pravda,* 26 May 1954, 4. This is typical of the model established in 1953: a beneficiary of the 1953 amnesty with a string of sentences behind him returns home to lead a "parasitic" life of crime. Other examples include "Likvidatsiia shaiki banditov," *Leningradskaia pravda,* 10 November 1954, 4; "Grabiteli," *Leningradskaia pravda,* 19 June 1954, 4; "Prestupniki nakazany," *Leningradskaia pravda,* 25 March 1954, 4; and "Grabiteli," *Moskovskaia pravda,* 7 September 1954, 4. By 1955 this kind of crime report was rarer.

[17] "V p'ianom ugare," *Moskovskaia pravda,* 7 August 1954, 4.

[18] "Khuligan," *Leningradskaia pravda,* 5 June 1954, 4.

Members of Soviet society were thus encouraged to take an active role in raising moral, healthy citizens of the future. The first responsibility naturally lay with the parents. Already in 1954 a feuilleton in *Moskovskaia pravda* showed how two young people slid toward crime as a result of their families' failure to teach them Soviet morality.[19] The article also suggested, however, that the wider Soviet community had a part to play. Unruly youths and inattentive parents were visible to everyone, the article concluded, and yet the vast majority of people said and did nothing. In the task of stamping out "unhealthy and amoral" tendencies among the young, the Soviet community had a great and, as yet, underused potential. When they witnessed abuses, Soviet citizens must henceforth speak out.

The role of the Soviet community (*obshchestvennost'*) became a key motif. All citizens were encouraged to be vigilant and to "whistle-blow" wherever they saw transgressions of Soviet *byt*. Initially the task was one of mutual surveillance. Over the course of 1956 a series of articles urged the Soviet community on to greater vigilance in the struggle against hooliganism, drunkenness, and other indiscretions. In the feuilleton "After Midnight . . . ," *Moskovskaia pravda* called on Muscovites to evince greater intolerance toward those who held responsible positions by day but indulged in public displays of drunkenness by night.[20] The railway station, a site of disruptive behavior for the bandits of 1953, was now reconfigured as a nighttime refuge for urban inhabitants who wanted temporarily to shed their identity as upstanding Soviet citizens. In its conclusion, the article entreated readers to "name and shame" all those who sought to turn the capital's stations into places of rowdy drunkenness: "We must speak out against them at full voice. At stations and in other places that remain open overnight, there are still those nocturnal heroes who roam in search of 'adventures.' If you meet them, don't just give these degenerate idlers a wide berth, proclaim their names, whoever they may be, whatever position they may hold."

Another typical article berated the inhabitants of Rybnikov lane who turned a blind eye to their neighbor's conspicuous consumption. Despite a quite ordinary job in a Moscow workshop, Leopol'd Glazenberg took manifest pleasure in his car and driver, the lavish décor of his home, his elegant clothing, and the long and expensive holidays he spent with his new, young wife. Why, the article demanded indignantly, did it take so long to discover his deceptions at work? How could a con man be at large for so long in Moscow?[21]

In 1956 several articles called for the public to denounce hooligans and brawlers: "The Community's Vital Task," "Don't Walk on By!" "The Duty of Each and Every One: Intensifying the Struggle with Violators of Social Or-

---

[19] "Kto vinovat?" *Moskovskaia pravda*, 29 October 1954, 3.
[20] "Posle dvenadtsati nochi . . . ," *Moskovskaia pravda*, 21 October 1956, 2.
[21] "Ne prokhodite mimo!" *Moskovskaia pravda*, 17 January 1956, 3.

der."[22] Public vigilance was plugged as a vital force in eradicating crime.[23] Local newspapers denounced not only those who had themselves committed antisocial acts but also those who had simply witnessed their excesses and carried on.[24]

In addition to the press campaign, volunteer brigades were established to fight the scourge of antisocial behavior. Encouraged by a speech made by Khrushchev in 1954, Komsomol organizations established volunteer youth brigades, charged with patrolling the streets and imposing order.[25] These supplemented the existing "police-assistance brigades," whose membership now grew, stimulated by new enthusiasm from the Komsomol.[26] In some cities, groups would go out several times a week to "raid" insalubrious spots where young people gathered, particularly parks, cinemas, "houses of culture," squares, canteens, shops, buses, dance floors, and certain notorious streets.[27] Some initiatives were immense in scale. One raid in the city of Baku involved 1,600 *Komsomoltsy* and saw 219 offenders arrested in a single night.[28] One of the Komsomol members' key roles was to aid in the act of arrest. In December 1955 the Kostroma Komsomol proudly informed the organization's Central Committee of the work carried out by its patrols, in which four thousand young people had already taken part and which had resulted in several arrests and convictions. In addition, a thousand had been involved in the "police-assistance brigades." Three of these Komsomol police-brigadiers had received rewards of 500 rubles each for their heroism in arresting two thieves armed with axes.[29]

A 1956 report to Komsomol headquarters on the effectiveness of these measures contained an extract from a letter, apparently intercepted in the city of Rostov. A criminal recently returned from the camps had written to a friend still serving time, describing the situation he now encountered: "They've taken the wind out of our sails. Everything's under wraps—the police-assistance brigades and Komsomol activists are everywhere. They speak freely, while we've been silenced. Take this little village. Even here there are three Komsomol groups, each with its own leader. And that's not counting those working for the police. It's a strong policy. The schemers have stitched

[22] "Krovnoe delo obshchestvennosti," *Leningradskaia pravda,* 7 September 1956, 2; "Krovnoe delo obshchestvennosti," *Pravda,* 26 August 1956, 3; "Delo vsekh i kazhdogo," *Moskovskaia pravda,* 4 September 1956, 2.

[23] "Ne prokhodite mimo!" *Moskovskaia pravda,* 17 January 1956, 3.

[24] In the city of Molotov *Molodaia gvardiia,* a newspaper produced by the local Komsomol, published an article "Kosvennye soobshchniki" ("Indirect Accomplices"), in which the author "heaped shame on philistines who walk straight past brawlers [*deboshiry*] and hooligans, thinking that it's not their duty to stop criminals or to help the police arrest them" (RGASPI f. M-1, op. 32, d. 811, l. 47).

[25] For a discussion of the origins of these initiatives, see Fürst, "The Arrival of Spring?" 146.

[26] RGASPI f. M-1, op. 32, d. 811, ll. 23–24, 35.

[27] RGASPI f. M-1, op. 32, d. 802, ll. 91–92; RGASPI f. M-1, op. 32, d. 950, l. 77.

[28] RGASPI f. M-1, op. 32, d. 811, l. 48.

[29] RGASPI f. M-1, op. 32, d. 802, ll. 61–63.

Fig. 3. "Tear the weeds out of the ground!" *Iunost'*
(January 1956). Courtesy Harvard College Library.

things up well."[30] Whether Gulag returnees were really so impressed by the new policing practices is questionable, but the report at least shows the desired result, from the perspective of the local Komsomol leaders. A net of voluntary law enforcers, they hoped, would protect the Soviet community, making criminal activity simply impractical.

A full-page drawing published in the magazine *Iunost'* in January 1956 suggested that the order of the day was still excision, or weeding: the picture showed a hand plucking out a selection of wrongdoers, depicted as weeds.[31] The idler, the hooligan, the drunkard, the *stiliaga,* the coward and the sneak (*iabednik*) must all be removed from the Soviet garden. And young people, the readers of *Iunost',* had a key part to play in this act of weeding (Figure 3).

From Vigilance to Salvation

In 1957 it seemed that public involvement in maintaining law and order was to become even greater. In August a draft law was proposed "On Intensifying the Struggle against Antisocial, Parasitical Elements," and its content was published in the press and read out at workplace meetings. The proposed initiative would grant communities the power to rid their localities of those deemed "antisocial." If passed, village assemblies or, in the city, meetings of residents from one housing block or street would now be able to impose exile on alleged parasites. Dispatched to distant locations within the Soviet Union, they would not be allowed to return for a period between two and five years.[32] According to two internal reports, many Soviet citizens responded favorably to the proposed measures. Some immediately took the opportunity provided by the public discussion of the law to give names of those local "parasites" they would like to see exiled. Others called for longer periods of exile, some suggesting that the sentence should be for life.[33] At this early stage, the very appeal of the proposal seemed to lie in its ambiguity. Everyone could imagine it being applied to their personal bugbear. Some imagined it would punish collective farmers who made a profit from their private plots; others hoped that war invalids caught begging would now get their comeuppance. Suggested targets also included: able-bodied people who did not work but made a living from fishing and mushroom picking; itinerant groups of builders who demanded high pay from collective farms short of manpower; young people who lived a decadent life off their parents' money; hooligans who had already been warned by the police; women leading an "indecent" way of life; people renting out living space; drunkards;

[30] RGASPI f. M-1, op. 32, d. 811, l. 38.
[31] B. Efimov, "Khudaia trava iz poliia von!" *Iunost'* (January 1956): unpaginated, between 64 and 65. I am grateful to Brian LaPierre for bringing this image to my attention.
[32] GARF f. 8131, op. 32, d. 6416, l. 146.
[33] GARF f. 8131, op. 32, d. 6416, l. 46.

women who stayed at home as housewives even though they did not have young children; and job-hoppers (*letuny*).[34] The discussion sparked criticism of existing criminal justice practices and the mild sentences courts were awarding, even in cases of murder.[35] Where there were doubts, they tended to concern the practicalities of assembling the required hundred citizens, rather than the notion of exile in itself.[36]

Despite apparent enthusiasm from some Soviet citizens, the law was not introduced in six of the fifteen republics until 1961: Russia (RSFSR), Ukraine, Belorussia, Lithuania, Estonia, and Moldavia.[37] Institutional opposition seems to have come in particular from the Ministry of Foreign Affairs (MID), where it was felt that the proposal risked contravening international human rights agreements.[38] Members of the legal profession also questioned the legitimacy of public gatherings issuing legally binding sentences.[39]

Two years later, a rather different solution to the problem of crime was introduced. On 2 March 1959 a joint decree from the Council of Ministers and the Central Committee "On the Participation of Workers in the Maintenance of Public Order" introduced a range of new measures.[40] Already established on an ad hoc basis in some areas, voluntary brigades were now to be organized in every factory and farm across the nation. Charged with patrolling the streets, they would identify troublemakers and, where necessary, inform the offender's workplace, or if necessary the police. Comrade courts were also revitalized, and instead of finding themselves in front of a Soviet judge, small-time offenders might now be tried by their own colleagues and

[34] RGASPI f. 556, op. 14, d. 89, ll. 159–162; GARF f. 8131, op. 32, d. 6416, ll. 44–59.

[35] GARF f. 8131, op. 32, d. 6416, l. 49.

[36] In Kursk and Novogorod oblasts workers suggested that village soviets could exile parasites without calling an assembly, while in the cities of Omsk and Cheliabinsk, in Voronezh and Novosibirsk oblasts, and in Altai krai (territory), it was suggested that local soviets, whether rural or urban, could be responsible for this legislation instead of public assemblies. In Krasnodar and Stavropol' krai, workers particularly emphasized the difficulty of assembling enough citizens in rural areas; in other localities, citizens suggested reducing the required quorum from one hundred to fifty. In Kaluga and Perm oblasts, some suggested that special commissions should be created. Such commissions would involve the public, but perhaps not in the mass form that the legislation had intended. See GARF f. 8131, op. 32, d. 6416, ll. 47–49.

[37] The law was adopted in Uzbekistan, Turkmenistan, and Latvia in 1957; in Tajikistan, Kazakhstan, Armenia, and Azerbaijan in 1958; in Kyrgyzstan in 1959; and in Georgia in 1960. See GARF f. 8131, op. 32, d. 6416, l. 88; and R. W. Makepeace, *Marxist Ideology and Soviet Criminal Law* (London, 1980), 249–257.

[38] On 14 October 1957 Rudenko wrote to the CC in response to a report made by the Ministry of Foreign Affairs the preceding month. Rudenko strongly supported the antiparasite legislation, arguing that international declarations and conventions were not observed in capitalist countries. For example, article 23 of the Declaration of Human Rights promised the right to work, yet Rudenko noted that unemployment existed in every capitalist country (GARF f. 8131, op. 32, d. 6416, ll. 39–42).

[39] Sheila Fitzpatrick, "Social Parasites: How Tramps, Idle Youth, and Busy Entrepreneurs Impeded the Soviet March to Communism," *Cahiers du monde russe* 47 (2006): 377–408 (384).

[40] "Voluntary Militia and Courts," *Soviet Studies* 11 (1959): 214–217.

neighbors.[41] Attached to every soviet, new commissions "for the protection of socialist legality and social order" were to implement, co-ordinate, and monitor these measures.[42] Although this promotion of popular participation showed continuity with the measures introduced in the preceding years, there were also key departures. Instead of arrest and imprisonment, the emphasis was now almost entirely on the notion of correction and re-education. Reflecting the belief that the force of collective disapproval was more effective than a prison term, noncustodial sentences were revived. A "collective"—such as a workplace or housing block—could save an offender from incarceration by offering to become his guardian, a long-established practice known in Russian as "poruka."[43] Likewise, a prisoner might be granted early release if a collective guaranteed to take responsibility for his "probation." The role of *obshchestvennost'* was rather different from that allowed by the anti-parasite legislation proposed in 1957: instead of meeting to judge and banish, citizens were now invited to participate in the task of redeeming those who erred.

Oleg Kharkhordin argues that the people's patrols and comrade courts created in the 1950s could be more ruthless than the police.[44] Whereas the police were—at least in theory—limited to apprehending those who breached Soviet laws, the patrols could reprimand passersby for wearing inappropriate clothing, throwing litter, playing cards, or even dancing "with unnatural, jerky movements." In addition, anyone could join in the censure, every passerby could "become a patrolman," potentially making "mutual surveillance" an absolutely ubiquitous force. Yet control was only one side to these measures. By 1959 the role of the volunteer brigades was less to aid in the arrest of lawbreakers than to assist in the task of transforming offenders into healthy and contented Soviet citizens.

The regime's decision to rely on public initiatives for not only *identifying* untoward behavior but also *correcting* it reflected growing concerns about the effect of the Gulag on those that passed through it. If even short sentences seemed to drag offenders deeper into the criminal milieu, then rehabilitation

---

[41] Yoram Gorlizki identifies three main categories of case heard in the comrade courts: first, justice officials could transfer minor offenses to the comrade courts; second, local soviets might refer cases where public order had been breached—for example, through drunkenness or playing loud music at night; and third, the courts might hear cases where no law had been broken but where moral norms were flouted, such as in domestic disputes or intra-apartment conflicts ("Delegalization in Russia: Soviet Comrades' Courts in Retrospect," *The American Journal of Comparative Law* 46 [1998]: 403–425).

[42] TsGAMO f. 2157, op. 1, d. 5311, l. 11.

[43] In pre-Petrine Russia the term *poruka* envisaged the responsibility of one person or group for the conduct of others. Horace Dewey and Ann Kleimola argue that whereas in western Europe the early modern period saw individualism flourish, in Russia the principle of collective responsibility survived ("From the Kinship Group to Every Man His Brother's Keeper: Collective Responsibility in Pre-Petrine Russia," *Jahrbücher für Geschichte Osteuropas* 30 [1982]: 321–335).

[44] Kharkhordin, *The Collective and the Individual*, 280.

programs within the community had an obvious appeal. They also fitted with Khrushchev's messianic vision. With the communist future allegedly approaching, Khrushchev focused on forging the "new man" and the imminent disappearance of crime. This shift was reflected in the metaphors and tropes used in the press. The new rhetoric confirmed communist eschatology but now rendered collective progress contingent on ensuring that every member was living in accordance with Soviet moral codes, not on fighting the enemy. Those already set on the correct path must look out for those who erred. Rather than catching villains, the community's main task was now to guide transgressors back onto the road that would lead them all happily toward communism.

A typical newspaper article on the activities of the newly formed *druzhiny* described the work of one brigade. In October 1959 the unit received a letter from a certain Shatrova who begged for help with her wayward brother who had recently indulged in some heavy drinking bouts, often cursing and threatening both her and her children. That same evening, members of the brigade visited the Shatrovs' apartment and rebuked the brother, thus demonstrating to him that the "collective" had firmly decided to "sober him up once and for all." The painstaking work of the volunteers did not stop there. In addition to further visits to the Shatrov residence, they ensured that the brother's work "collective" also discussed his misdemeanors. The story ended with Shatrov converted into a polite and sober individual. The article concluded: "This short story is just an episode. There are no 'brigands' involved, no talk of 'arrest,' or 'convictions' . . . But the deed is done. One man was prevented from veering off the path."[45] The very title of the article— "No Incidents to Report"—promoted the utopian dream that there would soon be no crimes at all.

Propaganda pieces showed how many individuals experienced radical personal transformation. The conversion of the worker O. S. Makarenkova was recounted under the headline "Collective Justice."[46] As forewoman in a workshop, she would swear at her team, humiliate them, and even slap subordinates. As the article reminded readers, the aim of the comrade courts was "not to punish, but to educate [*vospityvat'*], to deter from further, more serious acts." After many official warnings, the case was transferred to the comrade court, where the board heard her pleas and promises to reform. It was only when the case was heard in front of the whole collective that Makarenkova realized the error of her ways. In the half-year since her hearing, Makarenkova had stopped cursing and bad-mouthing other workers, becoming a sociable and friendly member of the team—"the past has been cancelled out."

Another article, optimistically titled "Toward Perfect Law and Order in

[45] "'Proisshestvii ne bylo . . . ,'" *Moskovskaia pravda*, 19 December 1959, 2–3.
[46] "Pravosudie kollektiva," *Moskovskaia pravda*, 30 June 1959, 2–3.

the Capital," recounted the reformation of several antisocial characters. In one workshop, the collective met to debate the behavior of the drunken worker Osipov a full three times; experienced and respected workmates talked with him; attention was paid both to his progress in the workplace and in his personal life. Soon Osipov also became a sober worker. In the same article a party member managed to "re-educate" the addled Morozov, whose transformation was so complete that he became a candidate member of the party himself. Eager to show how these tales of personal transformation related to the issue of eradicating crime in the capital, the article cited from A. F. Gorkin, chairman of the USSR Supreme Court:

> Listening to criminal cases in the peoples' courts it is evident that in the vast majority of cases lawbreakers can be dealt with by means of collective pressure. Instead of imprisonment, the pressure of the collective can in many cases be a more effective means to re-educate a man [*perevospitanie cheloveka*].
>
> Correcting a man who is on the slippery path, preventing him from going downhill, keeping him under a friendly but firm control, showing him the trust of the collective—this is the genuine battle for a man and for his moral education [*vospitanie*].[47]

Once more promoting the vision of the offender as "erring" or "slipping," Gorkin rejected the idea that prison could effectively correct offenders. Soviet society was now the preferred site for re-education.

The principle of "correction" was also advocated in cases of political error. In September 1959, an *Izvestiia* article told how students who formed an "anti-Soviet group" in the wake of the Secret Speech were not arrested but merely warned by the KGB; as a result of this generosity, their "defective souls" were cured, and they deeply regretted their earlier foolishness. It also recounted the story of a worker who had begun listening to foreign broadcasts in 1955 and spreading "rumors and gossip"; again the KGB decided against arrest, instead calling the man in for a meeting at the match factory where he worked; roundly criticized by his colleagues, he was nonetheless taken under their collective guardianship (*poruka*) for re-education, again with great success.[48]

In the Secret Speech Khrushchev had challenged the prevalence of the concept of *vrag naroda* (enemy of the people) within Soviet society and urged listeners to remember Lenin's commitment to re-educating and retraining those who made mistakes. By 1959 this approach was publicly endorsed with regard to those who committed offenses, whether they were antisocial acts or transgressions of a more political nature.

[47] "Za obraztsovyi obshchestvennyi poriadok v stolitse," *Moskovskaia pravda*, 2 December 1959, 2.
[48] "Sila i vera," *Izvestiia*, 6 September 1959, 4.

A Tale of Redemption

In May 1959 Khrushchev put his own personal stamp onto these campaigns. At the Third Writers' Congress, Khrushchev made a long speech that *Pravda* published on its front-pages.[49] In a long and convoluted introduction, Khrushchev first rebuked the writers for getting entangled in lengthy wrangles among themselves, only to remind them that while capitalism still existed in the world, conflict would always remain. Realizing the ambiguity of his words, he asked rhetorically, "You're probably wondering what I'm calling you to do—to ignite the passions of battle, or to promote reconciliation?" In response to his own question, he first answered, "If the enemy doesn't surrender—then destroy him." Following this battle cry, with its echoes of Stalinist rhetoric, Khrushchev repeated that in the class war with capitalism, the Soviets would never capitulate. Then, however, he used the adage "Don't kick a lying dog" to encourage a less ruthless approach *within* the Soviet Union itself. If the opponent shows a readiness to take the correct position, Khrushchev said, he should be given a helping hand, encouraged to join the ranks of Soviet society. He concluded: "I'd like to say that in our socialist society, where there are no enemy classes or groups, where our whole life is built on the principles of comradeship and friendship, we need to deal more sympathetically with those people who have let the devil get the better of them [*dat' sebia chertu zaputat'*]."

Combative only in relation to socialist society's relations to the external, capitalist world, Khrushchev portrayed the Soviet world as one that was internally harmonious. He encouraged his audience—both delegates at the congress and *Pravda* readers—to follow Feliks Dzerzhinskii (first chairman of the Cheka) in believing that every individual, "including both political opponents and criminals," could be re-educated. "We believe," he said, "that no such thing exists as a person who cannot be corrected." In choosing to frame the question as he did, Khrushchev suggested that those who made mistakes should no longer be treated as enemies. Real "enemies" existed only in the form of capitalists. His argument was thus absolutely in keeping with the Secret Speech, in which he had claimed that the threat of internal enemies had been greatly exaggerated. The policies of 1959 built on the principles of 1956: those who committed mistakes, even crimes, should be treated not as enemies but with concern and sympathy; *vospitanie* (moral education) and even *perevospitanie* (moral re-education) were the order of the day.

Even though he addressed writers, and not criminal experts, judges, or policemen, Khrushchev went on to devote yet more of his speech to the issue of criminality. Choosing the writers' congress as a suitable occasion to discuss the merits of "correction" over "imprisonment," he detached it from

[49] "Rech' N. S. Khrushcheva na III s″ezde pisatelei 22 maia 1959 goda," *Pravda*, 24 May 1959, 1–3.

the narrower issues of penal policy and presented the revised treatment of offenders as a profound, philosophical shift in how society defined itself. By addressing writers, the debate became a question of how society's "interpreters" should view the Soviet world and its inhabitants. The message was that instead of portraying society as a battleground, they should see it as a nursery for new citizens.

The candidate for re-education chosen by Khrushchev was rather different from Shatrova's drunken brother or any of the other stray individuals profiled in the press so far. Konstantin Nogovitsin was the author of a petition to Khrushchev—and a self-professed recidivist. A petition, that staple of the Soviet criminal justice system, was now used to broadcast his life story, and Khrushchev read out the letter in its entirety. From the age of twelve, Nogovitsin had committed thefts and as a result had been sentenced four times. Having recently finished a six-year stretch, he returned home to his mother, wife, and daughter and found work as a carpenter; but with his wife pregnant and his wages low, he quickly sank into debt and ran away to the "easy life." Somehow he found himself unwilling to take up his old life of thieving again yet was equally unable to return home to the family he had abandoned. In limbo, Nogovitsin sent in his petition, a plea for advice. As Khrushchev informed the congress, he invited the man to meet him. Additional biographical information was garnered at the interview: thirty years old, sensible and pleasant, Nogovitsin talked of how he had lost his father and of the negative environment that had influenced him. Explaining that he continued to be labeled a thief, which prevented him from finding normal work or acquiring reasonable lodgings, he concluded his little speech: "I promise you that I will become a decent man [*chestnyi chelovek*]. I will prove it to you."

Choosing to believe the man, Khrushchev offered him practical help. He telephoned the local gorkom, instructing them to help Nogovitsin find work and acquire qualifications. He offered him credit so he could build himself a little house (*domik*). When he checked on the progress of his protégé, Khrushchev learned that the man was working well. From his story, Khrushchev concluded that the days of draconian discipline were over. What would the old approach have achieved, he asked:

> It would have meant that a man who had erred from the correct path ended up back in prison, improving his professional qualifications only in the business of thieving, while all the time we are in need of extra men for our own matters. To return this man to the correct path, a different approach is needed. You need to believe in a man, in his good side. Can this man be an active participant in the construction of communism? He can, comrades! (Noisy applause).

Eyes set firmly on the future, Khrushchev painted a rosy picture of communism. In an environment of absolute harmony and prosperity, there would no longer be any temptation to commit crime. While he could not guarantee complete absence of criminals under communism, he suggested that such behavior would be so strange and rare, society would consider the perpetrators mentally ill.[50]

Up to the point of Khrushchev's intervention, Nogovitsin's story in itself was not uncommon. After losing his father, he came under the influence of a "bad" environment and started thieving during the dislocations of war. His lack of qualifications, coupled with society's distrust, made it difficult for him to build a normal life, and he became locked in a transitory existence, interspersed with stretches in the Gulag. In his desperate plea for readmission to society and his promises to be become a *chestnyi chelovek,* his petition had much in common with those described in chapter 2. In a highly public manner, Khrushchev chose to rewrite the ending to one of these broken life stories, allowing Nogovitsin to become a respected member of Soviet society.

In 1962 the full story of Nogovitsin's conversion was published in *Izvestiia.* It showed how a wayward, directionless life story could be happily concluded when society was prepared to take an active role in reforming the individual, cultivating in him the correct moral values, and educating him in the ways of the Soviet world.[51] The authors of "Konstantin Nogovitsin's New Life" describe their arrival at the Novorossiisk docks by impressing on the reader the stunning industrial landscape, deftly setting the scene for a socialist realist tale of personal transformation. The reader first glimpses the protagonist from afar, singing as he masterfully operates one of the huge cranes towering over the docks. Nogovitsin finishes his shift, greets the journalists, and begins to relate his story—not his life as a thief but the story of his conversion. His first days as a stevedore were painful. Physically unable to keep up the pace and ashamed by his weakness, he was dependent on the support of the collective. Their help was forthcoming; no one evinced curiosity about his past and members of his brigade were ready to tutor him. When he took his breaks alone, his workmates drew him into their group, offering him food and friendship. In his private life, important changes also occurred. When his wife and new baby came home from the maternity hospital, the family moved into a new little room. To celebrate their housewarming, the couple invited Nogovitsin's foreman to tea, and he not only showed great warmth toward the family but also encouraged Nogovitsin to train as a crane operator. Settled into a new home with his family around him, learning new skills at work, and attending night school, Nogovitsin was on track to become a model worker. No socialist realist conversion story could be resolved so easily, however, and our protagonist would have to undergo several trials and tribulations before he could fully emerge as *Homo sovieticus.*

[50] This principle was already leading to the abuses for which Soviet psychiatry was to become notorious. Sidney Bloch and Peter Reddaway, *Soviet Psychiatric Abuse: The Shadow over World Psychiatry* (London, 1984).

[51] "Novaia zhizn' Konstantina Nogovitsina," *Izvestiia,* 8 September 1962, 6.

A year went past, but Nogovitsin remained aware that he had not yet been fully transformed, later explaining, "I felt in my soul that I had not yet become a real working person." He still lacked the "proletarian consciousness" of which his new friend and workmate, Valentin Dubinin, spoke. When problems arose—arguments with his mother-in-law, financial worries, his daughter's ill-health—Nogovitsin embarked on a drinking binge. Old friends found him and took their former comrade-in-arms on a drunken train journey. Horrified by his friend's behavior, Dubinin identified it as the "lure of the old." Nogovitsin's life was thus configured as a battle between the forces of the "old" life—in which he was "Kos'ka," member of a vodka-drinking, criminal gang riding the rail network—and the new life, where he had become Konstantin Nogovitsin, a worker loyal to family, friends, and sobriety. Nogovitsin explained to the journalists, "it was as if I were reborn but didn't believe that everything was behind me." A full transformation of consciousness was required before he could truly become a new man.

Rejecting life on the trains, Nogovitsin immediately returned home, where he faced a frosty reception. Those who had assisted him were disgusted by his relapse. The foreman encouraged them to give him a second chance, however, rejecting the urge to cast Nogovitsin out: "We should fire Nogovitsin. But if we push him aside [*ottolknut'*], where will he go? Off thieving? And will we be able to sleep easy if he ends up in prison again? And after all, he did return to us. This shows that he is not a completely lost man." Paraphrasing Khrushchev's words from 1959, the foreman argued that the collective had a responsibility to save Nogovitsin from a life of crime and prison. Prison was clearly presented as a site of corruption and degeneration, Soviet society a breeding ground for healthy new citizens.

The first time, Nogovitsin had learned how to work; this second time, the transformation was a spiritual one. He became utterly dedicated to his work, remorseful for the wasteful way he had spent so many years. When he showed the journalists the certificate proving his status as a fully trained crane operator, Nogovitsin commented: "so it looks like I made myself into a person [*chelovekom sdelalsia*]." The story ended with a dramatic finale in which—like any good socialist realist hero—Nogovitsin triumphed against the natural elements. Though modest about the incident, he explained how in the middle of a ferocious storm he and three colleagues had battled to save the crane from ruin. When he saw a letter of thanks to the four workers hanging on the notice board the following day, pride welled up in him. At one now with Soviet society, Nogovitsin's story could end. His certificate and the notice-board tribute offered two official recognitions of his new identity as a Soviet worker. Khrushchev's intervention had made the story unusual, but the message was universal: even the most "fallen" of individuals could be restored to the Soviet family. The path may be thorny, but all could become respected members of Soviet society. The article praised those who made this transformation possible, those who saw their task in "saving" him, not rejecting him—*spasti*, not *ottolknut'*.

The article praised Khrushchev for having uncovered the good side underneath the "mask" of a criminal: "Under the heap of convictions, beneath the dirty skin of the criminal, Nikita Sergeevich Khrushchev saw the Man [*uvidel Cheloveka*]."[52] Whereas the rhetoric of the Stalinist era incited the public to "unmask" enemies concealed under the guise of ordinary Soviet citizens, here the reader was encouraged to find the "man" secreted within even the most unappealing of "dirty" criminals. The rhetoric of unmasking remained, but its new application revealed a significant change in Soviet philosophy. To build communism, the main task facing the collective was not to hunt out hidden enemies but rather to seek out the natural—if buried—good within each person. Published in 1962, this long article about Nogovitsin's life came at a time when attitudes toward crime were changing, but it embodied beautifully the spirit of 1959 when Khrushchev first turned Nogovitsin into a cause célèbre.

Building on the principles Khrushchev had laid out in his keynote address at the writers' congress in May, new measures were introduced over the coming months. A new wave of releases was announced. On 14 August 1959 the Supreme Soviet issued a decree creating commissions to reconsider the cases of those serving time for nondangerous crimes. Within just two months 158,074 prisoners had been released, almost half of whom had been serving time for theft and a quarter for hooliganism.[53] At the same time Moscow urged the courts to reduce the number of prisoners being sent to the Gulag. On 15 July 1959 a CC decree criticized the judicial system for continuing to convict first-time offenders, and members of the police force and workers at the Procuracy were instructed to invite offenders first for cautionary chats (*besedy*), rather than immediately initiating criminal proceedings.[54] Between June and September the number of prisoners dispatched to the Gulag each week was more than halved.[55] Overall, the number of convictions for 1959 dropped significantly in comparison with the previous year.[56]

These measures represented an important step toward implementing the principle of correction or re-education *within* Soviet society, rather than in a place of exclusion. In the first ten weeks after the August decree, 7 percent of the prisoners set free by the commissions were not given unconditional release but saw the remaining part of their sentence replaced with noncusto-

---

[52] Ibid.

[53] Of the 158,074 prisoners released, 41,831 had been sentenced for theft of state or public property, 32,083 for theft of personal property, and 40,629 for hooliganism (GARF f. 9401, op. 2, d. 507, ll. 24–25).

[54] Following the CC's criticisms, the Procuracy introduced a raft of reforms. These are detailed in Rudenko's report to the CC on 2 March 1960. See GARF f. 8131, op. 32, d. 6411, ll. 139–149.

[55] GARF f. 9401, op. 2, d. 506, l. 429.

[56] In 1959 the number of cases brought to court dropped by 23% compared with the preceding year. There was a particular reduction in the number of hooliganism, petty theft, violent assault, and home-brewing cases. See GARF f. 8131, op. 32, d. 6411, ll. 156–167.

dial punishment, such as "corrective work" (*ispravitel'nye raboty*) in their place of residence. For these 11,170 prisoners, redemption was thus still achieved through labor, but it was now performed on the offender's home turf. A further 5,533 released prisoners were taken under the guardianship (*poruka*) of a social organization, such as the local Komsomol organization or a workplace collective.[57] Over the course of 1959 the total number of people sentenced to imprisonment fell by 30 percent compared with the preceding year, while noncustodial sentences, including corrective work, fines and "social censure" (*obshchestvennoe poritsanie*), increased by 3 percent.[58]

The Komsomol's New Task

The Komsomol was particularly encouraged to take offenders under its guardianship. This role as "guardian" or "patron" to erring individuals was something of a departure from the members' earlier work as brigadiers. Admittedly, in its earlier campaign against criminal or antisocial behavior, the Komsomol had always noted the importance of educational measures, in particular lectures and talks on subjects such as "The Komsomol's Struggle for Healthy *Byt*" and "The Battle to Overcome Vestiges of the Past in People's Consciousness," but these seem somewhat overshadowed by more exciting means of combating crime.[59] In the years 1954–1956 particularly, the organization of "raids" seems to have been a key focus of Komsomol attention, perhaps because of the excitement they promised; after all, they offered membership in a close-knit group, training in the arts of *sambo* (unarmed combat), the possibility of winning local acclaim, and even substantial monetary prizes for successful arrests. In 1959 Komsomol members were asked to take a rather different approach. At the seventh plenum of the Komsomol CC in February 1960 *profilaktika* (prophylactics) was the order of the day. In the plenum's final resolution, there was explicit criticism of the organization's priorities: "It's still the case that not all Komsomol organizations actively participate in the work of the voluntary people's *druzhiny*. Young people often think that their main task is to arrest people who disturb public order and pass them over to the police. They don't undertake prophylactic work with the work collectives at factories, collective farms, state farms, and educational institutions in order to forestall antisocial behavior."[60] Although deemed heroic just a few years earlier, youthful enthusiasm for arresting offenders now aroused displeasure.

Two speeches from the plenum are indicative of the new approach the Komsomol took in the wake of the Twenty-First Party Congress and Khru-

[57] GARF f. 9401, op. 2, d. 507, ll. 24–25.
[58] GARF f. 8131, op. 32, d. 6411, ll. 156–167.
[59] RGASPI f. M-1, op. 32, d. 811, l. 152.
[60] RGASPI f. M-1, op. 32, d. 1024, l. 2.

shchev's speech on Nogovitsin. According to one Komsomol Central Committee secretary, L. V. Karpinskii, the focus of the organization's work should now be on the home. He said: "Many Komsomol committees are worried only about ensuring that young people are well-behaved outside, in public places, that is, where they are seen. Attitudes that form in everyday private life [*v povsednevnom bytu*], however, have a huge impact on the temperament of a young person."[61] Komsomol activists could no longer be concerned with ensuring that young people *acted* correctly when visible to the outside world; they must also be concerned about the attitudes, thoughts, and ideas the young person was developing out of view. This notion was echoed by other speakers at the plenum, including a Komsomol secretary at a factory in the town of Sormov who said, "The Komsomol must not only spend time with every worker, but more important, it must devote itself to the worker's thoughts."[62]

Karpinskii noted the importance of Khrushchev's speech at the Third Writers' Congress before stressing the need for the Komsomol to do more for those returning from the camps. Local committees must ensure that these young returnees had work and that their home life—their *byt*—was cared for. Karpinskii identified indifference toward other people as the "worst human evil," arguing that a lack of concern could easily lead young offenders to revert to their old ways. He used a story to illustrate this point. A girl raised in an orphanage committed an (undefined) offense and served time in prison. On release she went to live with an unwelcoming sister who soon kicked her out; the police found her work and a place in a dormitory, but the other young people living there, including Komsomol members, were uninterested in helping her. Her roommates put locks on their cupboards and told the girl her past was unforgivable. When she approached her superintendent for an advance on her first pay packet, he curtly refused. All this led to her reoffending. According to Karpinskii, the girl was destroyed, and all because no one could be bothered to save her. Following Khrushchev, Karpinskii emphasized the need to invest trust in those who returned from the camps, to see the real, good person buried within. Karpinskii finished his speech with a flourish: "Some people are comforted by the idea that every family has its black sheep. It would be far more appropriate for us to live by another principle: one for all, and all for one!"[63]

Comrade Kurbatova, secretary of the Ivanovo oblast Komsomol committee, was even more explicitly critical of the organization's priorities over recent years. In 1954, she said, Komsomol members joined the police-assistance brigades and organized their own raids, but they often forgot about what was most important—the *vospitanie* of young boys and girls who had

[61] RGASPI f. M-1, op. 2, d. 391, l. 83.
[62] RGASPI f. M-1, op. 2, d. 391, l. 204.
[63] RGASPI f. M-1, op. 2, d. 391, l. 105.

set off on the wrong track in life. In her region this had changed in October 1959, when a Komsomol rally decided to strengthen its "prophylactic" work.[64] She gave an example of this successful work: a leading figure in the local Komsomol took one Gulag returnee, Iurii Arkhireev, under his wing (*vzial nad shefstvo*). His patron took painstaking care with Iurii, accompanying him to the theater and giving presents on his birthday, as well as helping him find work. Fully transformed, the former offender was now about to join the Komsomol.[65]

Despite the support for the new emphasis on prophylactic work and the heightened concern for previous offenders, however, Komsomol leaders were still anxious about the influence of some Gulag returnees. Even though Kurbatova had just condemned the earlier emphasis on arresting offenders, she still seemed to find such approaches appealing. Indeed, she emphasized the need to protect young people from bad influences, recounting a recent incident in which the Komsomol played a heroic role in arresting offenders recently released from the camps. In the spring of 1959 a group of "thief-recidivists" had returned to the city of Ivanovo, leading to a spate of pickpocketing. Thirty-eight of the best Komsomol members, all with experience in fighting crime, joined the police effort. The results were impressive: twenty-three pickpockets were arrested, of whom nine were convicted and the remaining fourteen, all minors, released back to the custody of their parents. Following Kurbatova's speech, some speakers began to articulate concern about the practice of taking guardianship of offenders, arguing that not all collectives took their responsibilities sufficiently seriously, allowing their charges to relapse.[66]

Underneath the apparent enthusiasm for new prophylactic measures, cracks were thus already beginning to show. Kurbatova made a distinction between young people who needed to be nurtured and protected and gangs of experienced criminals who must be arrested and sentenced. This left important questions: Where should the line be drawn? Which offenders could safely be corrected within society? Could moral education really work? Which criminals needed to be shut away in the interests of protecting citizens?

Khrushchev had said that all human beings could be saved and imagined a future without prisons, but even at his most utopian he never suggested this day had already arrived. Although he condemned the Gulag as a place where offenders only become more skilled in the criminal arts, he never called for it to be disbanded entirely. It existed for the time being as a last resort and holding pen for those too dangerous to undergo correction within society. At the Komsomol plenum in February 1960, General Procurator

[64] RGASPI f. M-1, op. 2, d. 391, l. 143–144.
[65] RGASPI f. M-1, op. 2, d. 391, ll. 143–148.
[66] RGASPI f. M-1, op. 2, d. 391, l. 167.

Rudenko put a figure of 25 percent on this contingent of offenders: a quarter of criminals, he said, needed to be incarcerated for the safety of others.[67] Yet such a figure does not seem to have been widely accepted. The question of which offenders could safely be corrected within the midst of the Soviet community caused disagreement, with many legal experts and ordinary citizens alike arguing that people needed protection from a much larger proportion of the criminal population. Only a small number of young, first-time offenders, they would argue, made appropriate subjects for noncustodial forms of re-education.

Even within Khrushchev's own political vision there were contradictions. The ongoing use of the death penalty is difficult to reconcile with Khrushchev's promise, "We believe that no such thing exists as a person who cannot be corrected." Reintroduced in 1954 for intentional homicide with aggravating circumstances, its use was extended to include banditry in 1960.[68] Even in 1959, when Khrushchev made his most ambitious claims, cases involving Komsomol members found guilty of murder sometimes ended with the award of the death penalty.[69] Not all offenders were being given the opportunity to be corrected and re-educated, either within society or even in the isolation of the Gulag.

Although policy fell short of the most ambitious aspects of Khrushchev's speech at the writers' congress, particularly in regard to the death penalty, the spirit of 1959 was strikingly utopian. The press presented Khrushchev's concern for one fallen individual as part of the party's renewed commitment to building communism and its repudiation of Stalinist injustices. This utopian spirit, embodied in the various different policing and judicial measures studied in this chapter, had significant results in terms of the prison population. In 1959–1960 the Gulag continued to shrink dramatically. When the number of inmates in corrective labor institutions dipped to 550,882 in 1960, it was at its lowest since 1935.[70] By the end of the decade, therefore, the horrendous expansion of the Gulag caused by the worst years of Stalinist brutality had been undone.

[67] RGASPI f. M-1, op. 2, d. 391, l. 214.

[68] Principles laid out in the unionwide decree of December 1958 were used as the basis for the 1960 RSFSR Criminal Code, in which, under article 77, banditry was made punishable by death (Berman, *Soviet Criminal Law,* 61).

[69] For example, in Lipetsk oblast, two drunken Komsomol members, a metalworker and a schoolboy, visited the sovkhoz club in a drunken state and then allegedly behaved indecently, provoking arguments with other youths. Out on the street afterwards, they attacked a young worker, stabbing him twenty times. The metalworker was sentenced to death. In Kurgan oblast, two Komsomol members drank large quantities of vodka, kicked and beat a nine-year-old boy, then stabbed and killed an eighteen-year-old. They were both sentenced to death (GARF f. 8131, op. 32, d. 6579, l. 7). For crime reports where the death penalty was given, see, for example, "Two Men Locked in Combat," *Komsomol'skaia pravda,* 23 May 1959, 2, trans. and reproduced in *Current Digest of the Soviet Press,* 11: 25, 23–24.

[70] GARF f. 7523, op. 95, d. 109, l. 27.

Both among the Soviet public and the legal and policing professions there was significant concern regarding these new approaches to criminality. Yet, for a brief moment, Khrushchev could promote an optimistic vision in which criminal or antisocial behavior could be overcome not by incarceration, exile, or execution—not by the excisionary methods deployed by Stalin—but by the power of good emanating from Soviet society as it stood on the brink of its communist future.

6   A Return to Weeding

Show the bandit-enemies of the people no mercy!

—Letter to the Supreme Soviet from employees at the
Institute of Mining in Moscow, 1957

In 1948 Konstantin Slivkin was a twenty-two-year-old from Riazan' work-ing in Kamchatka's fishing industry.[1] He was arrested for theft of state prop-erty and sentenced to ten years' imprisonment. A reinvestigation in 1952 revealed his innocence, however, and he was set free. Upon release, Slivkin decided his experiences must be set to paper and, after acquiring a typewriter, wrote several stories based on his experiences in the camps. In October 1957 he accidentally left a manuscript in a restaurant in the town of Petro-pavlovsk. In the course of the investigation, both his manuscripts and pri-vate correspondence were meticulously scrutinized, and as a result, he was sentenced to six years' imprisonment under article 58. Several high-profile party members tried to intervene in the case, including Elena Stasova and A. V. Smirnov, a member of the governing board of the Writers' Union, who believed Slivkin to be an honest Soviet citizen whose desire to become a writer, coupled with his inexperience, had landed him in trouble.[2] Their ef-forts were unsuccessful, and he served his whole sentence.

In a petition written in June 1960, Slivkin tried to defend his writings, claiming that his criticisms of camp life and Soviet criminal justice were in keeping with current debates. To make his argument, he drew on the press:

[1] GARF f. 8131, op. 31, d. 86804.
[2] GARF f. 8131, op. 31, d. 86804, l. 30, l. 53.

156

The discussion that is developing on the pages of Soviet press has reflected the fact that Soviet public opinion on this subject is entirely in keeping with the ideas I expressed in my manuscripts. For example, public opinion has two tendencies:

Number one: This tendency is expressed in an article by V. Soloukhin "Killed in Peacetime" (*Literaturnaia gazeta*, 11 January 1959). This calls for greater severity in punishment. For example it says in the article: "The experience of imprisonment should be such that after release convicted criminals fear finding themselves in there once again . . ."

Number two: This tendency is expressed in an article by V. Leonokhov "If We Gave Up on Him" (*Literaturnaia gazeta*, 6 November 1959). This article calls for a more humane attitude toward those imprisoned. Here is an extract from the article: "Can we decide the problem of the battle against crime simply with the punitive sword of justice? No we can't!"[3]

Slivkin thus identified two conflicting trends, citing one article that fell before Khrushchev's Nogovitsin speech, and one that followed. In the second page of his petition he argued that it was the second stance that had become dominant, and his views coincided, he believed, with this approach to criminal justice and with the views expressed by leaders at the Twenty-First Party Congress. Slivkin quoted from Khrushchev's speech in which he invited social organizations to take a greater role in maintaining order and cited calls for more prophylactic measures in the fight against crime from A. N. Shelepin, chairman of the KGB.[4] His own works, he argued, reflected the spirit of the congress.

Earlier scholarship on the Khrushchev era tended to see it as a period of binary conflict between those who supported change and those who opposed it, and this would indeed be a plausible way to explain the vicissitudes of criminal justice reform in the late 1950s and early 1960s. The zigzags in Khrushchev's policy could be interpreted as the victories and defeats of competing factions of reformers and conservatives, well-defined groups with clear political identities. This chapter argues, however, that in the uncertain post-Stalin era fixed positions were rather hard to form or maintain. Instead of seeing Khrushchev as a man buffeted by vying factions, able to pursue his personal vision at one moment when his political capital was high, the next submitting to conservative forces, I argue that political agendas were fluid during these years. On the one hand, the Twentieth Party Congress and the denunciation of Stalin revived revolutionary fervor and inspired leaders to make rash promises regarding the imminence of communism; on the other, the far-from-utopian realities of Soviet life frequently undermined their messianic hopes. Throughout their history, the communists had been buoyed up by the beauty of the political vision they promised, yet at the same time angst-

---

[3] GARF f. 8131, op. 31, d. 86804, ll. 8–9.
[4] GARF f. 8131, op. 31, d. 86804, ll. 9–10.

ridden that this might be snatched away by imperialist enemies or submerged by the weight of the past. With various certainties shaken in the wake of Stalin's death, these tendencies were magnified. Renewed optimism, undercut by biting anxiety, was perhaps as much responsible for the shifting tides in criminal justice policy as the chronicles of Kremlin infighting. Moments of great optimism, such as Khrushchev's Nogovitsin lecture, could easily be drowned by a tide of neurotic doubt.

This chapter explores the evolution of policy and rhetoric toward crime between 1959 and 1962. At the Twenty-First Party Congress in 1959, Khrushchev had promised that Soviet society itself could transform all but the most toughened criminals without requiring their isolation or excision from the social body. At the Twenty-Second Party Congress, however, Khrushchev demanded a renewed "battle against idlers and parasites, hooligans, and drunkards" and claimed: "There is no place for these weeds in our life."[5] Three years after his ambitious promises at the Twenty-First Party Congress and the Third Writers' Congress, he was now suggesting that the Soviet garden was threatened not only by dangerous, hardened criminals but also by relatively minor offenders—idlers, parasites, hooligans, drunkards—who must be weeded out. It is not impossible that opponents of the reform had ultimately defeated Khrushchev, yet in many other areas the Twenty-Second Party Congress saw the first secretary impose his will.[6] Khrushchev seems to have had a change of heart, his earlier optimism dissolved by the problems his criminal justice reforms encountered almost as soon as they were introduced.

The new measures depended on the willingness of local officials to radically change the way they worked, and this in itself was no mean task. But the nature of the reforms meant that they were also dependent on the readiness of volunteers to devote energy and leisure time to the task of converting offenders into model citizens. While many people did become involved in voluntary activities in this period, they did not necessarily share Khrushchev's faith in their ability to transform recidivist criminals into respectable members of the community. Both law-enforcement officials and ordinary Soviet citizens repeatedly and vociferously expressed their concerns about the new direction criminal justice was taking, and their combined resistance fundamentally undermined the reforms' chance of success.

---

[5] "Doklad N. S. Khrushcheva," *Pravda,* 18 October 1961, 11.

[6] William Taubman writes: "The Twenty-Second Congress was another turning point. No longer constrained by Stalin, Molotov, or anyone else and armed with new authority on top of all his old power, Khrushchev set out to attack the problems that had been vexing him." Taubman identifies agricultural reform and the renewed attacks on Stalin as signs of Khrushchev's reforming zeal and the new power he enjoyed (*Khrushchev,* 516).

Optimism and Doubt

On 18 July 1959, just two months after Khrushchev's speech at the Third Writers' Congress, members of the new "observation committees" from across Moscow oblast came together to discuss the state of corrective-labor institutions and prisons in the province.[7] One member, G. U. Kalinin, made a long and impassioned speech. He reminded his audience that their work had become even more important in the wake of the Twenty-First Party Congress as the task of building communism was now urgent. "We won't be taking any thieves, bandits, or robbers forward with us to the future communist system," he told listeners.[8] In keeping with the utopian rhetoric articulated by Khrushchev in 1959, he thus opened his speech by configuring the issue of crime in relation to the creation of earthly paradise. Later in the speech he boasted that the Soviets had been the first in the world to build a socialist state, "the first to launch a satellite and a ballistic rocket," and would be the first to build communism, eradicate crime, and destroy prisons, camps, and labor colonies.[9] There was only one way to achieve this. As soon as possible, he said, we must liquidate all "deviations" (*otkloneniia*) by "engaging the carriers of these deviations [*nositeli etikh otklonenii*] in communist labor."

"Unfortunately," he said, "the majority of those carrying deviations are not recidivist thieves, bandits, and so on, whose whole existence is about crime. About 70–80 percent are white and blue-collar workers, collective farmers, members of the intelligentsia, and students." Sixty percent of those arrested in Moscow oblast were young people under the age of twenty-five.[10] Such figures suggested that a majority of offenders were ordinary Soviet citizens who might make suitable subjects for the various forms of social rehabilitation advocated in 1959. Kalinin said the work of the police was directed toward "prophylactics." Above all else, they must try to save an offender within the collective and his family home. If he ended up in the Gulag and came into contact with thieves with fifteen years' worth of experience, then all their re-educational work would be wasted. The first-time offender could not help but pick up the habits and behavior of the camp old hands.[11] Like Khrushchev, Kalinin saw the dangers of the prison and its potential to corrupt the offender further.

Yet there were important divergences from Khrushchev. Kalinin was worried about the impact of Khrushchev's speech at the Third Writers' Congress.

---

[7] TsGAMO f. 2157, op. 1, d. 5311, ll. 148–159. The "observation committees" were set up by a decree from the Council of Ministers on 24 May 1957. Their goal was to strengthen public (*obshchestvennyi*) control over the work of the corrective-labor institutions.

[8] TsGAMO f. 2157, op. 1, d. 5311, l. 153.

[9] TsGAMO f. 2157, op. 1, d. 5311, l. 156.

[10] TsGAMO f. 2157, op. 1, d. 5311, l. 153.

[11] TsGAMO f. 2157, op. 1, d. 5311, l. 155.

Lots of prisoners, he warned his colleagues, would try to manipulate Khrushchev's speech to plead for their own release. Such prisoners should be reminded that when Nogovitsin approached Khrushchev he had already reformed himself, having run away from his family but resisted the lure of crime, thus proving his determination to give up his old habits. Charging fellow committee members to be more cautious in considering prisoners' requests for early release, he told them:

> Among them [the prisoners], there are people who can't be made out [*razgadany*] at first glance, who try to hide their face from us, and often they hide it so well that it is initially difficult to figure them out. It is hard to know how this group will behave after release. . . .
>
> It is our first task to master this difficult group so that when they are released from the camps or prison, they will be on the correct working path and won't lead our young people astray. But now they are beginning to behave in a very cunning way. When they are released from the prisons and camps, they don't immediately go about their shady business themselves, but instead try to involve our young people.[12]

Kalinin was concerned that the authorities would not be able to distinguish the repentant offender from the recidivist criminal. Where Khrushchev believed that they had the power to unearth the "man" buried within the criminal, Kalinin worried that a cunning villain might hide behind the mask of a reformed citizen. He might successfully deceive members of the committee. In Kalinin's view, therefore, early release should not be granted too freely: collective initiatives to "correct" and "save" an offender were appropriate for young people who had committed a single error, but the application of "early release" should be more restrained than at present.

Kalinin tried to follow Khrushchev in his utopian vision, wanting to believe that society was well on its way to constructing a communist paradise without crime. Yet he saw more significant obstacles on the road ahead. He agreed with Khrushchev on the corrupting influence of the Gulag, but this made him more aware than ever of the need to safeguard ordinary citizens from those who had been there. He himself was a member of one of the administrative bodies created in the 1950s to reclassify the criminal population, to decide who could be corrected within society and who must be isolated, but he worried that they might be getting it all wrong. The results of the next two years would suggest that officials did struggle to find the balance. Time and again, internal reports complained that dangerous criminals had been allowed to remain at large, while ordinary, if flawed, citizens were being unfairly packed off to the Gulag.

---

[12] TsGAMO f. 2157, op. 1, d. 5311, l. 154.

Implementing the New Measures

On 8 April 1959 a meeting was organized by Leningrad's head procurator to discuss the introduction of new policies, and initially debate progressed smoothly as delegates planned the new volunteer brigades and shared their experiences of setting up "socialist legality" committees. The emphasis on re-educating offenders *within* society, however, caused consternation. Comrade Lototskaia, the procurator of Zhdanov raion, said that she did not understand the new practice of transferring offenders to the guardianship of community organizations. "Don't these measures indicate a tendency to undermine our fight against dangerous criminals?" she asked the assembled. The procurator of Moscow raion declared that the practice would not be adopted in his dominion.[13]

Six months later, the Leningrad oblast procurator reported to Moscow headquarters on the implementation of the new measures.[14] In many places, the new *druzhiny* were working well, and in many places public drunkenness and misbehavior had apparently decreased as a result of the patrols. The *druzhiny* exposed offenders to public shame by placing their pictures in local newspapers, an apparently effective method: one drunkard promised to reform, begging for his photograph to be removed and claiming he had lost 6 kilos from the shame of it all! The situation varied, and the procurator admitted that in some areas the brigades still required better leadership and organization. It was a similar story with the comrade courts. In many areas the courts had impressive successes in correcting drunken, unruly behavior and poor work discipline, whereas in others they existed on paper alone, again as a result of poor management. In this memo the procurator devoted much greater space to the question of "guardianship," the practice of charging social organizations (such as a workplace, housing block, or Komsomol organization) with responsibility for an offender's re-education (a practice known as *poruka*). The results seem remarkable: there had been only one case of re-offending, a young man who had been taken under the care of his school but was reconvicted of pickpocketing a few months after his first offense. Despite this apparently impressive strike rate, the procurator's report went on for several pages to detail failings in the way the measure was being implemented. He complained of many problems: poor communication between the local procuracy and the social organizations charged with carrying out re-education; the procuracy's habit of passing on cases for re-education without a petition from the collective; the failure of procuracy officials and police to take an interest in the further development of the case; the tendency for organizations to petition for the guardianship of offenders who were clearly unsuitable. Courts were accused of making insensitive decisions, as

[13] GARF f. 8131, op. 32, d. 6199, ll. 130–131.
[14] GARF f. 8131, op. 32, d. 6199, ll. 208–229.

in the case of A. N. Subbotina, who was assigned to her housing collective for re-education, even though these were the very people whom she had drunkenly mistreated in the first place. One court failed to transfer any of their cases for re-education by the collective, whereas at the other end of the spectrum some courts were releasing serious offenders back into the community. Considering the near absence of reoffending, it is perhaps surprising that the procurator felt driven to write such a detailed and critical report. It does not seem that the Leningrad oblast procurator opposed the initiative per se, but he could already identify all kinds of uncertainties in the attitudes of the people putting it into practice and many inconsistencies in the way it was implemented across his province.

Officials elsewhere were aware of these problems: some procurators were ridiculously cautious, others almost reckless. In the fall of 1959, a report from Kalinin oblast criticized local procurators for their failure to implement the new policies in a coherent manner. In one raion individuals guilty of attempted murder, rape, and grievous bodily harm might be granted reprieve and bailed out for *poruka*, while in a neighboring district a man was brought to trial for failing to pay alimony for two months.[15] An inquiry in Moscow found similar problems. The author of the report queried why some cases had reached court at all, questioning the appropriateness of convicting a factory worker who stole a jar of jam worth 14 rubles or of sentencing a deaf and mute woman whose "offense" was to knock down the partition dividing the room she shared with her ex-husband.[16] At the same time, some organizations were trying to bail out entirely the wrong kind of people. For example, the Kuntsevo Komsomol applied for guardianship of Danilov, a drunk driver with previous convictions who had killed a young woman in a hit-and-run incident.[17] In the city of Cheliabinsk one local procurator criticized the choice of candidates taken for re-education. "Party organizations prepare for meetings inadequately," he said at a raikom plenum in September 1960, "meaning that they don't take guardianship of the right people but instead those who know how to play the game."[18]

One of the key difficulties with the new measures, it seems, was how to distinguish those wrongdoers who could safely be re-educated within society (according to Rudenko in 1960, 75 percent of offenders), and those who must be put behind bars. The inconsistency noted in the procurators' reports is perhaps unsurprising. For a quarter of a century, the promise to correct criminals within the community had been quietly withdrawn. Within the socialist realist models promoted under Stalin, the hero might make mistakes before his final moral victory, but the extent of his deviation was limited; he might be rude or insensitive, but the new Soviet man did not commit

15 GARF f. 8131, op. 32, d. 3200, ll. 42–45.
16 GARF f. 8131, op. 32, d. 6226, l. 9.
17 GARF f. 8131, op. 32, d. 6226, l. 8.
18 GU OGAChO f. 94, op. 2, d. 389, l. 132.

crimes.[19] Now, however, law-enforcement officials were told that collective practices could deal with a much greater range of offenses and they were encouraged to see imprisonment as a last resort. At the same time, however, they were told to remain on their guard, because dangerous recidivist criminals might still infect and contaminate their society, given half the chance. It was a thin line to tread, with little guidance offered. If anything, the Nogovitsin story only served to muddy the water: it suggested that repeat offenders who showed repentance might be suitable candidates for re-education within the community, and yet oblast procurators were critical when recidivists were given noncustodial sentences.[20] Like Kalinin in Moscow, officials in the provinces worried that offenders might pretend to repent but in fact be fooling them.

Even once the courts had decided which offenders could be reprieved from the Gulag, the new measures proved problematic. The second difficulty lay with the social organizations charged with reforming the delinquents. Social organizations, such as the Komsomol and work collectives, were criticized not only for choosing the wrong people but also for failing to work effectively with them. Some reports suggested that the mechanism was used by organizations wanting to save friends from prison, without any real intention of engaging in their charge's moral education. In January 1960 S. P. Pavlov, first secretary of the Komsomol, received a report from the section of the RSFSR Procuracy dealing with youth crime. The author of the report complained that there were cases where Komsomol organizations requested guardianship over young people but did not carry out the necessary work. For example, in Cheboksary in July 1959, a minor convicted of pickpocketing was transferred to the care of the work collective at a local factory. Apart from writing the petition, however, the workers left their charge to his own devices and he reoffended a few months later.[21] In one raion of Cheliabinsk, the procurator attacked one of the local trade schools which had taken on a certain Penkin but made no efforts to re-educate him, with the result that he had gathered together a group of kids and organized three violent robberies. Incredibly, the school had again applied for guardianship.[22] Reports from across Vladimir oblast give a similar picture. In January 1960, for example, N. N. Chuzlov was released early from prison on the grounds that Workshop No. 10 at the Ordzhonikidze factory in Kol'chugun would become his "guardian" and take responsibility for his re-education.[23] For almost two months, however, he was without work and so reoffended. According to the report, delays in finding work for returnees were not uncommon.

In other cases offenders and ex-convicts themselves were blamed, and this

---

[19] Clark, *The Soviet Novel*, 167–176.
[20] GAVO, f. r-3789, op. 1, d. 2007, l. 49.
[21] GARF f. 8131, op. 32, d. 6579, l. 10.
[22] GU OGAChO f. 94, op. 2, d. 389, l. 132.
[23] GAVO, f. r-3789, op. 1, d. 2007, l. 68.

points to a third area of difficulty. Even when the collective showered them with help, some offenders apparently refused to change. After serving five sentences, A. I. Feniushin was granted early release in May 1959; he was found work and in October of the same year was even given a sanatorium holiday worth 1,200 rubles with a further 130 rubles for travel expenses. Despite the generosity shown him, he reoffended in January 1960. Another returnee from the Gulag, Telegin, managed to reoffend in little over three weeks after his release, even though he received 100 rubles to tide him over until he was allocated work.[24]

Even before the first year of the experiment was over, therefore, widespread misgivings had arisen among those charged with its implementation. Difficulties dogged the new measures in three main areas: first, local procurators, judges, and social organizations alike struggled to identify suitable candidates; second, organizations charged with the work of re-education did not always find it easy to muster the necessary enthusiasm; third, not all returnees turned out like Nogovitsin, however much effort was invested in them. Even where the measures were relatively successful and reoffending rates low, judicial officials articulated deep anxiety.

The failure of these initiatives to fire public enthusiasm does not suggest indifference to the question of crime per se. Crime was a highly divisive issue within Soviet society. Some young people seem to have found the criminal lifestyle appealing and romantic, and this cult of criminality only served to alarm other Soviet citizens further. After years of violent upheaval many feared any threat to the fragile stability achieved in the 1950s. These anxieties were not confined to the older generation, however, for while some youths were enamored of the criminal subcultures, others sought to become heroes in the fight against crime. With passions running high, many citizens were ready to put pen to paper to inform the powers-that-be of their views on the subject of crime. They certainly hoped for new measures to tackle the problem, but they were not necessarily the ones that Khrushchev had introduced in 1959–1960.

Calls for Banishment

The press is often blamed for "moral panics," but the crisis of confidence regarding law and order that occurred in the Soviet Union after Stalin's death seems to have followed a rather different pattern—perhaps ironic considering the dominant and didactic role played by the Soviet media.[25] Despite the

---

[24] GAVO, f. r-3789, op. 1, d. 2007, ll. 60–68.

[25] In his study of "mods" and "rockers" in 1960s Britain, Stanley Cohen argues that the over-reaction of the media was central to the escalation of the "moral panic" (*Folk Devils and Moral Panics* [London, 1972]). For a review of the different interpretations of moral panics, see Erich Goode and Nachman Ben-Yehuda, "Moral Panics: Culture, Politics, and Social Con-

doubts articulated by law-enforcement officials and political figures behind the scenes, in the late 1950s Soviet newspapers tried to convince their readers that criminals could be saved and returnees from the Gulag were not the dangerous enemies feared. Readers' anxieties do not seem to have been assuaged, however. Reporting on the influx of letters about crime, a Supreme Soviet official wrote in December 1955: "after a significant rise in the numbers of these letters in 1953 and the beginning of 1954, the numbers gradually decreased until the present time when it has started to grow again."[26] This epistolary outcry did not abate as the decade went on. Letter writers continued to present the Soviet world as one where honest, respectable citizens were under threat from an army of recidivist, degenerate enemies, even though official sources actively deterred them from such a reading.

Sometimes letter writers identified the offenders as young people recently demobilized from the army or studying at a local trade school, and one long letter to Rudenko claimed many culprits were the children of rich parents.[27] More often than not, though, letter writers believed that the problem lay with those released from the camps.[28] A letter addressed to Voroshilov informed him that the city of Stavropol' was taken over by criminals at night: "It is no secret that the morgues are full of the corpses of people murdered. After nine o'clock in the evening, life stops for peaceable citizens. Those who have spent their whole lives in the camps come out onto the streets. They don't allow us to live peacefully."[29] Another described recent attacks, complaining that people "return from the camps and begin their dark deeds again."[30]

Letter writers were concerned about a whole variety of unsavory behaviors. F. Ia. Filonov from Khar'kov, complained that his neighbor's home had become a hangout for scores of layabouts. Instead of working, these people "play cards for days on end, and if the weather permits, chase doves . . . they throw sticks, stones and lumps of earth at them." In the evenings, Filonov lamented, they drank and engaged in hooligan activities, including poking out dogs' eyes.[31] Iurii Smirnov from Krasnodar said he was frightened to leave his house because of the groups of men openly drinking vodka and cursing on the streets, even encouraging young people to use the "same foul language."[32] The inhabitants of Shchekino in Tula oblast wrote: "They attack decent [*chestnyi*] Soviet citizens, insult them, steal, and even kill."[33]

---

struction," *Annual Review of Sociology* 20 (1994): 149–171. Following their schema, my interpretation would come closest to the "grassroots" model.

[26] GARF f. 7523, op. 107, d. 189, l. 65.
[27] GARF f. 8131, op. 32, d. 5663, l. 11.
[28] RGANI f. 5, op. 30, d. 186, ll. 74–77.
[29] GARF f. 7523, op. 107, d. 189, l. 74.
[30] GARF f. 7523, op. 107, d. 189, l. 70.
[31] GARF f. 7523, op. 107, d. 189, l. 87.
[32] GARF f. 7523, op. 107, d. 189, l. 67.
[33] GARF f. 7523, op. 107, d. 189, l. 66.

Bracketing together less serious transgressions like swearing with grave ones such as murder, the letters suggested that public anxiety was not always occasioned by specific acts but reflected a more general malaise about the presence within their communities of individuals they regarded as outsiders. A collective letter from thirty-one people living in Cheliabinsk began by saying that people hated thieves, hooligans, bandits, and other criminal elements and then continued: "There can be no clear distinction between them as they are all as disgusting, amoral, and inhumane as it is possible to be. People hate them as their most evil enemies who darken our life, terrorizing and robbing innocent, honest Soviet citizens."[34]

These criminal "elements" were presented not as erring members of their own Soviet family but as outsiders, and even as political enemies. In 1955 a group of citizens wrote that, "a hooligan-bandit who has been convicted two or three times, should be isolated from society as an enemy of the people [*vrag naroda*]."[35] A collective letter written in 1957 by employees at the Institute of Mining in Moscow began by listing a series of attacks suffered by colleagues over the past two years before cautioning its readers: "We shouldn't forget the fact that the hands of bandits are often being directed by foreign spies and are acting for the benefit of foreign enemies."[36] They concluded their letter with a slogan worthy of any Bolshevik agitator: "Show the bandit-enemies of the people no mercy!" (*Banditam—vragam naroda— ne mozhet byt' poshchady!*).[37] V. V. Polynev from Dnepropetrovsk lamented that after forty-three years of Soviet rule, the nation was failing to follow Lenin's orders to wage a "relentless battle against enemies of the people— hooligans, parasites [*tuneiadtsi*], speculators, and so on."[38] Attacking official policy as a betrayal of Leninism, Polynev argued for an approach that treated lawbreakers of any description as enemies. He called for battle, not reconciliation.

In addition to labeling offenders as "bandits" and "enemies," letter writers also vilified them as "parasites." As early as 1955, two years before the proposed antiparasite measures of 1957, such metaphors were common in letters addressed to the Supreme Soviet. One letter began by praising the high "ideological and moral" level of Soviet people, which it quickly contrasted with the murky ways of thieves and bandits—"morally fallen people who have lost all appearance of being human [*poteriavshikh oblik cheloveka*]." They wrote: "They hold nothing sacred, they are parasites on the body of society."[39] Calling for more dramatic measures to be taken against a broad and often ill-defined group of offenders, letter writers frequently wrote of the

---

[34] GU OGAChO f. 288, op. 21, d. 93, l.13.
[35] GARF f. 7523, op. 107, d. 189, l. 73.
[36] GARF f. 7523, op. 89, d. 7272, ll. 7–8.
[37] GARF f. 7523, op. 89, d. 7272, ll. 7–8.
[38] GARF f. 7523, op. 95, d. 73a, l. 184.
[39] GARF f. 7523, op. 107, d. 189, l. 80.

need to "isolate these parasites."[40] In 1960 a certain S. E. Taranov, aged
sixty-six, a former miner and war veteran, wrote from Novocherkassk: "The
people aren't happy with such mild measures against parasites, and I think
that a bandit and anyone who kills a man are class enemies. We need to wipe
them from our earth."[41] The Cheliabinsk letter writers wrote: "We need to
rip out this terrible and rotten ulcer [*s kornem vyrvat' tu strashnuiu i parshi-
vuiu iazvu*] that discredits our society and brings it incurable and irreversible
ills which darken and poison our life."[42] Offenders were thus imagined both
as parasites eating away at society's healthy body and as an incurable growth
that must be cut out: biomedical metaphors were thus used to present criminality as an incurable ill that must be excised to preserve society's well-being.

Letter writers frequently expressed their dissatisfaction with the "humaneness" of the new laws. A certain Smirnov from Minsk exclaimed:
"How much grief these swine [*merzavtsy*] inflict on our people! And this
needn't be, if it wasn't for our humane laws."[43] A group of workers from
the Nikol'skii factory in Taganrog told the Moscow authorities that the
"workers are deeply indignant that they as decent people are valued so little, while bandits are shown such humanity."[44] "Humaneness," a concept
embraced by the regime when it embarked on its criminal justice reforms in
1953, was here rejected as a misguided policy that left respectable Soviet citizens hopelessly at risk.

The tales of correction and re-education promoted in the press in the late
1950s also fell on stony ground. From the town of Turinsk in Sverdlov
oblast, a certain Stizhevskii wrote: "If severe measures aren't taken against
those who disrupt the lives of decent citizens, then other measures of moral
education [*vospitanie*] won't help."[45] Members of the Komsomol organization in the town of Cherepovets, Vologda oblast, collectively wrote to express their anxiety with the state of affairs in their hometown: "The police
in our town probably aren't in a position to cope with such widely developed banditry, which makes people live in fear, as they did during the war."
The terror of war had left its scars even on the younger generation, and they
dreaded any new threat. Their letter continued: "All this is the fault of hooligans, let out from prison before the end of their sentence and without learning their lesson. We know that our country is now conducting significant
work in the sphere of moral education [*vospitatel'naia rabota*], but we
mustn't choose to educate some at the cost of others' lives."[46] More tem-

---

[40] Letters from Arzamassk oblast and Stavropol' wrote of the need to isolate parasites
(GARF f. 7523, op. 107, d. 189, ll. 73–74).
[41] GARF f. 7523, op. 95, d. 73a, l. 180.
[42] GU OGAChO f. 288, op. 21, d. 93, l. 14.
[43] GARF f. 7523, op. 95, d. 109, l. 13.
[44] GARF f. 7523, op. 95, d. 99, l. 55. See also GARF f. 7523, op. 95, d. 73a, l. 180.
[45] GARF f. 7523, op. 89, d. 7494, l. 104.
[46] GARF f. 7523, op. 95, d. 73a, l. 174.

perate than some letter writers, the Komsomol members did their best to acknowledge the merit of early release and re-education but still believed that the policies of correction endangered their own lives as law-abiding Soviet citizens. Almost before the policies of re-education and correction were implemented, the public insisted enough was enough.

Not only did letter writers scorn the idea that offenders could be corrected within the Soviet community, they also rejected the Belomor model, disputing any claims that the Gulag corrected its inmates. One citizen from the city of Molotov complained that young offenders scorned the courts because they knew that even a fifteen-year sentence could see them out in three. Referring to one hooligan released by the amnesty, the letter writer asked rhetorically: "And has he been corrected? Not a bit of it. He causes havoc and says he's not scared of prison because he's better off there than at home."[47] Another said: "People released from the camps early commit serious crimes knowing that they won't be in prison for long."[48] The solution was to banish them forever. One letter writer considered prison a "breeding-ground for infection" (*rassadniki zarazy*); and he therefore suggested keeping hooligans, thieves, murderers, and pillagers in special camps where they would live "in strict isolation from society" for the rest of their lives.[49] Polynev, from Dnepropetrovsk, suggested that "hooligans" should not be allowed to return to the south, but "be sent off only to the north, and after the end of their sentence, be made to stay there for ever."[50]

Rather than thinking that it was within the powers of their local community to transform these criminal elements, letter writers instead called for outside help. Expressing serious dissatisfaction with the failure of local authorities to ensure public safety, miners from Stalinskii oblast asked Voroshilov to send them a "battalion of good soldiers from the MVD's internal forces."[51] Another letter writer suggested it was necessary to "bring in the army to eradicate banditry, as was done in Moscow immediately after the war—but this time throughout the country."[52] A former army officer proposed setting up temporary sentry posts on trams, in shops, and on the streets, which would be manned at night by armed communists—a far more militant version of the *druzhiny*.[53] One citizen wrote that the volunteer brigades introduced in 1959 were simply "not strong enough to stand up to the armed bandits."[54]

Calls for the death sentence to be applied more frequently were widespread. One letter demanding murderers be sentenced to death was signed

[47] GARF f. 7523, op. 89, d. 4403, l. 8.
[48] GARF f. 7523, op. 89, d. 4403, l. 9.
[49] GARF f. 7523, op. 89, d. 7494, l. 103.
[50] GARF f. 7523, op. 95, d. 73a, l. 184.
[51] GARF f. 7523, op. 89, d. 7494, l. 105.
[52] GARF f. 7523, op. 89, d. 7272, ll. 7–8.
[53] GARF f. 7523, op. 107, d. 189, l. 81.
[54] GARF f. 7523, op. 95, d. 73a, l. 168.

by 625 citizens.[55] A collective letter from Ivanovo oblast argued that the time for re-education was over: "We workers ask you to grant us a quiet life. Apply the most severe measures to banditry—public execution. Moral education has already gone far enough—it's time to punish!"[56] Not only did these letter writers want the death sentence as a means to rid the country of its worst criminals, but they also hoped for a public spectacle which would allow the collective to express its antipathy to those who broke its laws.[57] One letter writer suggested that people who had committed murder be publicly shot, "as they do in China."[58] From the city of Tula, workers demanded that "criminals who slaughter people" be "hanged in front of the whole people on the town square."[59] A collective letter from Novosibirsk stated: "In Leningrad at the end of the war four Germans were hung on the central square for their evil deeds. Why can't the bandits be punished for their bestial [*zverskii*] crimes in the same way? We Soviet citizens demand public punishment like this."[60] Even harsher proposals came from E. A. Zotova, an inhabitant of Stalino, who had been robbed of her savings. In a somewhat confused sequence of events, she wanted "these animals . . . executed, quartered, and exiled for life."[61] References to China and wartime executions of Germans remind us that there was little precedent for public execution even under Stalinist rule.[62] Now, however, some Soviet citizens wanted a spectacle that could be reproduced in their own localities and in which they could personally participate. It was perhaps seen as a means to reaffirm their identity as "decent citizens" or "decent workers" in stark contrast to the "animals" so violently contesting their control of public space.

Many writers set pen to paper to defend the imagined boundary between law-abiding citizens, on one hand, and offenders, on the other. They claimed that such widespread criminality undermined the amazing progress the Soviet Union had achieved, with one complaining that in a country that had become so strong, cultured, and creative, incidents of banditry, theft, rape,

[55] GARF f. 7523, op. 95, d. 73a, ll. 168–169.

[56] GARF f. 7523, op. 89, d. 7494, l. 108.

[57] In 1960 officials at the Supreme Soviet noted that many letters included requests for murderers and recidivists to be given the death sentence publicly (GARF f. 7523, op. 95, d. 73a, l. 167).

[58] GARF f. 8131, op. 32, d. 5663, l. 12.

[59] GARF f. 7523, op. 95, d. 73a, l. 76.

[60] GARF f. 7523, op. 95, d. 73a, l. 172.

[61] GARF f. 7523, op. 95, d. 73a, l. 179.

[62] In April 1942 a GKO (State Committee of Defense) resolution stated that "German-fascist villains who are guilty of murders, torture of the Soviet civil population and captured Red Army men," spies, and traitors could be sentenced to public hanging; the bodies of the hanged men must be left on the gallows for several days as a lesson to others. On the wartime decrees, see Pavel Polian, "The Internment of Returning Soviet Prisoners of War after 1945," in *Prisoners of War, Prisoners of Peace: Captivity, Homecoming, and Memory in World War II*, ed. Bob Moore and Barbara Hately-Broad (Oxford, 2005), 123–139 (128). On the postwar executions in Leningrad, see A. Z. Vakser, *Leningrad poslevoennyi. 1945–1982 gody* (St. Petersburg, 2005), 134–135.

and speculation were an incredibly bitter pill to swallow.[63] Some felt that they, as good Soviet citizens, deserved better protection. There were references to the sacrifices made during the war and the need for a quite, peaceful life in its wake.[64] Although the existence and preservation of these texts does not mean that all citizens experienced such extreme hostility toward offenders, the growing number of such letters suggests that these anxieties did become more widespread and entrenched over the course of the 1950s.[65] Moreover, the linguistic commonalities among these letters suggest that within the Soviet community there were well-defined alternatives to the official rhetoric concerning crime and correction. Thirty years earlier, anxieties that the criminal was a source of infection and contamination had been an important current in NEP thinking and such notions had evidently not been eroded from the popular imagination.[66] The Stalinist vision of a world beset by deadly foes provided a template for further vilification of the criminal as an alien and enemy to Soviet society. Although these visions of the offender were not articulated in official sources in the 1950s, they recur with remarkably similarity in a large number of citizens' writings.

Public concerns over law and order might be a common feature to many postwar societies where citizens thirst for stability and an end to violence. The specific linguistic forms they took in the Soviet popular imagination in the 1950s, however, were a unique hybrid which included NEP-era ideas about crime as disease and Stalinist rhetoric about enemies as well as express opposition to the concepts of correction, re-education, and humaneness promoted in the press. Increasingly distressed by what they saw as the government's failure to protect them, some members of the public also came to draw on a concept from the prerevolutionary past: the *samosud,* which translates as self-trial, or sometimes as "mob law."

Angry Crowds in the Fight for Law and Order

Amir Weiner has shown that in the western regions of Ukraine the authorities sometimes encouraged lynch-mob attitudes. Local bosses were keen to

[63] GARF f. 7523, op. 107, d. 189, l. 78.

[64] One letter began: "We, pilots, technical staff, and service personnel at the aviation section of the Civil Air Defense returned from the Great War to peaceful work, and we are proud that we aid the Motherland, assisting the harvest in our airplanes and helping to save people." It went on to describe in detail the brutal murder of a fifteen-year-old near Tambov, recounting how locals had caught the culprit and handed him to the police. The authors of the letter were anxious that he be given the death penalty. In the conclusion to the letter they reminded their reader that they came from the same region as the wartime martyr Zoia Kosmodem'ianskaia (GARF f. 7523, op. 85, d. 33, l. 26).

[65] As already suggested, officials at the Supreme Soviet said that the numbers of letters they received began to increase from the end of 1955. In June 1956 officials at the party's CC reported that they too had been receiving more correspondence on the subject of crime (RGANI f. 5, op. 30, d. 186, ll. 74–77).

[66] Beer, *Renovating Russia*, 165–204.

incite widespread antipathy toward the former nationalists returning from the Gulag and places of exile: in 1959, for example, five men charged with heinous crimes (including countless murders against civilians in the years 1943–1944) were the subject of a public trial in Rivne oblast which was attended by over five hundred men and women, many of whom screamed and cried when the death sentence was read out.[67] Elsewhere, however, Moscow's criminal justice policies meant that more lenient punishments were being awarded; and popular outbursts, far from being stage-managed by the local party or KGB, in fact slipped beyond their control.

In Stalingrad on 6 July 1957 a man named Shiianov, once the head of the local air defense unit and now retired, spotted an intruder in his garden and shot at him with his hunting rifle. He was soon arrested for the death of the teenage trespasser but when the case came to court, he was sentenced to only one year in the corrective labor camps. Even considering the drive toward shorter custodial sentences at this time, this was an unusually mild punishment, perhaps reflecting Shiianov's standing in the community. The teenager's family and relatives attending the trial were outraged, and eight of them were led out of the courtroom for causing a disturbance. Instead of going home, however, they gathered outside, where they were soon joined by other sympathetic bystanders. When the day's shift was over, workers leaving the local factory added to the crowd, which grew to about one thousand. The police were out in force but failed to disperse the throngs, among whom there were several individuals demanding that Shiianov be handed over for reprisals (*rasprava*). Even with the arrival of the raikom secretary and the town procurator, order could not be restored. According to a subsequent report, "at around nine o'clock, a significant number of citizens, among whom a number were drunk, threw stones at the police, swarmed toward the building, broke three doors, and forced their way into the courtroom in search of Shiianov." Shiianov tried to make good his escape by jumping through a window but was intercepted by members of the crowd. He was beaten and stoned to death. Certain unidentified individuals then dragged Shiianov's body to a piece of wasteland and set light to it.[68]

The incident points to a surprising breakdown in law and order with the police powerless to restore peace to the city streets or even protect the courthouse. This rapid escalation of crowd violence following a local incident has some parallels with the uprisings that were to occur a few years later in the towns of Aleksandrov and Murom in Vladimir oblast.[69] There were very sig-

[67] Weiner, "The Empires Pay a Visit," 369–370.

[68] GARF f. 9401, op. 2, d. 492, ll. 63–64.

[69] Disorders occurred in the cities of Murom and Aleksandrov in Vladimir oblast over the summer of 1961. The cities were just over 100 km from Moscow, the nearest that former prisoners with passport restrictions could get to the capital, and this meant that both places had a larger than average contingent of returnees. In Murom the police's decision to arrest a worker injured during a drunken accident, and then to let him perish untreated in his cell, led to rioting and the storming of the police station. Disorders occurred in Aleksandrov the following month, inspired by events in Murom. See Kozlov, *Mass Uprisings*, 193–214.

nificant differences, however: in place of a crowd that stormed the police station as the site of persecution and the police's *excessive* use of force, as was to happen in Aleksandrov and Murom, here the courtroom was attacked because of the extremely *mild* justice it had meted out. In this case, the local outrage might point to resentment of the power held by a high-ranking figure in the local military who had been able to get off almost scot-free. Another riot that took place three years later clearly suggests, however, that such disorders might rather be the result of popular anger toward the current policies of reduced sentencing.

The incident took place in the Zheleznodorozhnii raion of Cheliabinsk, a large industrial city in the southern Urals. On Monday, 8 August 1960, a group of local residents arrested V. I. Nemytov and locked him into a worker's apartment. Their anger is understandable: a man with several previous convictions, Nemytov had raped a four-year-old girl the previous day. By taking an active role in arresting a criminal, the Cheliabinsk citizens perhaps sought to fulfill their civic duty in the fight against crime. Yet there was a twist: the residents refused to hand the man over to the police. A swelling crowd around the apartment prevented police access and demanded the right to hold a *samosud*. According to the report submitted by N. V. Laptev, first secretary of the Cheliabinsk obkom, this demand was "motivated by a lack of faith in the sentences given by judges in similar cases."[70]

By the evening the crowd grew to some 2,000 "workers and housewives." Some of the men wanted to break into the apartment and began attacking the roof and walls of the building. The police were able to prevent them reaching the arrested man, and he managed to escape Shiianov's horrid fate. Yet here too the police clearly struggled to bring order back to the streets. Despite the presence of the police force, 150 members of the *druzhiny,* and several high-ranking figures from the local party apparatus, it was not until ten o'clock at night that the authorities could safely escort Nemytov away from the building.[71] Laptev offered the CC his own interpretation of events:

> In connection with the incident that occurred, I consider it necessary to inform the CC that during my conversations with workers and housewives I was told, as secretary of the party obkom, member of the CC, and deputy to the Supreme Soviet, that people were unhappy with the liberal [*liberal'nye*] decisions of the courts with regard to especially dangerous criminals, especially murderers and rapists. They said that the awarding of milder punishments creates a situation in which especially dangerous criminals can be released early, and that they often commit serious crimes again. There was specific reference to the case of Utkin, who was sentenced in 1954 to ten years' imprisonment for raping women but released early in 1958, when he again committed heinous crimes. The work-

[70] RGASPI f. 556, op. 14, d. 166, l. 57.
[71] RGASPI f. 556, op. 14, d. 166, ll. 57–58.

ers asked me to convey their opinions to the party's CC and ask for more severe and merciless punishment of murderers, bandits, and rapists who are poisoning the life of honest workers.[72]

Laptev's decision to include such analysis of the causes of the unrest in part reflects his own point of view: a report from the MVD was much less sympathetic and made reference to the drunkenness of many of those involved.[73] Laptev agreed with the opinions he had summarized, referring to the "unwarranted mild sentences" which arouse "legitimate indignation toward the Soviet justice system."[74] Noting that in the first half of 1960 there had been an increase in the number of murders, violent assaults, and rapes, he suggested the CC should consider a hardening (*ozhestochenie*) in the way dangerous criminals were treated.

When the Zheleznodorozhnyi raikom met on 17 August 1960, their approach was slightly different.[75] Their emphasis was on the sheer poverty of the area. Referring to the "workers' gathering" of the previous week, the chairman of the raikom's executive committee, Comrade Bashkin, began by criticizing the low levels of political work and the failure of local party and trade union activists to visit local residents, to speak with them, and to explain policies. The party was also failing to respond to workers' complaints regarding their glaringly bad living conditions. Roads were in disrepair, pavements unfinished, workers' barracks decrepit, shop shelves bare (without even basics such as bread, vegetables, kerosene, and milk), and there were no children's play areas. According to Bashkin, crime was a particular problem in this area, with high levels of hooliganism, and no effective *druzhiny* patrols in place.[76] In subsequent meetings, the raikom would return to the issue of crime, the ongoing failure of the voluntary brigades, and the difficulties posed by the presence of the city's major railway station, which not only brought many itinerants to the neighborhood but also provided shelter for them, the empty carriages becoming temporary homes for large numbers of tramps and vagrants.[77] It is not insignificant that those who were most distressed about the apparent breakdown in law and order and the state's failure to punish crime were not necessarily those whose position within the Soviet world was most secure. Rather it was those who lived on the edge, in outlying districts, next to stations, and in poverty, who were most outspoken in their anger.

While the implications of this one incident should not be taken too far, they provide interesting insights into the nature of the "moral panic" that

---

[72] RGASPI f. 556, op. 14, d. 166, l. 58.
[73] RGASPI f. 556, op. 14, d. 166, ll. 60–61.
[74] RGASPI f. 556, op. 14, d. 166, l. 59.
[75] GU OGAChO f. 94, op. 2, d. 399, ll. 138–143.
[76] GU OGAChO f. 94, op. 2, d. 399, ll. 139–140.
[77] GU OGAChO f. 94, op. 2, d. 399, ll. 122–150.

seized Soviet society in the late 1950s and early 1960s. In Cheliabinsk oblast at least, there were other incidents, if less serious. The procurator reported that the oblast court was hearing fewer murder cases in the localities where the crime had been committed because "current sentencing practice does not coincide with public opinion." When judges failed to give the death sentence, the crowd often expressed displeasure. In February 1960, for example, two men and a woman were convicted of murder with intent to steal at a trial held in the city of Bakal and attended by five hundred people. On hearing that none of the three would be given the death sentence, the crowd broke out in loud indignation, some shouting that the offenders would return and slaughter their children, others that the judges themselves should be killed.[78]

The disorders that occurred in both Cheliabinsk and Stalingrad are the other side of the coin to the riots that took place in Murom and Aleksandrov.[79] Instead of resenting the power of the police, the participants railed against what they saw as the weakness of the local authorities and the breakdown of order. By referring to *samosud,* the participants associated their actions with the practices of popular justice that existed under the prerevolutionary regime. If, as Stephen Frank has argued, *samosud* was almost exclusively a rural phenomenon by the end of the nineteenth century, it is surprising to find it occurring in two Soviet cities in the second half of the twentieth century.[80] Their use of the concept appears reluctant, however. According to Frank, peasants believed that the official courts did not punish severely enough, and he suggests the practice of *samosud* was fueled by a sense that "he's our criminal and it's up to us to punish him."[81] Yet such mentalities may have already been on the wane by the turn of the century. Jane Burbank argues that in the years running up to the First World War *samosud* was no longer a dominant feature of rural justice and shows that peasants were turning in droves to the township courts to resolve their legal issues.[82] The inhabitants of Cheliabinsk and Stalingrad certainly had firm ideas about the role the official legal system should be playing and, as modern citizens, they believed law and order were the preserve of the state. Unlike the peasants described by Frank, they did not seem to want to be left to their own devices and were deeply angered that the court system was failing them: as the outbursts in Bakal show, citizens articulated violent anger toward the judges who let them down. Participants in the disorders did not necessarily

---

[78] GU OGAChO f. 288, op. 24, d. 108, ll. 24–25.

[79] There was at least one other case in which *samosud* was demanded. This occurred in the city of Minsk, but during recent visits to Moscow the pages of the file were unavailable. See GARF f. 9401, op. 2, d. 505, ll. 241–243.

[80] Stephen P. Frank, "Popular Justice, Community, and Culture among the Russian Peasantry," *Russian Review* 46 (1987): 239–265 (240).

[81] Ibid., 260.

[82] Jane Burbank, *Russian Peasants Go to Court: Legal Culture in the Countryside, 1905–1917* (Bloomington, 2004).

want to be involved in administering justice, but in moments of rage they invoked the prerevolutionary notion of *samosud* to protest against state policies that they believed put ordinary citizens at risk.

From Redemption to Excision Once More

In 1960, a year after the introduction of the new measures, law-enforcement officials noted some worrying trends. The Moscow procurator recorded a rise in the number of crimes committed in the city in 1960, and in the oblast the number of crimes had increased by 27 percent in just one year.[83] In the city of Cheliabinsk, the first half of 1960 saw the number of crimes committed rise by a staggering 36 percent in comparison with the preceding six months. For the whole of the RSFSR the rise was rather less dramatic, though still a substantial 5.4 percent.[84] Over the first half of 1960, the recorded number of grievous bodily harm incidents in Russia had increased by 31.2 percent compared with the second half of 1959, while theft was up by 36 percent.[85]

Not for the first time, officials pointed the finger at returnees, and specifically at those who had been released by the 14 August 1959 decree. The Moscow procurator noted that of all the crimes committed in Moscow 42 percent were by previous offenders and 17 percent by those released by the August resolution.[86] Dudorov, minister of the interior, was also concerned about the impact of the latest round of releases. In a report to the CC on 24 December 1959, he recounted a whole stream of incidents in which recent returnees had been rearrested, often for quite serious crimes.[87] The extent to which the release of small-time offenders in the second half of 1959 actually contributed to the following year's rise in crime is debatable, but, as ever, the return of prisoners was one of the favored explanations put forward.

The new sentencing practices were also identified as a key factor. As we have seen, there were particular doubts about the practice of placing offenders under the guardianship of their workplace collective, local Komsomol cell, or other social organizations instead of a custodial sentence. The procurator of Cheliabinsk oblast blamed the rise in crime on those returning from the camps and on the failure of the *poruka* system and noted that by August 1960, 92 of the 2,016 people passed on for *poruka* in the first half of 1960 had already reoffended.[88] One might question the significance of these figures, as they suggest that in Cheliabinsk under 5 percent of those

[83] GARF f. 8131, op. 32, d. 6612, l. 28.
[84] GU OGAChO f. 288, op. 24, d. 108.
[85] RGASPI f. 556, op. 23, d. 106, cited in Gorlizki, "Delegalization in Russia," 418.
[86] GARF f. 8131, op. 32, d. 6612, ll. 2–3.
[87] GARF f. 9401, op. 2, d. 507, l. 85.
[88] GU OGAChO f. 288, op. 24, d. 108.

placed under probationary guardianship reoffended. The figure was even lower elsewhere. In Moscow only 2.5 percent of those placed under the *poruka* system in 1960 reoffended in the following months (though the procurator warned that the figures were incomplete).[89] In the Soviet Union as a whole, figures suggest that only 0.8 percent of those under *poruka* in 1960 had reoffended.[90]

Considering the climate of doubt and uncertainty among those charged with implementing the new practices, it is perhaps unsurprising, however, that the innovative measures introduced in 1959 were blamed when things went wrong. In addition to the difficulties they encountered in their work, law-enforcement officials could not help but be aware of the public's anxieties surrounding the new criminal justice policies. In addition to the rumors and opinions that they—like any Soviet citizen—might hear from friends, acquaintances, or neighbors, they were also privy to the growing number of letters that the Supreme Soviet and various party organs received, read, and processed in the 1950s. The authorities seemed to take the views of their correspondents seriously. In December 1957 Voroshilov considered a letter from the Institute of Mining of sufficient importance to forward it to the general procurator, the minister of the interior, the chairman of the KGB, and the chairman of the Supreme Court.[91] By 1958 officials at the Supreme Soviet charged with handling these letters believed the increased correspondence worthy of a memo to the CC and drew attention to the worrying levels of crime across the nation and the public outrage that accompanied it.[92] On 7 March 1961 senior officials within the Supreme Soviet wrote to Leonid Brezhnev, Voroshilov's successor as chairman, voicing concerns about both crime itself and the epistolary outcry it had generated. Initially praising the measures adopted in 1959, they swiftly moved on to doubt their effectiveness, noting rising crime in 1960 and the accompanying influx of letters, mostly coming from large industrial cities in Russia and Ukraine. This led them to question the practices of re-education within society. Weak participation on the part of the collective, they wrote, frequently resulted in those on probation reoffending.[93]

The worrying rise in crime recorded in 1960, the uncertainties encountered in the administration and application of the new measures, and the public's lack of enthusiasm for its new role as moral guardians led to a speedy

---

[89] GARF f. 8131, op. 32, d. 6612, l. 9.

[90] GARF f. 8131, op. 32, d. 6588, l. 30.

[91] GARF f. 7523, op. 89, d. 7272, ll. 7–8. Serov (chairman of the KGB), Vasil'ev (deputy minister of the interior), Rudenko (general procurator), and Gorkin (chairman of the USSR Supreme Court) wrote responses to the letter. No one endorsed the call for greater use of the death penalty. Both Gorkin and Rudenko emphasized the need for greater involvement of the community (*obshchestvennost'*) and greater attention to cultural, educational work (*kul'turno-vospitatel'naia rabota*).

[92] GARF f. 7523, op. 89, d. 7266, l. 21.

[93] GARF f. 7523, op. 95, d. 99, ll. 49–53.

rejection of the new policies. By 1961 the heyday of re-education *within* society was already over. The years 1961–1962 saw a raft of laws and decrees that included the extension of the death penalty, lengthening of prison sentences, the decline of the *poruka* system, and a campaign to banish all those who acted as "parasites" on society's healthy body.

In the new Criminal Code introduced in the RSFSR in 1960 the death penalty was applicable to a range of political acts (treason, espionage, terrorism, participation in anti-Soviet organizations) as well as to banditry, intentional homicide committed under aggravating circumstances, and certain crimes committed in time of war or in a combat situation. In 1961 and 1962 new legislation extended its use to include disrupting work within corrective labor institutions, making or passing counterfeit money, violating rules on currency transactions, stealing state or social property on an especially large scale, committing rape, receiving bribes, and taking or attempting to take the life of a policeman or *druzhinnik*.[94] The last amendment, introduced in February 1962, was soon used freely: in the following month, twenty-one people were convicted under the new clause, and in April 1962 as many as eighty-five.[95] The *druzhinniki* were once more encouraged to become action heroes; they must stop the criminal in his tracks at all costs, even when this led to a fatal shoot-out.[96]

The use of custodial sentences rose rapidly. In a report written in June 1962, Rudenko spoke of a new direction in criminal justice practice in the second half of 1961 that corrected earlier errors, in particular rulings that gave serious recidivists overly "liberal" sentences while first-time, petty offenders had often been given unnecessary prison terms.[97] In reality there was simply a decline in the use of noncustodial sentences. In 1960, 34 percent of offenders convicted were handed over to comrade courts and collectives for guardianship and re-education, but by the following year only 16 percent benefited from this measure.[98] The crackdown hit minor offenders hard. In 1960 sentences of under a year accounted for 11.7 percent of all convictions, but this figure rose to 18 percent in the first few months of 1961.[99] In 1961 the number of convictions for hooliganism rose by 95.6 percent compared

---

[94] Berman, *Soviet Criminal Law*, 61–62.

[95] GARF f. 8131, op. 32, d. 6748, l. 235.

[96] A pamphlet produced by the Ukrainian MVD criticized several decisions made by local courts in which members of the *druzhiny* had been given custodial sentences for shooting criminals while on duty. Instead, it suggested, they should be rewarded for their bravery. See I. A. Gel'fand and N. T. Kuts, *Neobkhodimaia oborona po sovetskomu ugolovnomu pravu* (Kiev, 1962).

[97] GARF f. 8131, op. 32, d. 6748, l. 241.

[98] GARF f. 8131, op. 32, d. 6748, l. 239. There was significant variation among republics. The community re-education practices were used more extensively in western republics such as Belorussia, Latvia, and Estonia than in Uzbekistan, Azerbaijan, Tadzhikistan, Armenia, and Georgia.

[99] GARF f. 8131, op. 32, d. 6748, l.87.

with the preceding year, while convictions for home-brewing rose nearly fourteen times.[100]

The introduction of antiparasite measures in the RSFSR in 1961 clearly indicated that the small-time offender was going to be hit hard by the new backlash. On 4 May 1961 the law "On Intensifying the Battle against Anti-Social, Parasitic Elements" was finally passed in the RSFSR.[101] As Sheila Fitzpatrick's work indicates, different types of "undesirables" were targeted: the subsidized children of wealthy parents ("gilded youth"), religious sectarians, and those making their living on the "shadow economy," as well as beggars, tramps, and drunks.[102] In its 1961 formulation the standard court system was given responsibility for applying the antiparasite measures to able-bodied people who were without work (and therefore deemed to be making their living illicitly), but the idea of popular participation was retained in the case of people who *did* have employment but who were nonetheless deemed idle and antisocial.[103] A public meeting of workers at the enterprise, workshop, institution, or kolkhoz where the "parasite" was employed had the jurisdiction to send him or her into exile for a period of up to five years (though the conviction had to be formally confirmed by the executive committee of the raion or city soviet).[104] This represented another highly important shift in the way community action was understood. Instead of acting as mentors to the "erring," community activists were now encouraged to act as judge and jury. They could play a decisive role in ejecting undesirables from the Soviet "family."

Party, trade union, and Komsomol meetings were held to discuss the new law, as well as assemblies in the workplace and living quarters.[105] According to a report to the CC following the publication of the antiparasite measures, the Supreme Soviet received many letters from citizens who were delighted by its introduction. Comrade Butenko, a Stalingrader, said: "In fact we couldn't bear it any longer that among the Soviet people marching toward communism, there were all kinds of scoundrels [*proidokhy*] and tricksters [*pronyri*] getting under our feet. They live off the state and don't give anything back. That's why we approve this measure wholeheartedly and will help implement it."[106] Alongside the reams of praise there were also reservations: some people expressed concern that the legislation might be applied

---

[100] GARF f. 8131, op. 32, d. 6748, ll. 85–88.

[101] Harold Berman, *Justice in the USSR: An Interpretation of Soviet Law* (Cambridge, Mass., 1963), 291–298.

[102] Fitzpatrick, "Social Parasites."

[103] R. Beermann, "The Parasites Law," *Soviet Studies* 13 (1961): 191–205.

[104] The fact that community participation was intended is evident in a memo written by Rudenko in July 1963, which expressed disappointment that most of the sentences against parasites were being made though the standard court system and not by the community agencies (GARF f. 8131, op. 32, d. 6913, ll. 122–135).

[105] RGASPI f. 556, op. 14, d. 189, l. 92.

[106] RGASPI f. 556, op. 14, d. 189, l. 92.

to housewives and those who temporarily rented out rooms during the holiday season. The main concern, though, was that the government had still not gone far enough. One Muscovite worried that the government could still do more in the fight against crime, as the decree included the possibility of the exile being shortened as a result of good behavior. A group of letter writers from Kazan' agreed: "Thanks to the word '*dosrochno*' [before the end of the term], courts have long since lost any kind of authority."[107] It seems the practice of exiling small-time offenders was not in itself widely questioned in these public debates.

As with previous reforms, newspapers publicized the new departure in criminal justice policies. The headline "Murderer Shot" reappeared.[108] Following the extension of the death penalty to bribe takers, a high-profile case was chosen for press purposes: the arrest and execution of K. T. Degtiarev, a senior official at the Ministry of Finance who had been convicted of large-scale bribe taking.[109] The small-time offender was given even greater coverage. The introduction of the antiparasite measures brought a whole series of articles in which readers were warned that even small infractions of law and order could lead to the eviction and exile of the perpetrator to distant parts of the country.

The Antiparasite Campaign

As the nation's leading satirical journal, *Krokodil* had been targeting various social ills throughout the 1950s, including both young hooligans and the lazy citizens who turned a blind eye to their misdemeanors.[110] The utopianism of Khrushchev's vision in May 1959 seemed to cause the magazine's editors to take stock; and although they published a long article in defense of satire in the wake of the Third Writers' Congress this was followed by a drought in which hooligans and other offenders were almost entirely absent from the magazine's pages, as if no longer suitable targets for mockery.[111] In the beginning of 1960, however, the problem of crime already re-emerged as a humorous subject. Not only were offenders themselves lampooned, but even the new measures which apparently let them get off so lightly. On 10 Janu-

---

[107] RGANI f. 5, op. 30, d. 373, l. 30.

[108] "Ubiitsa rasstrelian," *Leningradskaia pravda*, 9 June 1962, 4.

[109] On 13 July 1962 Rudenko reported to the CC that Degtiarev had received 26,500 rubles in bribes from people wrongly sentenced for counter-revolutionary crimes who, once rehabilitated, had sought financial compensation for confiscated possessions. Rudenko prepared a short article for the press, though the piece did not make reference to the status of his victims. GARF f. 8131, op. 32, d. 6749, ll. 30–34. For the press coverage, see "Vziatochnik prigovoren k rasstrelu," *Izvestiia*, 26 July 1962, 4.

[110] See, for example, the following articles in *Krokodil*: 10 January 1956, 1; 20 July 1956, 12; 20 July 1956, 13; 10 September 1956, 15; and 30 October 1956, 8.

[111] "Eshche raz o smekhe," *Krokodil*, 20 June 1959, 9.

Fig. 4. "They helped him out," *Krokodil*, 10 January 1960. Courtesy SSEES Library, London.

ary 1960 *Krokodil* criticized collectives for using guardianship as a means to get friends out of hot water (Figure 4). In Russian, the caption is a play on words: instead of "They took him under their guardianship" (*Vziali na poruki*), it reads "They helped him out" (*Vziali na poRUCHKI*).[112]

In February, a cartoon showed how offenders themselves might manipulate the new measures (Figure 5). The caption reads: "Citizens, I am good! Take me under your guardianship!"[113] In October of the same year, a *Krokodil* article entitled "How They Re-educated Me: The Story of a Recidivist," described how a cynical prisoner played on the concept of "humaneness" to take advantage of the new measures.[114]

Newspapers followed a similar pattern. After a summer of propaganda materials proclaiming the merits of re-education, the end of 1959 saw the first tentative challenge to the prevailing rhetoric of rehabilitation. On 20 December 1959 *Moskovskaia pravda* tentatively voiced criticism of the new policies. Under the rubric "From the Courtroom," the story of Pavel Lavrukhin challenged the whole rhetoric of "re-education."[115] A drunkard and hooligan, Lavrukhin had been taken into police custody six times. He

[112] "Vziali na poruchki," *Krokodil*, 10 January 1960, 7.
[113] "Glas vypiiushchego," *Krokodil*, 10 February 1960, 16.
[114] "Kak menia perevospitali: Rasskaz retsidivista," *Krokodil*, 20 October 1960.
[115] "Kogda obshchestvennost' ne mozhet poruchitsia," *Moskovskaia pravda*, 20 December 1959, 3. It is perhaps significant that this article appeared after the negative reports arrived from the provincial procurators in December 1959.

НОМЕРА 1 р. 20 к.

Рисунок Е. ЩЕГЛОВА.

ГЛАС ВЫПИЮЩЕГО...

Fig. 5. "The voice of a drinker," *Krokodil*, 10 February 1960. Courtesy SSEES Library, London.

appeared drunk at work, created scandals at home, and assaulted his neighbors. Despite workplace meetings devoted to his behavior, he failed to change and after a particularly violent evening, he was arrested and sentenced to three years' imprisonment. At odds with the message so often proclaimed in the press articles earlier in 1959, reforming a drunken hooligan was here placed beyond the scope of the collective organs. When the community met to discuss his misdemeanors, Lavrukhin made a "speech of repentance," promising not to touch a drop of vodka ever again but by describing his violently drunken state the very same evening, the article invited the reader to treat such confessions as mere theatrics. At his trial, the accused complained that he "wasn't given a moral education" (*menia ne vospityvali*). In Lavrukhin's mocking manipulation of the rhetoric of "correction," the concept itself was undermined. Just as back-page crime reports had subverted the official commitment to "humanity" in 1953, depicting those amnestied as out-and-out criminals, the rubric now began to question the party's commitment to correction within the community.

The following June an article in *Leningradskaia pravda* entitled "'I Want Probation,'" was even more emphatic.[116] The story told of four offenders who sought to avoid incarceration by persuading their work collective to apply for guardianship over them. The criminals were varied and included the deputy director of a shop who consistently swindled the firm, a burglar, a con man, and a young factory worker who had attacked a group of young girls and threatened to knife them. In each case, the article not only showed how their crimes made them totally unsuitable for rehabilitation within the community but also demonstrated how each offender manipulated the rhetoric of "re-education." The shop deputy director, for instance, begged the local procurator to let him be adopted by his old workplace, asking "Why are you planning to sentence me, if the 'people' [*narod*] will take responsibility for my probation? I need to be re-educated, not judged!" Out of the mouth of such a reprehensible character, the words were clearly meant to be distrusted. Meanwhile the burglar was told to "re-educate himself," but "do it behind bars!" Correction was thus relocated to the site of imprisonment. In the place of the rhetoric of conversion, a highly antagonistic approach was taken to these offenders. The reader was told that the burglar was a "swine who should be isolated from society and punished with all the severity of the law!" Even though the article conceded that, "when a man has stumbled, not understanding that he has erred onto the slippery slope of crime, it is possible and necessary to rehabilitate him within society," it firmly concluded that this "does not mean that we should mollycoddle hardened bandits." While still paying tribute to the practice of social rehabilitation, this 1960 article already began to adopt a position of greater severity, calling for the isolation of bandits and swine.

---

[116] "'Khochu na poruki . . . ,'" *Leningradskaia pravda*, 26 June 1960, 2–3.

By the summer of 1961, newspaper headlines publicized a far more severe rhetoric. Typical articles proclaimed "Parasite, Get out of Leningrad!" and "The People Convict a Parasite."[117] In these tales, the protagonists were not on trial for any specific crime but for their failure to conform to the profile of a good, hard-working citizen. In "Parasite Brought to Justice" the reporter opened with a courtroom scene, pouring scorn on Oleg Oparin for the way he was sitting, his bored expression, and his generally lackadaisical attitude in the courtroom.[118] The reader was told that Oparin had already been sentenced for several crimes in the past, including hooliganism, possession of firearms, and contravention of the passport regime. As he did not have any official work, the court deduced that he must be making money out of illegal activities. His persona and past record were sufficient grounds for exiling him from Leningrad for five years. In "Parasite, Get out of Leningrad!" the leading man was a beneficiary of the 1953 amnesty, and although he was not depicted as a dangerous criminal, this dubious past contributed to his negative profile. Returning to the city, the young man had been repeatedly fired from jobs for drinking and had relied on the limited resources of his aging mother to support his dissolute lifestyle. In both cases, the individual's life story included previous convictions, and this was very important in constructing such people's profile as un-Soviet individuals. Even if they had not committed major new crimes, those once cast out were considered unworthy to be members of the Soviet family.

The type of negative behavior the "parasite" demonstrated was often little different from the protagonist's transgressions in the conversion tales of 1959. With a previous conviction for hooliganism, Anatolii Selenkov, the antihero in "The People Convict a Parasite" was already a marked man. His antisocial activities were catalogued: he rarely stayed more than a few days at one job; he stole his mother's belongings and sold them at the market; he drank heavily and beat his mother and wife. These might contravene Soviet laws and norms, but in 1959 a newspaper article might easily have told of Selenkov's reprehensible actions and subsequent rehabilitation. No longer was he offered the sanctuary of "correction" or "re-education." When the collective met to judge him, one factory worker spoke out against him, shouting, "He has lost his conscience. My opinion is this: parasite—get out of Leningrad!" There was no longer any hope of a sinner reforming, and he must be ejected from the Soviet city.

"Parasite—get out of Leningrad!" (or Moscow, Dnepropetrovsk, Stalingrad, etc.) became a frequent formulation. The imagined Soviet realm was once more divided into two "zones"—one an urban enclave for decent, hard-working Soviet citizens, the other an ill-defined wilderness for offend-

---

[117] "Narod sudit tuneiadtsa," *Leningradskaia pravda,* 7 June 1961, 4; "Tuneiadets von iz Leningrada!" *Leningradskaia pravda,* 17 July 1961, 4.
[118] "Tuneiadets privlechen k otvetsvennosti," *Moskovskaia pravda,* 3 June 1961, 4.

ers, parasites, and all other undesirables. This new topography pointed to a general decline of the more radical aspects of reform. Belief in the inherent goodness of every Soviet citizen, however much he had erred, lost out to widespread fears of social degeneration.

In 1953 "socialist legality" referred to the new controls placed on the legal and security apparatus and the end to arbitrary terror. This meaning resurfaced in the early 1960s with new campaigns to ensure that the police and judicial system acted in full accordance with the law.[119] Yet in the utopian days of 1959 "socialist legality" had acquired additional meanings. At that point, the term was also used to refer to the new measures aimed at correcting the offender *within* society: comrade courts, *druzhiny,* and non-custodial guardianship of offenders were coordinated by the "commissions for socialist legality." The notion that "socialist legality" was about non-custodial, prophylactic measures was called into question by 1962. Detailing a workplace scam in which crooks underweighed products and pocketed the spare, one journalist wrote: "When these and other criminals were punished with all the severity of the law, they began to scribble off petitions, reckoning [*spekuliruia*] on the words "legality" [*zakonnost'*], humaneness [*gumannost'*], and so on. But in fact they were sentenced for the sake of socialist legality, for the sake of genuine humaneness and justice."[120] Ridiculing the offenders' invocation of legality and humanity as acts of cunning and deceit, the author of the article claimed that maintaining "socialist legality" was more about enforcing strict discipline than about ensuring due process. A similar pattern emerged with the concept of "humaneness": where once being humane meant extending sympathy to the offender, this article now suggested that "humaneness" was about protecting the average citizen from any possible danger. With this shift, the derision some citizens had expressed toward the notion of "humaneness" ever since 1953 had finally made its way into print.

Popular anxieties about crime and social breakdown were perhaps unsurprising considering the recent experience of total war and the fragile nature of postwar stability. One letter writer complained about pickpocketing: "In no other country is there so much theft. The only solution is to shoot them. This is a contagion [*zaraza*]. We work for 300 rubles a month, and they deprive us of a crust of bread."[121] Such sentiments, articulated in letters to the authorities and in occasional outbursts of crowd disorder, could not easily be ignored. The new measures could succeed only with social support: if vol-

---

[119] On 30 June 1962 the general procurator of the USSR issued an order entitled "On Measures to further Improve the Procuracy's Work in the Fight against Crime and Violations of Legality," targeting policemen and procuracy workers who allowed citizens to be unlawfully arrested (GARF f. 8131, op. 32, d. 6911, ll. 12–19).

[120] "Poimany!" *Leningradskaia pravda,* 15 June 1962, 3.

[121] GARF f. 7523, op. 107, d. 191, l. 5.

untary initiatives were to successfully play the role ascribed to them in 1959, then widespread enthusiasm for the *perevospitanie* project was needed. According to the reports made by law-enforcement officials, such enthusiasm was at best sporadic. Moreover, although they expressed themselves in rather different ways, law-enforcement officials were not immune to these anxieties. The task of distinguishing the small-time offender who could still be saved from the dangerous recidivist who must be banished seemed a daunting one. When the number of registered crimes exploded in 1960 it confirmed their doubts: Soviet society was not yet ready for this next step toward the communist utopia.

While the policy shift of the early 1960s has long been noted in the criminal justice literature, it has remained largely absent from more general accounts of the period.[122] It seems to go against the grain of everything that is normally associated with the Twenty-Second Party Congress, apparently the highpoint of de-Stalinization. In fact, key aspects of de-Stalinization were already being revoked by 1961. If the release of prisoners and the massive downsizing of the Gulag are to be considered important elements in Khrushchev's reform package, then it is significant the earlier trends were being reversed in 1961, the year he was understood to be at the peak of his political career. In 1960 the number of prisoners in corrective labor institutions had been at its lowest in thirty-five years (550,882), but by 1961 it was back up to 674,080 and by early 1962 had reached as high as 968,080.[123]

---

[122] Berman, *Soviet Criminal Law*, 60–64; Berman, *Justice in the USSR*, 85–86; Yoram Gorlizki, "De-Stalinisation and the Politics of Russian Criminal Justice, 1953–1964," Ph.D. Diss., University of Oxford, 1992, 114–118; Makepeace, *Marxist Ideology*, 262.

[123] GARF f. 7523, op. 95, d. 109, ll. 25–27.

III
A FRAGILE SOLUTION?

From the Twenty-Second Party Congress

to Khrushchev's Ouster

7 *1961*

Clearing a Path to the Future

> The party proudly proclaims: Today's generation of Soviet people
> will live under communism.
>
> —"Program of the Communist Party of the Soviet Union,"
> *Pravda*, 30 July 1961

In July 1957 a *listovka* was stuck to a post in a Kursk park. The leaflet read:

> Comrade Communists, Komsomol members, citizens! When they say on the ra-
> dio that all communists and all the people unanimously approve the Central
> Committee resolution on the antiparty activities of Comrades Molotov, Malen-
> kov, and Kaganovich, they are lying. The majority of communists and citizens
> do not believe the plenum's decree. It is the work of the adventurist [*avantiurist*]
> Khrushchev. Communists vote in favor only because they are afraid of being ex-
> pelled.[1]

On 16 March 1958, on the day elections were being held for the Supreme
Soviet, two anti-Soviet *listovki* were hung up at Vologda station. One read:
"We hate the party. The party has insulted its best sons like Stalin, Malenkov,
Molotov, Zhukov, and others, and now it is conspiring against the people of
all countries. Down with Khrushchev, Mikoian, Pospelov." Nearby, another
read: "Comrades! Khrushchev is soon going to have a child. His belly is big-

---

[1] GARF f. 8131, op. 31, d. 80406, ll. 18–19. The culprit was sentenced to ten years' imprisonment under article 58–10, with an additional year for a pistol discovered at his home
during the arrest. In November 1957 the Supreme Court decided to reduce the ten-year sentence to three (l. 23).

ger than that of a pregnant woman."[2] The two authors were very different: the author of the first was Iosif Snegirev, a party member in his late forties who had served in the Soviet army for twenty-four years; the second was nineteen-year-old Valentin Kushkov who, though a trained metalworker, was currently without a job or fixed abode. They expressed their ideas in quite different ways, one focusing on responses within the party, the other expressing a more visceral animosity toward the new leader. Yet both were distressed not only by Stalin's demotion but also by the subsequent attacks on his former colleagues.

Molotov, Malenkov, and Kaganovich were dismissed from both the Presidium and the CC on 29 June 1957 and lost their posts in the Council of Ministers on the same day.[3] The content of the decree was published on the front page of *Pravda* on 4 July 1957. The newspaper told its readers that over the previous three to four years, while most of the party leaders had been actively correcting mistakes and inadequacies generated by the cult of personality, the members of the antiparty group had sought to subvert this new direction.[4] This attack on three of Stalin's former colleagues often seems overshadowed by the preceding year's Secret Speech, yet its implications were also highly disturbing. By demoting these former heroes, the CC brought into question the honor and reputation of a whole generation of leaders. At a party meeting in Sverdlov oblast, a physical education teacher said that he agreed with the resolution against the antiparty group but could no longer believe in the CC. The party leadership no longer held any "authority" (*avtoritet*) for him.[5] Many were simply confused: did this make Stalin less, or more, guilty? Was Stalin an enemy or a genius? Were the lower

---

[2] Valentin Kushkov admitted to writing the *listovki* and was sentenced to seven years' imprisonment (GARF f. 8131, op. 31, d. 85245, ll. 1–3).

[3] Malenkov had been deputy chairman of the Council of Ministers and minister of electric power stations; now he was made director of a hydroelectric power station in northern Kazakhstan. Kaganovich was demoted from his positions as minister for the building materials industry, chairman of the State Committee for Work and Salaries, and deputy chairman of the Supreme Soviet to take over the directorship of a group of asbestos-producing enterprises in the Southern Urals. Molotov, deputy chairman of the Soviet of National Commissars and minister of state control, was sent to Mongolia as Soviet ambassador. Others were also disgraced. D. T. Shepilov's positions as a candidate member of the Presidium and as full member of the CC Secretariat were both revoked, M. G. Pervukhin was demoted from full member to candidate member of the Presidium, M. Z. Saburov was removed from the Presidium, and N. A. Bulganin was issued a "severe reprimand" and warning by the plenum. See "'Tovarishch Kaganovich pretenduet na osoboe k sebe otnoshenie': Ural'skaia ssylka opal'nogo soratnika I. V. Stalina. 1957–1958 gg.," *Istoricheskii arkhiv* (July–August 2005): 4–26; Artizov et al., eds., *Reabilitatsiia: Kak eto bylo*, vol. 2, 866–867; N. Kovaleva, A. Korotkov, S. Mel'chin, Iu. Sigachev, and A. Stepanov, eds., *Molotov, Malenkov, Kaganovich. 1957. Stenogramma iiun'skogo plenuma TsK KPSS i drugie dokumenty* (Moscow, 1998).

[4] "Postanovlenie plenuma TsK KPSS ob antipartiinoi gruppe Malenkova G. M., Kaganovicha L. M., Molotova V. M.," *Pravda*, 4 July 1957, 1.

[5] "Tovarishch Kaganovich pretenduet," 13.

ranks of the party going to be purged as in 1937–1938? How, and why, had the defects of these leading party figures come to light only now?[6]

As after the Secret Speech, meetings were held at every level of the party hierarchy to explain these political developments in more depth. The kind of distress articulated by Snegirev and Kushkov was also palpable at many of these gatherings. At a joint meeting for communists at the Khrushchev Collective Farm and a nearby MTS (Machine Tractor Station) in Tambov oblast, a mechanic, a joiner, and a tractor driver did their utmost to disrupt proceedings throughout, with the mechanic eventually shouting: "In this county there is no democracy. I'll say this openly—let them convict me! The CC Plenum was undemocratic. I don't believe the CC Plenum. Let Malenkov, Kaganovich, Molotov speak on the radio and admit their mistakes."[7] At a party meeting in Iaroslavl', a Komsomol secretary defied the CC line, arguing that the three ex-leaders were highly popular and had done a great deal for the "people," citing Malenkov's lowering of agricultural taxes.[8] Dissension was not always limited to one or two lone voices but even came to dominate at some meetings. At the Voroshilov factory in Kuibyshev the meeting had to be abandoned completely. During the speeches, all carefully choreographed beforehand, several notes were passed up from the floor from a young worker named Lazarev who wanted to speak. Frustrated at being ignored, he jumped onto the platform and demanded to be heard, receiving noisy support from some sections of the audience. Despite attempts to bring the meeting to order, the audience refused to be quiet, demanding that Molotov be allowed to speak on the radio or visit the factory in person. Only then, they said, could they decide if the CC plenum decree was correct or not. The meeting was cut short, and the microphones switched off to prevent any more impromptu speeches.[9]

Of course, most party meetings ultimately came up with the right answers. A report on the outcome of the meetings submitted to the CC on 26 July 1957 stated that 3,771,352 had voted in favor of the plenum's decision, with only 20 voting against, and 243 refraining from voting.[10] Yet even where the

---

[6] On 24 July 1957 Penza obkom submitted several pages to the CC listing the different questions being asked at party meetings. See RGASPI f. 556, op. 14, d. 73, ll. 80–96.

[7] RGASPI f. 556, op. 14, d. 72, l. 8.

[8] RGASPI f. 556, op. 14, d. 73, l. 252.

[9] It is difficult to know why workers at this one factory should prove so much more subversive than at another. The party officials believed Molotov's visit to the factory in 1955 was the cause of the workers' loyalty toward him (RGASPI f. 556, op. 14, d. 72, ll. 12–15).

[10] The report, produced by V. Churaev, head of the Party Organization Department of the CC CPSU for the Russian Federation, focused on the primary meetings held in factories, collective farms, MTS, state farms, and institutions in the Russian Federation. A total of 3,771,615 communists had attended meetings, 84.6% of the members and candidate members registered for these party cells. Meetings remained to be held at 4,411 primary organizations, mostly based in schools and educational institutes, as many members were on vacation (RGASPI f. 556, op. 14, d. 72, ll. 2–10).

decision was approved, meetings were not necessarily harmonious occasions. In fact, many meetings went much further in their condemnation of the antiparty group than the CC had stipulated. The initiative taken at lower levels of the party is perhaps surprising: almost a third of primary party meetings passed resolutions asking the CC to exclude the members of the antiparty group from the party. A further 7 percent requested that the CC dealt with the guilt of Malenkov, Kaganovich, and Molotov more severely, believing that they should be brought to justice for their role in the purges.[11] The calls for retributive justice heard at some obkom and gorkom meetings in 1956 became more widespread now that the party had identified culprits. At the Kirov factory, also in Leningrad, where 2,100 communists met to hear Kozlov's address, a lathe operator said: "A poisonous snake has wormed its way into the CC and the Presidium. First we need to destroy the snake's head, but we should not leave its tail. . . . Putilovite-Bolsheviks were, and will be, the stronghold of communism."[12]

Not all party members were so bellicose. Many were simply uncertain what to make of the situation, wondering why, if the crimes of the accused were as heinous as suggested, the CC had not advocated more radical action. During a joint meeting held for various medical institutes in Iaroslavl' oblast, a proposed resolution asking the CC to exclude Molotov, Malenkov, and Kaganovich from the party was put to the vote; of the 138 attending, only 24 voted, the vast majority abstaining. At a factory meeting in the same oblast, a certain Kirillov refused to vote, saying that the CC knew best what measures should be taken.[13] Demands for more information, which were articulated in the wake of the Twentieth Party Congress, resurfaced stronger than ever. Many asked whether the disgraced former leaders would be able to speak on the radio.[14] One communist from Iaroslavl' oblast asked: "Why did Comrades Molotov, Kaganovich, and Malenkov not speak on the radio? Why did they not confess their incorrect behavior to the people, so that the people could judge their actions?"[15] In Molotov oblast, another party member asked why the newspapers included speeches only from Khrushchev and not from Molotov, Kaganovich, and Malenkov. Surely people should be allowed to read the speeches themselves and make up their own minds, he argued.[16] As in the 1930s when prized heroes were suddenly unmasked as enemies, people expressed disbelief that former leaders could fall from grace so quickly.[17] Perhaps now people's incredulity was even greater because the

[11] RGASPI f. 556, op. 14, d. 72, l. 4.

[12] RGASPI f. 556, op. 14, d. 72, l. 174.

[13] RGASPI f. 556, op. 14, d. 73, l. 252.

[14] RGASPI f. 556, op. 14, d. 73, l. 81 (report from Penza obkom); RGASPI f. 556, op. 14, d. 73, l. 9 (report from Magadan obkom).

[15] RGASPI f. 556, op. 14, d. 73, l. 255.

[16] RGASPI f. 556, op. 14, d. 73, l. 25.

[17] On reactions to the arrest of party leaders in the 1930s, see Sarah Davies, *Popular Opinion in Stalin's Russia: Terror, Propaganda, Dissent, 1934–1941* (Cambridge, 1997), 118–119.

accusations against the erstwhile leaders were oblique and their status—chastened but not condemned—equivocal.

For four years, these questions were left hanging. From mid-1957 until the buildup to the Twenty-Second Party Congress, the party leadership remained largely silent on the subject of Stalin's reputation, the status of the antiparty group, the terror, and the fate of purge victims.[18] At the Twenty-Second Party Congress, Khrushchev once more condemned the three leaders of the antiparty group, focusing in particular on their role in the purges of 1936–1938. Khrushchev remained moderate in the language he employed, but other speakers at the tribune were less restrained. A leading figure in the Kazakh party raged: "The members of the antiparty group have been called dogmatists. This is correct. But what they tried to do in June 1957 was not dogmatism, it was banditry, it was robbery in broad daylight [*razboi sredi belogo dnia*]. And for robbery we need to respond with all the severity the law allows."[19] The editor of *Pravda* went further still, calling them "swamp creatures grown used to slime and dirt."[20]

In many of the party meetings that followed, demands for the three men to be excluded from the party or even put on trial were once more articulated. At the meetings of the Ivanovo obkom, one pensioner shared his reminiscences of Kaganovich's role in the local purges, finishing his speech with a call for all three to be charged. As the meeting drew to a close, the delegates voted for all three to be excluded from the party and for Kaganovich, whose role was so significant in the Ivanovo party repressions, to be charged.[21] Demanding that this "beast in human form be sentenced," one delegate anonymously declared that Kaganovich's deeds were not "mistakes" but "crimes against the people and against the fatherland, the like of which have not been seen since the Middle Ages."[22] At the meeting of the Moscow obkom, delegates also proposed that the members of the antiparty group be put on trial for committing such "grave crimes." When party activists met in the town of Vyborg, Kondukov, a retired railway worker and party member since 1917, talked of the "unlawful acts" Kaganovich had committed, concluding: "Kaganovich, Malenkov, and Molotov's hands are stained with the blood of many honorable and loyal Soviet people. I propose excluding Kaganovich, Malenkov, and Molotov from the party and handing them over to the people's court."[23] Although calls for these three men to be

---

[18] A careful reader of the Soviet press could find references to the purge victims, though not generally in the main newspapers such as *Pravda* and *Izvestiia*. Encyclopedias began to include entries on party figures purged under Stalin, while historians started to reintegrate the names of revolutionary and Civil War heroes wiped out during the Stalinist terror into their accounts. See Albert P. Van Goudoever, *The Limits of Destalinisation in the Soviet Union: Political Rehabilitations in the Soviet Union since Stalin*, trans. Frans Hijkoop (London, 1986), 101–117.

[19] "Rech' tovarishcha N. N. Rodionova," *Pravda*, 31 October 1961, 3.

[20] Cited in Taubman, *Khrushchev*, 514.

[21] RGANI f. 5, op. 32, d. 174, l. 178.

[22] RGANI f. 5, op. 32, d. 174, l. 179.

[23] RGANI f. 5, op. 32, d. 175, l. 116.

put on trial were not met, the process of expelling them from the party began almost immediately after the congress. Kaganovich and Malenkov were out by the end of the year. The holder of party card number 00000005, Viacheslav Molotov, appealed, but without success, and he was stripped of his membership in the summer of 1962.[24]

The other pressing issue for the party leadership was still Stalin's body. In the wake of the Secret Speech, many people had asked for it to be removed from the Mausoleum and now, in the course of the Twenty-Second Party Congress, the body was reburied in the wall of the Kremlin. Stalin's body was thus not cast out entirely but relegated to a site symbolically on the margins of Red Square's sacred space. This move went at least some way to resolving the confusion of 1956. Stalin's new location came closer to what Khrushchev was trying to say: Stalin was not an enemy of the people, but he was by no means a hero of Lenin's ilk.

This was momentous stuff: by the end of 1961 Stalin's body had been removed from the Mausoleum, leading Bolshevik heroes had been forced out of the party in disgrace, and the subject of the terror had entered the realm of permitted discourse. Without a doubt, some communists were distressed by the new course of action. In the case of Boris Livanov, for example, the congress proved the final straw. Having served in both the army and party ranks for many years, Livanov was an exemplary communist, and in the mid-1950s he had given up his cushy Kiev life to volunteer as a thirty-thousander.[25] Yet even as he was transforming the kolkhoz he had been assigned (once considered a backward, undisciplined failure) into a so-called "millionaire-farm" praised in the local press, he had begun nurturing grave doubts about the course the party leadership was taking. In January 1962 this devoted communist cut out a photograph from the newspaper *Sel'skaia zhizn'*, drew on a gallows and hangman's noose, scribbled slanderous comments and death threats toward "one of the leaders" (presumably Khrushchev), and sent it on to the editors of *Pravda*.[26] Following his conviction under article 58, Livanov wrote a petition to Khrushchev in which he reported that among his fellow prisoners there were several long-standing party members, a well-known partisan fighter, and two retired colonels driven to commit political offenses by their frustration with de-Stalinization.[27] A deep sense of anger and distress must have motivated these loyal party men to re-

---

[24] RGANI f. 6, op. 5, d. 607, l. 34, 140–160, reproduced in Artizov et al., eds., *Reabilitatsiia: Kak eto bylo*, vol. 2, 378–392.

[25] The thirty-thousanders campaign sent cadres with a higher and specialized education into the countryside. See Cynthia S. Kaplan, "The Communist Party of the Soviet Union and Local Policy Implementation," *Journal of Politics* 45 (1983): 2–27 (17).

[26] GARF f. 8131, op. 31, d. 93800.

[27] GARF f. 8131, op. 31, d. 93800, ll. 23–25. For the case of one of the retired colonels he mentions, see GARF f. 8131, op. 31, d. 92549.

sort to such actions, but their discontent does not seem to have been articulated openly within the ranks of the party. Although the records of party meetings in 1956 and 1957 describe unpredictable and even unruly occasions, reports describe rather more restrained responses from the party ranks in 1961.[28] It was not a sign of consensus necessarily but a reflection of the much clearer guidelines that the party leadership had now provided for its members.

The speeches made at the Twenty-Second Party Congress, then reproduced in all main organs of the Soviet press, contained far less that could shock their audience, for much had been presaged in the revelations of 1956–1957. Although there was some variation in the way the leaders spoke of the members of the antiparty group—and some leading figures found it impossible to eschew Stalinist demonizing practices in speaking of these "swamp creatures"—a common line on the terror was presented. For the first time since Stalin's death, the leadership made a concerted effort to provide its citizens with a coherent set of myths about the Soviet past, which it linked into a clear and appealing vision of the future. The errors of the past were not to be a source of shame but part of the Soviet Union's trajectory toward the shining future.

The Congress: A Roadmap to the Future

As first secretary and the party's appointed exegete, it was incumbent on Khrushchev to interpret the repressions in a way that confirmed the party's odyssey toward communism.[29] In 1961 he embraced this task with new conviction. In his speeches at the Twenty-Second Party Congress, Khrushchev constructed a coherent eschatological myth in which revelations about the terror fortified the party in its struggle toward the communist utopia. Rather than detailing the flaws in Stalin's character, Khrushchev simply labeled him a "brake" (*tormoz*), whose guilt lay in slowing the party in its inexorable journey forward.[30] Commending the party for courageously correcting its wrong turns (*izvrashcheniia*) and returning to the path set by Lenin, he condemned the antiparty group for trying to divert the course of revolution. Successful revolution involved three stages, he reminded the congress: first, the overthrow of the exploiters and the establishment of the dictatorship of the

[28] Polly Jones also suggests that the party meetings of 1961 were calmer than those of 1956 in her "From the Secret Speech," 55.

[29] According to Igal Halfin, "the Marxist metanarrative assigned a beginning and end to history and marked out the landmarks between the two points," and so, "no event escaped the Marxist eschatological prism" (*From Darkness to Light: Class, Consciousness, and Salvation in Revolutionary Russia* [Pittsburgh, 2000], 8–9).

[30] "Doklad N. S. Khrushcheva," *Pravda*, 18 October 1961, 9.

proletariat; second, the building of socialism; and third, the creation of communist society. Identifying the Soviet Union's location on the timeline, he told his audience that "our party and people have already completed the first two stages," and he attributed their successes to the fact that the party had a "faithful compass" (*vernyi kompas*)—the doctrines of Marxism-Leninism.[31] In the press the congress was repeatedly labeled a "compass" or "beacon."[32] The Twenty-Second Party Congress was thus presented as a key landmark: truth was restored, Lenin revived, and the relentless advance toward the communist future back on track. After the doctrinal uncertainties engendered by the Secret Speech, the party once more had a roadmap directing them toward the communist paradise they sought.

Throughout his speeches, Khrushchev consistently presented history as a journey, using topographical metaphors to show the party moving forward. The cult of personality was presented as a dangerous leg of that journey, but one that had now been successfully traversed. In his concluding speech, Khrushchev said: "The time will come when we will all die, for we are all mortal. Until then we must do our work, and we can and must tell the party and the people the truth. We need to do this so that nothing like this can ever be repeated."[33] Khrushchev's emphasis on individual mortality served to remind the party of its own *im*mortality: repetition of the past was impossible, history was linear, the ranks of the party were moving collectively and inexorably toward the promised future. As in revolutionary lore, the individual may die, but the party lives on, going forward to the light of communism. Khrushchev's sound bite would be repeated frequently over the coming months.

Inspired by Khrushchev, many leading party members made sense of the horrors of the party's past by locating them on the historical timeline. At the congress, P. N. Demichev, first secretary of the Moscow gorkom, claimed that the party had traversed a "difficult but glorious and victorious path" (*nelegkii, no slavnyi pobednyi put'*). He continued: "the Party Program has opened up even wider horizons before the people. It is almost as if Soviet people have grown wings on their backs."[34] Perhaps inspired by cosmonaut German Titov's recent achievement, Demichev drew on the prevalent images of flight, imagining the boundless horizons opening up to the Soviet people.[35] Yet he also rendered the "difficult" past a source of pride: having sur-

---

[31] "Doklad N. S. Khrushcheva," *Pravda*, 19 October 1961, 1.

[32] For example, on 18 November 1961 *Pravda* carried an article on the Twenty-Second Party Congress written by a Canadian communist entitled "Workers' Beacon." On 14 October 1961 the *Pravda* front page depicted a large ship, called Lenin, sailing through rocky seas. From the ship, searchlights are directed upward to form the letters XXII against the night sky, across which whiz three rockets. Next to it, read the headline "Faithful Compass."

[33] Tvardovskii's preface to "One Day in the Life of Ivan Denisovich," *Novyi mir* (November 1962): 8.

[34] "Rech' tovarishcha P. N. Demicheva," *Pravda*, 20 October 1961, 2.

[35] German Stepanovich Titov piloted the Vostok-2 spacecraft, launched on 6 August 1961.

vived an arduous stage on the journey toward the light, the party had new reason to be confident in the legitimacy of its mission. The first secretary of Ukraine, N. V. Podgornyi, used similar formulations: "We communists are proud that the honor fell to us to build mankind's bright future. Whatever kind of obstacles we encounter on the way, they will be overcome, because our party is the party of Lenin, the party of unstoppable movement forward, the party of victory in the name of communism and the happiness of all the people of the earth."[36] Reiterating the inexorable nature of their mission, these leading communists assured their audience that the dismantling of the personality cult confirmed the party's capacity to overcome any difficulties placed in its way.

All across the Soviet Union, party meetings appropriated these myths of fortitude and reiterated their faith in the advent of the communist future. At the Amur obkom meeting, for instance, the party secretary was jubilant that by criticizing the cult of personality and overcoming the distortions and mistakes of the past, the party had ensured a better future.[37] A letter from Tambov party members embraced the new eschatology even more euphorically. The gorkom wrote to Moscow commending the congress's repudiation of the cult of personality, adding that now "the path has been cleared for an even quicker advance forward toward communism."[38] In some meetings, accounts of the purges at local level were given. In Tula an obkom secretary, Mochalov, praised the Party Program as a "true compass," before recounting the arrest and shooting of twenty-four high-ranking obkom figures, an atrocity in which Malenkov had played a key role. Mochalov noted that since the Twentieth Party Congress, two hundred members had been readmitted to the party in Tula oblast, some of them posthumously.[39] Both terror and rehabilitation were presented as completed stages in the party's history.

For the first time since Stalin's funeral, party leaders staged a confident and reassuring performance, and members of the public responded emotionally. When the Martirosian family in Moscow wrote to Khrushchev telling him "we have just listened to your concluding speech on the radio, and listened to your every word without breathing," they might easily have been describing their response to Molotov's graveside speech in 1953.[40] Others explicitly stated that their greatest joy lay in the fact that the official sources now seemed to give them a clear and comprehensible message.[41] On 28 October 1961 R. Shtil'mark wrote: "Why should I hide it? I'm writing, and

---

[36] "Rech' N. V. Podgornogo," *Pravda*, 20 October 1961, 4.

[37] RGANI f. 5, op. 32, d. 175, l. 201.

[38] RGANI f. 5, op. 32, d. 174, l. 46.

[39] RGANI f. 5, op. 32, d. 174, l. 135.

[40] RGANI f. 1, op. 4, d. 87, l. 35.

[41] One citizen wrote that after Khrushchev's speech "everything is clear and comprehensible" (RGANI f. 1, op. 4, d. 87, l. 33).

tears get in my way. I listened to the concluding words standing next to the loudspeakers, not daring even to sit down. I couldn't hold back my burning tears. Then I got hold of a newspaper, and I read it through again and again, word for word, and again I was crying. I had to write to you. In all my long working life, I never felt such agitation and never had such feeling toward a political leader. I simply couldn't *not* write!"[42] Later in the same letter, he wrote: "Please understand me correctly. I didn't hear anything that was new factually or anything unexpected, but I couldn't believe that I was hearing it all on the radio from the party's first secretary." Shtil'mark's sense of triumph came not from the acquisition of new information but from the party's resumption of its authoritative voice. He claimed, "when, in the auditorium of the Twenty-Second Party Congress, delegate no. 1 told the whole people, things previously divulged to the 'faithful' [*posviashchennye*], then *truth* came."[43] In similar terms, the son of a Ukrainian purge victim, now rehabilitated, wrote a short telegram of congratulations to Khrushchev, euphoric that his father had been rehabilitated a "second time, in front of the whole people," and "truth has triumphed" (*pravda vostorzhestvovala*).[44] Even for those whose close families had suffered from Stalinist terror, the new myths of the past offered at the congress might prove meaningful; and some, at least, embraced the notion that this was a moment of truth reaffirming the nation's march forward to a shining future.

Public Rehabilitation and Commemoration of Victims

In his letter to Khrushchev, Shtil'mark wrote: "Do you remember how in olden times, believers used to greet each other at Easter with the words 'Christ has risen.' Today I feel like saying: 'Congratulations, Lenin has risen!' [*pozdravliaiu, Lenin voskres!*]."[45] Here he echoed the sentiments of D. A. Lazurkina, a Leningrad Old Bolshevik and Gulag survivor who spoke at the congress of Lenin's return to life. She presented herself as a true revolutionary heroine: imprisoned under both tsarism and Stalinism, she had survived with her faith intact. At the end of an emotional speech, she explained: "The only reason I survived is that Il'ich was in my heart, and I sought his advice, as it were. (Applause.) Yesterday I asked Il'ich for advice, and it was as if he stood before me alive and said. 'I do not like being next to Stalin, who inflicted so much harm on the party.'"[46] With Lenin speaking through Lazur-

---

[42] RGANI f. 1, op. 4, d. 87, l. 22.

[43] RGANI f. 1, op. 4, d. 67, l. 23.

[44] RGANI f. 1, op. 4, d. 67, l. 23, l. 27. In another message to Khrushchev, a Moscow communist used the same "truth has triumphed" formulation, here referring to the removal of Stalin's body from the Mausoleum. See RGANI f. 1, op. 4, d. 67, l. 23, l. 33.

[45] RGANI f. 1, op. 4, d. 67, l. 23.

[46] "Rech' tovarishcha D. A. Lazurkinoi," *Pravda*, 31 October 1961, 2.

kina's intercession, the Twenty-Second Party Congress rather dramatically played out the notion "Lenin lives." In these metaphors of resurrection, the "death" endured during the "cult of personality" became a prerequisite for today's spiritual rebirth and the rehabilitation of purge victims beautifully symbolized the party's return to life.

By 1960, 715,120 people once convicted of counter-revolutionary crimes had been legally rehabilitated.[47] Over thirty thousand repressed communists also had their party membership restored.[48] Some former enemies of the people integrated their own stories of suffering and rehabilitation into the regenerative narratives the party leadership was crafting. At a meeting of party activists in the Dzerzhinskii raion of Moscow held on 21 November 1961, a pensioner, Comrade Gruzinskaia, spoke of her family history. In 1937 her husband was arrested and died as a result of torture. At their last meeting he told her that he was honorable (*chesten*) and without guilt, and according to Gruzinskaia, he, like thousands of others, "preserved his Bolshevik cleanliness [*Bol'shevistskaia chistota*]." Although she and her daughter had suffered nineteen years of prison and exile, she was grateful for their rehabilitation and finished her speech triumphantly: "Under the leadership of the Communist Party and its Leninist CC we are moving forward toward the triumph of communism, which, without a doubt, we will live to see."[49] When party members in Chuvash oblast met, a party member since 1917, Comrade I. E. Efimov, a victim of repression, said:

> Thank you to the great Leninist party, and from the bottom of my heart thank you to the Leninist Central Committee and personally to Comrade N. S. Khrushchev, for making it possible for us old communists, whose lives hung by a thread, to live to see these happy and triumphant days, when the banner of Lenin's party is emblazoned with the words: "The present generation of Soviet people will live under communism." Glory to the Leninist Twenty-Second Party Congress for paving the way to communism![50]

[47] Between 1954 and 1960, 892,317 counter-revolutionary cases were reconsidered and decisions overturned and amended. Of these, 715,120 were granted full rehabilitation. The documentation does not specify how many of these were posthumous rehabilitations (GARF f. 7523, op. 95, d. 109, l. 11). Marc Elie notes that these figures do not include a further 16,849 who had been rehabilitated by the commissions of 1954 and 1956 ("Les anciens détenus du Goulag," 346–347).

[48] Between the congresses, 30,954 communists had been rehabilitated into the party. Again the documentation does not show how many of these rehabilitations were posthumous. Records from the Party Control Commission, however, show that in Moscow in 1956, 45 out of 196 party rehabilitations were posthumous. If Moscow was typical, this would suggest that 77% (or approximately 24,000) of those rehabilitated were living. In addition, 16,223 former POWs who had been expelled from the party—though not legally convicted—had their party cards returned. For the Moscow figures, see RGANI f. 6, op. 6, d. 6, l. 15; for overall figures, see RGANI f. 6, op. 6, d. 1165, ll. 1–15, 30–32, 40, reproduced in Artizov et al., eds., *Reabilitatsiia: Kak eto bylo*, vol. 2, 354–365.

[49] TsAODM f. 65, op. 46, d. 28, ll. 41–43.

[50] RGANI f. 5, op. 32, d. 174, l. 270.

Even victims of repression could thus interpret their own suffering in terms of the collective journey toward communism.

Their stories were embraced enthusiastically at many obkom and gorkom meetings. At the meeting of the Ivanovo obkom party *aktiv,* one delegate suggested that local factories be renamed after rehabilitated members of the local party apparatus. In his proposal, the Ivanovo machine factory could be named after A. S. Kiselev and the Zhidelev Factory could once more become the Bubnov factory, while educational institutions should be named after Postyshev, A. S. Bubnov, and N. N. Kolotilov, also a terror victim.[51] Another party member present asked for more information about local *Ezhovshchina* victims, while a third suggested that collected memoirs of local Bolsheviks be published.[52] At the Leningrad obkom, a party member asked whether a monument would be erected to the victims of the Leningrad Affair.[53]

These calls for public commemoration of the victims did not go unheeded. In December 1961 a group of six communists (including the elderly Elena Stasova, who had supported many purge victims through the rehabilitation process), wrote to Khrushchev requesting that the ninetieth anniversary of N. A. Skrypnik's birth be commemorated in the press. A close colleague of Lenin's from the earliest days of the party, Skrypnik had been arrested eight times under tsarism before going on to hold leading positions in Ukraine from 1920 to 1933 when, as colleagues began to be arrested, he committed suicide. This small group of high-status petitioners asked for biographies of Skrypnik to be published, for various educational and cultural institutions to be named after him, for commemorative meetings to be held—perhaps at the Ukrainian Academy of which he had been vice-president—and for his portrait to be displayed.[54] The Presidium agreed to publish anniversary articles on 25 January 1962 in *Pravda, Izvestiia, Pravda Ukrainy,* and *Radian'ska Ukraina* and instructed the Ukrainian Council of Ministers to consider the publication of his works and the erection of a monument.[55]

In February 1962 the press commemorated the life of I. E. Iakir and condemned his death, using citations from his final letter to prove his honor and courage (just as Khrushchev had done with purge victims' letters in the Se-

---

[51] A. S. Kiselev held high party positions during the revolution and, though involved with the Workers' Opposition in 1921, had broken with them after the Tenth Party Congress. Arrested and shot in 1937, he was posthumously rehabilitated in 1956. Born in Ivanovo-Voznesensk, A. S. Bubnov went on to become the RSFSR people's commissar of enlightenment. Arrested in 1937 and sentenced to death in 1938, he was posthumously rehabilitated and readmitted to the party in 1956 (Artizov et al., eds, *Reabilitatsiia: Kak eto bylo,* vol. 2, 14–15, 834, 855). On Bubnov, see also Van Goudoever, *The Limits of Destalinisation,* 183–199.

[52] RGANI f. 5, op. 32, d. 174, l. 178.

[53] RGANI f. 5, op. 32, d. 175, l. 34.

[54] APRF f. 3, op. 24, d. 445, ll. 2–4, reproduced in Artizov et al., eds., *Reabilitatsiia: Kak eto bylo,* vol. 2, 370–371.

[55] RGANI f. 3, op. 18, d. 25, l. 7, summarized in Artizov et al., eds., *Reabilitatsiia: Kak eto bylo,* vol. 2, 815. See A. Snegov, "Vidnyi deiatel' partii i gosudarstvo: K 90-letiiu s dnia rozhdeniia N. A. Skrypnika," *Pravda,* 25 January 1962, 2.

cret Speech six years earlier).[56] The following year, ten years to the day since Stalin's death, the Council of Ministers issued a decree instructing the Ministry of Defense's publishing house to issue editions of selected works by Tukhachevskii and ordering the Moscow city authorities to rename one of the capital's streets after the purged military commander and to place a commemorative plaque on the house where he had lived in his final years.[57] While *Pravda* had carried no articles commemorating the rehabilitated before 1961, it published seven in 1962, ten in 1963, and eleven in 1964, before decreasing to a mere two pieces in 1965.[58] In the Soviet press, there had been a total of 10 commemorative articles in 1961, rising to 55 in 1962, 131 in 1963, before reaching a peak of 165 in 1964.[59]

For those who survived, the postcongress mood even allowed the possibility of celebrity, as the case of A. V. Snegov demonstrates. A high-ranking victim of Stalinist terror who had spent seventeen years in prison, camps, and exile, Snegov was rehabilitated, reinstated in the party, and made deputy director of the political section (*politotdel*) of the Gulag in 1954. Over the coming years he re-established friendships and acquaintances with members of the political elite, including the Mikoian family.[60] On 30 November 1961 Snegov made his first speech at a meeting of Old Bolsheviks at the Lenin Museum, followed by six or seven similar appearances across the Soviet Union. According to an Old Bolshevik present on one of these occasions, a certain N. G. Alekseev—also a victim of Stalinist terror—rumors had spread that as a result of his popularity, Snegov would soon speak at a meeting for Old Bolsheviks at the Kremlin Palace of Congresses. Concerned that Snegov went too far in his condemnation of Stalin, Alekseev wrote to the CC expressing his concern. His letter is highly revealing: while it suggests his own dislike for Snegov's anti-Stalin position, it also unwittingly informs us of the party's appetite for stories of the terror in the early 1960s.[61]

At this time, survivors' experiences of imprisonment also began to make their way into print. A short story entitled "Samorodok" promoted the im-

[56] S. Burdianskii, "Podvig komandarma," *Izvestiia,* 6 February 1962, 4.

[57] RGANI f. 3, op. 18, d. 140, l. 12; d. 141, l. 31, reproduced in Artizov et al., eds., *Reabilitatsiia: Kak eto bylo,* vol. 2, 419–420. See A. Todorskii, "Slavnyi sovetskii polkovodets," *Pravda,* 16 February 1963, 4. The article described Tukhachevskii's social origins, his contribution to the Civil War, and the unjust nature of his arrest and death in 1937, referring to the accolades Khrushchev had given him at the Twenty-Second Party Congress. The author, Todorskii, was also a purge victim, released from the camps in 1955.

[58] Appendix D, Van Goudoever, *The Limits of Destalinisation.*

[59] The first articles had appeared in 1956. Before the Twenty-Second Party Congress, the year with the highest number of commemorative articles was 1957, when twenty-one had appeared (ibid., 120).

[60] For an overview of Snegov's life, and the role he played during de-Stalinization, see Kathleen E. Smith, "Gulag Survivors and Thaw Policies" (paper presented at the conference on "The History and Legacy of the Gulag," Harvard University, November 2006). See also Roy A. and Zhores A. Medvedev, *Khrushchev: The Years in Power* (Oxford, 1977), 11; S. A. Mikoian, "Aleksei Snegov v bor'be za 'destalinizatsiiu,'" *Voprosy istorii* (April 2006): 69–84.

[61] RGANI f. 5, op. 30, d. 402, ll. 38–40.

age of the terror victims as true revolutionary heroes, devoted to the party at whatever cost to themselves. Printed in *Izvestiia* in 1962, Georgii Shelest's tale of four purged party members sent to the Kolyma gold mines provided its readers with an example of ideal communist behavior. Having unearthed a huge nugget of gold, the heroes are tempted to hide it, allowing them to sliver off small pieces each day and thus meet their targets with less exertion. As dutiful Bolsheviks they resist this urge, however, handing it all in immediately to help the war effort.[62]

In 1963–1964 the "thick journals" published a handful of select memoirs that depicted party members who succeeded in retaining their Bolshevik faith even when arrested and tortured. *Novyi mir* published the recollections of A. V. Gorbatov, a Red Army General briefly repressed at the height of the purges, who returned to take up a leading position in the Soviet Army. Gorbatov made light of his physical suffering, laying great emphasis on the sense of honor that sustained him.[63] The journal *Zvezda* published a twenty-page memoir by a communist, Boris D'iakov, who stated in the introduction: "Some of the people who appear in this story prematurely and tragically died, taking in their soul their faith in the party and the motherland. The majority has had their good name—once cruelly slandered—returned to them. They are now working for the good of communism. . . . My chief aim was to show true communists always remain communists no matter what terrible experiences are thrown at them."[64] In keeping with the image of the purge victim that Khrushchev had first created in 1956, the journals presented the victims as unerring believers in the communist cause however great their suffering.

This specific profile of the purge victim required by the party meant that there were limits on publication. In 1963 the camp survivor Semen Vilenskii, who went on to become a human rights activist, first attempted to publish an anthology which included writings by people who had been repressed, but his initiative was blocked at the last moment.[65] Many purge victims who submitted pieces to journals and newspapers simply had their work returned. Yet even when their manuscripts were rejected for publication, the authors were not wholly rebuffed. In December 1962 Aleksandr Zuev wrote to *Novyi mir* with his recollections of 1938, asking if the time had come for the publication of such material—and if not, for his manuscript to be returned to him.[66] The journal's editor, Aleksandr Tvardovskii, replied that he read the text with interest but was unable to publish it, partly because the journal was simply inundated with such memoirs, partly because Zuev named

---

[62] Georgii Shelest, "Samorodok," *Izvestiia*, 6 November 1962, 6.

[63] A. V. Gorbatov, "Gody i voiny," *Novyi mir* (March 1964): 133–156; (April 1964): 99–138; (May 1964): 106–153.

[64] Boris D'iakov, "Perezhitoe," *Zvezda* (March 1963): 177–196.

[65] Simeon Vilensky, ed., *Till My Tale Is Told* (Bloomington, 1999), x.

[66] Memorial f. 2, op. 1, d. 68, l. 1.

his persecutors, which created "additional problems for the editors." Despite
the impossibility of publishing his work, however, Tvardovskii told Zuev
that it was still "correct and necessary" that these pages had been written.[67]
When one of Tvardovskii's colleagues wrote a rejection letter to another
purge victim turned memoirist, he too claimed that the journal had received
"hundreds" of such pieces over the past year but assured the author that even
if it remained unpublished, "the manuscript was worth writing."[68] Although
the journal's editors could not publish material relating to the purges if it fell
outside certain closely defined parameters (and certainly not if the author
named the guilty), they considered the act of writing in itself valuable. Some
returnees at least, shared this enthusiasm for writing about their ordeal, even
when it did not result in publication.

Recovering a Sense of Self

One of the first returnees to write her memoirs was Mariia Ioffe, wife of
Adol'f Ioffe, who committed suicide in 1927 in protest against Trotskii's expulsion from the party. She endured exile, prison, and labor camps from
1929 to 1957 and lost her only child to the purges in 1937. Written in 1958
on her return to Moscow, though published abroad only much later, her
memoirs are testimony to the destructive nature of the Gulag: disorienting
and desperate, the text launches straight into the horrors of camp life, giving the reader little sense of the author's life before arrest or her own personality. Recounting a moment when she was close to death, she wrote: "I
am not, I will not be. A human being is destroyed. Turned in to *nothing.*"[69]
Traumatic experiences do not always translate easily into language, for they
are—to use Michael Humphrey's formulation—"encoded not in verbal narrative and context but in sensations and images." For some people, however,
the act of writing may become a way to overcome the silencing effect of violence, allowing the victim to regain voice and re-establish "self-identity
through narration."[70] The party's own attempts to make sense of the terror
in 1961 perhaps helped. In one memoir written by a purge victim in the wake
of the Twenty-Second Party Congress, the author explained that for a long
time he had jotted down recollections on scraps of paper but could bring
these fragments together into a whole only now.[71]

Encouraged by the Twenty-Second Party Congress, some former purge

[67] Memorial f. 2, op. 1, d. 68, l. 2.
[68] Kondratovich wrote to Boris Oliker, a rehabilitated party member from Minsk, in May
1963 (RGALI f. 1702, op. 9, d. 109, l. 20).
[69] Maria Joffe, *One Long Night: A Tale of Truth*, trans. Vera Dixon (New York, 1978), 167.
[70] Humphrey, *The Politics of Atrocity,* 112.
[71] RGASPI f. 560, op. 1, d. 11.

victims did set to work on their autobiographies.[72] Most did not write to condemn the party for its cruelty. Quite the opposite: many submitted their manuscripts directly to party headquarters for approval and safekeeping. The former spy, Dmitrii Bystroletov, donated his manuscript straight to the CC and chose to see his whole experience of imprisonment in terms of service to the Soviet cause, at one point describing the forced labor he carried out as his "patriotic duty" (*otchii dolg*).[73] Not all were so extreme in their formulations, but many repressed communists did see the act of writing as part of their service to the party. Scores of these donated autobiographies were brought together to form a collection labeled "manuscript materials relating to miscarriages of justice committed during the cult of Stalin's personality," housed at the central party archive at the Institute of Marxism-Leninism.[74] In one manuscript from this collection, the author, Fedor Lisitsin, claimed he had no view to publication but hoped that by describing his own experiences of repression in 1938–1939, he could clarify exactly what happened within the "walls of the NKVD." Writing in December 1963, he felt that the terms "lawlessness" and "arbitrariness" found in the press were still vague, and he hoped to give a clearer understanding of what they meant in reality.[75]

A similar sense of duty pervades the memoir of M. A. Panich, a party member since 1928 and Red Army engineer, who submitted an account of his "dark past" to the party in 1964. Entitled "Letter to a Friend," his memoirs began:

> Finally I have picked up my pen. It is hard for me to do, for I find it difficult to remember my dark and terrible past. Yet I must tell everything to my comrades, friends, and acquaintances at work, as this all has a socio-political importance.
>
> At the Twenty-Second Party Congress they said that it was our duty to carefully and thoroughly deal with cases like this, which relate to the abuse of power. A time will come, we will die, we are all mortal, and while we live, we can and must explain a lot and say the truth to the party and people. . . . We must do this so that this kind of phenomenon can never be repeated in the future.
>
> For many years before this I could not talk to you of this. Now I will try and put everything briefly.[76]

---

[72] There is an emerging scholarship on memoir literature. See, in particular, Leona Toker, *Return from the Archipelago: Narratives of Gulag Survivors* (Bloomington, 2000). Many memoirs were written later: either in the Brezhnev era for the "desk drawer" or in the perestroika and post-Soviet period with a view to publication. The Memorial archive contains many memoirs (f. 2, op. 1), but the majority of these were written after the Khrushchev era.

[73] According to Sergei Milashov's introduction to the first volume, he gave copies to the CC in 1962 and to the manuscript section of the state library in 1966. See Dmitrii Bystroletov, *Pir bessmertnykh* (Moscow, 1993), 4, 125; and *Puteshestvie na krai nochi* (Moscow, 1996).

[74] Now housed at RGASPI f. 560, op. 1.

[75] RGASPI f. 560, op. 1, d. 24, l. 2.

[76] RGASPI f. 560, op. 1, d. 30, l. 1.

The congress encouraged Panich to think that his contribution to the party's history was important, and despite the pain involved, he came to believe that remembering and articulating his ordeal was valuable. As he recounted his emotional response to rehabilitation in the concluding pages of the memoir, Panich wrote that he sobbed "out of happiness that *truth* had triumphed, genuine Leninist truth."[77] This was a moment of symbolic rebirth. During imprisonment it was as if he had been buried alive (*pogreben zazhivo*), not least because his sentence robbed him of his Bolshevik honor. His release in 1941 had been a kind of a resurrection (*voskres posle rasstrela*) but his return to life was not complete until 1961, and he said that he had remained in a semi-conscious, "dreamlike" state until the Twenty-Second Party Congress aroused him from his somnolence.[78]

The Twenty-Second Party Congress was also a turning point for Georgii Chebanov, although his relationship with his past was a little more troubled. Having spent over fifteen years in the camps, he was legally rehabilitated in 1956 and readmitted to the party in 1959. A letter sent to both the Odessa obkom and the CC in August 1961 suggests that his return to the party ranks had not been easy, with some local figures apparently still wary of him: his requests for tickets to the May and October festive ceremonies were repeatedly turned down, as were his pleas to be included in the annual raion conference.[79] Bitter that he was not allowed to take a full role in party life, he wrote: "Have I not traveled long enough on this thorny path? Why must they still pick at my pain-ridden soul!!! [*Zachem eshche nuzhno kovyriat'sia v moei nabolevshei dushe!!!*] Why, and for whom, is this necessary?!! Do they not trust me because I am a former prisoner? Now nobody needs me! I was needed in 1917 when I had a gun in my hand, but not now I'm old and sick."[80] Gradually, however, he seemed to gain a sense of his triumph for surviving against the odds. In memoirs submitted to the CC archive in December 1965 he presented a rather different version of postcamp life and rehabilitation.[81] In one chapter of the memoirs, he described the great spiritual and emotional importance of his first trip to the CC headquarters in 1955. Powerless to check his emotions, he had broken down in tears in front of the official dealing with his case. The CC instructor immediately recognized him as a genuine terror victim and spoke to him reassuringly, like a doctor to his patient: "Only he, Comrade Bukhanov, understood my spiritual state."[82] In the version of events he wrote in 1964–1965, he no longer remembered feelings of discrimination but instead described how local party members had welcomed him back: "Life had become more joyous, life had become eas-

[77] RGASPI f. 560, op. 1, d. 30, l. 25.
[78] RGASPI f. 560, op. 1, d. 30, l. 3; l. 18; 26.
[79] RGASPI f. 560, op. 1, d. 41, ll. 39–40.
[80] RGASPI f. 560, op. 1, d. 41, l. 40.
[81] RGASPI f. 560, op. 1, d. 41, ll. 43–52.
[82] RGASPI f. 560, op. 1, d. 41, ll. 45–46.

ier," he wrote, echoing Stalin's 1935 slogan without apparent irony.[83] In 1965 a relationship that had begun ten years earlier in the CC offices in Moscow office resulted in the Bukhanov family visiting the Chebanovs for a holiday at their home in the Odessa region. In the concluding page of this chapter, he wrote: "I am seventy-three, and the road to the cemetery is already showing a green light! . . . But I want to pass on my warm, heartfelt words, to say a big thank you to Comrade N. A. Bukhanov and to the former first secretary of Reni raikom, M. V. Posel′nikov, for all the good they did for me in the difficult moments of my life. . . . They eased my suffering, and extended my life! They brought great happiness to our house!"[84] The dissatisfaction he had articulated in August 1961 seemed to have been forgotten by 1964–1965 when he wrote his memoirs, as if wiped away in the pleasure of his new comradeship with these two party men, Bukhanov and Posel′nikov.

The memoirs of both Panich and Chebanov suggest that in the wake of the Twenty-Second Party Congress these Gulag survivors were able to think of their lives not only in terms of the suffering they had endured but also in terms of their service to the party and their survival as true, committed Bolsheviks. For some returnees, then, the early 1960s were good years. This is certainly how Z. L. Serebriakova, the daughter of two "enemies of the people" and a terror victim in her own right, chose to remember the late Khrushchev era. Rehabilitated in 1956, she flourished under Khrushchev, defending a candidate's dissertation in history and receiving an invitation to join the Academy of Sciences. She later recalled this period as one of great optimism, in which the rehabilitated were treated as "heroes."[85] Influenced by such stories, Vladlen Loginov, a historian and colleague of Serebriakova, has argued that returnees were given a "hero's reception."[86]

In her study of survivors' experiences Nanci Adler challenges this picture, focusing on the experiences of many less high-ranking victims of Stalinist terror who did not enjoy this kind of privileged status. She is certainly right that only a limited group of returnees were fêted in this way: few were invited to speak at the Lenin Museum or hosted CC officials on their summer vacation.[87] In fact, both perspectives are possible: it was a time when some purge victims could, rather unexpectedly, become heroes (in Snegov's case perhaps even celebrities), and a small number seized this chance. But this was certainly not the case for the majority.

[83] RGASPI f. 560, op. 1, d. 41, l. 50. At the First All-Union Conference of Stakhanovites in 1935 Stalin said, "Life has improved, comrades. Life has become more joyous. And when life is joyous, work goes well."

[84] RGASPI f. 560, l. 1, 41, l. 51.

[85] See Adler, *The Gulag Survivor*, 184–186, for an account of Serebriakova's life; and Artizov et al., eds., *Reabilitatsiia: Kak eto bylo*, vol. 2, 889–892, for short biographies of her relatives.

[86] Adler, *The Gulag Survivor*, 186.

[87] Ibid.

When party leaders invited Lazurkina to speak at the party congress in 1961, they took control of the "truth-telling" process and decided who would be acknowledged as victims.[88] High-ranking *Ezhovshchina* victims were the ideal group for this honor, not least because in their petition letters so many of them had articulated their readiness to rejoin the party with renewed enthusiasm and commitment. The Soviet leadership encouraged a specific narrative of Stalinist terror: one in which the victims' moral rectitude and noble heroism not only ensured survival but even spiritual resurrection. By emphasizing the bravery of the victims, these stories of survival sought to "dissolve" the violence of the purges, and in stressing their symbolic rebirth in the present moment they deflected attention from the atrocities of the past—and from the guilt some must bear for them.[89]

The party's version of the past clearly influenced the way some returnees chose to remember their experiences. Those who fitted the party's profile of the "purge victim" were encouraged to create a meaningful and perhaps uplifting version of their lives, sometimes based around the symbolic pattern of death and resurrection found in official texts. Yet by singling out this select group for rituals of commemoration the party leadership was severely restricting how many of Stalin's outcasts were recognized as victims. Full readmission into the Soviet family became the right of a privileged few. It is no coincidence that at the same time as it celebrated the "resurrection" of selected purge victims, the party leadership was creating increasingly stringent social boundaries.

Banishing the Un-Soviet

The Twenty-Second Party Congress condemned Stalin, reaffirmed the party's commitment to "legality," and extolled the virtue of purge victims, but this did not mean that the leadership was simply continuing and deepening the de-Stalinizing policies it had been pursuing since 1953: in fact important re-

---

[88] This pattern is not unique to the Soviet Union. In Argentina, for example, kidnappings, disappearances, and torture became prominent in the public commemoration of the "dirty war" (1976–1983) not least because the victims largely came from the middle classes; collective massacres, which were more representative of the working classes, were largely ignored (Humphrey, *The Politics of Atrocity,* 109).

[89] Frank Biess's work suggests that in postwar Germany POW narratives of survival (found in the press, film, or other official forums) served a similar function. By turning their experiences into "universal tales of moral regeneration," these public narratives enabled postwar society to distance itself from the violent remnants of the war. Biess's work also shows that although these narratives helped shore up a sense of national community in the fragile aftermath of war, in the longer term these redemptive narratives prevented a real confrontation with, or "working through," of the trauma of war. The same could be said of the purge narratives. It is from Biess that I borrow the notion of "dissolving" the violence of the past. See Frank Biess, *Homecomings: Returning POWs and the Legacies of Defeat in Postwar Germany* (Princeton, 2006), 97–152, 227–231.

forms were in the process of being reversed in 1961. Whereas in 1960 the population of corrective labor institutions had been at its lowest in twenty-five years, by 1961 it had climbed to 674,080, and by early 1962 it reached as many as 968,080.[90] Although such figures were never made public, the general principle behind them was certainly not hidden; nor was it at odds with the eschatological tropes found in the congress speeches and accompanying newspaper articles.

At the congress Khrushchev called for a more aggressive "battle against idlers and parasites, hooligans, and drunkards," claiming that there was no room for such "weeds" in Soviet life. "Some people," he complained in his inimitable style, "seem to think that under communism, man won't have to sow or reap but will just sit about eating pies."[91] Khrushchev now seemed to have few qualms about ejecting such people from Soviet society. There was apparently no contradiction between the severe line he was advocating toward "antisocial elements" and his anti-Stalinist agenda. Quite the opposite: ridding society of troublemakers and correcting past injustices were presented as part and parcel of a single mission to cleanse society of the impurities that currently prevented the country's advance toward communism.

The ground had been prepared in preceding months by the antiparasite campaign and the Party Program that was published with great fanfare in the run-up to the congress. The new Party Program was to replace the now outdated program of 1919, and a first draft was printed in an extended edition of *Pravda* on 30 July 1961. It contained an explanation of the Soviet past, identified the country's current location on its journey toward communism, and described the steps necessary to ensure successful arrival at that destination.[92] Pictures in the press linked the new program with the country's technological advances and the Soviet conquest of space (Figures 6 and 7).[93] This was the year's seminal text, the tract that the nation's leaders most hoped to impress on the ranks of the party and on the nonparty public. It was quite different from the key political speeches and announcements of 1956 and 1957, in which the party had admitted to its failings, asked for forgiveness, and even suggested that the lines between good and evil, hero and enemy, were blurred and uncertain. Now the focus, as at the congress, was on the transition to communism.

As had been the case throughout the 1950s, improving the behavior and morals, or *byt*, of ordinary citizens was presented as an integral part of building communism. The program contained a long section devoted to "incul-

---

[90] GARF f. 7523, op. 95, d. 109, ll. 25–27.

[91] "Doklad N. S. Khrushcheva," *Pravda*, 18 October 1961, 11.

[92] "Programma Kommunisticheskoi Partii Sovetskogo naroda," *Pravda*, 30 July 1961, 1–9.

[93] "Programja," *Pravda*, 7 August 1961, 5; "Tri programmy—tri epokhi," *Pravda*, 8 August 1961, 5.

ВЕЛИКОЛЕПНО СКОНСТРУИРОВАННЫЙ КОСМИЧЕСКИЙ КОРАБЛЬ

Fig. 6. "Programja," *Pravda,* 7 August 1961. Courtesy SSEES Library, London.

ТРИ ПРОГРАММЫ — ТРИ ЭПОХИ.

Fig. 7. "Three Programs—Three Epochs," *Pravda,* 8 August 1961. Courtesy SSEES Library, London.

cating communist consciousness," with a twelve-point Moral Code that listed the essential characteristics of the new Soviet man. These were:

1. Devotion to communism and love for the socialist fatherland and socialist countries.
2. Conscientious labor for the good of society; he who does not work does not eat.
3. Concern for protecting and accumulating communal property.
4. A developed sense of social duty, intolerance toward those who violate collective interests.
5. Collectivism and a comradely attitude to helping others; all for one and one for all.
6. Humane relationships and mutual respect among people: each human being is a friend, comrade, and brother to all.
7. Decency and truthfulness [*chestnost' i pravdivost'*], moral cleanliness, simplicity, and modesty in public and private life.
8. Mutual respect within the family, attention to the upbringing of children.
9. Intolerance toward injustice, parasitism, dishonesty, and careerism.
10. Friendship and brotherhood among all the peoples of the USSR; intolerance of any kind of nationalist or racial hostility.
11. Intransigence toward the enemies of communism.
12. Brotherly solidarity with all the workers of all peoples.[94]

The new Soviet man was to be patriotic, industrious, law-abiding, family-minded, helpful, and decent (*chestnyi*). He was not only required to "work on himself," however, but also to take a tough line on those whose behavior was found lacking. The Moral Code urged the new Soviet man to rebuff those who failed to meet the high standards it set: articles 4 and 9 both spoke of "intolerance" (*neterpimost'*) toward those who violated the social order in some way. In keeping with both the antiparasite campaign and the speeches Khrushchev made at the congress, the Party Program suggested that the transition to communism required a new battle with antisocial elements.

The regime did everything it could to make the public aware of the message set out in the Party Program. In August and September party meetings were held in every workplace to propagate the messages contained within the Party Program and to involve rank-and-file members in the act of endorsing the new party dogma. Activists also went door-to-door to convey the importance of the Party Program to the nonparty public and to gauge their reactions. In Moscow alone, four hundred thousand propagandists and agitators were set to work.[95] Excerpts of letters from ordinary Soviet citizens on the subject of the Party Program filled the pages of *Pravda* throughout

---

[94] "Programma Kommunisticheskoi Partii Sovetskogo Soiuza," *Pravda*, 30 July 1961, 8.
[95] RGANI f. 1, op. 4, d. 27, l. 1.

the early fall.[96] The campaign elicited a significant response, with a total of 123,000 letters sent to party organs and newspaper editors.[97]

Because of the broad nature of the Party Program, the meetings and doorstep discussions led by agitators provided an unusual occasion for members of the public to express their views on a range of topics. Many took the opportunity to complain about living standards: agitators recorded calls for better housing, for gray and black bread to be given out freely, for wage differentials to be decreased, for working women to be given more support.[98] Some collective farmers demanded pensions.[99] There were frequent complaints against excessive bureaucracy.[100] More radical political commentary also arose, with some suggesting a party purge was due, while others called for more power to be devolved to the local party organizations.[101] Letters addressed to the CC contained, on one hand, requests for the program to include stronger "formulations" against the cult of personality and, on the other, demands for Stalin's role in the crushing of Trotskyists and other opponents of the party to be given full credit.[102] Some feared that the behavior cultivated under Stalin had not yet disappeared from Soviet officialdom.[103] Yet of the issues raised in the draft Program, the Moral Code produced the most passionate responses.[104] One worker from the Krasno-presenskii construction complex in Moscow proposed writing the Moral Code out in golden letters and hanging it in public places.[105] Perhaps he envisaged it as a surrogate for Stalin's watchful gaze: replacing the dictator's portrait, copies of the Moral Code would serve as a constant reminder of the rules of conduct citizens must follow if they wished to reach the communist paradise.

The Moral Code proved so important because it was here that the party gave encouragement to those who wanted to see a more aggressive fight waged against antisocial behavior. Perhaps unsurprisingly, the ninth point of the Moral Code proved particularly popular, especially the reference to "par-

---

[96] From 16 September 1961 onward, *Pravda* devoted the third page of most issues to the Party Program, and almost daily it contained the rubric "Lines from Your Letters" (*Stroki iz pisem*). In a period of just two weeks, *Pravda* received 1,290 letters, of which 61 were published in some form (RGANI f. 1, op. 4, d. 73, l. 5).

[97] RGANI f. 1, op. 4, d. 23, l. 46.

[98] RGANI f. 1, op. 4, d. 27, ll. 4–15.

[99] RGANI f. 1, op. 4, d. 27, l. 7.

[100] RGANI f. 1, op. 4, d. 52, l. 20.

[101] Some communists suggested that local party organizations should be able to decide on whether to expel members without interference (RGANI f. 1, op. 4, d. 51, l. 22, 76). A report from B. N. Ponomarev, a CC secretary, said that many letters had been received with suggestions for a *chistka* within the party, though he does not give more detail (RGANI f. 1, op. 4, d. 27, l. 14).

[102] RGANI f. 1, op. 4, d. 27, l. 31.

[103] RGANI f. 1, op. 4, d. 27, ll. 31 and 219.

[104] This is highlighted in Ponomarev's report (RGANI f. 1, op. 4, d. 27, l. 13).

[105] RGANI f. 1, op. 4, d. 27, l. 13.

asites." One person was reported as saying: "We should clean society [*ochishchat' obshchestvo*] of parasites and petty thieves. Instead of taking them on probation, we should judge them with the full severity of the law and banish them from the towns, so that the negative influence of these elements does not harm young people."[106] Another read: "Where it [the code] talks about parasites, it should add that these people are liable to be shunned by the workers of communist society and sent to distant places in the country to take care of themselves."[107] In Magadan oblast demands for a "tougher battle against parasites" coexisted with pleas for cheaper cinema tickets, better books for students, and free breakfast for children. One Leningrad official noted that when the party conducted discussions across the city and province, they frequently encountered calls for the revised draft to include "more concrete statements about the measures to be taken in the struggle to strengthen social order."[108] While the ninth point simply stated that the "new man" should show intolerance toward certain negative features of Soviet life, some members of the public hoped for stronger formulations.

Articulating these demands for more stringent "punitive measures" was not deemed at odds with the rhetoric of de-Stalinization. Severe punishment of those who displayed criminal or antisocial behavior was rarely considered an indication that the state was acting "repressively." V. Belousov, chairman of a village soviet in Saratov oblast, called for greater severity by invoking the party's own commitment to the future: "In a society that is building communism, there should be no place for lawbreaking and criminality. But while criminal incidents still occur, it is necessary to punish severely those people who commit dangerous crimes, who break the rules governing the socialist community and who don't wish to be a part of a decent working life."[109] One Leningrader praised the Party Program for devoting such attention to "raising people of the communist tomorrow" (*vospitanie liudei kommunisticheskogo zavtra*) but also wanted something added about the "use of force against those who maliciously prevent us from moving forward."[110] A certain Domacheva, a cook in a communal dining room, commented: "In our country there should be no place for parasites, idlers, skivers, and other parasitical elements which hinder the building of communism. If these types won't respond to educational measures [*ne poddaiutsia vospitatel'nomu vozdeistviiu*], they should be punished by judicial means."[111]

In a retrospective account of the 1960s, two Russian émigrés Aleksandr Genis and Petr Vail asserted, "with all the mastery of an experienced

---

[106] RGANI f. 1, op. 4, d. 29, l. 121.
[107] RGANI f. 1, op. 4, d. 28, ll. 120–122.
[108] RGANI f. 1, op. 4, d. 51, l. 16.
[109] RGANI f. 1, op. 4, d. 72, l. 39.
[110] RGANI f. 1, op. 4, d. 51, l. 38.
[111] RGANI f. 1, op. 4, d. 52, ll. 7–8.

preacher, the Party Program touched the right spot in every soul."[112] In the light of public anxieties regarding crime through the 1950s, Khrushchev's pledge to cleanse Soviet space of the "undesirable" while at the same time promising the advent of communism was perhaps particularly well calculated.

In the early 1960s the party allowed some men and women formerly labeled enemies of the people to speak publicly of their ordeals. Over the course of the first decade since Stalin's death, some communists like Snegov, Lazurkina, and Serebriakova had made it back from the darkest edges of the Soviet Union to the very heart of Moscow. They were praised for their courage and fortitude and restored to the party, and many were grateful that their honorable nature had finally been recognized. Briefly, at least, it seemed possible to rethink the party's history in a way that made the terror not shameful but potentially revitalizing. The power of this new myth lay in its offer of a single narrative of this difficult past, which began with the party's suffering in 1936–1938 and ended with its recovery in 1956–1961. This version of the past of course excluded many of Stalin's outcasts. Of the many different kinds of prisoner who had been returning from the camps since 1953, only a small group was incorporated into this grand narrative of the party's history.

In the summer of 1962, *Pravda* published an article entitled "By Way of an Exception."[113] The piece suggested that long-standing fears about identity fraud were still prevalent.[114] The reader was introduced to Kirill Marikutsa, who had adopted a false identity and claimed to be a purge victim, even though he was a common criminal and jailbird. "A citizen of crystal-clear purity, Marikutsa was treated badly: 'he was repressed' [*repressirovali*]. Not now, of course, but 'in those times.'" The days of "unmasking," it seems, were not over after all. Admonished for a lack of vigilance, the public was taken to task for not seeing through Marikutsa's cunning disguise. In 1959 Khrushchev had encouraged people to look for the good "man" hidden underneath the mask of criminal, but in this newspaper article readers' vigilance was required once more, and they were asked to uncover enemies masquerading as deserving citizens. In part, this shows the regime's concerns to restrict the heroic status—and the (limited) material recompense—that had been promised to purge victims, but it also demonstrates the kind of people it feared most.[115] Where "unmasking" in the Stalinist era had revealed

[112] Petr Vail' and Aleksandr Genis, *60-e: Mir sovetskogo cheloveka* (Ann Arbor, 1988), 6.
[113] "V poriadke iskliucheniia," *Pravda*, 23 August 1962, 3.
[114] On the figure of the "confidence man" in Stalinist Russia, see Sheila Fitzpatrick, "The World of Ostap Bender: Soviet Confidence Men in the Stalin Period," *Slavic Review* 61 (2002): 535–557.
[115] In September 1955 the Presidium CC decreed that those rehabilitated receive only two months' salary in recognition of their ordeal (RGANI f. 3, op. 8, d. 296, ll. 177–180, reproduced in A. Artizov et al., eds., *Reabilitatsiia: Kak eto bylo*, vol. 1, 257–259).

Trotskyists, rightists, and foreign spies, here the press used the same practices to unearth a "common criminal." The message of the article and other similar pieces was that the prime threat to Soviet well-being came not from the hirelings of the capitalist west but from its own uncivilized masses, here represented by the criminal returning from his Gulag exile.[116] The enemy was not the political provocateur of old but rather a shady criminal.

In exploring the rhetoric of the Twenty-Second Party Congress, and reactions to it from both in and outside the party, this chapter reveals complexities to Khrushchev's political vision that have been overlooked to date. At the moment when he was most confident in his dismantling of the personality cult, his condemnation of Stalin's former colleagues, and his repudiation of the terror, Khrushchev was also encouraging intolerance toward all kinds of petty offenders and introducing policies that punished them severely. It was a reversal of policies that Khrushchev had been promoting just two years earlier. Instead of preaching forgiveness and reintegration for all manner of sinners, Khrushchev now promised to restrict membership in the Soviet community. He brought together two quite different strands—the overcoming of the terror and the renewed severity of law and order—weaving them into a single narrative in which the impurities of the past were to be purged to secure tomorrow's happiness. This melding of two quite distinct themes was not unproblematic, however, and although Khrushchev ingeniously presented them as part of the same de-Stalinizing package, the union was to prove a fragile one.

---

[116] *Izvestiia* carried a similar piece in January 1963. A certain Igor' Bostrikov had allegedly claimed to be the son of a military commander killed during the purges, whereas in fact his father was still alive and he himself had already served time for forging documents. Having condemned the fraudster, the article finished by reassuring readers that justice had already been done for the real relatives of Marshal Aleksandr Bostrikov ("Podaite, ottsa radi . . . ," *Izvestiia*, 4 January 1963, 3).

8 Literary Hooligans and Parasites

What socialist legality? When they shoot Baldie, that'll be social-ist legality. What they had was nothing but lousy corruption, not legality. The state they reduced the country to! . . . Nowadays everybody writes about the camps. As if there weren't any other subjects. They let everybody do whatever they want.

—Algaya in Vladimir Voinovich, *Monumental Propaganda*, 2002

While the movement toward the rule of law, which had begun "from the top," thus gradually bogged down in a bureaucratic swamp, suddenly voices demanding the observance of the laws were heard "from below."

—Andrei Amalrik, *Will the Soviet Union Survive Until 1984?* 1970

"In Kharkov I have seen all kinds of queues—for the film 'Tarzan,' butter, women's drawers, chicken giblets, and horse-meat sausage," wrote a certain Mark Konenko, describing urban life under Khrushchev. He continued: "But I cannot remember a queue as long as the one for your book in the li-braries. . . . I waited six months on the list and to no avail. By chance I got hold of it for forty-eight hours."[1] The author he addressed was Aleksandr

---

[1] Aleksandr Solzhenitsyn, "How People Read *One Day*: A survey of Letters," in *Solzheni-tsyn: A Documentary Record*, ed. Leopold Labedz (Harmondsworth, U.K., 1974), 48–66 (50). While many readers addressed letters to the editors of *Novyi mir* (now preserved at the Russian State Archive of Art and Literature), others wrote directly to the author himself. Small snippets of these letters are printed in Labedz's collection.

Solzhenitsyn; the book was *One Day in the Life of Ivan Denisovich*, published in the November 1962 issue of the literary journal *Novyi mir*.[2] A former prisoner himself, Konenko had a personal interest in the work, yet his comments suggest that his fascination was far from unique. According to Konenko, the urge to read about life in Stalin's prison camps proved stronger than even the usual hunger for sausage and American movies. The struggle to obtain a copy of the coveted text required stamina, luck, and connections. Another of Solzhenitsyn's correspondents wrote: "I am only a nurse, and there were professors and university teachers in the queue for the book. But because I know someone in the library, and because I was there myself, I was given it for the New Year without waiting in the queue."[3]

In the winter of 1962–1963, citizens across the Soviet Union voraciously read Solzhenitsyn's bleak depiction of life in one of Stalin's labor camps. Whether incensed by Solzhenitsyn's audacity or by the horrors he revealed, few could respond with indifference. Many felt compelled to set their reactions down on paper. As established writers, literary critics, and leading party members wrote reviews for a variety of Soviet newspapers and journals, the pages of *Novyi mir, Ogonek, Literaturnaia gazeta, Izvestiia, Literaturnaia Rossiia, Oktiabr', Don,* and *Pravda* became the site of a major polemic between what Ivan Lakshin, a contemporary critic, dubbed the "friends and foes of Ivan Denisovich."[4] The nation's leading literati and politicians may have battled it out publicly in the Soviet press, but ordinary citizens were no less opinionated. The journal *Novyi mir* received an unprecedented number of letters from readers who wished to articulate their views on the controversial new work. As readers sought to understand its significance, they discussed not only the text itself but also the important political and social changes that had occurred in the decade since Stalin's death. The discussion that followed the publication of *One Day in the Life of Ivan Denisovich* became part of a rather more complex dialogue about the nature of change in the post-Stalin era, for it led many readers to reflect not only on the crimes of the past but also on current issues, in particular the changing status of the Gulag since Stalin's death.

Many readers, including Gulag survivors, responded enthusiastically to the publication of Solzhenitsyn's novella as an indicator of the regime's

---

[2] Aleksandr Solzhenitsyn, "Odin den' Ivana Denisovicha," *Novyi mir* (November 1962): 8–74.

[3] Solzhenitsyn, "How People Read *One Day*," 50.

[4] See, for example, Konstantin Simonov, "O proshlom vo imia budushchego," *Izvestiia*, 18 November 1962, 5; "Vo imia pravdy, vo imia zhizni," *Pravda*, 23 November 1962, 7–8; N. Kruzhkov, "Tak bylo, tak ne budet," *Ogonek*, 2 December 1962, 28–29; Lidiia Fomenko, "Bol'shiie ozhidaniia," *Literaturnaia Rossiia*, 11 January 1963, 6–7; "V redaktsiiu Literaturnoi gazety," *Literaturnoi gazeta*, 22 January 1963, 3; Fedor Chapchakhov, "Nomera i liudi," *Don* (January 1963): 155–159; N. Sergovantsev, "Tragediia odinochestva i 'sploshnoi byt,'" *Oktiabr'* (April 1963): 198–206; and V. Lakshin, "Ivan Denisovich, ego druz'ia i nedrugi," *Novyi mir* (January 1964): 223–245.

ongoing commitment to repudiating Stalinist terror and the triumph of "truth."[5] The praise was not universal, and Solzhenitsyn's depiction of the horrors of Stalin's Gulag proved deeply troubling for some readers. For some it served as a reminder of the limitations that had been placed on discussion of the terror: the *Novyi mir* mailbag brought calls for the atrocities committed under Stalin to be examined further, and at least one letter writer expressed frustration that the perpetrators had not been brought to justice, asking why all the witnesses, judges, and procurators implicated in the terror were still walking around as free men, "often with a party card in their pocket."[6] Solzhenitsyn's shocking account of Gulag life was simply too painful for others, perhaps particularly those whose lives had been damaged by the terror.[7] Among these varied responses to Solzhenityn's novella, however, no one attacked the key premises of the Twenty-Second Party Congress: none of the letters to *Novyi mir* praised Stalin or challenged the principle that *Ezhovshchina* victims deserved sympathy.[8]

The narrative of the terror presented at the Twenty-Second Party Congress slotted the party's bloody history into a triumphant myth of regeneration and rebirth, but it was a narrative that worked for only a small proportion of Gulag survivors. One of the key polemics emerging from the correspondence addressed to the *Novyi mir* editors concerned the status of the many prisoners and former prisoners whose life stories escaped the narrow parameters set by this version of the country's past. In her letter to *Novyi mir,* E. A. Ignatovich, a worker in a chemical laboratory in Tula oblast, put the case trenchantly: "With regard to Solzhenitsyn, I want to ask the question: Why? Why did you write in the introduction to *One Day in the Life of Ivan Denisovich* that it was about 1937 people? No; here there wasn't even one 1937 person. From my point of view they were wartime deserters, criminals, and cowards. To my mind, the story was well written, but the heroes are trash [*drian'*]."[9] For Ignatovich, the victims of 1937 had been identified as members of a special category whose status as victims she did not challenge. She believed Solzhenitsyn's text was seditious, however, because it extended the heroic status outside this particular cohort to include people arrested during

---

[5] For a more extensive examination of responses to *One Day in the Life of Ivan Denisovich,* see Denis Kozlov's dissertation ("The Readers of *Novyi mir,* 1945–1970: Twentieth-Century Experience and Soviet Historical Consciousness," Ph.D. Diss., University of Toronto, 2005, 301–361).

[6] RGALI f. 1702, op. 9, d. 109, l. 44.

[7] A seventy-five-year-old named Spasskaia, whose husband and brother had both been arrested in 1938, wrote to the *Novyi mir* editors arguing that it was unnecessary and painful to see accounts such as Solzhenitsyn's published (RGALI f. 1702, op. 9, d. 107, ll. 34–35).

[8] While Kozlov's analysis of the letters stresses the varied and contested nature of readers' responses to the work, his findings also seem to suggest that there was little explicit defense of Stalin or his use of terror. He notes that even the three negative letters preserved in the archives of *Novyi mir*'s conservative rival, the journal *Oktiabr',* did not defend Stalin's repression ("The Readers of *Novyi mir,*" 301–361).

[9] RGALI f. 1702, op. 9, d. 109, l. 152.

the war. Gal'chenko and Petrov, party members from Zagorsk, also objected to the characters Solzhenitsyn created, particularly the kind of people who were now being presented as "Soviet."[10] They produced a blistering tirade:

> Can they really be Soviet people who simply fell into the camps as a result of Stalin's cult of personality? Where is their organization, ideas, culture, and humanity? Ivan Denisovich Shukhov—the main hero of the "story"—is supposed to be seen as a good person but in actual fact he is shown to be a petty crook/ odd-jobber [*mel'kii zhulik/masterok*] who swindles two extra bowls of soup from hungry comrades, a glutton, a toady (in his relations toward Tsezar'), who doesn't have a single friend or a single honest thought. Is this really a "hero," is this realism? This is in fact an alien [*chuzhak*]!

Like Ignatovich, Gal'chenko and Petrov were anxious to define who could be considered "heroes." In their eyes, Shukhov was so lacking in positive attributes he could not even be identified as a Soviet person. He should remain an outsider and an alien, belonging not to the Soviet collective but to some unnamed "other" (*chuzhoi*).

In both letters, the authors worried that Khrushchev's de-Stalinizing rhetoric was being applied too broadly. Criticism of the "cult of personality," they maintained, should not be used to revise the status of all those cast out during the Stalinist era. Readmission into Soviet society should be granted only to party members victimized at the height of the terror. Setting themselves up as defenders of Soviet moral values, the letter writers intimated that many who "fell into the camps" were indeed there for a reason— they were not truly Soviet people. As formulated by Gal'chenko and Petrov, key issues included: Who was Soviet, and who was "alien"? How were such identities to be decided?

A discussion regarding the boundary between belonging and alienation developed in the early 1960s in relation to literature in terms of both the text and the author's life. Two cases are examined here: the polemic surrounding Solzhenitsyn's novella in the fall of 1962; and the trial and exile of the young Leningrad poet Iosif Brodskii in 1964. On both occasions, the writers and their work provoked a widespread debate about what it meant to be Soviet and un-Soviet in the post-Stalin world. Both testify to a sense of crisis, with some citizens fearful that certain aspects of their civilization were under threat from uncultured, vulgar, or nonconformist behavior. The Brodskii case also suggests that by the last year of Khrushchev's rule, the regime's commitment to the concept of "legality" was becoming shaky, even though it had been one of the founding concepts of the post-Stalin era.

[10] RGALI f. 1702, op. 9, d. 107, ll. 97–100.

The Threat of Poshlost'

Introducing Solzhenitsyn's work in the November 1962 issue of *Novyi mir,* the journal's editor, Aleksandr Tvardovskii, seemed to predict some aspects of the ensuing debate. In the opening paragraph of his preface, he encouraged readers to approve the work as a necessary part of breaking with the past, citing from Khrushchev's speech at the Twenty-Second Party Congress: "We can and must tell the party and the people the truth. . . . We need to do this so that nothing like this can ever be repeated."[11] Extolling Solzhenitsyn's work as a necessary contribution to the party's quest for "truth," Tvardovskii appeared unable to countenance any fundamental opposition to the work. No one, he seemed to claim, could deny the necessity of speaking openly about the horrors of Stalin's Gulag. Yet in the closing words of his preface, Tvardovskii did acknowledge that some might be shocked, and even angered, by Solzhenitsyn's text. Some overly "persnickety" (*priveredlivyi*) people, he feared, would object to some words and expressions taken from the "milieu" in which the story takes place. Tvardovskii already realized that the issue of language would be central.

Though initial reviews had been positive, dissenting voices emerged by the New Year, and the question of language did indeed prove important.[12] Writing in the literary journal *Don* in January, the critic Fedor Chapchakhov criticized Solzhenitsyn's use of "convict slang," or literally "convict music" (*blatnaia muzyka*).[13] Nevertheless, none of the published critics focused on the problem of language with quite the tenacity shown by ordinary readers. In the letters located in the *Novyi mir* archive, it appears to be one of the most distressing aspects of *One Day in the Life of Ivan Denisovich.*[14] One pensioner described how he almost laughed at the made-up criminal (*blatnye*) words but was then overcome with confusion as to how this kind of "concoction" came to be published.[15] A Russian teacher complained that in all sixty-five pages the reader would not find a single phrase written in the literary language he had been taught.[16] Meanwhile, a captain in the Soviet army expressed his indignation that someone who had received a higher education, served as an officer, and was now a teacher and novice author,

---

[11] Tvardovskii's preface to "Odin den' Ivana Denisovicha," *Novyi mir* (November 1962): 8.
[12] Fomenko, "Bol'shie ozhidaniia."
[13] Chapchakhov, "Nomera i liudi."
[14] I appreciate Kozlov's constructive criticism of an earlier version of this chapter; and he is right that the issue of language is not only the aspect of Solzhenitsyn's work discussed in readers' letters. Even according to Kozlov's figures, however, 73 (or 14%) of the 532 letters addressed to *Novyi mir* in response to Solzhenitsyn's work in the years 1962–1969 contained critical remarks about the author's language. This strikes me as a sufficient proportion to warrant examination, particularly considering the trends in popular opinion identified in earlier chapters of this book. See Kozlov, "The Readers of *Novyi mir*," 310–317.
[15] RGALI f. 1702, op. 9, d. 108, ll. 10–12.
[16] RGALI f. 1702, op. 9, d. 107, l. 71.

should use words that most readers would take "years to learn."[17] For him, Solzhenitsyn's status identified him as a respectable member of Soviet society, a fact that should be reflected in the language he employed.

Even readers who passionately denounced the atrocities committed under Stalin were nonetheless aghast at the author's use of slang and profanity. Such a response is best illustrated by a letter from a certain Grinberg, a *Novyi mir* reader from the city of Ukhta in the republic of Komi. Grinberg identified himself as a keen follower of both Khrushchev and of the journal's liberal editor, Tvardovskii.[18] He welcomed the repudiation of the cult of personality and believed that the new openness was valuable: he expressed admiration for the recent film *Clear Skies*, in which an innocent victim of wartime repression endured suffering without losing faith in the party.[19] He also praised Shelest's short story in which, he said, the heroes—communists consigned to one of Stalin's prison camps—displayed great fortitude and "moral cleanliness."[20] Grinberg had good reason to appreciate Khrushchev's policies: once a leading party cadre, he had been repressed in 1937 and endured eight years in the camps.

As a purge victim himself, Grinberg hardly fits the profile of a conservative pro-Stalinist, but he was, nonetheless, deeply concerned by the publication of *One Day in the Life of Ivan Denisovich*. For him, the work represented a distortion of Khrushchev's new rhetoric: "N. S. Khrushchev did not mean in any way for all this dirt to be raked up under the guise of truth." Although a "foe" of Solzhenitsyn and Ivan Denisovich, Grinberg presented himself as a friend of Khrushchev and a defender of the "truth." He believed that Solzhenitsyn had exploited the current quest for truth to "rake up" dirt, and, as Tvardovskii had predicted, it was indeed the language of the text that he contested. The whole tale, wrote Grinberg, was composed in the jargon of the "thief, the recidivist, and the bandit." He cited various examples of this slang, which, he claimed, "makes you sick." Why, he asked, do we need to make a cult out of thieves' jargon? In addition to labeling Solzhenitsyn's language "the lexicon of thieves and bandits," he also repeatedly designated it as vulgar (*poshlyi*) or vulgarities (*poshliatina*). *Poshlost'*—derived from the Russian word *poshlo* originally meaning "traditional" or "ancient"—represented a direct challenge to the "new" Soviet values.[21] Grinberg's dread of vulgarity revealed both the significance he attached to the new mores of Soviet society and his deep anxiety that they were now under threat.

Grinberg feared the appearance of bad language as a threat to Soviet *kul'turnost'*, especially as this "vulgarity" was now apparently condoned by

[17] RGALI f. 1702, op. 9, d. 107, l. 65.

[18] RGALI f. 1702, op. 9, d. 107, ll. 58–61.

[19] *Chistoe nebo*, directed by Grigorii Chukhrai, 1961, USSR.

[20] Georgii Shelest, "Samorodok," *Izvestiia*, 6 November 1962, 6.

[21] Svetlana Boym, *Common Places: Mythologies of Everyday Life in Russia* (Cambridge, 1994), 41–42.

the nation's cultural luminaries. Throughout the Soviet era, literature had been one of the prime sites for the promotion of "cultured" behavior and language.[22] It was hardly a surprise therefore that Grinberg was so aghast to discover examples of the criminal jargon promoted in a leading literary journal. He asked the editors of *Novyi mir,* "Do you really have to be a 'persnickety' person to disapprove of an approach to literature that flaunts the most vulgar examples of the thieves' lexicon in our high-minded Soviet literature?" A few lines later he again questioned why Tvardovskii encouraged "actual vulgarity" (*nastoiashchaia poshliatina*) in literature.

Grinberg's linguistic quibbles reflected the broader anxieties engulfing Soviet society in the first post-Stalin decade. Many seemed to fear that if the millions of prisoners released from the Gulag spoke and thought in the same way as Ivan Denisovich, the cultured behavior that the party had fought so hard to inculcate was at risk. Grinberg apparently believed the boundaries between respectable Soviet society and the dirty underworld of the criminal should remain sealed. Expressing his concerns that "this jargon and vulgarity" would reach "the lexicon of callow youths," he argued that *poshlost'* represented the "harmful influence of an alien ideology" (*chuzhaia ideologiia*). If the jargon spoken within the camp was "alien," its use—according to Grinberg—exposed Soviet youth to dangerously foreign influences. Soviet respectability was thus at risk from a foreign culture which had been fostered within the segregated zone of the Gulag, and which the process of de-Stalinization now allowed to filter back into society.

Such anxieties were even more explicit in a letter addressed to the Chairman of the Supreme Court by a certain A. Mel'nikov. Mel'nikov opened fire on Solzhenitsyn's use of "criminal words" (*blatnye slovechki*), words that he found shameful and disgusting. With echoes of Grinberg, he wrote:

> This kind of vulgarity is clearly only permissible abroad, but here in the USSR the man of the future is being raised, and not the man of the obsolete past, when the older children taught the younger ones to say disgusting swear words to their own mothers. . . . Why then is the journal *Novyi mir* not pulling the reader toward the good but instead dragging him toward the mire [*boloto*]?[23]

Mel'nikov structured his text on certain oppositions; between the good and the "mire," here and abroad, the new and the old. Abroad "vulgarity" might flourish, but there was no place for it within the Soviet Union. Similarly, in the "old" Russia, children had been raised in the uncouth and vulgar ways

---

[22] "The culture of speech derived from good literature," writes Vadim Volkov in his study of the campaigns for *kulturnost'* in the 1930s, and "reading was also directly connected with the acquisition of culturedness." See Volkov, "The Concept of *Kul'turnost'*," 223. See also Michael S. Gorham, *Speaking in Soviet Tongues: Language Culture and the Politics of Voice in Revolutionary Russia* (DeKalb, 2003), 120–140.

[23] RGALI f. 1702, op. 9, d. 107, l. 76.

of their older brothers and sisters, but now, according to Mel'nikov, they were educated to be citizens of the communist future.[24] He was happy that the nuclear family was no longer able to pass on unsavory behavior to the new generation and cherished the Soviet state's interest in child rearing. For him, the publication of *One Day in the Life of Ivan Denisovich* was at odds with the official commitment to raising this new man. He found it contradictory that even as the state struggled to combat the problem of hooliganism, it allowed this work full of foul words, written by a "criminal hoodlum" (*zlostnyi khuligan*), to be published. In choosing to address his letter to the Supreme Court, Mel'nikov intimated that this was not a matter only for the literary experts at *Novyi mir* but also for the government bodies responsible for maintaining law and order.

In another letter, this time addressed to the editors of the satirical journal *Krokodil,* a lawyer praised Solzhenitsyn for "telling the truth" but condemned his use of bad language, writing graphically: "Some phrases in the book are disgusting, like typhus louses on the human body."[25] With Soviet citizens fearful that the immoral behavior of the Gulag was set to contaminate society, criminal argot was repudiated as the means by which this dreaded contagion might spread.

Anxiety about the *blatnoi* lexicon in Solzhenitsyn's novella played into broader fears about the Gulag releases and rising levels of crime, and the letters addressed to the editors of *Novyi mir* can be seen as part of more general letter-writing practices. Solzhenitsyn's apparent infatuation with *blatnaia muzyka* enraged those who were already deeply fearful that criminal culture might soon drown out their own respectable voices.[26]

The Disillusionment of the *Zek*

Despite the concerns of the Soviet public, the party had spent much of the 1950s loudly proclaiming its commitment to transforming all criminals into decent Soviet citizens. Yet by 1962, when *One Day in the Life of Ivan*

---

[24] In his work on swearing in late imperial Russia, Steve Smith has suggested that for "conscious" workers striving to acquire *kul'turnost'*, swearing was so strongly associated with a perceived "lack of culture" that it came to serve as a "recognised marker of Russian ethnicity." It is revealing that half a century after the revolution, Mel'nikov regarded bad language as a hangover from the past, an unsavory kind of behavior that was Russian and not Soviet. See S. A. Smith, "The Social Meanings of Swearing: Workers and Bad Language in Late Imperial and Early Soviet Russia," *Past and Present* 160 (1998): 167–202 (181).

[25] RGALI f. 1702, op. 9, d. 109, l. 66.

[26] Denis Kozlov suggests that it was particularly older readers who objected to Solzhenitsyin's language. Of the seventy-three letters concerning Solzhenitsyn's language, thirty-one mentioned the writer's age; twenty-four of these were over fifty-five. While I agree that an older generation might be more concerned with questions of social conformity, Komsomol members were also engaged in the fight for law and order. Moreover, it is possible that pensioners were more likely to consider their age of significance and therefore to mention it in their letter, perhaps as proof of their experience and wisdom. Over half of the letter writers critical of Solzhenitsyn's language did not mention their age. See Kozlov, "The Readers of *Novyi mir,*" 315–316.

Denisovich was published, this policy was already being reversed. The party had sanctioned a return to a more severe approach to criminal justice by 1961. With the tide already turning against the notion of re-education, the responses to *One Day in the Life of Ivan Denisovich* are all the more noteworthy. Mel'nikov, for one, welcomed the changes, admitting that there had recently been some successes in the fight against crime and "you don't see the rampant hell-raisers who spew out foul language on the streets any more. Now they quickly take them off to sober up at the police station."[27] The state's volte-face did not, however, receive support from everyone.

Several prisoners wrote to the editors of *Novyi mir* over the course of 1962–1963, perhaps inspired by a letter published in *Literaturnaia gazeta,* allegedly from a former recidivist thief named Minaev.[28] Yet where Minaev was full of disgust for the criminal world he had once inhabited, the prisoners who dispatched letters to the editors of *Novyi mir* sought some kind of vindication. Seizing on the publication of Solzhenitsyn's novella as an opportunity to express their own views on the subject of crime and punishment, they railed against their renewed exclusion from Soviet society. Of the five prisoners whose letters survive in the *Novyi mir* archive, only one believed that the Soviet system might still welcome him home. Singularly optimistic, Aleksandr Sergachev asked the editors to find him a ghostwriter willing to transform his experiences—which included a series of sentences for theft and hooliganism—into a publishable autobiography.[29] The four other prisoners, serving time for nonpolitical crimes, no longer believed that the Soviet regime would engage in the rewriting of their life stories. Unlike the purge victims whose autobiographies ended with rehabilitation and readmission to the party, these prisoners recognized their chances of a new life were slim. Increasingly convinced that their reintegration into society had become impossible, they realized that the days when rehabilitation was promised to *all* had come to an abrupt end. One prisoner, Mikhail Fadeev, commented pointedly that prisoners were now "doomed not to correction but to physical destruction by means of hunger, calculated deprivation, and suffering in the camps of the USSR."[30]

A fellow prisoner, V. A. Lovtsov, firmly believed that the government now lacked any kind of commitment to its erstwhile goal of re-education. Describing in detail the barbarity of life in the camps, he was highly critical of the Soviet penal system for failing to "correct" prisoners. According to Lovtsov, prisoners in 1951—the year in which *One Day in the Life of Ivan Denisovich* was set—would commonly say that as soon as they were free they would try to steal a little bit more money, commit a robbery, or even kill someone. "Neither re-education nor correction had touched them," averred Lovtsov. While the Gulag allowed them to become master card play-

[27] RGALI f. 1702, op. 9, d. 107, l. 76.
[28] "V redaktsiiu Literaturnoi gazety," *Literaturnaia gazeta,* 22 January 1963, 3.
[29] RGALI f. 1702, op. 9, d. 107, ll. 49–51.
[30] RGALI f. 1702, op. 9, d. 107, l. 79.

ers, it denied them access to newspapers, study, or training. Penal reform was still painfully slow in the post-Stalin years, he said, and not until Khrushchev's speech at the Third Writers' Congress in 1959 did the prisoner begin to hope for change. Hearing Khrushchev's promises of "faith in man" (*vera v cheloveka*), every prisoner felt that he too "could become a human being" (*stat' chelovekom*).[31] Soon, however, this became another broken promise. Commenting on the failure of the amnesties and the high levels of reoffending, Lovtsov argued that the authorities had betrayed their own pledge to "correct" prisoners. Applied only to petty offenders, the decree of 14 August 1959 had ignored those serving longer terms, which, according to Lovtsov, suggested that the government did not believe the more dangerous criminals could be "reforged."[32] Denouncing this approach, Lovtsov emotionally claimed that the criminal should be "forgiven," however grave his first offense had been: "If you believe in him once, if you forgive him, he will never be a criminal again." According to Lovtsov, Khrushchev's promises of "faith in man" had never materialized, and the practices of the Gulag remained sharply at odds with the advertised rhetoric of 1959. Lovtsov grew despondent and at one point wrote: "I am a son of the Gulag, if you can put it that way."[33] The reforms of the early Khrushchev era had promised "reforging," but Lovtsov now seemed to think of himself as an innate outsider, his membership to the other world of the Gulag almost a birthmark—a part of his identity he would never shed.

Railing against his exclusion, Lovtsov realized the difficulty inherent in proving that he had reacquired the moral qualities needed to participate in Soviet life once more. He wrote: "Do you really think that I don't want to be respectable [*chestnyi*], that I don't want to live well, like millions of Soviet citizens? But how to obtain this? How and to whom shall I prove that I want to live respectably [*chestno*], that I won't commit any more crimes? . . . Nobody wants to deal with my case."[34] Lovtsov repeatedly used the adjective *chestnyi* in his letter. As he understood it, *chestnost'* was the prime quality used to distinguish members of Soviet society from those banished as outcasts. In his usage, it can perhaps be read as an antonym for *poshlost'*. With some Soviet citizens loudly insisting on the *poshlost'* of Gulag culture, those inhabiting this other world realized that their chances of being recognized as a *chestnyi chelovek* were increasingly remote.

The unobtainable nature of *chestnost'* was also a key theme for A. Makarov, a prisoner serving a twenty-five-year sentence in the Komi ASSR. From the outset, Makarov problematized the notion of "correction" and "re-education":

---

[31] RGALI f. 1702, op. 9, d. 108, l. 5.
[32] On the 14 August 1959 decree, see chapter 5.
[33] RGALI f. 1702, op. 9, d. 108, l. 2.
[34] RGALI f. 1702, op. 9, d. 108, l. 7.

Having read [Solzhenitsyn]'s story, one can't but help thinking not only about those who endured those *terrible years* but also about those who are enduring the *tortures* of "Correction" even now. In addition to this book, I have also read many books and brochures on moral education, and I have decided to use these brochures in writing this letter, so that with your help I can find answers to some of the questions which as a prisoner I somehow can't figure out.[35]

Well versed in Soviet theories on re-education, he began by citing at length from a brochure by A. Kovalev, *The Psychology and Personality of the Prisoner and the Individual Approach to the Process of Re-education.* Using the regime's own texts to condemn it, he noted its failure to live up to the grand claims of the 1950s. Having repeatedly read that Soviet justice was committed to returning prisoners to life within the Soviet collective, Makarov asked sardonically: "In a few years' time, will I really be working in some collective or other, if out of the forty-three years of my life, I've spent five and half of them serving in the army and seventeen in prison?" Concluding that redemption was simply not possible, he dismissed the notion of correction as merely a "pretext" which hid the Gulag's true function as a site of infinite suffering. "I can't find any answer to the question," he wrote. "Who needs these camps, why do they exist? Are they really a method of 're-education,' or a means of spiritual and physical corruption?"[36] By the end of the letter Kovalev came to the radical conclusion that he would never be allowed back: "There's only one way out: death! To die is far simpler than meeting the daily norms. The only pity is that so many still have to meet the norms and I have to ask: What is all this for, and who needs it? If I have still not become respectable [*chestnyi*] in the eyes of the people, and atoned for my crime with seventeen years of imprisonment, then are the people respectable in my eyes?" Makarov had already reached the bitter conclusion that a return to Soviet society was impossible, the regime's promises of re-education empty. He would never be recognized as *chestnyi*. And if readmission into the Soviet community was not possible, he renounced life.

One of the most astute writers, Makarov clearly realized that by the early 1960s two different approaches were being taken: one approach for criminals, another for party members. Later in his letter he cited from a 1963 tract that already embodied the regime's new stance on crime. In this work, *In a Society Building Communism, There Should Be No Place for Lawbreaking and Crime,* A. L. Remenson had even begun to undermine the notion of *vospitanie,* a fact that Makarov was quick to note. The passage that most vexed Makarov began: "Some prisoners claim that: 'I'm not the one who's guilty: it was the war, I got a poor upbringing [*plokhoe moe vospitanie*], the wrong kind of teachers, and so on. Poor, unhappy old me—I'm not to

---

[35] RGALI f. 1702, op. 9, d. 109, l. 139.
[36] RGALI f. 1702, op. 9, d. 109, l. 141.

blame.' We should say straight out to these people: 'Don't deceive your-self!'"[37] Makarov went on to argue that the same line could logically be taken toward purge victims. Reworking the passage cited above, Makarov suggested that even purge victims like Solzhenitsyn himself could be told: "Don't deceive yourself, not all communists ended up in camps under Stalin. In fact, many were able to 'overcome' these difficulties rather than bowing down before them, and so they didn't end up in a camp." Makarov was deeply bitter that political prisoners were vindicated, while those sentenced under Stalin for nonpolitical crimes were doomed to seemingly eternal incarceration. In dealing with the great body of Stalin's outcasts, the state was now making important distinctions among different categories. As Makarov noted, the promise of readmission was no longer universal but restricted primarily to political prisoners and party members such as Solzhenitsyn.

A. G. Baev took a slightly different approach, but the beliefs underpinning his letter were similar. Writing on 22 December 1962 while serving his fifth sentence, Baev opened his letter with a long description of conditions in a labor camp. In it he hoped to prove to his reader that the hardships and injustices endured by Ivan Denisovich had not yet been eradicated.[38] Rotten meat, neglect for the sick, and official corruption were still the staples of camp life. Such experiences led Baev to believe that no prisoner could emerge reformed. A prisoner was typically so corrupted by his ordeals in the camps and by the loss of his family and home, he wrote, that there was little chance he would do anything other than reoffend upon release. Baev realized that as a nonpolitical criminal he would have little chance of successfully returning to Soviet society, so he sought to be reclassified as one of Stalin's victims. According to Baev, his errors—which he did not deny—had been grossly exaggerated by an unjust system that wanted to turn him into an "eternal *zek*." Denying that he was born a criminal, Baev sketched out his life story:

> During the war, I lost my parents and became a street child at the age of twelve. While I was still a minor, I joined the army and received many awards. I was in the partisan forces. But after the war, a "crack" appeared in my life, and the stamp of Stalin's cult of personality was imprinted on my life. And so I served fifteen years in prison, experiencing all the "joys" of a life without any happiness and without any hope for the future.[39]

Baev could have decided to construct his story solely around his wartime losses and failed *vospitanie* like some of the petition writers described in chapter 2, but he clearly feared that this tale would receive an unsympathetic hearing. In Baev's eyes, his only chance to rejoin the Soviet collective was to

---

[37] A. L. Remenson, *V obshchestve, stroiashchem kommunizm, ne dolzhno byt' mesta pravonarusheniiam i prestupnosti* (Moscow, 1963), 19.

[38] RGALI f. 1702, op. 9, d. 107, ll. 8–14.

[39] RGALI f. 1702, op. 9, d. 107, l. 12.

align himself with the regime's new priorities. In the wake of the Twenty-Second Party Congress, it seemed the only credential for a successful readmission into Soviet society was to be a victim of Stalin's cult of personality. Baev's attempt at reclassification was not, however, entirely successful. A reply from the *Novyi mir* editors noted pointedly: "It seems to us that you wrongly compare your life in the camps with the life of the prisoners in Solzhenitsyn's story *One Day in the Life of Ivan Denisovich*. Ivan Denisovich and his comrades were sentenced unlawfully, whereas you have been sentenced five times and you don't deny that you were guilty. What kind of victim of the cult were you? Did the period of the cult really lead people to commit crimes?"[40] Baev wrote a second angry letter.[41] Again he asserted that as someone born and raised under Soviet power, he should not have turned out a criminal; the fact that he did reflected the inadequacies of the Stalinist period. This time the editors did not reply. Having determined that Baev was a criminal and not a victim of political repression, the editors saw no need to prolong the dialogue. Any suggestion that the faults of the Stalinist era extended to child rearing and education was now firmly off-limits.

These prisoners concurred that the promises of redemption blazoned across the newspapers in the late 1950s had now been broken. None of them could really cherish any hope that they would emerge from the camps as new men and respected members of Soviet society. While some purge victims could hope to share in the euphoric mood of 1961–1962, the "criminal" who had been wooed with notions of correction in recent years remained isolated and excluded.

Some prisoners even realized that it was not only the state that had rejected them but also—and perhaps most vociferously—the Soviet public. One prisoner wrote to Solzhenitsyn:

> We who are serving twenty-five years are the bread and butter for those who are supposed to teach us virtue, corrupt though they are themselves. Did not the colonizers make out that Indians and Negroes were not fully human in this way? . . . It takes nothing at all to arouse public opinion against us. It is enough to write an article in the paper called "Man in a Cage," or to describe how a degenerate criminal violated a five-month-old baby girl, and tomorrow the people will organize meetings to demand that we be burnt in furnaces.[42]

Although acknowledging the role the media played, the prisoner also appreciated the high levels of collective anger emanating from Soviet citizens.[43]

[40] RGALI f. 1702, op. 9, d. 107, l. 7.
[41] RGALI f. 1702, op. 9, d. 107, ll. 1–6.
[42] Solzhenitsyn, "How People Read *One Day*," 56.
[43] The prisoner might be referring here to *Sovetskaia Rossiia*'s publication in September 1960 of extracts from readers' letters written in response to an earlier article condemning the allegedly lax nature of camp discipline. The editors' introduction to the correspondence stated that the

According to this prisoner-correspondent, the reluctance to view outcasts as fully human came not only from the state but from deep within society itself. The identification and branding of outcasts was not just a state-led enterprise, but one in which the newspaper-reading public also played an important part.

These letters provide an unexpected angle on the Ivan Denisovich debate. As the post-Stalinist world sought to redefine the boundary between insiders and outsiders, those cast out did not always remain silent. Instead of accepting their renewed exclusion, they used the notions of "re-education" and "reforging" promoted during the 1950s to claim their rightful return to society. With the state engineering a dramatic turn away from a rhetoric that had never successfully caught the public imagination, however, the prisoners built their protest on promises that were already being retracted.

A Zealous *Druzhinnik* and a "Parasite"

The enthusiasm some citizens displayed for policing society's moral boundaries was highly instrumental in the campaigns against the Leningrad poet Iosif Brodskii, in which both the secret police and voluntary brigades were involved. Since at least 1960 Brodskii had been under the scrutiny of the Leningrad KGB as a result of his involvement with the illegal underground collection *Sintaksis*, for which Aleksandr Ginzburg had been arrested.[44] Although neither officially trained in literature nor a member of the Writers' Union, Brodskii continued to devote his time to writing and translating poetry and his apparently unorthodox lifestyle became the main focus of the campaign against him, particularly for the *druzhinnik* who spearheaded the campaign of persecution.

The Leningrad poet Natal'ia Grudinina, who was closely involved in the defense of Brodskii, later described how Iakov Lerner, the bursar at Leningrad's Giproshakht Institute and a leading activist in the Dzerzhinskii raion *druzhina,* led a campaign against Brodskii from the fall of 1963.[45] Lerner

---

press had received a thousand letters supporting their view that the detention regime should be made tougher, and only a hundred extolling the opposite view (apparently almost exclusively from recidivist criminals themselves). In the published extracts, repeat offenders were condemned as "internal enemies" and the "overly humane" nature of the law criticized. For the original article, see "Men behind Bars," *Sovetskaia Rossiia,* 27 August 1960, 2–3, translated and reproduced in *Current Digest of the Soviet Press,* 12: 39, 18–20; for the letters, see "Men behind Bars," 17 September 1960, 2–3, translated and reproduced in *Current Digest of the Soviet Press,* 12: 40, 16–18.

[44] GARF f. 8131, op. 31, d. 99616, l. 2. A later KGB report from November 1964 suggested that Brodskii had first been invited for a "chat" in 1957, though other documentation suggests he first came under KGB scrutiny only in 1960. The report cited comments verbatim and referred to "operational information" (*operativnye dannye*), suggesting that he had been under close surveillance (GARF f. 8131, op. 31, d. 99616, ll. 35–38).

[45] Nikolai Iakimchuk, *Kak sudili poeta (delo I. Brodskogo)* (St. Petersburg, 1990), 6–7. Efim

had already appeared in newsreels as an exemplary activist devoted to the task of morally educating young people. Initially obsessed with catching and "re-educating" youths involved in black market transactions, Lerner then turned his attention to those young people among whom supposedly "anti-Soviet moods" flourished. Prior to the Brodskii case, Lerner had already organized one campaign against three young poets at the Technological Institute and presided over the trial of a young teacher who had left the Herzen Pedagogical Institute and was without employment.[46] In his first sally against Brodskii, Lerner used his contacts at the editorial offices of *Vechernii Leningrad* to publish a long condemnation of the young poet.[47]

In the article the *druzhinniki* wrote for the Leningrad evening newspaper, it was Brodskii's nonconformity that seemed to rankle most. Although insinuations about Brodskii's political allegiances were also made, he was primarily condemned for his appearance and unconventional behavior. Entitled "A Pseudoliterary Parasite," the article began by sketching out an image of the young poet. From the outset the reader was given to understand that this youth deliberately fashioned himself as something out of the ordinary: he wore corduroy trousers and walked the streets without a hat in winter, his red hair covered in snow. Thus even before the authors touched on his poetry, Brodskii had been painted as an outsider.

The way in which he spent his days was also unorthodox. Brodskii tended to sleep late before strolling down the Nevskii, where he liked to flirt with a young shop assistant in the bookstore. By evening, he would apparently find himself in a café or restaurant, drinking cocktails, often in the company of someone called "Jeff" or "Jack" and some girl "in glasses with a shock of disheveled hair." This daily routine demonstrated the two approaches taken in the attack against Brodskii. On one hand, he was a good-for-nothing, an idler who failed to get out of bed in the morning; on the other, he had American friends, a shady type with a questionable sense of patriotic duty. To slur his patriotism further, Lerner and his cowriters recounted how Brodskii almost betrayed his fatherland during a trip to Samarkand to visit his friend Shakhmatov. Having met with an American acquaintance at the Samarkand Hotel, Brodskii handed over copies of another friend's work for publication abroad. Brodskii and Shakhmatov then went to the aerodrome, where they apparently planned to steal an airplane and fly it over the border, until they

---

Etkind also describes Lerner as Brodskii's main persecutor. Etkind claims that Lerner regularly extorted huge sums of money from the black marketeers (*fartsovshchiki*), and that in 1973 he was arrested and sentenced to six years' imprisonment as a swindler (*moshennik krupnogo mashtaba*). See Efim Etkind, *Protsess Iosifa Brodskogo* (London, 1988), 47.

[46] The young teacher was sentenced to exile from Leningrad. Grudinina explains that when he traveled to Moscow to plead for intervention by the Komsomol's CC, they instructed the young man to return home and find himself a job, mocking Lerner's overzealous activism (Iakimchuk, *Kak sudili poeta*, 7).

[47] "Okololiteraturnyi truten'," *Vechernii Leningrad*, 29 November 1963, reproduced in Etkind, *Protsess Iosifa Brodskogo*, 16–22.

realized there was insufficient gasoline for the trip. As Brodskii also chose to take the manuscripts back from the American, no actual crime was committed even within the bounds of this constructed narrative, yet Lerner and his accomplices left no doubts about Brodskii's intended treachery.[48]

This profile of a traitor was somewhat secondary to the portrayal of Brodskii as a lazy, antisocial youth leading a quasi-criminal life. The reader learns that his companion on the Samarkand adventure had since been sentenced for a criminal act, and that many of his other friends led marginal lives: Geikhman was a criminal (*ugolovnik*), while Shveigol'ts, a bully who refused to work, had already been named and shamed on various *druzhiny* posters; Efim Slavinskii was labeled a good-for-nothing, while Mariamma Volnianskaia had abandoned her elderly and needy mother for the sake of the bohemian lifestyle, hanging out with a girlfriend who was fanatical about yoga and any sort of "mysticism." Brodskii was thus indicted as part of a youth subculture that rejected official Soviet values such as hard work and devotion to family and where criminal behavior was the norm.[49] Claiming that Brodskii had been unresponsive to "educational work," the article drew on the prevailing rhetoric of the antiparasite campaign to call for his exile: "Clearly we need to stop fussing over pseudoliterary parasites [*perestat' nianchit'sia s okololiteraturnym tuneiadtsem*]. There is no place for types like Brodskii in Leningrad."

To begin the process of removing Brodskii from Leningrad, the procurator of Dzerzhinskii raion turned to A. A. Prokof'ev, head of the Leningrad Writers' Union, in December 1963, requesting that the members organize a trial. Lerner personally visited Prokof'ev and the leadership of the union to explain the case, trying to whip up a frenzy of hatred toward the young poet. Following his visit, a document was produced by the leaders of the Leningrad Writers' Union in February 1964 which stated that Brodskii was not a writer but a "person attempting to compose verse." His writings were the result of a bored idler, though they also showed signs of "antipopulist" attitudes (*antinarodnye pozitsii*), and if disseminated among impressionable young people ran the risk of "corrupting their souls" (*rastlevat' dushi*).[50] As Brodskii was not a member of the union, however, no public trial was held among the Leningrad writers. Instead, the raion procurator, head of the local police, the chairman of the raion court, Lerner and other local dignitaries opted to try

---

[48] For Brodskii's account of this incident, see Solomon Volkov, *Conversations with Josef Brodsky*, trans. Marian Schwartz (New York, 1998), 61–63. Brodskii says that during the time he was staying in Samarkand, he came up with a plan to hijack an airplane and fly to Afghanistan. He intended to knock out the pilot, and his friend would take the controls. At the last moment, though, he suddenly became horrified by the idea of inflicting violence on the pilot, and the plan was abandoned.

[49] Etkind also notes that the names of many of the friends listed in the article are typically Jewish, making antisemitism an additional means used to attack Brodskii (*Protsess Iosifa Brodskogo*, 28).

[50] GARF f. 8131, op. 31, d. 99616, ll. 5–6.

Brodskii as a parasite through the standard court system.[51] On 18 February 1964 Brodskii was brought before the Dzerzhinskii local court (*narsud*), but the session was aborted to obtain medical reports from the psychiatric hospital where Brodskii was a registered patient.[52] On 13 March 1964 the court reconvened. At the trial, several writers spoke in defense of his writing, but there were also witnesses ready to testify to his harmful social influence. One witness told the court that Brodskii's poetry had a demoralizing effect on his son who no longer wanted to work. Others, handpicked by the leaders of the local *druzhina*, did not know Brodskii personally but spoke against him in court "on the basis of public opinion and the written evidence they had seen."[53] Brodskii was sentenced to five years' exile from Leningrad.[54]

This was not the result of a one-man crusade, and Lerner-the-*druzhinnik* was not the sole instigator of the affair. The Leningrad KGB had been following Brodskii's life for several years prior to his trial in 1964 and an internal memorandum preserved in his personal dossier states that on 23 October 1963 the head of the "public order" section within the Leningrad city Komsomol *apparat* had instructed Lerner to take action against Brodskii. Lerner was provided with Brodskii's diary and poetry by the KGB, which had confiscated his personal papers during a search of his apartment in January 1962 following the arrest of Shakhmatov and Umanskii.[55] Even if he was prompted into action, however, Lerner was clearly zealous about his task. Indeed, although he had been slated to speak himself at the March trial, the trial's organizers decided at the last minute that he lacked the necessary impartiality. He attended the trial nonetheless and taped the testimony of Brodskii's defendants. Passed on to Prokof'ev, the recording became the basis for a reprimand awarded to three members of the Leningrad Writers' Union who had spoken at the trial in defense of Brodskii—Grudinina, E. G. Etkind, and V. Admoni.[56]

Several of those involved in Brodskii's defense identified the zealous *druzhiny* as an important and unsavory social phenomenon in these years. Admitting that he did not know Brodskii at all, Surkov, first secretary of the Writers' Union of the USSR, argued that if there really were incriminating

---

[51] GARF f. 8131, op. 31, d. 99617, l. 116.

[52] A medical report written on 11 March 1964 found that he showed "psychopathic character traits," but that he was fit to stand trial and was able to work (GARF f. 8131, op. 31, d. 99616, ll. 58–59).

[53] GARF f. 8131, op. 31, d. 99617, l. 127.

[54] GARF f. 8131, op. 31, d. 99616, ll. 18–54.

[55] GARF f. 8131, op. 31, d. 99617, ll. 115–116. In 1962 he was interrogated following the arrest of two of his acquaintances, A. A. Umanskii and O. I. Shakhmatov, under charges of anti-Soviet activity. The report also mentions his contact with various foreigners, including at least one whom the KGB suspected of involvement with espionage. On the arrest of his two acquaintances, see GARF f. 8131, op. 31, d. 99616, ll. 35–38.

[56] GARF f. 8131, op. 31, d. 99617, l. 117. Grudinina noted in one of her letters that the tape had been destroyed and that snatches of their testimony were reworked into an "absurd text." GARF f. 8131, op. 31, d. 99616, l. 76.

materials he should be put on trial for anti-Soviet activity, but Surkov strongly objected to the use of the antiparasite legislation and to the "farcical trial" that had been staged. In a letter to General Procurator Rudenko, Surkov wrote: "Always there in the background of this case are the people's brigadiers [*druzhinniki*]. For me, a man who has read and seen a lot, their behavior triggers certain associations, though I can't bring myself to spell them out."[57] Not many went so far as to imply that these armbanded brigadiers might be compared with fascist thugs, but others were also highly critical of the role played by some of the *druzhinniki*, particularly Lerner. According to a collectively authored letter from Grudinina, Etkind, and N. G. Dolinina, he was a fanatic who stopped and searched any "suspicious" passersby, "frightening and blackmailing those he apprehended."[58] Describing the March trial, Zoia Toporova, Brodskii's legal defense attorney, later wrote that the courtroom was absolutely full, with scores of *druzhinniki* on one side and young poets and members of the intelligentsia on the other.[59] A conflict was thus emerging between those who feared a breakdown in the country's moral order and those who dreaded a return to the extralegal measures of policing that had flourished under Stalin.

Fighting for Legality

In the battle to see Brodskii set free, many of the petitioners were themselves writers, but they did not focus predominantly on Brodskii's work except to mention that he had not in fact authored many of the snippets of poetry interspersed into the *Vechernii Leningrad* article.[60] One of his defenders, E. Gnedin, himself a victim of Stalinist terror, wrote to the Procuracy to stress the damage being done to Brodskii's health by his enforced exile in Arkhangel'sk oblast where he was denied medical attention.[61] Other petitioners mentioned Brodskii's health, but this did not become the mainstay of their defense, however, and two other explanatory frameworks seemed to prevail: one asserted that he had erred but was not irredeemable; the second that there had been a gross miscarriage of justice which had parallels with the abuses of legality that had occurred under Stalin.

The first approach thus employed terms and principles that had been promoted in the press so enthusiastically in the late 1950s. In the aftermath of the trial, Frida Vigdorova wrote a petition asking for a review of the case

[57] GARF f. 8131, op. 31, d. 99616, ll. 65–66.

[58] GARF f. 8131, op. 31, d. 99616, l. 53.

[59] Iakimchuk, *Kak sudili poeta,* 11.

[60] Grudinina asserted that the true author, D. Bobyshev, had written to the Writers' Union claiming the poetry as his own (GARF f. 8131, op. 31, d. 99616, l. 71).

[61] GARF f. 8131, op. 31, d. 99617, l. 18. Evgenii Gnedin would later write about his experiences in prison in *Katastrofa i vtoroe rozhdenie!* (Amsterdam, 1977).

and objecting to the fact that references to Brodskii's friendship with Umanskii and Shakhmatov *before* their conviction in the spring of 1962 were still being used to convict him. Although he had at one time been "under their influence," he had "broken with them" even before they were arrested, she claimed. This played into established models in which young people might temporarily come "under the influence" of older, criminal types but then see the light. According to Vigdorova, Brodskii had been saved: "Thanks to the kind intervention of various adults, Brodskii and other young people who had been under the influence of Umanskii and Shakhmatov, began to correct themselves, to work productively, to study. Brodskii also got back on his feet and tried his hand at literary translation: he studied Polish and translated a cycle of poems by the Polish writer Galchinskii." Nefarious influences had been deflected, bad habits corrected, and Brodskii had now found "his path in life, the path of honesty and hard work."[62] The court case had only served to knock him off course. Grudinina also argued that after his "past mistakes and sins" he had stood on "the correct path of socially useful literary work" for more than a year.[63] In the fall of 1964, she and other writers suggested a solution that was in keeping with the principles promoted in the late 1950s. Drawing on the concept of *poruka,* they offered to become guardians to Brodskii, meaning that a process of correction and rehabilitation could happen in Leningrad itself.[64] This suggestion did not seem to meet with much enthusiasm from the authorities, perhaps reflecting the fact that such ideas were already somewhat passé.

The second approach focused on the methods employed by prosecutors and judge to secure Brodskii's conviction: they had referred to earlier incidents, such as Brodskii's involvement with Ginzburg's samizdat and friendship with Umanskii and Shakhmatov, even though he had been officially cleared of any wrongdoing; they claimed he had not been working, even though he had contracts for freelance work; and they generally did all they could to tarnish his reputation. All this smacked of the unlawful practices that had been common under Stalin but recently condemned so fully by the party. Writing to Rudenko in March 1964, Surkov said that, the "habits and customs of 1937–1938 are clearly visible." "No one involved in organizing this case could have read the materials from the Twentieth Party Congress, nor the new Party Program approved at the Twenty-Second," he argued.[65] In an unpublished article for *Literaturnaia gazeta,* Lidiia Chukovskaia wrote: "When I read the first article about him, published in the newspaper *Vechernii Leningrad* on 29 November 1963, it seemed to me that by some miracle I had been transported back from 1963 to 1937. Or, let's say,

---

[62] GARF f. 8131, op. 31, d. 99616, ll. 67–68.
[63] GARF f. 8131, op. 31, d. 99616, l. 69.
[64] GARF f. 8131, op. 31, d. 99617, l. 18 and l. 58.
[65] GARF f. 8131, op. 31, d. 99616, ll. 65–66.

1949."[66] In the wake of the Twenty-Second Party Congress connections with Stalinist justice represented the most damning of condemnations.

Brodskii did not easily fit the profile of the 1937 victim that had been promoted by the party in the early 1960s. Not even a party or Komsomol member, he was by no means a martyr to the Bolshevik cause, and even those who supported him did not make this claim. A member of the Composers' Union, G. Ia. Iudin, admitted that, "of course, Brodskii is far from being an ideal young Soviet person."[67] At the party congresses of 1956 and 1961, however, Stalinist terror had been indicted not *only* because it culled a generation of heroes, but also because it failed to observe Soviet laws. Although it had been violated in the past, the authorities had been promising since 1953 that legality, or *zakonnost'*, would be observed. Iudin was outraged that the law could even now be flouted: "It is beyond belief that such a shameful kangaroo court [*pozornoe sudilishche*] should happen these days. . . . The trial was a violation of the most elementary foundations of Soviet legal proceedings and communist morality."[68] Even before the court had sentenced Brodskii, Ol'ga Chaikovskaia, a Moscow journalist, raised the alarm, telling Rudenko that the newspaper article was "distorted and libelous." She implored the general procurator: "I beg you to intervene in this case and to restore legality."[69] In a letter written to Khrushchev himself, Grudinina asked: "Where will it all end? The party and you personally promised the strictest observation of the law. Why has the law been broken in Leningrad without any consequences?"[70]

Over the course of 1962–1963, the General Procuracy had launched a campaign to ensure that its own organs, as well as the police and courts, were aware of the importance of acting in strict conformity with the law.[71] Now the accusations of violated legality apparently touched a nerve, at least among some leading figures in the law-enforcement agencies. According to a report from November 1964, the writers' petitions led to the formation of a commission to review the case, and the members decided that many of the accusations against Brodskii were unfounded. The authors objected in particular to the way earlier incidents were now resurrected, and they lamented the absence of "concrete proof."[72] In December 1964 Rudenko, Chairman of the Supreme Court Gorkin, and KGB Chairman V. E. Semichastnyi wrote

[66] Iakimchuk, *Kak sudili poeta*, 8.

[67] GARF f. 8131, op. 31, d. 99616, l. 96.

[68] GARF f. 8131, op. 31, d. 99616, l. 96.

[69] GARF f. 8131, op. 31, d. 99616, ll. 8–9.

[70] GARF f. 8131, op. 31, d. 99616, l. 95.

[71] On 30 June 1962 the general procurator of the USSR issued an order entitled "On Measures to further Improve the Procuracy's Work in the Fight against Crime and Violations of Legality." Subsequent reports described cases in which citizens had been arrested unlawfully and even convicted groundlessly. Some police officers were censured for beating citizens. See GARF f. 8131, op. 32, d. 6911, ll. 12–19.

[72] GARF f. 8131, op. 31, d. 99616, ll. 121–129.

to the CC recommending that the sentence be reduced. According to this memo, they were worried not only by the way the case was being reported in France, West Germany, and the United States but also by the uproar that it had caused among writers in Moscow and Leningrad, who had written many letters that "call into doubt whether Brodskii's conviction as a parasite is justified."[73]

There was, however, resistance to this new line from Leningrad. Important figures in the city and oblast party leadership and the local KGB believed Brodskii had been correctly sentenced. Rather than worrying about the writers' responses, these figures turned their attention to a slightly different constituency. Declaring a review of the case unwarranted, they argued that it was likely to provoke a "negative reaction from the public." At best they could envision Brodskii released from administrative exile but still banished from Leningrad.[74] Keen to defend their actions, local leaders were also sensitive to the fact that some sectors of the public were anxious to see the courts take a more severe stance in the fight against any form of unorthodox behavior.

Rudenko, Semichastnyi, and Gor'kin, the defenders of legality triumphed —at least for a while. In September 1965 the RSFSR Supreme Court reduced Brodskii's exile from five years to one year and five months, the time already served.[75] The reprieve was only temporary, however: in 1972 Brodskii was forced into exile abroad, and Solzhenitsyn followed two years later.[76]

The disgust evinced by readers of *One Day in the Life of Ivan Denisovich* and the zeal Leningrad *druzhinniki* showed in their hunt for "parasites" share the same origin: pride in "Soviet" values, concern for law and order, the fear of otherness. Anxieties about Soviet respectability, voiced at many times during the 1950s, resurface in these two cases. Brodskii's lack of headwear and Solzhenitsyn's *poshlost'* were both read as signs of their failure to follow the prescriptions of Soviet *byt;* both were anathema to citizens who found the experience of change in the post-Stalin era highly disturbing and feared that their "civilized" world was now under threat.

At the Twenty-Second Party Congress Khrushchev had tried to meld two strands in post-Stalinist thinking into one political vision: labeled an "obstacle" that had been overcome, Stalinist terror was incorporated into a narrative of the glorious Bolshevik journey toward the shining future, a future now dependent on cleansing and purifying society of all that impeded this progress. Already by 1963–1964, however, the fragility—perhaps the impossibility—of this union became apparent. Khrushchev's repudiation of

[73] GARF f. 8131, op. 31, d. 99617, ll. 91–93.
[74] GARF f. 8131, op. 31, d. 99617, ll. 117–118.
[75] GARF f. 8131, op. 31, d. 99617, l. 218.
[76] Volkov, *Conversations with Josef Brodsky;* and D. M. Thomas, *Aleksandr Solzhenitsyn: A Century in His Life* (London, 1998).

Stalinist terror included stinging indictment of his predecessor's abuse of legality, but the campaign against nonconformist or deviant behavior itself imperiled the sanctity of *zakonnost'*. By the final year of Khrushchev's rule, the contradictions inherent in his promise to purify the Soviet world of dubious elements while establishing a law-based society were evident, at least to some.

The crux of the problem lay in agreeing on the criteria by which those unfit to be members of the community would be identified. Some seemed to argue that there were obvious, external signifiers that marked out the un-Soviet: the wrong clothes, uncouth language, excessive time spent in cafés drinking cocktails. According to others, however, it was easy for these signs to be wrongly interpreted. Khrushchev had promised to move away from the Stalinist model in which convictions could be based on the "type" of person someone was, promising a law-based society in which criminal convictions were the result of specific, proven crimes. The RSFSR Criminal Code of 1960 had endorsed this principle.[77] Yet the antiparasite law and the campaign against Brodskii showed that by the early 1960s a criminal conviction could be based on a person's profile, on the persona they presented to the world, rather than on specific unlawful actions. And with this, the government's commitment to *zakonnost'*, pledged ever since Stalin's death, was severely undermined.

---

[77] Harold Berman explains that Article 3 of the 1960 Criminal Code stated that no person could be subjected to criminal responsibility and punishment unless he had committed a crime, defined as a socially dangerous act provided for by law. This eliminated the doctrine of analogy (embodied in the 1926 code) whereby a person could be sentenced for committing a "socially dangerous act" which was *not* specifically provided for in the code (Berman, *Soviet Criminal Law*, 24–25).

Conclusion

In April 1953 a group of former prisoners serving out a term of exile in Siberia wrote to the Supreme Soviet expressing their gratitude for the amnesty decree. Soon, they said, Muscovites, Leningraders, Kievans, and other city dwellers would go out to the stations with flowers and welcome back the returnees. "The sons of the Motherland are going home!"[1] Yet these were not soldiers returning heroic from war. Their position was far more ambiguous, their service to the nation—which these exiles wished to emphasize—always questionable. The realities of their return doubtless proved quite different from their expectations.

Anna Akhmatova's image of two Russias "eyeball to eyeball" suggested that the opening of the Gulag gates would engender scenes of silent accusation and guilt between released prisoners and those who had denounced them. Such encounters are described in the diaries and memoirs of the artistic intelligentsia and in literary accounts of the period, such as Vasilii Grossman's *Forever Flowing* and Nekrasov's *Kira Georg'evna*.[2] In Iulii Daniel's short story "Atonement," an old acquaintance of the protagonist, returning from imprisonment, wrongly accuses him of being an informer and spreads rumors to this effect; the moral opprobrium of the intelligentsia milieu he inhabits, although ungrounded, eventually forces him into self-imposed exile from Moscow.[3] In keeping with Akhmatova's claim, the tale suggests the guilt not only of those directly responsible for the terror but of those who were simply part of the "Russia" that allowed them to be sent there. This book has argued, however, that the encounter between two Russias was even more complicated and messy. The return included a whole contingent of pris-

---

[1] GARF f. 7523, op. 85, d. 235, l. 8.
[2] Chukovskii, *Dnevnik*, 222; Vasily Grossman, *Forever Flowing*, trans. Thomas P. Whitney (Evanston, Ill., 1997); Viktor Nekrasov, "Kira Georg'evna," *Novyi mir* (June 1961): 70–126.
[3] Yuly Daniel [Nikolai Arzhak], "Atonement," *This Is Moscow Speaking* (London, 1968).

oners, including recidivist criminals, petty thieves, one-off offenders, as well as those wrongfully convicted (of both political and nonpolitical crimes). Encounters did not take place only in the corridors of party buildings, at theaters, or in writers' apartments but also on trains, in parks, and on station platforms. Not all the returnees were the noble martyrs to the cause found in much of the memoir literature, nor sincere artists, as in *Kira Georg'evna:* some were broken men, drunk and violent; some had come to hate the regime that had so destroyed their lives. Many simply did not have a family or home to which they could return.

These encounters excited some young people, thrilled at their glimpse into the other world of the Gulag. Others, however, felt profoundly threatened. In a climate of hardship and adversity—and this was the experience of most Soviet citizens even if the 1950s saw some economic recovery—many worried that the releases put their own welfare at risk. With the brutal chaos of war not yet a distant memory, the public was desperate for stability; and as crime rates began to climb, some set pen to paper to articulate their concern about both those coming back from the camps and the young people who seemed to find criminal behavior alluring. Khrushchev had attempted to discard the more violent elements of Stalinist political culture, but letter writers continued to use established formulations, often labeling returnees as "enemies of the people" and "bandits."

According to Zygmunt Bauman, modernity's promise was to bring order to the chaos of the world, and its vision of order was dependent on identifying and degrading all that it sought to replace: the creation of a civilized, law-abiding "us" relied on establishing a deviant, barbaric "other."[4] Under Stalin the state launched repeated campaigns to bring *kul'turnost'* to the Soviet Union and to destroy the "uncultured" and disorderly. Ideally, this chaotic "other" resided in capitalist regions of the world or in the past. The Soviet regime dismissed any signs of disorder in contemporary society as vestiges of the prerevolutionary era. As the revolutionary era receded into history, however, this tactic proved increasingly problematic. Citizens who had accepted the Soviet regime's order-building mission did not always rely on the state to identify the disturbing "other," and many of them were unhappy that vestiges of the past remained a blemish on Soviet life long after 1917. The principles of "correction" and "re-education" which the leadership promoted in the mid to late 1950s thus failed to resonate with these members of Soviet society. In their binary vision of the world, their own respectable community was under mortal threat from within, particularly from the new arrivals from the Gulag.

In 1961 the party leader tried a different solution. At the Twenty-Second

---

[4] Zygmunt Bauman, *Modernity and Ambivalence* (Cambridge, 1991), 14. See also Wendy Holloway and Tony Jefferson, "The Risk Society in an Age of Anxiety: Situating the Fear of Crime," *British Journal of Sociology* 48 (1997): 257–266.

Party Congress, Khrushchev presented a vision of the world that sought to answer many of the difficulties and complexities thrown up by the previous eight years of change. He revisited the subject of Stalinist terror, a topic that had caused great difficulties when first broached in a semipublic fashion in February 1956. In pointing the finger at key culprits (Molotov, Kaganovich, and Malenkov, as well as Stalin), Khrushchev hoped to stem the unsettling tide of questions about accountability generated by the first releases and the Secret Speech. As well as clarifying who was responsible for past miscarriages of justice, he identified the victims far more clearly, focusing almost exclusively on party repressions, in particular the generation of 1936–1938. The symbolic rebirth of the Old Bolsheviks culled in the Great Terror was appropriated as a symbol of the party's revival. Khrushchev thus turned the party's repudiation of terror into one of the party's great victories on the road to full-blown communism, a goal that was apparently now imminent. And if the communist paradise was so near, he could allow no toleration of those who failed to live up to his ideal of the new Soviet man and woman and antisocial parasites must be ejected from the community. It was a clever argument: it brought together a version of the Stalinist past in which the party was cleared of any wrong-doing during the purges, the revolutionary spirit was renewed, and the imminent advent of communism promised, while reassuring anxious citizens that criminal or deviant behavior would no longer be allowed. In the same year that Stalin's body was removed from the Mausoleum, the Gulag population began to climb once more, but the two were ingeniously presented as part of a single purgative process: the condemnation of terror apparently purified the party, while the new commitment to banishing offenders and criminals allowed society to rid itself of potential contaminants of the next generation.

Some groups in Soviet society objected to Khrushchev's revised vision. Some members of the intelligentsia, including writers and lawyers, became aware that the new "cleansing" of Soviet society conflicted with one of the pledges made in the 1950s, the regime's adherence to *zakonnost'*. Prisoners objected to the revoking of earlier promises to allow them to return to the Soviet family. These were not powerful voices in the early 1960s, but Khrushchev's ouster from the leadership in 1964 suggests a wider recognition of the failure of his reform program. Although the solutions of 1961 were presented using triumphant and euphoric rhetoric, oratory could not disguise Khrushchev's failure to find a satisfactory solution to one of the most difficult Stalinist legacies. In allowing the Gulag population to grow, Khrushchev himself backtracked on his most significant reform.

By the early 1960s Stalin's successors had approved a new expansion of the Gulag and had allowed the concept of "legality" to be sacrificed for the sake of more stringent law-and-order measures. They also seemed to abandon the revolutionary goal of transforming human nature: Khrushchev's belief, professed in 1959, that "no such thing exists as a person who cannot be corrected" was quietly discarded. With it went the promise that every individual, however sinful, could be turned into a healthy citizen fit to live in communist society. The late 1950s perhaps saw the last gasp of the revolution, a final attempt to craft the perfect world, this time without relying on excessive use of violence. Instead the Gulag was here to stay. Now the network of prison camps was no longer even *imagined* as a site for re-education and cure, and instead served as a mirror that reassured the Soviet community that it was indeed orderly, cultured, and respectable.

Bibliography

PRIMARY SOURCES

ARCHIVAL SOURCES

Below I give the title of each archive I visited, and the *fond*s from which I have cited material. Where I feel it would be helpful for the reader, I give detail of each *delo,* but for others—for example, the *fond*s at GARF and RGANI which I used extensively—I simply give the title of the *opis'.*

Gosudarstvennyi arkhiv Rossiiskoi Federatsii (GARF)

f. 7523 USSR Supreme Soviet, 1937–1985
op. 58, op. 85, op. 107 Documents from the structural sections of the Presidium of the Supreme Soviet apparatus
op. 69, op. 89 Documents relating to the review of pardon appeals
op. 95 Group for the Preparation of Pardon Appeals

f. 7863 USSR Supreme Soviet: Commission for Complaints and Appeals, 1938–1958
op. 20 (1953); op. 21 (1954); op. 22 (1955); op. 23 (1956)

f. 8131 USSR Public Prosecutor's Office, 1924–1980
op. 31 Section for the Verification of Investigations
op. 32 Office (*kantseliariia*) of the General Procuracy

f. 9401 USSR Ministry of Internal Affairs, 1918–1960
op. 1a Collection of orders, decrees, directives, and circulars from the NKVD-MVD
op. 2 Khrushchev's "Special Files"

Rossiiskii gosudarstvennyi arkhiv noveishei istorii (RGANI)

f. 1 Party congresses
op. 4 Materials relating to the Twenty-Second Party Congress

f. 2 General Section of the CC CPSU
op. 1 Plenums

f. 5 Apparatus of the CC CPSU
op. 30 General Section of the CC CPSU
op. 32 Party Organs Department, RSFSR

f. 6 Committee of Party Control (KPK)
op. 6 Reports, references, verbatim accounts, protocols

Collection 89 "The Communist Party on Trial"

Rossiiskii gosudarstvennyi arkhiv sotsial'no- politicheskoi istorii (RGASPI)

f. 82 Molotov, V. M.
op. 2, dd. 1443–1464 Letters and telegrams; d. 1466 Anonymous letters; d. 1470 Summaries (*svodki*) of letters

f. 356 Stasova, E. D., 1887–1973
op. 2, d. 37 Letters from E. D. Stasova to N. S. Khrushchev and G. M. Malenkov; d. 25 Correspondence with M. A. Shaver; d. 34 Correspondence with E. M. Rikhter; d. 41 Correspondence with S. E. Shpits

f. 556 CC CP *biuro* for RSFSR, 1954–1966
op. 1 Protocols and stenograms, d. 197 Vladimir obkom (1956); d. 243 Gor'kii obkom (1956); d. 304 Irkutsk obkom (1956); d. 601 Leningrad obkom (1956); d. 638 Magadan obkom (1956); d. 691 Moscow obkom (1956); d. 705 Moscow gorkom (1956); d. 875 Rostov obkom (1956); d. 881 Rostov gorkom (1956); d. 1031 Stalingrad obkom (1956)
op. 14 Party Organs Department

f. 560 Violations of the law under Stalin: manuscript material, 1935–1980
op. 1, d. 2 (I. Bogdanovich); d. 19 (I. Kochergin); d. 23 (Leskov-Ongudinov); d. 24 (F. E. Lisitsin); d. 30 (M. I. Panich); d. 41 (G. I. Chebanov)

f. 599 Journal *Kommunist*
op. 1 (single *opis'*, not categorized)

f. M-1 Komsomol CC
op. 32 Propaganda and Agitation Section, 1941–1965

Rossiiskii gosudarstvennyi arkhiv literatury i iskusstva (RGALI)

f. 1702 Journal *Novyi Mir*
op. 9, dd. 107–109 Readers' letters regarding works published in the journal

Tsentral'nyi arkhiv obshchestvennykh dvizhenii Moskvy (TsAODM)

f. 65 Dzerzhinskii raikom
op. 46, d. 28 Stenogram of the party *aktiv* meeting following the Twenty-Second Party Congress

f. 82 Sverdlov raikom
op. 34, d. 12 Information on work of primary party cells following the Twentieth Party Congress

f. 8132 Party organization of the Moscow Writers' Union
op. 1, d. 6 Stenogram of party meeting (30 March 1956)

Tsentral'nyi gosudarstvennyi arkhiv Moskovskoi oblasti (TsGAMO)

f. 2157 Moscow Oblast Soviet of Workers' Deputies
op. 1, d. 5311 Permanent Commission for the Maintenance of Socialist Legality and Social Order

Gosudarstvennyi arkhiv Vladimirskoi oblasti (GAVO)

f. p-830 Vladimir obkom
op. 3, dd. 212–213 Reports from the gorkoms and raikoms (1956); d. 824 Reports from the gorkoms and raikoms (1961)

f. r-3789 Vladimir Oblast Soviet of Workers' Deputies
op. 1, d. 2004, d. 2007 Commission for the Maintenance of Socialist Legality and Social Order

f. r-2172 Aleksandrov City Soviet of Workers' Deputies
op. 4, d. 64 Protocols (1955)

Ob'edinennyi gosudarstvennyi arkhiv Cheliabinskoi oblasti (GU OGAChO)

f. 288 Cheliabinsk obkom *biuro*
op. 21, d. 93 Information and correspondence regarding socialist legality and the fight against crime
op. 24, d. 108 Materials relating to the obkom *biuro* meeting of 26 August 1960

f. 94 Zheleznodorozhnyi raikom
op. 2 *Biuro* protocols

Tsentral'nyi arkhiv dokumental'nykh kollektsii Moskvy (TsADKM)

f. 85 Personal files of N. I. Kochin

Memorial

f. 2 Personal memoirs

NEWSPAPERS AND PERIODICALS

Current Digest of the Soviet Press
Don
Iunost'
Izvestiia
Krokodil
Leningradskaia pravda
Literaturnaia Rossiia
Literaturnaia gazeta
Molodaia gvardiia
Moskovskaia pravda
Novyi mir
Ogonek
Oktiabr'
Pravda
Prizyv (Vladimir oblast)
Zvezda

LITERARY WORKS, PAMPHLETS, MEMOIRS, SOURCE COLLECTIONS

Amalrik, Andrei. *Will the Soviet Union Survive until 1984?* London: Penguin, 1970.
Artizov, A., Iu. Sigachev, I. Shevchuk, and B. Khlopov, eds. *Reabilitatsiia: Kak eto bylo. Dokumenty prezidiuma TsK KPSS i drugie materialy, mart 1953–fevral' 1956.* Vol. 1. Moscow: Demokratiia, 2000.
———. *Reabilitatsiia: Kak eto bylo. Fevral' 1956–nachalo 80-kh godov.* Vol. 2. Moscow: Demokratiia, 2003.
Bardach, Janusz, and Kathleen Gleason. *Surviving Freedom: After the Gulag.* Berkeley: University of California Press, 2003.
Bystroletov, Dmitrii. *Pir bessmertnykh.* Moscow: Granitsa, 1993.
———. *Puteshestvie na krai nochi.* Moscow: Sovremennik, 1996.
Chukovskaia, L. K. *Zapiski ob Anne Akhmatovoi.* Vol. 2, 1952–62. Paris: YMCA, 1980).
Chukovskii, Kornei. *Dnevnik, 1930–1969.* Moscow: Sovremennyi pisatel', 1994.
Daniel, Yuly [Nikolai Arzhak]. *This Is Moscow Speaking.* London: Collins, 1968.
Dzhekobson, Mikhail, and Lidiia Dzhekobson. *Pesennyi fol'klor GULAGa kak istoricheskii istochnik (1940–1991).* Moscow: Sovremennyi gumanitarnyi universitet, 2001.
Etkind, Efim. *Protsess Iosifa Brodskogo.* London: Overseas Publications Interchange, 1988.
Ezhegodnik knig SSSR 1954: II-polugodie. Moscow: Izdatel'stvo vsesoiuznoi palaty, 1955.
Ezhegodnik knig SSSR 1955: II-polugodie. Moscow: Izdatel'stvo vsesoiuznoi palaty, 1956.
Erenburg, Il'ia. *Ottepel': povest'.* Moscow: Sovetskii pisatel', 1954.
Feifer, George. *Justice in Moscow.* London: Bodley Head, 1964.
Gel'fand, I. A., and N. T. Kuts. *Neobkhodimaia oborona po sovetskomu ugolovnomu pravu.* Kiev: Vysshaia shkola MVD USSR, 1962.
Gnedin, Evgenii A. *Katastrofa i vtoroe rozhdenie!* Amsterdam: Seriia biblioteka, no. 8, 1977.
Gor'kii, Maksim, L. Auerbach, and S. G. Firin, eds. *Belomor: An Account of the Construction of the New Canal between the White Sea and the Baltic Sea.* Translated by Amabel Williams-Ellis. London: John Lane, 1935.
Grossman, Vasily. *Forever Flowing.* Translated by Thomas P. Whitney. Evanston, Ill.: Northwestern University Press, 1997.
Iakimchuk, Nikolai, ed. *Kak sudili poeta (delo I. Brodskogo).* St. Petersburg: Soiuz kinematografistov RSFSR Sankt-Peterburgskaia organizatsiia, 1990.
Istoriia Stalinskogo Gulaga: Konets 1920-kh–pervaia polovina 1950-kh godov. 7 vols. Moscow: ROSSPEN, 2004.
Joffe, Maria. *One Long Night: A Tale of Truth.* Translated by Vera Dixon. New York: New Park Publications, 1978.
Khlevniuk, Oleg V. *The History of the Gulag: From Collectivization to the Great Terror.* New Haven: Yale University Press, 2004.
Khrushchev, N. S. *Khrushchev Remembers.* Translated by Strobe Talbott. London: Andre Deutsch, 1971.
Khrushchev, Sergei. *Rozhdenie sverkhderzhavy: Kniga ob ottse.* Moscow: Vremia, 2000.
Kokurin, A. I., and N. V. Petrov. *Gulag (Glavnoe upravlenie lagerei) 1918–1960.* Moscow: Demokratiia, 2002.
Kovaleva, N., A. Korotkov, S. Mel'chin, Iu. Sigachev, and A. Stepanov. *Molotov,*

Malenkov, Kaganovich. 1957. Stenogramma iiun'skogo plenuma TsK KPSS i drugie dokumenty. Moscow: Demokratiia, 1998.

Kozlov, V. A., and S. V. Mironenko, eds. *58–10: Nadzornye proizvodstva prokuratury SSSR po delam ob antisovetskoi agitatsii i propagandy, mart 1953–1991.* Moscow: Demokratiia, 1999.

Labedz, Leopold, ed. *Solzhenitsyn: A Documentary Record.* Harmondsworth, U.K.: Penguin, 1974.

Loginov, V. T., ed. *XX S″ezd: Materialy konferentsii k 40-letniiu XX s″ezda KPSS.* Moscow: Aprel'-85, 1996.

Makarenko, A. S. *The Road to Life: An Epic of Education (Putevka v zhizn': Pedagogicheskaia poema).* Translated by Ivy Litvinov and Tatiana Litvinov. Moscow: Foreign Languages Publishing House, 1951.

Medynskii, G. A. *Chest'.* Moscow: Sovetskii pisatel', 1960.

Mihajlov, Mihajlo. *Moscow Summer.* London: Sidgwick and Jackson, 1966.

Molchanov, Gennadii. "Lagernyi kanon: popytka opredeleniia zhanra." *Volia: zhurnal uznikov totalitarnykh system,* 2–3 (1994): 381–388.

Moullec, Gaël, and Nicolas Werth, eds. *Rapports secrets soviétiques: La société russe dans les documents confidentiels, 1921–1991.* Paris: Gallimard, 1994.

Nekrasov, Viktor. "Kira Georg'evna." *Novyi mir* (June 1961): 70–126.

"O kul'te lichnosti i ego posledsvtiiakh: Doklad Pervogo sekretaria TsK KPSS tov. Khrushcheva XX s″ezdu Kommunisticheskoi partii Sovetskogo Soiuza 25 fevralia 1956 goda." In *Doklad N. S. Khrushcheva o kul'te lichnosti Stalina na XX s″ezde KPSS: dokumenty.* Moscow: ROSSPEN, 2002, 51–119.

Raleigh, Donald J., ed. and trans. *Russia's Sputnik Generation: Soviet Baby Boomers Talk about Their Lives.* Bloomington: Indiana University Press, 2006.

Remenson, A. L. *V obshchestve, stroiashchem kommunizm, ne dolzhno byt' mesta pravonarusheniiam i prestupnosti.* Moscow: Politotdel MZ MOOP RSFSR, 1963.

Russian Criminal Tattoo Encyclopaedia. Vol. 1. London: Steidl/Fuel, 2003.

Russian Criminal Tattoo Encyclopaedia. Vol. 2. London: Fuel, 2006.

Schlesinger, Rudolph, ed. *Changing Attitudes in Soviet Russia: The Family in the USSR.* London: Routledge and Kegan Paul, 1949.

Shepilov, D. T. "Vospominaniia." *Voprosy istorii* (March 1998): 3–24.

Siegelbaum, Lewis, and Andrei Sokolov, eds. *Stalinism as a Way of Life: A Narrative in Documents.* New Haven: Yale University Press, 2004.

Solzhenitsyn, Aleksandr. *The Gulag Archipelago, 1918–1956: An Experiment in Literary Investigation.* 2 vols. Translated by Thomas P. Whitney. New York: Harper and Row, 1975.

Stalin, I. V. *Sochineniia.* 3 vols. Edited by Robert H. McNeal. Stanford: Hoover Institution Foreign Language Publications, 1967.

Sudoplatov, Pavel. With Anatoli Sudoplatov, Jerrold L. and Leona P. Schecter. *Special Tasks: The Memoirs of an Unwanted Witness—A Soviet Spymaster.* London: Little Brown, 1994.

Tertz, Abram [Andrei Siniavskii]. *Goodnight!* New York: Viking, 1989.

"'Tovarishch Kaganovich pretenduet na osoboe k sebe otnoshenie': Ural'skaia ssylka opal'nogo soratnika I. V. Stalina. 1957–1958 gg." *Istoricheskii arkhiv* (July–August 2005): 4–26.

Vail', Petr, and Aleksandr Genis. *60-e: Mir sovetskogo cheloveka.* Ann Arbor: Ardis, 1988.

Vilensky, Simeon, ed. *Till My Tale Is Told.* Translated by John Crowfoot. Bloomington: Indiana University Press, 1999.

Voinovich, Vladimir. *Monumental Propaganda*. Translated by Andrew Bromfield. New York: Alfred A. Knopf, 2004.

Volkov, Solomon. *Conversations with Josef Brodsky*. Translated by Marian Schwartz. New York: Free Press, 1998.

FILMS

Chistoe nebo. Directed by Grigorii Chukhrai. USSR, 1961.

Kholodnoe leto 53. Directed by Aleksandr Proshkin. USSR, 1988.

Partiinyi bilet. Directed by Ivan Pyr′ev. USSR, 1936.

Putevka v zhizn′. Directed by Nikolai Ekk. USSR, 1931.

SECONDARY SOURCES CITED

BOOKS AND ARTICLES

Adler, Nanci. *The Gulag Survivor: Beyond the Soviet System*. New Brunswick: Transaction, 2002.

Aksiutin, Iu. V. *Khrushchevskaia "Ottepel′" i obshchestvennye nastroeniia v SSSR v 1953–1964 gg.* Moscow: ROSSPEN, 2004.

———. "Novoe o XX s″ezde KPSS." *Otechestvennaia istoriia* (March–April 1998): 108–123.

———. "Popular Responses to Khrushchev." In *Nikita Khrushchev*, edited by William Taubman, Sergei Khrushchev, and Abbott Gleason, 177–208. New Haven: Yale University Press, 2000.

Aksiutin, Iu. V., and A. V. Pyzhikov. *Poststalinskoe obshchestvo: Problema liderstva i transformatsiia vlasti*. Moscow: Nauchnaia kniga, 1999.

Alexopoulos, Golfo. "Amnesty 1945: The Revolving Door of Stalin's Gulag." *Slavic Review* 64 (2005): 274–306.

———. *Stalin's Outcasts: Aliens, Citizens, and the Soviet State, 1926–1936*. Ithaca: Cornell University Press, 2003.

Altshuler, Mordechai. "More about Public Reaction to the Doctors' Plot." *Jews in Eastern Europe* 2 (1996): 22–57.

Attwood, Lynne, and Catriona Kelly. "Programmes for Identity: The 'New Man' and the 'New Woman.'" In *Constructing Russian Culture in the Age of Revolution: 1881–1940*, edited by Catriona Kelly and David Shepherd, 256–290. Oxford: Oxford University Press, 1998.

Barnes, Steven A. "'In a Manner Befitting Soviet Citizens': An Uprising in the Post-Stalin Gulag." *Slavic Review* 64 (2005): 823–850.

Bauman, Zygmunt. *Modernity and Ambivalence*. Cambridge: Polity, 1991.

———. *Modernity and the Holocaust*. Cambridge: Polity, 1989.

Beer, Daniel. *Renovating Russia: The Human Sciences and the Fate of Liberal Modernity, 1880–1930*. Ithaca: Cornell University Press, 2008.

Beermann, R. "The Parasites Law." *Soviet Studies* 13 (1961): 191–205.

Berman, Harold. *Justice in the USSR: An Interpretation of Soviet Law*. Cambridge, Mass.: Harvard University Press, 1963.

———. *Soviet Criminal Law and Procedure: The RSFSR Codes*. Cambridge, Mass.: Harvard University Press, 1966.

Biess, Frank. *Homecomings: Returning POWs and the Legacies of Defeat in Post-war Germany*. Princeton: Princeton University Press, 2006.

Bittner, Stephen V. *The Many Lives of Khrushchev's Thaw: Experience and Memory in Moscow's Arbat*. Ithaca: Cornell University Press, 2008.

Bloch, Sidney, and Peter Reddaway. *Soviet Psychiatric Abuse: The Shadow over World Psychiatry*. London: Victor Gollancz, 1984.

Bloomfield, David, Teresa Barnes, and Luc Huyse. *Reconciliation after Violent Conduct: A Handbook*. Stockholm: IDEA, 2003.

Bonnell, Victoria. *Iconography of Power: Soviet Political Posters under Lenin and Stalin*. 2d ed. Berkeley: University of California Press, 1999.

Boym, Svetlana. *Common Places: Mythologies of Everyday Life in Russia*. Cambridge, Mass.: Harvard University Press, 1994.

Breslauer, George W. *Khrushchev and Brezhnev as Leaders: Building Authority in Soviet Politics*. London: George Allen and Unwin, 1982.

——. "Khrushchev Reconsidered." In *The Soviet Union since Stalin*, edited by Stephen F. Cohen, Alexander Rabinowitch, and Robert Sharlet, 50–70. Bloomington: Indiana University Press, 1980.

Brooks, Jeffrey. *Thank You, Comrade Stalin! Soviet Public Culture from Revolution to Cold War*. Princeton: Princeton University Press, 2000.

——. *When Russia Learned to Read: Literacy and Popular Literature, 1861–1917*. Princeton: Princeton University Press, 1985.

Brown, Deming. *The Last Years of Soviet Russian Literature: Prose Fiction 1975–1991*. Cambridge: Cambridge University Press, 1993.

Bruner, Jerome. "Life as Narrative." *Social Research* 54 (1987): 11–32.

Brusilovskaia, L. B. *Kul'tura povsednevnosti v epokhu "ottepeli": Metamorfozy stilia*. Moscow: URAO, 2001.

Buchli, Victor. *An Archaeology of Socialism*. Oxford: Berg, 1999.

Buckley, Mary. "The Untold Story of *Obshchestvennitsa* in the 1930s." *Europe-Asia Studies* 48 (1996): 569–586.

Buck-Morss, Susan. *Dreamworld and Catastrophe: The Passing of Mass Utopia in East and West*. Cambridge, Mass.: MIT Press, 2000.

Burbank, Jane. *Russian Peasants Go to Court: Legal Culture in the Countryside, 1905–1917*. Bloomington: Indiana University Press, 2004.

Burds, Jeffrey. "Bor'ba s banditizmom v SSSR v 1944–1953 gg." In *Sotsial'naia istoriia. Ezhegodnik 2000*, 169–190. Moscow: IRI RAN, 2000.

Carleton, Greg. "Genre in Socialist Realism." *Slavic Review* 53 (1994): 992–1009.

Clark, Katerina. *The Soviet Novel: History as Ritual*. 3d ed. Bloomington: Indiana University Press, 2000.

Clarke, John, Stuart Hall, Tony Jefferson, and Brian Roberts. "Subcultures, Cultures, and Class." In *Resistance through Rituals: Youth Subcultures in Post-War Britain*, edited by Stuart Hall and Tony Jefferson, 9–74. London: Routledge, 1993.

Cohen, Stanley. *Folk Devils and Moral Panics*. London: MacGibbon and Kee, 1972.

Cohen, Stephen F. "The Friends and Foes of Change: Reformism and Conservatism in the Soviet Union." In *The Soviet Union since Stalin*, edited by Stephen F. Cohen, Alexander Rabinowitch, and Robert Sharlet, 11–31. Bloomington: Indiana University Press, 1980.

——. "The Stalin Question since Stalin." In *An End to Silence: Uncensored Opinion in the Soviet Union*, edited by Stephen F. Cohen, 22–50. New York: W. W. Norton, 1982.

Condee, Nancy. "Body Graphics: Tattooing the Fall of Communism." In *Consum-

ing Russia: Popular Culture, Sex, and Society since Gorbachev, edited by Adele Marie Baker, 339–361. Durham: Duke University Press, 1999.

———. "Cultural Codes of the Thaw." In *Nikita Khrushchev,* edited by William Taubman, Sergei Khrushchev, and Abbott Gleason, 160–176. New Haven: Yale University Press, 2000.

Davies, Sarah. *Popular Opinion in Stalin's Russia: Terror, Propaganda, Dissent, 1934–1941.* Cambridge: Cambridge University Press, 1997.

Davis, Natalie Zemon. *Fiction in the Archives: Pardon Tales and Their Tellers in Sixteenth-Century France.* Stanford: Stanford University Press, 1987.

Dewey, Horace W., and Ann M. Kleimola. "From the Kinship Group to Every Man His Brother's Keeper: Collective Responsibility in Pre-Petrine Russia." *Jahrbücher für Geschichte Osteuropas* 30 (1982): 321–335.

Dobson, Miriam. "Letters." In *Reading Primary Sources: The Interpretation of Texts from Nineteenth- and Twentieth- Century History,* edited by Miriam Dobson and Benjamin Ziemann, 57–73. London: Routledge, 2008.

———. "POWs and Purge Victims: Attitudes towards Party Rehabilitation, 1956–7." *Slavonic and East European Review* 86 (2008): 328–345.

Eakin, Paul John. *How Our Lives Become Stories: Making Selves.* Ithaca: Cornell University Press, 1999.

Edele, Mark. "Strange Young Men in Stalin's Moscow: The Birth and the Life of Stiliagi, 1945–53." *Jahrbücher für Geschichte Osteuropas* 50 (2002): 37–61.

Elie, Marc. "Les politiques à l'égard des libérés du Goulag: amnistiés et réhabilités dans la région de Novosibirsk, 1953–1960." *Cahiers du monde russe* 47 (2006): 327–348.

Febvre, Lucien. *The Problem of Unbelief in the Sixteenth Century: The Religion of Rabelais.* Translated by Beatrice Gottlieb. Cambridge, Mass.: Harvard University Press, 1982.

Field, Deborah. *Private Life and Communist Morality in Khrushchev's Russia.* New York: Peter Lang, 2007.

Fitzpatrick, Sheila. *Everyday Stalinism: Ordinary Life in Extraordinary Times. Soviet Russia in the 1930s.* New York: Oxford University Press, 1999.

———. "How the Mice Bury the Cat: Scenes from the Great Purges of 1937 in the Russian Provinces." *Russian Review* 52 (1993): 299–320.

———. "Readers' Letters to *Krest'ianskaia gazeta,* 1938." *Russian History* 24 (1997): 149–170.

———. "Social Parasites: How Tramps, Idle Youth, and Busy Entrepreneurs Impeded the Soviet March to Communism." *Cahiers du monde russe* 47 (2006): 377–408.

———. "Supplicants and Citizens: Public Letter-Writing in Soviet Russia in the 1930s." *Slavic Review* 55 (1996): 78–105.

———. "The World of Ostap Bender: Soviet Confidence Men in the Stalin Period." *Slavic Review* 61 (2002): 535–557.

Fitzsimons, Dermot. "'Shoot the Mad Dogs!': Appellation and Distortion during the Moscow Show Trials, 1936–8." *Slovo* 13 (2001): 172–187.

Foucault, Michel. "About the Beginning of the Hermeneutics of the Self: Two Lectures at Dartmouth." *Political Theory* 21 (1993): 198–227.

———. "The Ethic of Care for the Self as a Practice of Freedom." In *The Final Foucault,* edited by James Bernauer and David Ramussen, 1–20. Cambridge, Mass.: MIT Press, 1988.

Frank, Stephen P. "Popular Justice, Community, and Culture among the Russian Peasantry." *Russian Review* 46 (1987): 239–265.

Friedgut, Theodore H. *Political Participation in the USSR*. Princeton: Princeton University Press, 1979.

Fursenko, Aleksandr, and Timothy Naftali. *Khrushchev's Cold War: The Inside Story of an American Adversary*. New York: W. W. Norton, 2006.

Fürst, Juliane. "The Arrival of Spring? Changes and Continuities in Soviet Youth Culture and Policy between Stalin and Khrushchev." In *The Dilemmas of De-Stalinization: Negotiating Cultural and Social Change in the Khrushchev Era*, edited by Polly Jones, 135–153. London: Routledge, 2006.

Gardzonio, Stefano. "Tiuremnaia lirika i shanson. Neskol′ko zamechaniia k teme." *Toronto Slavic Quarterly*, 14 (2005). www.utoronto.ca/tsq/14/garzonio14.shtml.

Getty, J. Arch, and William Chase. "Patterns of Repression among the Soviet Elite: A Biographical Approach." In *Stalinist Terror: New Perspectives*, edited by J. Arch Getty and Roberta T. Manning, 225–246. Cambridge: Cambridge University Press, 1993.

Getty, J. Arch, and Oleg V. Naumov. *The Road to Terror: Stalin and the Self-Destruction of the Bolsheviks, 1932–1939*. New Haven: Yale University Press, 1999.

Getty, J. Arch, Gabor T. Rittersporn, and Victor N. Zemskov. "Victims of the Soviet Penal System in the Pre-War Years: A First Approach on the Basis of Archival Evidence." *American Historical Review* 98 (1993): 1017–49.

Glotov, Aleksandr, and Natal′ia Guliaigrodskaia. "Russkaia fol′klornaia tiuremnaia pesnia i pesni Iuza Aleshkovskogo." *Studia Metodologica* 12 (2003): 74–81.

Goode, Erich, and Nachman Ben-Yehuda. "Moral Panics: Culture, Politics, and Social Construction." *Annual Review of Sociology* 20 (1994): 149–171.

Gorham, Michael S. *Speaking in Soviet Tongues: Language Culture and the Politics of Voice in Revolutionary Russia*. DeKalb: Northern Illinois University Press, 2003.

Gorlizki, Yoram, and Oleg Khlevniuk. *Cold Peace: Stalin and the Soviet Ruling Circle, 1945–1953*. Oxford: Oxford University Press, 2004.

Gorlizki, Yoram. "Delegalization in Russia: Soviet Comrades' Courts in Retrospect." *American Journal of Comparative Law* 46 (1998): 403–425.

Gorsuch, Anne E. *Youth in Revolutionary Russia: Enthusiasts, Bohemians, Delinquents*. Bloomington: Indiana University Press, 2000.

Graziosi, Andrea. "The Great Strikes of 1953 in Soviet Labor Camps in the Accounts of Their Participants: A Review." *Cahiers du monde russe et soviétique* 33 (1992): 419–445.

Hagenloh, Paul M. "'Socially Harmful Elements' and the Great Terror." In *Stalinism: New Directions*, edited by Sheila Fitzpatrick, 286–308. London: Routledge, 2000.

Halfin, Igal. "The Demonization of the Opposition: Stalinist Memory and the 'Communist Archive' at Leningrad Communist University." *Kritika* 2 (2001): 45–80.

———. *From Darkness to Light: Class, Consciousness, and Salvation in Revolutionary Russia*. Pittsburgh: University of Pittsburgh Press, 2000.

———. *Terror in My Soul: Communist Autobiographies on Trial*. Cambridge, Mass.: Harvard University Press, 2003.

Halfin, Igal, and Jochen Hellbeck. "Rethinking the Stalinist Subject: Stephen Kotkin's 'Magnetic Mountain' and the State of Soviet Historical Studies." *Jahrbücher für Geschichte Osteuropas* 44 (1996): 456–463.

Hellbeck, Jochen. "Fashioning the Stalinist Soul: The Diary of Stepan Podlubnyi, 1931–9." In *Stalinism: New Directions*, edited by Sheila Fitzpatrick, 77–116. London: Routledge, 2000.

Hoffmann, David L. *Stalinist Values: The Cultural Norms of Soviet Modernity, 1917–1941*. Ithaca: Cornell University Press, 2003.

Hoggart, Richard. *The Uses of Literacy*. Harmondsworth, U.K.: Penguin, 1958.

Holloway, Wendy, and Tony Jefferson. "The Risk Society in an Age of Anxiety: Situating the Fear of Crime." *British Journal of Sociology* 48 (1997): 257–266.

Holquist, Peter. "'Information Is the Alpha and Omega of Our Work': Bolshevik Surveillance in Its Pan-European Context." *Journal of Modern History* 69 (1997): 415–450.

Hosking, Geoffrey. *A History of the Soviet Union 1917–1991*. 3d ed. London: Fontana, 1992.

Humphrey, Michael. *The Politics of Atrocity and Reconciliation: From Terror to Trauma*. London: Routledge, 2002.

Ivanova, Galina Mikhailovna. *Labor Camp Socialism: The Gulag in the Soviet Totalitarian System*. Translated by Carol Flath. Armonk, N.Y.: M. E. Sharpe, 2000.

Johnson, Priscilla. *Khrushchev and the Arts: The Politics of Soviet Culture, 1962–4*. Cambridge, Mass.: MIT Press, 1965.

Jones, Polly. "From Stalinism to Post-Stalinism: De-Mythologising Stalin, 1953–6." In *Redefining Stalinism*, edited by Harold Shukman, 127–148. London: Frank Cass, 2003.

———. "From the Secret Speech to the Burial of Stalin: Real and Ideal Responses to De-Stalinization." In *The Dilemmas of De-Stalinization: Negotiating Cultural and Social Change in the Khrushchev Era*, edited by Polly Jones, 41–63. London: Routledge, 2006.

Kaplan, Cynthia S. "The Communist Party of the Soviet Union and Local Policy Implementation." *Journal of Politics* 45 (1983): 2–27.

Kelly, Catriona. *Refining Russia: Advice Literature, Polite Culture, and Gender from Catherine to Yeltsin*. Oxford: Oxford University Press, 2001.

———. "'Thank You for the Wonderful Book': Soviet Child Readers and the Management of Children's Reading, 1950–1975." *Kritika* 6 (2005): 717–753.

Kharkhordin, Oleg. *The Collective and the Individual in Russia: A Study of Practices*. Berkeley: University of California Press, 1999.

Knight, Amy. *Beria: Stalin's First Lieutenant*. Princeton, N.J.: Princeton University Press, 1993.

Korey, William. "Continuities in Popular Perceptions of Jews in the Soviet Union." In *Hostages of Modernization: Studies on Modern Anti-Semitism 1870–1933/39*, edited by Herbert A. Strauss. Vol. 2, 1383–1405. Berlin: de Gruyter, 1993.

Korolenko, P. "Ot 'strashnogo' Iudka k 'nestrashnomu' Beilisu: V. G. Korolenko. Noch'iu. Delo Beilisa." *Russkii zhurnal* (March 2001), www.russ.ru/krug/razbor/20010330.html.

Kotkin, Stephen. *Magnetic Mountain: Stalinism as a Civilization*. Berkeley: University of California Press, 1995.

Kozlov, Denis. "Naming the Social Evil: The Readers of *Novyi mir* and Vladimir Dudinstev's *Not by Bread Alone*, 1956–59 and Beyond." In *The Dilemmas of De-Stalinization: Negotiating Cultural and Social Change in the Khrushchev Era*, edited by Polly Jones, 80–98. London: Routledge, 2006.

Kozlov, V. A. "Kramola: Inakomyslie v SSSR pri Khrushcheve i Brezhneve, 1953–1982." *Otechestvennaia istoriia* (July–August 2003): 93–111.

———. *Mass Uprisings in the USSR: Protest and Rebellion in the Post-Stalin Years*. Translated by Elaine McClarnand MacKinnon. Armonk, N.Y.: M. E. Sharpe, 2002.

Kramer, Alan. "'Law-Abiding Germans'?: Social Disintegration, Crime, and the

Reimposition of Order in Post-War Western Germany, 1945–9." In *The German Underworld: Deviants and Outcasts in German History,* edited by Richard J. Evans, 238–262. London: Routledge, 1988.

Krylova, Anna. "The Tenacious Liberal Subject in Soviet Studies." *Kritika* 1 (2000): 119–146.

Lane, Christel. *The Rites of Rulers: Ritual in Industrial Society—The Soviet Case.* Cambridge: Cambridge University Press, 1981.

LaPierre, Brian. "Making Hooliganism on a Mass Scale: The Campaign against Petty Hooliganism in the Soviet Union, 1956–1964." *Cahiers du monde russe* 47 (2006): 349–376.

Lawton, Anna. *Kinoglasnost: Soviet Cinema in Our Time.* Cambridge: Cambridge University Press, 1992.

Lenoe, Matthew E. "Letter-Writing and the State: Reader Correspondence with Newspapers as a Source for Early Soviet History." *Cahiers du monde russe* 40 (1999): 139–170.

Linden, Carl A. *Khrushchev and the Soviet Leadership.* Baltimore: Johns Hopkins University Press, 1966.

Livshiz, Ann. "De-Stalinizing Soviet Childhood: The Quest for Moral Rebirth." In *The Dilemmas of De-Stalinization: Negotiating Cultural and Social Change in the Khrushchev Era,* edited by Polly Jones, 117–134. London: Routledge, 2006.

Lorey, David E., and William H. Beezley, eds. *Genocide, Collective Violence, and Popular Memory: The Politics of Remembrance in the Twentieth Century.* Wilmington: SR Books, 2002.

Makepeace, R. W. *Marxist Ideology and Soviet Criminal Law.* London: Croom Helm, 1980.

McCauley, Martin, ed. *Khrushchev and Khrushchevism.* Basingstoke, U.K.: Macmillan, 1987.

McReynolds, Louise. *The News under Russia's Old Regime: The Development of a Mass-Circulation Press.* Princeton: Princeton University Press, 1991.

Medvedev, Roy A. "The Stalin Question." In *The Soviet Union since Stalin,* edited by Stephen F. Cohen, Alexander Rabinowitch, and Robert Sharlet, 32–49. Bloomington: Indiana University Press, 1980.

Medvedev, Roy A., and Zhores A. Medvedev. *Khrushchev: The Years in Power.* Oxford: Oxford University Press, 1977.

Merridale, Catherine. *Night of Stone: Death and Memory in Russia.* London: Granta, 2000.

Mikoian, S. A. "Aleksei Snegov v bor'be za 'destalinzatsiiu.'" *Voprosy istorii* (April 2006): 69–84.

Minow, Martha. *Between Vengeance and Forgiveness: Facing History after Genocide and Mass Violence.* Boston: Beacon Press, 1998.

Moeller, Robert G. "What Has 'Coming to Terms with the Past' Meant in Post-World War II Germany? From History to Memory to the 'History of Memory.'" *Central European History* 35 (2002): 223–256.

Morrissey, Susan. *Heralds of Revolution: Russian Students and the Mythologies of Radicalism.* New York: Oxford University Press, 1998.

Murav, Harriet. "The Beilis Ritual Murder Trial and the Culture of Apocalypse." *Cardozo Studies in Law and Literature* 12 (2000): 243–263.

Murto, Kari. *Towards the Well Functioning Community: The Development of Anton Makarenko and Maxwell Jones' Communities.* Jyväskylä: University of Jyväskylä, 1991.

Naumov, V. P. "N. S. Khrushchev i reabilitatsiia zhertv massovykh politicheskikh re-pressii." *Voprosy istorii* (April 1997): 19–36.

———. "Sud'ba voennoplennykh i deportirovannykh grazhdan SSSR. Materialy Komissii po reabilitatsii zhertv politicheskikh repressii." *Novaia i noveishaia istoriia* (March–April 1996): 91–112.

Neuberger, Joan. *Hooliganism: Crime, Culture, and Power in St. Petersburg, 1900–1914.* Berkeley: University of California Press, 1993.

Papovian, Elena. "Primenenie stat'i 58–10 UK RSFSR v 1957–1958 gg.: po materi-alam Verkhovnogo suda SSSR i Prokuratury SSSR v GARF." In *Korni travy: Sbornik statei molodykh istorikov,* edited by L. S. Eremina and E. B. Zhemkova, 73–87. Moscow: Zven'ia, 1996.

Papovian, Elena, and Aleksandr Papovian. "Uchastie Verkhovnogo suda SSR v vyrabotke repressivnoi politiki, 1957–1958 gg." In *Korni travy: Sbornik statei molodykh istorikov,* edited by L. S. Eremina and E. B. Zhemkova, 54–72. Moscow: Zven'ia, 1996.

Pearson, Geoffrey. *Hooligan: A History of Respectable Fears.* Basingstoke, U.K.: Macmillan, 1983.

Poiger, Uta G. "A New, 'Western' Hero?: Reconstructing Masculinity in the 1950s." In *The Miracle Years: A Cultural History of West Germany, 1949–1968,* edited by Hanna Schissler, 412–427. Princeton: Princeton University Press, 2001.

Polian, Pavel. "The Internment of Returning Soviet Prisoners of War after 1945." In *Prisoners of War, Prisoners of Peace: Captivity, Homecoming, and Memory in World War II,* edited by Bob Moore and Barbara Hately-Broad, 123–139. Oxford: Berg, 2005.

Reid, Susan E. "Cold War in the Kitchen: Gender and the De-Stalinization of Consumer Taste in the Soviet Union under Khrushchev." *Slavic Review* 61 (2002): 211–252.

———. "The Meaning of Home: 'The Only Bit of the World You Can Have to Yourself.'" In *Borders of Socialism: Private Spheres of Soviet Russia,* edited by Lewis H. Siegelbaum, 145–170. Basingstoke, U.K.: Palgrave Macmillan, 2006.

———. "Women in the Home." In *Women in the Khrushchev Era,* edited by Melanie Ilič, Susan E. Reid, and Lynne Attwood, 149–176. Basingstoke, U.K.: Palgrave Macmillan, 2004.

Rogger, Hans. "The Beilis Case: Anti-Semitism and Politics in the Reign of Nicholas II." *Slavic Review,* 25 (1966): 615–629.

Rosenberg, Tina. *The Haunted Land: Facing Europe's Ghosts after Communism.* London: Vintage, 1995.

Roth-Ey, Kristin. "'Loose Girls' on the Loose?: Sex, Propaganda, and the 1957 Youth Festival." In *Women in the Khrushchev Era,* edited by Melanie Ilič, Susan E. Reid, and Lynne Attwood, 75–95. Basingstoke, U.K.: Palgrave Macmillan, 2004.

Shearer, David. "Elements Near and Alien: Passportization, Policing, and Identity in the Stalinist State, 1932–1952." *Journal of Modern History* 76 (2004): 835–881.

Sherlock, Thomas. "Shaping Political Identity through Historical Discourse: The Memory of Soviet Mass Crimes." In *After Mass Crime: Rebuilding States and Communities,* edited by Béatrice Pouligny, Simon Chesterman, and Albrecht Schna-bel, 215–240. Tokyo: United Nations University Press, 2007.

Shrader, Abby M. "Branding the Exile as 'Other': Corporal Punishment and the Construction of Boundaries in Mid-19th Century Russia." In *Russian Modernity: Politics, Knowledge, Practices,* edited by David L. Hoffman and Yanni Kotsonis, 19–40. Basingstoke, U.K.: Macmillan, 2000.

——. "Branding the Other/Tattooing the Self: Bodily Inscription among Convicts in Russia and the Soviet Union." In *Written on the Body: The Tattoo in European and American History*, edited by Jane Caplan, 174–192. London: Reaktion Books, 2000.

Smith, Gerald Stanton. *Songs to Seven Strings: Russian Guitar Poetry and Soviet 'Mass Song.'* Bloomington: Indiana University Press, 1984.

Smith, Kathleen. *Remembering Stalin's Victims: Popular Memory and the End of the USSR.* Ithaca: Cornell University Press, 1996.

Smith, S. A. "The Social Meanings of Swearing: Workers and Bad Language in Late Imperial and Early Soviet Russia." *Past and Present* 160 (1998): 167–202.

Solomon, Peter H. *Soviet Criminal Justice under Stalin.* Cambridge: Cambridge University Press, 1996.

——. *Soviet Criminologists and Criminal Policy: Specialists in Policy-Marking.* Basingstoke, U.K.: Macmillan, 1978.

Sosin, Gene. *Sparks of Liberty: An Insider's Memoir of Radio Liberty.* University Park: Pennsylvania State University Press, 1999.

Spechler, Dina. *Permitted Dissent in the USSR: Novyi Mir and the Soviet Regime.* New York: Praeger, 1982.

Stewart, Philip D. *Political Power in the Soviet Union: A Study of Decision-Making in Stalingrad.* Indianapolis: Bobbs-Merrill, 1968.

Stites, Richard. *Revolutionary Dreams: Utopian Vision and Experimental Life in the Russian Revolution.* New York: Oxford University Press, 1989.

Stolee, Margaret K. "Homeless Children in the USSR, 1917–1957." *Soviet Studies* 11 (1988): 64–83.

Taubman, William. *Khrushchev: The Man and His Era.* London: Free Press, 2003.

Teitel, Ruti G. *Transitional Justice.* Oxford: Oxford University Press, 2000.

Thomas, D. M. *Aleksandr Solzhenitsyn: A Century in His Life.* London: Little, Brown, 1998.

Tikhonov, Aleksei. "The End of the Gulag." In *The Economics of Forced Labor: The Soviet Gulag*, edited by Paul R. Gregory and Valery Lazarev, 67–73. Stanford: Hoover Institution Press, 2003.

Toker, Leona. *Return from the Archipelago: Narratives of Gulag Survivors.* Bloomington: Indiana University Press, 2000.

Tucker, Robert C. "The Rise of Stalin's Personality Cult." *American Historical Review* 84 (1979): 347–366.

Tumarkin, Nina. *Lenin Lives! The Lenin Cult in Soviet Russia.* Cambridge, Mass.: Harvard University Press, 1983.

Vakser, A. Z. *Leningrad poslevoennyi. 1945–1982 gody.* St. Petersburg: Ostrov, 2005.

Van Goudoever, Albert P. *The Limits of Destalinisation in the Soviet Union: Political Rehabilitations in the Soviet Union Since Stalin.* Translated by Frans Hijkoop. London: Croom Helm, 1986.

Varese, Federico. "The Society of the *Vory-v-Zakone*, 1930s–1950s." *Cahiers du monde russe* 39 (1998): 515–538.

Varga-Harris, Christine. "Forging Citizenship on the Home Front: Revising the Socialist Contract and Constructing Soviet identity during the Thaw." In *The Dilemmas of De-Stalinization: Negotiating Cultural and Social Change in the Khrushchev Era*, edited by Polly Jones, 101–116. London: Routledge, 2006.

Verdery, Katherine. *The Political Lives of Dead Bodies: Reburial and Postsocialist Change.* New York: Columbia University Press, 1999.

Volkov, Vadim. "The Concept of *Kul'turnost'*: Notes on the Stalinist Civilizing Process." In *Stalinism: New Directions,* edited by Sheila Fitzpatrick, 210–230. London: Routledge, 2000.

"Voluntary Militia and Courts." *Soviet Studies* 11 (1959): 214–217.

Weiner, Amir. "The Empires Pay a Visit: Gulag Returnees, East European Rebellions, and Soviet Frontier Politics." *Journal of Modern History* 78 (2006): 333–376.

—— *Making Sense of War: The Second World War and the Fate of the Bolshevik Revolution.* Princeton: Princeton University Press, 2001.

Amir Weiner, ed. *Landscaping the Human Garden: Twentieth-Century Population Management in a Comparative Framework.* Stanford: Stanford University Press, 2003.

Yampolsky, Mikhail. "In the Shadow of Monuments: Notes on Iconoclasm and Time." Translated by John Kachur. In *Soviet Hieroglyphics: Visual Culture in Late Twentieth Century Russia,* edited by Nancy Condee, 93–112. Bloomington: Indiana University Press, 1995.

Yurchak, Alexei. *Everything Was Forever, Until It Was No More: The Last Soviet Generation.* Princeton: Princeton University Press, 2006.

Zelnik, Reginald E. *The Perils of Pankratova: Some Stories from the Annals of Soviet Historiography.* Seattle: Donald W. Treadgold Studies on Russia, East Europe, and Central Asia, University of Washington, 2005.

Zemskov, V. N. *Spetsposelentsy v SSSR 1930–1960.* Moscow: Nauka, 2005.

Zubkova, Elena. *Obshchestvo i reformy, 1945–1964.* Moscow: Rossiia molodaia, 1993.

——. *Poslevoennoe sovetskoe obshchestvo: Politika i povsednevnost'.* Moscow: ROSSPEN, 1999.

——. *Russia after the War: Hopes, Illusions, and Disappointments, 1945–1957.* Translated by Hugh Ragsdale. Armonk, N.Y.: M. E. Sharpe, 1998.

Unpublished Dissertations

Barnes, Steven Anthony. "Soviet Society Confined: The Gulag in the Karaganda Region of Kazakhstan, 1930s–1950s." Ph.D. dissertation, Stanford University, 2003.

Elie, Marc. "Les anciens détenus du Goulag: libérations massives, réinsertion et réhabilitation dans l'URSS poststalinienne, 1953–1964." Ph.D. dissertation, École des Hautes Études en Sciences Sociales, 2007.

Gorlizki, Yoram. "De-Stalinisation and the Politics of Russian Criminal Justice, 1953–1964." Ph.D. dissertation, University of Oxford, 1992.

Kozlov, Denis. "The Readers of *Novyi mir,* 1945–1970: Twentieth-Century Experience and Soviet Historical Consciousness." Ph.D. dissertation, University of Toronto 2005.

Roth-Ey, Kristin. "Mass Media and the Remaking of Soviet Culture, 1950s–1960s." Ph.D. dissertation, Princeton University, 2003.

Smith, Aminda M. "Reeducating the People: The Chinese Communists and the 'Thought Reform' of Beggars, Prostitutes, and other 'Parasites.'" Ph.D. dissertation, Princeton University, 2006.

Varga-Harris, Christine. "Constructing the Soviet Hearth: Home, Citizenship and Socialism in Russia, 1956–1964." Ph.D. dissertation, University of Illinois at Urbana-Champaign, 2005.

Unpublished Conference Papers

Smith, Kathleen E. "Gulag Survivors and Thaw Policies." Paper presented at "The History and Legacy of the Gulag" Conference, Harvard University, November 2006.

Index

Page numbers in italics refer to figures.